NUMBER 15 OF THE COLUMBIA STUDIES IN AMERICAN CULTURE

Edward Bellamy

Edward Bellamy

Edward Bellamy

by ARTHUR E. MORGAN

COLUMBIA UNIVERSITY PRESS

New York

MGE

COPYRIGHT 1944

COLUMBIA UNIVERSITY PRESS, NEW YORK

First printing 1944
Second printing 1945

Foreign agent: OXFORD UNIVERSITY PRESS, Humphrey Milford,
Amen House, London, E.C. 4, England, AND B. I. Building, Nicol
Road, Bombay, India

MANUFACTURED IN THE UNITED STATES OF AMERICA

58997
920-B435m

Preface

AN AUTHOR wrote me recently that after working through several years on a biography of a well-known contemporary of Edward Bellamy in social pioneering, he had dropped the project because the personality of his subject continued to shrink as his acquaintance became more intimate. My experience has been exactly the opposite. This biography of Bellamy was begun as a relaxing diversion from active days, but as the undertaking proceeded a remarkable personality came into view, whose widespread influence is not a caprice of circumstance but a natural outcome of a life of signal quality.

The reader who takes up this book expecting to find simply the story of the author of the world's most widely read utopia may be surprised to discover how large a part deals with other interests. Bellamy was not just a utopian. His was one of the most ranging and penetrating minds America has produced. This real Edward Bellamy was a very different and far more interesting personality than the public has known. The fact that he was well along in his thirties before he became committed to a life of social and economic pioneering does not mean that his earlier years were lightly spent. Already he had done original and significant thinking on more than one major human issue.

One of these other interests might well have become the chief contribution of his life. From boyhood his mind had played upon a problem of such universal import that even economic well-being would scarcely take a higher place. Bellamy observed men everywhere to be living under a dread burden of the past. They have felt themselves to be relentlessly pursued by their weaknesses and errors. This dire shadow was the *nemesis* of the Greek, the *sense of guilt* of the Jew, the *sense of sin* of the Christian, and that feeling of servitude to the past which has lain heavy on the spirits of men of many times, races, and religions, and which chills the life of many men today. Edward Bellamy was born under the spell of the Calvinist doctrine of innate depravity, which is but one variety of this widespread servitude. His spirit revolted from that incubus. He began to explore it, to criticize it, to analyze it. He observed it from many different and novel points of view.

Gradually he developed a conviction that crude and bungling efforts of men to explain how and why they suffer for their mistakes had led to harmful exaggeration of the sense of guilt or of nemesis. He came to believe that this excessive feeling of nemesis was an unnecessary burden which men had made for themselves. He began to glimpse possibilities of a spiritual freedom, and with it a great refreshment and renewal of the human spirit, which would go far to make life good. Some of his tentative approaches to this problem he published in story form, but no one seemed to catch their deeper implication, partly because they were but brief fragments of a structure of thought that was slowly being created in the author's mind. Bellamy found the public but little interested in this subject. Like the slave who never had known freedom, and therefore had no craving for it, men experienced this kind of servitude so universally that there was almost no awareness of it or rebellion against it. At some time in the future the heat of men's attention may be focused on that issue. Had Bellamy's early life been in such a period he might have become a great leader in the understanding and mastery of those forces which control the spirits and attitudes of men.

Sigmund Freud, in spite of his lapses from responsible scientific processes, has left an enduring imprint on the world. Edward Bellamy, in his penetrating and significant thinking on the nature of personality, of which his treatment of nemesis is but one phase, has made a contribution to human thinking hitherto largely unrevealed. Had that field continued to be his dominant life interest, his insight, his sanity, and his objectiveness might have made his work even more significant than that of Freud.

The struggle with the doctrine of nemesis was far from being Bellamy's only interest aside from economics. If one were appraising Ralph Waldo Emerson, his concern would be with the ideas, intuitions, and flashes of insight, and the well-disguised Yankee adaptation of Indian philosophy, which constitute perhaps his chief significance. Edward Bellamy had a mental life in many respects like that of Emerson and, like the sage of Concord, seems to have been deeply influenced by the wisdom of the East.

Henry Thoreau found much of the meaning of his life in unity with nature, and that element must be the chief burden of any biography of the man who immortalized Walden Pond. Edward Bellamy had a sensitiveness to nature scarcely less acute than that of Thoreau, though it ran more to over-all aesthetic appreciations and philosophical inferences than to observation and cataloguing of details.

Nathaniel Hawthorne was the outstanding American genius of his time in romance and fantasy. Before Bellamy gave up that field for social philosophy, he was coming to be Hawthorne's legitimate successor. He had a quality of philosophic insight far superior to that of Hawthorne and was achieving at least an equal power of unadorned, realistic expression.

A biography of Henry George would have as its subject almost solely the social and economic philosopher and reformer. In that field the mind of Edward Bellamy has been no less far-reaching, while his grasp of the problem was much fuller and more fundamental, and his program was more comprehensive.

Edward Bellamy lived not one life but several. Each was enriched by the carrying over of the spirit and skills he had developed when other interests were dominant.

Much of the effect of what he wrote on economics was due not only to the ideas expressed but to the manner and skill of expression. Others had similar ideas, but he had readers by the million. How did it come about that a large number of the men who later became significant in social thought and action received their initial impetus from him? It is desirable, if possible, to discover the secret of his literary style. Few men have so clearly disclosed the process by which they became effective writers. In the chapter "The Writer," he is allowed to tell his own story of that mastery.

Some of those interested solely in Bellamy's social and economic philosophy may feel that that phase of his life should have a monopoly of attention. To them, and to a large part of the public, *Looking Backward*, the book which made him famous, *is* Edward

Bellamy. The two utopias, *Looking Backward* and *Equality*, and the Nationalist movement may deserve the dominant place in this biography, but nothing less than an all-around view of the man is adequate.

Bellamy was an artist and an original thinker before he was a reformer. The wholesomeness of his social vision is due somewhat to that fact.

In the long run the significance of his social and economic theories will be judged partly by the fact that they are the product, not of a one-track mind, but of a ranging and universal type of personality—almost a modern Leonardo da Vinci. As he himself expressed it in one of his early notebooks, "The Religion of Solidarity requires in all cases the fulfillment of the instinct of the whole, obedience to that universal which may indifferently coincide with the assertion or abrogation of my individuality." [1] To do justice to such a personality is far more difficult than to treat of a mind with a single dominant manner or a few modes of expression, as was the case with Emerson, Thoreau, Freud, Hawthorne, or Henry George.

I have endeavored to throw light on Bellamy's life and work and to appraise them objectively, rather than to make converts to his views. Let us hope that his devotees do not consider this to be disregard for his social views. These have had a more widespread influence than even Bellamy's disciples have realized.

In February, 1870, a short time before his twenty-first birthday and eighteen years before the publication of *Looking Backward*, Edward Bellamy prepared an address, apparently for the village Lyceum of his home town of Chicopee Falls, on the subject of world government. In that address he wrote:

A faith in the good time coming might, I think, be set down as among those innate ideas with which, as certain philosophers insist, every soul is born impregnated. Assuredly, no idea has been more common to all men and all ages than the belief that the world has before it an era of perfection, when every obstacle of physical nature, and the far more stubborn obstacles of human ignorance, having been removed, every

[1] Unpublished papers of Edward Bellamy (B2-4-13). The wholist school of philosophy can find in Edward Bellamy a pioneer and a prophet.

possibility of political and social amelioration shall be effected, and every human faculty shall have free course and be glorified. And indeed it is impossible to conceive how anyone could zealously labor for the weal of men unless his soul were cheered and guided by some scintillations of this hope—some glimpse of this distant dawning.

. . . in my faith in the good time coming I do not rest for evidence upon the mystical hyperboles of Jewish seers, whence many draw great but indefinite comfort, nor yet upon any of the subjective transcendental philosophies produced in such number by the dreamers of our day, but upon what appear to me natural deductions from undoubted facts.

But this universal faith of which I have spoken is very general in its terms, and does in no wise specify the particular elements of this anticipated perfection, and, on account of this peculiarity, has been deemed by some skeptical minds as so altogether hazy and undefined as to be undeserving of any respect. . . . Certainly, then, this great principle of faith in the future stands in great need of a vindication against the capital charge of indistinctness. [2]

It was the genius of Edward Bellamy that he took Utopia out of the region of hazy dreamland and made it a concrete program for the actual modern world. A reviewer of *Looking Backward* wrote: "Men read the Republic or the Utopia with a sigh of regret. They read Bellamy with a thrill of hope." [3] His picture of a better world, and the hope and expectation of its fulfillment, were transmitted through the years until those who looked to him as the source of their initial inspiration consituted an important part of the army of social progress.

In 1935, at a request from Columbia University, three men undertook, each from his own appraisal, to make a list of the twenty-five books of the preceding half century which had most influenced the thought and action of the world. The three men were John Dewey, philosopher; Charles Beard, historian; and Edward Weeks, editor of the *Atlantic Monthly*. When the three lists appeared, at the head of each was Karl Marx's *Das Kapital*, and second in each list was Bellamy's *Looking Backward*. That statement in brief indicates the opinion of representative men as to the place of Edward Bellamy in recent world history.

[2] *Ibid.* (B3B—Miscellaneous Fragments).
[3] H. P. Peebles, "The Utopias of the Past Compared with the Theories of Bellamy," *Overland Monthly*, 2d series, XV, No. 90 (June, 1890), 574.

In a similar appraisal published at about the same time in the *Wilson Library Bulletin*, *Looking Backward* is included in a list of twenty-six books of the past four hundred years "that have changed the modern world."

At about the turn of the century Dr. Rudolph Broda, a young Austrian of means, read *Looking Backward*, which gave direction to his thinking and started him on an interesting career. He began to consider how he could be most useful in improving the economic order. He made many acquaintances, and in 1906 traveled over Europe developing an association of young liberals which took the name "The League for the Organization of Progress." Among the members of this League were Eduard Beneš, then a young law student, since known to the world as Czechoslovakia's Minister of Foreign Affairs and President; Emile Vandervelde, member of the Belgian parliament, who in succeeding years held several important cabinet posts as the foremost Belgian liberal of his day; Ramsay MacDonald, a labor member of the British House of Commons at that time, later to emerge as Prime Minister of England; Aristide Briand, a member of the French parliament, preparing himself for his later place as Premier; and Karl Renner, a liberal member of the old Austro-Hungarian parliament, who later became the first Chancellor of the Austrian Republic. Until the World War this organization published *Records of Progress*, a magazine of social affairs, edited by Dr. Broda and published in French, German, and English. At his suggestion the "International Institute for the Exchange of Social Experience" was organized in Paris in 1909. Its success surpassed the expectation of its founders, and soon more than forty experts of national or international reputation spent part of their time each year traveling all over Europe as lecturers of the Institute. Thus the humane spirit of Bellamy had its expression in much of the work of Dr. Broda and his associates.

Thorstein Veblen ranks as one of America's most original and creative thinkers in the fields of sociology and economics. As a young man he was at a loss to choose a life calling. Philology seemed most feasible, and in 1888 he had made a translation of an Icelandic saga, for which he had been unable to find a publisher. Then he and his wife read *Looking Backward* together. She wrote of the experience, "I believe that this was the turning point in our lives." [4] Veblen thereupon adopted the social sciences as the field of his life work, and, in one of his first pieces of economic writing, *Some Neglected Points in the Theory of Socialism,* he took an idea presented in *Looking Backward* and developed its significance with greater detail and emphasis. This idea—that social injustice is partly due to the fact that men strive not only for physical needs but for favorable economic standing as compared with other men—was the most widely recognized theme of Veblen's provocative and creative career. His *Theory of the Leisure Class,* and his discussions of "conspicuous waste" as a method of social competition, are little more than elaborations of Bellamy. He found the remedy for existing social evils to be Bellamy's program of the public conduct of industry, and equal division of income. With such division, he held, as did Bellamy, that economic emulation would cease, and that ambition would find more useful channels of expression.

William Allen White has described the effect of *Looking Backward* and *Equality* during the late nineteenth century:

Edward Bellamy had written a book called *Looking Backward,* filled with what his generation regarded as prophetic folderol. Yet out of his vision for the young men of yesterday we elders of today dream our dreams.[5]

. . . .

I remember the tremendous thrill I had from reading the books from the late Eighties and the early Nineties. I was a young man passing out of my teens. I went into life a thoroughgoing conservative but before I had been ten years out of college I was crossing the deadline into an open-minded attitude about the political, social, and economic problems. Probably this was the yeast of Edward Bellamy working in me. I have never been permanently cured. The book had a tremendous influence on my generation. Young men in high school and college, serious young men in those days, were talking about it.[6]

There are many men whose memories support that of William Allen White. Stephen Leacock has written:

I am one of the many people to whom his *Looking Backward* came as a sort of an illumination of a world that might be. I know now that

[4] Joseph Dorfman, *Thorstein Veblen and His America,* p. 68.
[5] Commencement Address, University of Kansas, June 11, 1934.
[6] Letter to the author.

humanity is not as yet fit to live in a Bellamy commonwealth, that old age is not as wise as he thought it or the instinct of work for all as strong as he imagined it. But even if his Commonwealth is a soap bubble, at least it had in it those iridescent colors which will in some long day light up the world. *Looking Backward* made an impression on my mind never to be effaced.

Adolph A. Berle, Jr., Assistant Secretary of State in the Franklin D. Roosevelt administration, whose Bellamy-like views on economic organization have been widely discussed, also is one of that large company. His father was a member of the Bellamy Club of Boston. According to Adolph A. Berle, Jr., "It is unnecessary to say that any one who ever followed Bellamy could never remain uninfluenced by his ideas." Various New Deal policies and proposals would seem to have been taken almost directly from the pages of *Looking Backward*.

Many a socially minded man or woman of the last generation could say with John Palmer Gavit, "Edward Bellamy's *Looking Backward*, with Henry George's *Progress and Poverty*, was my first experience of economic heresy." Jasper McLevy, the several-times Socialist mayor of Bridgeport, Connecticut, who by the competence of his administration has made himself respected among all classes, got his first social interest from *Looking Backward*. Norman Thomas, several times Socialist candidate for President, has said, "The first book I ever read which could be called Socialist was *Looking Backward*, and it made a deep impression on me."

Hamlin Garland wrote, "Mark Twain was profoundly touched by *Looking Backward*." Mark Twain's own little utopia, *The Curious Republic of Gondour*, was written before *Looking Backward*, and *A Connecticut Yankee at King Arthur's Court* was written just afterward, and apparently after he and Bellamy had discussed *Looking Backward*. On this visit to Mark Twain's home Bellamy was much impressed by his seriousness of purpose. The great increase in depth of feeling and of understanding in *A Connecticut Yankee at King Arthur's Court*, as compared with Mark Twain's earlier utopian sketch, lends color to the widespread opinion that he was much influenced by Bellamy.

In his biography of Bernard Shaw, Archibald Henderson wrote:

"It is highly significant of the advance of the American Socialists, known as Nationalists, beyond Shaw's view of that period, that Edward Bellamy was advocating in 1894 [and he might have said in 1887, and even in 1871] the very principle which Shaw did not discover to be fundamental to Socialism until almost two decades later." [7] Again, in discussing the development of Shaw's outlook he wrote:

During the hottest days of Lloyd Georgism, when Old Age Pensions were the chief bone of contention, Shaw suggested to his friend, the Socialist and artist, Cobden-Sanderson, that the people should have "Universal Old Age Pensions" for everybody. With a flash of insight, Cobden-Sanderson replied: "Why not Universal Pensions for Life?" Thus Cobden-Sanderson, in a phrase, furnished a substitute for Capitalism and a solution of the industrial problem at a stroke. But the conception was original with neither Shaw nor Cobden-Sanderson, having been advanced by the brilliant American novelist and Utopist, Edward Bellamy, as early as 1897. In his Utopian novel, *Equality,* which was overshadowed by the world-sweeping success of his *Looking Backward,* Bellamy previsioned a society in the year 2000 in which "all alike were in the service of the nation working for the common fund, which all equally shared."

"We took it for granted," Shaw reminisced to me, "that we knew all about *Equality* and did not read it. We rather turned up our noses at Utopias as cheap stuff until Wells stood up for them; and by that time Bellamy was a back number. Later on, we found that we had underrated him, and that he had made many converts." Shaw followed in Bellamy's footsteps.[8]

For half a century there has been a conflict between the American spirit as expressed by Edward Bellamy, and the spirit of irreconcilable class conflict which finally took definite form in the Russian regime. John Dewey has expressed a significant opinion of this issue:

I was moved by the particular Utopia presented by Bellamy, and derived from it the belief that the world was coming into possession of the technical means for a much better, more humane social order than existed. Succeeding years have deepened my belief that if the type of ideas represented by Bellamy had continued to be presented from his

[7] Henderson, *Bernard Shaw, Playboy and Prophet*, p. 182.
[8] *Ibid.,* pp. 240–41. Reprinted by permission of the publisher.

standpoint, rather than from a European one, they would have had a more prosperous career than they have had.

This interest was not confined to America. David Joffo, a member of the Kerensky regime in the early days of the Russian revolution, has described the same conflict in Russia, and the part which the ideas of Bellamy played in it before the failure of the Russian moderate and progressive revolutionary program, and the emergence into power of the doctrines of an irreconcilable class conflict. As to the influence of Bellamy on himself and his associates, Joffo wrote:

Looking Backward was quite popular in advanced intellectual circles and, though regarded as a Utopia, it nevertheless had a great influence on me as well as on a great many of the youth of my day who were interested in the advancement of Russia on social and economic lines.

He has given the author considerable detailed information to support this statement. The last Russian Duma was moving in Bellamy's direction, as was the Kerensky regime.

Only rarely, and often by chance, do we have a record of the influences which were most important in setting a man on his life course. If we could have a complete census of the men and women prominent in social and economic thought in America and Europe during the past fifty years who received their initial social vision from Edward Bellamy, the list doubtless would be greatly extended.

We must not think of Bellamy simply as an "inspirational" writer, who waked men up and started them thinking. Because he wrote in the language of the common man, so that boys and girls of fifteen eagerly read *Looking Backward;* because he avoided technical terminology, and so did not use the mystic passwords of the cult of economists, frequently he has been passed over with a smile by the professionals. As compared with *Looking Backward*, those other classics—More's *Utopia* and Bacon's *New Atlantis*—are light and casual tracts. The pseudo-erudition which includes these and Campanella's *City of the Sun* in collections of significant utopias while omitting *Looking Backward* will pass away in time. The substantial quality of Edward Bellamy is coming to be recognized. For instance, H. Stanley Jevons in discussing utopian writings in his *Economic Equality in the Co-operative Commonwealth* says: "I have gained more from Bellamy than from any single author. He deserves more attention from economists than he has received. The economic system he outlines does stand a rigid examination for workability in its essential features." [9]

The most immediate handicap to human progress is lack of a vision and of expectation, hope, desire, and will, rather than lack of those forms of intelligence which are expressed in formal reasoning. Unless a picture exists of what might be, formal reasoning will concern itself with other and familiar issues. While it was Bellamy's great contribution to provide that vision, he did it with such responsible consistency, and with such creative inventiveness, that his work is not only an inspiration, but in many respects is a practical guide to the organization of the public business.

Contrary to general opinion, and quite to my surprise, evidence has been disclosed that *Looking Backward* and, what is more unexpected, its great progenitor, the *Utopia* of Thomas More, are not just fanciful stories of an ideal society; but that in their essential features they describe a system of social organization which operated successfully for a long period, over a vast extent of territory, and for a greater population than that of any European nation of the time. Recent disclosures of the original discovery of ancient Peru from the Atlantic, very much as described by More in his utopia, and detailed comparison of *Utopia* and Peru seem to leave little basis for doubt that More's great book was patterned after this ancient society. Evidence similarly indicates that Peru was Bellamy's chief pattern. The story of this utopia in action is presented in a succeeding book, *Nowhere Was Somewhere*. In the light of the facts there assembled, the age-old criticism of More's *Utopia* and the more recent criticism of Bellamy's *Looking Backward*—that they are "contrary to human nature"—falls to the ground.

At best this biography is incomplete, partly because much of

---

[9] *Economic Equality in the Co-operative Commonwealth*, p. xx.

the material relating to Bellamy's life has been lost. One of the greatest works of Thomas Carlyle is his spiritual autobiography, *Sartor Resartus*. As a reading of this life of Bellamy will indicate, the spiritual odyssey of the author of *Looking Backward* covered much of the same territory, with the same types of desperate spiritual adventures, as those experienced by the great Scotsman who donned the disguise of Diogenes Teufelsdröckh.

Carlyle's masterpiece includes a fanciful description of a heterogeneous mass of scarcely legible Diogenes Teufelsdröckh manuscripts from which the essence had to be deciphered and pieced together. In the preparation of Bellamy's biography this process actually took place. A jumbled mass of notebooks, manuscripts, and scraps of paper, sometimes almost hopelessly unreadable, constituted much of the raw material. Three assistants worked on this material intermittently through several years, reading it and reducing it to usable form.

Edward Bellamy's large library was scattered after his death. A dozen persons were invited to take such books as they wanted, and then about two tons of books and magazines, and three barrels of manuscripts and correspondence, were sold in bulk, the latter as old paper. As a result, we know very little about the books he owned or read, and still less of his correspondence, though it was very extensive and included many interesting persons, among them Mark Twain, William Dean Howells, German Socialists, and many American liberals. Fortunately, a number of notebooks and a box of notes and manuscripts were preserved. It is from these fragments that much of the content of Bellamy's mind was recovered. We have gathered up and presented the surviving records, trusting to their quality to preserve them from oblivion until they have infected other minds and so have entered into the stream of human thought and intuition.

The writings of Edward Bellamy in the field of philosophy, psychology, and related interests were too extensive to be included in this biography. They have been assembled and edited by the writer, and are being published concurrently with this biography by the King's Crown Press, under the title *The Philosophy of Edward*

Bellamy. This little volume includes both his "Religion of Solidarity" and his treatment of the subject of nemesis.

Charges of plagiarism, so frequently made against Bellamy and other utopians, led to a study by the author of the continuity of the utopian tradition. The resulting story is published separately by the author, under the title *Plagiarism in Utopia.* It discloses interesting and hitherto unrecognized personal relations between Bellamy and contemporary utopians and, the author believes, clears Bellamy of the charges frequently made by superficial critics.

In the preparation of this biography the writer has received information and assistance from so many sources that acknowledgments are recorded in an appendix.

The unpublished writings of Edward Bellamy which are quoted in the text and referred to in footnotes have been placed in the Harvard College Library, where they are available for reference. Typed copies of most of these have been placed also in the Library of Congress, the Huntington Library and the Library of Antioch College. Details concerning this material are included in an appendix to this volume.

A bibliography of books and articles by and about Edward Bellamy also is included in an appendix, together with a bibliography of writings cited in the text.

A. E. M.

Yellow Springs, Ohio
April, 1944.

Contents

Illustrations

Edward Bellamy

I · The New England Setting

EDWARD BELLAMY was a very natural product of New England. He looked penetratingly and without evasion both at the excellencies and at the sordid realities which were about him, and then he attacked the ugliness with a spiritual commitment which long was a common New England trait.

If a virgin area identical with New England should today be added to the continental United States, probably it would be classed as "submarginal" and unfit for human habitation and it might be converted into a national forest. Boston harbor might be developed as a railroad terminal, the lower Connecticut Valley might be cleared for agriculture, and the beaches and lakes would be highly regarded as summer resorts. The land of New England as a whole, however, would not be worth clearing for agriculture. In fact, much of that which was subdued by generations of backbreaking labor has been abandoned as not worth even its maintenance.

Without coal or oil, almost without iron or other minerals or navigable streams, it would not be advantageous for industry, except for its timber resources, water power, and harbor facilities. As compared with the more favored parts of America, the rugged hills and barren sandy plains and swamps of New England would appear uninviting. With fish in the ocean and timber for ships, the Yankee was driven to the sea and then into foreign commerce, to compete with all the world in sheer energy and acumen.

Yet few spots on earth have made greater contributions to human culture or have been centers of more concentrated material wealth. The first volumes of *Who's Who in America* were issued toward the end of Bellamy's life. These early volumes listed more natives of each of the New England states, except Rhode Island, than of any other state. Only Delaware and New York had even half as many names in *Who's Who* in proportion to their native-born white population, and many of the New York notables were of New England stock. As compared with Pennsylvania, Ohio, and Michigan, which had the next largest per capita representation, the New England states mentioned had from three to six times as large representation in *Who's Who*. As compared with some others of the most populous states, the representation from New England was as high as thirty to one.[1]

According to an unconfirmed statement in the press at about the same time, approximately 10 per cent of all the invested wealth in America was owned within fifty miles of Boston. The entries in the Hall of Fame in New York have been chosen with great care. Of the 65 native-born Americans who have places there, 36 were born in New England, and others are of New England descent.

In New England a certain element of utopian adventure, though greatly diluted by commonplace components, nevertheless had a substantial degree of success. Had New England shut itself away from the rest of the world for a few centuries, as did Japan, and worked out the implications of its genius, the results might have been striking.

If the purposes and plans for the original settlement of New England had failed, they would be remembered as quixotic, utopian schemes to create communities in which ideals would be effective along with material considerations. Because those plans did not fail, the settling of New England is a case where ideals were to a significant degree effective. The settlers included men of all motives. There was an unusual proportion of men and women who came definitely in hope of achieving civil and religious freedom. Others were men of adventurous, constructive temperament who sought opportunity to build lives for themselves. Still others, though vigorous and aggressive, were inclined to exploit society, rather than to be producers. Some upper-class New Englanders would have been willing to reproduce an old-world feudalism. Others were brought as servants or menials and had the temper and outlook of inferiors. All these lived together and became intermixed. The element which came with religious or humane convictions and

[1] *Who's Who in America, 1903–1905,* p. xxi; *The World Almanac and Encyclopedia* (1903), p. 376.

purposes was not strong enough to dominate, but it was strong enough to provide some degree of leadership and to define standards by which the deficiencies of society as a whole could be measured. When the typical New Englander was not acting from good motives, at least he was uncomfortable acting from bad ones.

In philosophers, historians, poets, educators, reformers, and scientists, New England has been pre-eminent. Massachusetts led in founding and developing the American public school system and in training teachers. In social legislation she has pioneered in limiting hours of work, controlling child labor, establishing the eight-hour day for public works, requiring wholesome employment conditions, and developing savings banks and savings-bank life insurance. She led America in regional public works, such as the Metropolitan Water Board in eastern Massachusetts.

Because of widespread education and the democratic structure of her society, her early achievement was not dominantly metropolitan but was diffused through many small communities. The village of Concord, holding a place as the home of philosophy, is an example of that decentralization. The region was not stricken with the temper of futility. New Englanders expected life to be significant.

Because of its pioneering initiative, New England tended to succeed in whatever it undertook. With the industrial revolution it became the foremost manufacturing region of America. Here, as almost everywhere, modern industry developed without a long cultural background and was immature, crude, primitive. The business life of New England had the typical evils of young industry, although those faults were somewhat tempered by legislation and by a sense of decency. At first there were very long hours with very low pay, child labor which now seems intolerable, crowding of industrial labor into tenements, and exploitation of newly arrived immigrants. Because Massachusetts was a pioneer in industry, it was among the first to develop some of these abuses, as it was among the first to curb them.

Chicopee Falls, the village where Edward Bellamy was born, a suburb of Springfield, Massachusetts, was typical of New England. Most of the virtues were there, and most of the evils. It was "a fine old New England village," with broad, maple- and oak-shaded streets, with environs of primeval forest, and with rugged hills and the Chicopee River to give it a distinctive setting.

One hundred and fifty years had transformed a breed of hard-headed and hardhanded Indian fighters into "solid business leaders" of the community. Much of the old-time neighborliness was still there, with the observance of everyday practical Christianity, personal responsibility, and exacting standards of living. Alongside it in the same community there was developing an entrenched wealthy class whose members were assuming social exclusiveness, mildly ostentatious living, and a subconscious feeling of divine right in their superior status. Not lacking in energy and intelligence, some of these men mixed exploitation with production, and thereby became industrial leaders, while other manufacturers were public-spirited, creative-minded, and highly efficient producers.

At the time Edward Bellamy was born, Chicopee Falls and the adjoining village of Chicopee Center had just united to form the city of Chicopee, with a population of about eight thousand. Twenty-five years before his birth the falls in the Chicopee River had been developed to provide power for two textile mills. These expanded and united until, when Edward Bellamy was becoming interested in industrial and labor conditions, they occupied a single building about a third of a mile long, no small industrial plant for a nineteenth-century village. In 1834 an armament factory was established, which made sabers, largely for European armies. The great bronze doors of the national Capitol were cast in Chicopee.

Intellectual life and liberal interests were not absent. Discussion clubs dealt with live contemporary issues. Education was held in high regard. The local library, in the quality of its books, would rank among the better of those in small New England cities. Abolitionist sentiment was strong for two decades before the Civil War.

Thus the community provided a cross section of New England life. There was rigorous, dogmatic Calvinist theology, along with the most liberal Unitarianism and freedom of inquiry and criticism.

There was neighborliness and the habit of looking after the sick and unfortunate, not as extending charity to the unprivileged, but as Christian co-operation. The descendants of pioneers were becoming the elite. A century before, the scheming exploiters among them had grabbed the farms of soldiers who were away fighting for American freedom. While Christian neighborliness prevailed very generally, this grasping acquisitiveness in a few laid the basis for economic dominance.

Steam, water power, and machinery on the one hand, and ignorant, impecunious immigrants on the other, arrived together, providing the ingredients for industrial expansion and for exploitation. When Edward Bellamy was a small boy, mechanics and operatives in the mills received about a dollar a day for twelve hours' work. Women received wages of $1.75 a week and board, which cost about as much. Workers lived in long rows of drab two- or three-story tenements, with large families crowded together in a few rooms, though even so they were far better housed than industrial workers today in many Southern mining towns. On these wages and under such working conditions the industrialists made large fortunes, built spacious homes, and developed beautiful estates.

The thrifty, lower-middle-class New England Yankees tended to look down on the ignorant, unwashed, foreign-looking workers and had little companionship with them. Yet, while the industrialists were achieving wealth and dominance, the average self-respecting New Englander was troubled. The Cabot Institute, a literary and social organization of Chicopee, struggled with this strange new phenomenon of the industrial revolution. We find its meetings discussing the question, "Will the increase of the manufacturing interests in New England tend to depress the condition of the laboring class?" [2] The feeling against exploitation did not originate with immigration from Ireland and from eastern Europe, but preceded it by half a century. As in other parts of the thirteen states, the rich merchants of the coast cities had ex-

[2] Burnham, "The City of Chicopee," *New England Magazine,* n.s. XVIII (May, 1898), 361–79.

ploited the agricultural communities a hundred miles to the west, and in the middle classes of western Massachusetts there was strong feeling against that use of economic power.

In this western Massachusetts community, turbulently changing from a quiet New England village to an actively growing manufacturing town, with foreign quarters, slums, and strikes, as well as with growing social and intellectual interests, Edward Bellamy was born on March 26, 1850.

II · Family Backgrounds

As a boy, Edward Bellamy seems to have been of a conservative turn of mind on the subject of heredity and to have felt very keenly the need of support of an appropriate ancestry. His father and his mother's father were preachers, and his most famous ancestor, Joseph Bellamy, also followed that calling. However, preachers did not entirely meet the craving of a boy whose heroes were warriors and other men of action, so he took great pride in a romantic character reputed to be a member of the family tribe, Captain Samuel Bellamy, sometimes also referred to as Charles or Joseph Bellamy, a New England filibuster and pirate. Here was a relative for a boy in a preacher-ridden family to be proud of—not only a daring pirate captain, but socialist, philosopher, and orator as well. Philip Gosse, in *The Pirates' Who's Who*, gives a picture of this forceful personage, whose active career lasted from about 1717 to 1727:

> Procuring a ship, he sailed up and down the coast of Carolina and New England. . . .
> Bellamy had considerable gifts for public speaking, and seldom missed an opportunity of addressing the assembled officers and crews of the ships he took, before liberating or otherwise disposing of them. His views were distinctly socialistic.[1]

Captain Bellamy met his fate when a captive pilot, who had been forced to steer the flagship of the pirate fleet, purposely ran it onto a sand bank at night on the Massachusetts coast, while the other pirate ships following it were dashed upon the rocks and destroyed. All the crews, apparently including Captain Bellamy, were drowned, except seven, who were caught, tried, and hanged at Boston in 1726, but not until after their souls were saved by "the special grace of God" through the ministration of "a pious

[1] *The Pirates' Who's Who*, p. 47. Reprinted by permission.

and learned divine." As a boy in a Baptist minister's home, young Edward made the entire family aware of his pride in this evidence of family virility.

Pioneer Americans intuitively assumed that it is those inborn traits common to us all which are fundamental and significant, while the special differences so much emphasized by dominant families are relatively superficial. People having this attitude held that it is enough to be born a sound, unblemished member of the human race, or at most, of European stock. Given that, they felt, a man's life was his own making.

That opinion has some support in present-day biology. Thomas Hunt Morgan, the distinguished geneticist, has declared that good inherited quality is so generally distributed that most American communities of European descent are rich in genetic potentialities. In his later years Bellamy gave expression to a similar view when he said:

The man who denies that all men owe one another the duties of brothers denies the duties of natural brothers. . . . The immediate parents of any man are but the last pair of an untraceable ancestry, which, at no remote period, becomes inextricably blended with that of the entire community or nation, and eventually with the race itself. Everyone has not only two but millions of parents. He is, in fine, the offspring of mankind, and his mother is humanity. The complex parentage, identical with humanity, is that which has formed him and determined him from the very rudiments of human nature. His immediate parents have done little more than to transmit to him, with a few superficial impressions from themselves, the moral, physical and intellectual inheritance of the race.[2]

Everyday experience supports biological and social science in convincing us that if a man shows special excellence, either in inherited traits or in qualities acquired after birth, somewhat similar excellence generally will be found also in his antecedents. When on rare occasions we do find what appears to be sheer creation of new personal qualities, the occurrence is important, and merits very careful observation.

[2] Mason Green's unpublished biography of Edward Bellamy, hereafter referred to simply as Green.

THE BELLAMY FAMILY

	Birth	Death	Marriage	
John Bellamy [a]	?	1647	?	
Matthew Bellamy	?	1692?	1671	Bethia Ford
Matthew Bellamy	1677	1752	1705	Sarah Wood
Joseph Bellamy	1719	1790	1744	Frances Sherman
Samuel Bellamy	1756?	1802	?	Anna Steele
Jonathan Bellamy	1781	1845	1804	Phoebe Stiles
Rufus King Bellamy	1816	1886	1839	Maria Louisa Putnam [b]
Edward Bellamy	1850	1898	1882	Emma Sanderson

THE PUTNAM FAMILY

	Birth	Death	Marriage	
John Putnam [c]	1580	1662	1611	Priscilla Gould (or Deacon)
Nathaniel Putnam	1619	1700	?	Elizabeth Hutchinson
Benjamin Putnam	1664	1715	1686	Elizabeth (or Hanna) Putnam
Israel Putnam	1699	1760	1720	Sarah Bacon
Tarrant Putnam	1733	1804	1756 (or 1758)	Mary Porter
Eleazer Porter Putnam	1758	1813	1781	Rebecca Smith
Benjamin Putnam	1788	1845	1811	Joanna Weaver

[a] Came to New England some time before 1644.
[b] Daughter of Benjamin Putnam and Joanna Weaver Putnam.
[c] Settled at Salem in 1634.

Much that passes for originality or for greatness is no more than sound human quality in a strikingly new situation, or with exceptional opportunity. The really important work in most cases is not the sudden burst into conspicuous achievement, but the long, slow process of selection and of discipline which largely eliminated weakness in that human stock, and gradually tempered it to discipline and to discrimination.

The New England minister, as represented by Edward Bellamy's father, was an excellent example of the selection and discipline which supply the foundation for great achievement. He was descended from a long line of men of responsibility. In charge of a large parish, he was business manager of a considerable property. His wife was an equal, if not the dominant, partner. They were neighbors and counselors to many. There was need to be arbiter, and sometimes judge, in pleading with or even disciplining wayward members, with a discipline in which tact and good will must prevail. Each week as minister he went through the ordeal of exposing his mind to an intelligent congregation, perhaps contributing to the cultural tradition. He was the principal channel by which learning and books were transmitted. He and his wife had constantly to aid unfortunates without infringing on their self-respect. They had much to do with determining social usage. The minister was constantly called on by farmers for business advice.

Such families have traveled, in obscurity, most of the way from mediocrity to greatness. They have achieved a foundation in biological inheritance and in cultural discipline which only awaits exceptional incentive or outlook or circumstance to emerge in outstanding accomplishment. Most human families are constantly producing sports or mutations which, if supported by general physical and mental stamina and by a tradition of personal discipline, may emerge as genius. Moreover, time and circumstance repeatedly call for or stimulate great endeavor which is within the capacity of almost any sound, intelligent person.

Most preparation for greatness is made in obscurity, where reserves of nervous energy and of physical stamina can accumulate. Quite generally the period of conspicuous success is not a time of biological creation, but of rapid consumption of the slowly accumulated resources of breeding, of discipline, and of physical reserves. But for the accumulation in comparative obscurity of many reservoirs of human excellence, the cultural and genetic resources of society would quickly be consumed. In fact, one of the chief reasons for the decay of human cultures may well be the periods of conspicuous achievement which outrun and exhaust reserves of quality which had been slowly and quietly acquired.

We have reason, therefore, to be interested in tracing the background of Edward Bellamy, both as to his ancestors and as to the spirit and conditions of the times. In many of his traits we can trace the diverse parentage of what might be called a hybrid personality. In other respects what seemed at first to be originality may be disclosed as unconscious imitation. Some of his characteristics were a motley combination of those of his parents.

Yet after accounting for his characteristics as best we can by observing family traits, there remains still an important residue of qualities that cannot be explained by personal or family background but which seem to be peculiarly his own. This streak of original quality was essential to the effectiveness of his writing.

An examination of the antecedents of Edward Bellamy supports that commonplace remark of the conventional biographer, "He came of good stock." Though the name, from *belle amie,* "good friend," implies French origin, it is found in English records, with nearly a score of different spellings, since the thirteenth century. No evidence has been found to support the statement of Mason Green that he was from a Huguenot family. The name appears in New England some time previous to 1644. John Bellamy, a merchant, came from London to Connecticut, settling at New London. It is said he was lost at sea while returning from a journey to London about 1647. The next Connecticut Bellamy was Matthew. It is not clear that he was the son of John. *The New England Historical and Genealogical Register* says of him:

Matthew Bellamy was one of the first settlers of New Haven. He signed the plantation covenant of 1639, and took the oath of fidelity in 1644. He was evidently an educated man, and acted as schoolmaster at various times. . . . The people of New Haven seem to have manifested some jealousy of him. At a court at New Haven in 1652 he is called a "new comer" and reproached with an excitable and litigious spirit.[3]

This first Matthew had a son and three daughters. The son, Matthew, "owned an interest in the copper mines there [near Cheshire, Connecticut] and appears to have worked them." [4] That he was like his father is indicated from the comment, "He was of a somewhat litigious character." [5] He was married twice and had eleven children.

The son of Matthew the second, who was in the direct line of the author of *Looking Backward,* was the noted preacher and educator, Joseph Bellamy. Born at New Cheshire, Connecticut, in 1719, Joseph was graduated from Yale at the age of sixteen, and when less than twenty began to preach at Bethlem, Connecticut, where he was ordained in 1740 and spent most of his life. It is reported that Mark Hopkins was one of his pupils. In 1768 he was given the degree of Doctor of Divinity by the University of Aberdeen. He had studied under Jonathan Edwards and became his lifelong friend. Like that famous divine, he had great influence through his spoken and written sermons. He was "a large, well built man, with voice to match."

There is a family tradition that he was influential in introducing into the Federal Constitution the provision for separating church and state. Though he must have been a powerful personality and had a marked influence on the theological opinions of his day, both in America and in Scotland, that influence may not have been due always to "sweetness and light." Dr. Ezra Stiles, a president of Yale, said to be his brother-in-law, was a neighbor and occasional companion through many years, spent many evenings at Joseph Bellamy's home, and repeatedly asked Bellamy to preach for him. Yet when Joseph Bellamy died, Dr. Stiles entered the following harsh appraisal of him in his diary:

---

[3] Smith, R. D., "Matthew Bellamy of New Haven, Conn., and His Descendants," *The New England Historical and Genealogical Register,* LXI, No. 244 (October, 1907), 338–39. Reprinted by permission.

[4] *Ibid.,* p. 339.   [5] *Ibid.,* p. 339.

March 16, 1790. . . . Died 6th Inst. Rev. Joseph Bellamy D.D. at Bethlem aet. 71. . . . He was but an indifferent Scholar in the Languages & Sciences. Began preaching about aet. 19, was highly carried away with New Lightism 1741. But soon recovered himself from the Extravagancies of those Times by the friendly Councils of President Edwards, to whom he was greatly attached. . . . He was a powerful Preacher, wholly absorbed in the Novelties & Peculiarities of New Divinity. He was of a haughty domineering Temper & till of late years unmercifully censorious of his Brethren in the Ministry & others who opposed him. He meliorated in his Temper in the latter part of Life. . . . He was boisterous & vociferous in Preaching, of a dogmatical & overbearing Disposition, severe, rigid & uncharitable towards all who differed from him, even tho' in the general in the same System with himself. He set his Face against every one, & had many Enemies & many Friends. . . . His Morals were rigid, regular, virtuous & pious. He forceably affected Philanthropy & Benevolence but they were foreign from his Temper. In ecclesiastical Matters he was very litigious & impatient. This was natural to him. His Father was litigious in Law Matters, & the son in religious Matters. He did much good, & occasioned considerable Hurt to the Churches. He needed much Grace, & was blessed with a considerable Share of it. He was however a mixt Character of such a Borgian Complexion as one would not wish often to appear in the Churches. . . . He wished to be oràcular, but he was not. . . . His numerous noisy Writings have blazed their day, & one Generation more will put them to sleep.[6]

Others spoke of Joseph Bellamy in different terms. It was said of him:

His benevolent feelings were not confined to a narrow circle, but were as extensive as the globe. . . . His acquaintance, as well with the political, as moral state of the world, was general, and especially of his native country . . .

As a preacher he had, perhaps, no superior, and very few equals. His voice was manly, his manner engaging . . . In the desk he appeared to understand human nature to perfection . . . He was master of his subject when he spake, and had a singular faculty of adapting himself to the meanest capacity. . . . His field was boundless . . . No subject escaped his notice, or that was not at proper times, held up to the view of his people. . . .[7]

[6] Dexter, ed., *The Literary Diary of Ezra Stiles*, III, 384–85. Reprinted by permission of the publisher.

[7] *The Works of the Rev. Joseph Bellamy, D.D.*, I, 23–24.

The committee of eleven distinguished ministers who assembled his writings and recommended them for publication said, "We consider him as one of the most distinguished and useful writers of the last age." [8]

He spent much time as a traveling preacher under the difficult pioneering conditions of the day. He established a divinity school at Bethlem, Connecticut, and developed a course of study of such thoroughness and with pedagogical methods so carefully designed and effective as to create a new standard. "He had an excellent talent at composing differences, and preventing or healing breaches in churches, and was much employed in such cases." [9]

Joseph Bellamy's first wife, and ancestor of Edward Bellamy, was Frances Sherman, supposed to be of the family of Roger Sherman, a signer of the Declaration of Independence. (Edward Bellamy was given the middle name of Roger in honor of this man, but changed it to Sherman. In later years he was inclined to omit his second name or initial.) Joseph Bellamy had five sons and three daughters by his first wife. One of his sons, Jonathan, a lawyer, served on Washington's staff and died in that service. Samuel, another son, was born in 1756. His son Jonathan, born in 1781, worked his way via New York City up to Kingsbury, Washington County, New York, where he built up a business through a general merchandise store, made what for those days was called a fortune, and had a handsome home. Of his five sons, Rufus King Bellamy, the father of Edward Bellamy, was the youngest. He was born at Kingsbury, on July 11, 1816, and was named after Rufus King, a patriot in New York during the American Revolution, active during the period of the Confederacy, and one of the first two Senators from New York after the adoption of the Federal Constitution. Rufus Bellamy was graduated from Middlebury College in 1835 or 1836, took a theological course at Hamilton, and was ordained as minister in 1838. Edward Bellamy's mother, Maria Louisa Putnam, daughter of a Baptist minister, was born at Royalton, Vermont, on April 9, 1816. They were married on November 5, 1839, at Lebanon, New York. After holding four pastorates in nine years, Rufus was appointed minister to the Baptist Church

[8] *Ibid.*, p. iii.   [9] *Ibid.*, p. 36.

at Chicopee Falls in 1848, and remained in that pulpit for thirty-four years. He died at Chicopee Falls in 1886, at the age of seventy. His wife survived him six years.

Thus we have a record of two centuries of paternal ancestors who were among the successful and leading members of their communities, following such varied callings as merchant, preacher, teacher, organizer and administrator of a theological school, and mine operator. Although this is only one line of an ever-expanding ancestry, in view of the habit of people in stable societies like that of New England of marrying into families of similar position, we can safely assume that this two-hundred-year-long sample is somewhat characteristic of the ancestral pattern during that period. If we trace the family line of Edward Bellamy's mother, we find a similar record. The Putnams, Weavers, and Porters show substantial quality, and great names along the way.

Leaving out of account any inherited superiority of blood, such a family background is a great resource to a young man. Two centuries of substantial success inculcates the habit and expectation of success. Preferred places in the community open the way to other preferred places. Financial resources in the family enable young people to live comfortably while getting financial footholds for themselves. Contact with parents of business experience tends to the transmission of business judgment to the next generation. Association with educated people may lead even to intelligent diet and eating habits, so that for generations prosperous people may be more vigorous and may have better physical development. Even if men were equal in inborn quality, exceptionally favorable environment would produce the appearance of a superior breed.

Let no one suppose that the cultural pattern is unimportant. It is the very stuff of which civilization is made. Of exceedingly slow growth, it requires perhaps as long a time for reaching maturity as is taken in developing inborn traits. Those qualities of character which marked Edward Bellamy had their roots in a long past, not only of inborn traits but also of family and community discipline and education, which for generations may be exerting their influ-

ence in inconspicuous places. Wherever that process is under way
and wherever the innate quality is strong enough and fine enough
to support it, we have the makings of history.

Edward Bellamy possessed a rare quality of intellectual and
emotional independence. He passed under various powerful influences without surrendering to them, and, what is no less unusual, without extreme reaction in the process of freeing himself
from them. He grew up in a New England Calvinist family in which
the rigors and dogmatism of Calvinism were associated with simple Christian living. He broke free entirely from Calvinist theology,
and—as many religious liberals did not—from Calvinist psychology; but he discriminated in retaining the ethics and spirit of
brotherhood. He grew up in a Republican-party environment, but
departed quite completely from the conservative elements and
attitudes of that party. Among his early associates were manufacturers, businessmen, and families with large inherited income,
but he freed himself almost entirely from their class outlook, and
pitilessly exposed their exploitation of labor. Unlike some men
from families of wealth or social standing who espouse liberal purposes, he did not turn on his old associates with venom. He spent
about two years in a lawyer's office, and was admitted to the bar;
but rejected entirely the lawyer psychology and the emoluments of
legal practice. In this he differed from the great utopian, Thomas
More, who, although he denounced lawyers and would not have them
in his ideal commonwealth, continued to develop an enviable law
practice in London.

Edward Bellamy came under the influence of Marxian socialism brought over from Europe, but though it would have furnished
his movement with powerful momentum, he selected what seemed
true and vital to him, and deliberately rejected the class hatred,
the theory of class warfare, and the extreme materialism with
which early Marxian socialism was infected.

When we observe his rare ability both to hold to a course which
is in accord with his discriminating and hard-won philosophy and
to resist powerful current influences, we are curious to learn how
he came by that capacity for self-direction. The mind of Edward
Bellamy provides an interesting opportunity to observe the proc-

esses by which independence of thinking and intellectual freedom are achieved.

There are at least three factors in freedom—absence of compulsion, the presence of alternatives from which to choose, and the inner impulse to appraise and to select. Simply to be unconscious of restraint or compulsion does not constitute freedom. Only in the presence of alternatives, with the opportunity or necessity for choosing between them, does freedom have practical meaning. Where there is no choice there can be no freedom. This holds true in the developments of habits, motives, and intuitions. Obviously the presence of alternatives is not by itself enough to bring about independent, creative thinking. There also must be vigor and toughness of mind which persists in developing ideas in accordance with the nature of things, and aggressive vitality to transcend conventions and regimentations of thinking.

The most fundamental traits of personality generally are deeply fixed in very early life, before a child is greatly conscious of his environment beyond the home and the immediate community circle. A boy living in a home where father and mother think and feel alike may be unaware of any lack of freedom of choice; yet, except as he meets with actual alternatives, he is not free. If the early environment presents great variety and personal contrasts, then conditions favoring critical choice are present, and the habit of discriminating selection may be deeply rooted in the personality.

As a boy in his parents' home Edward Bellamy was faced with great contrasts. His father and mother were such strikingly different personalities that the process of unconscious imitation, by which every child acquires speech, habits, manners, and convictions, was made unusually complex. He could not, in all things, be like them both. Consciously or unconsciously it was necessary for him to compare, to appraise, and to select.

The contrasting traits between which he must choose were not superficial differences. Between Rufus and Maria Bellamy there was no great gulf in education or social background, or even in intelligence. There were no striking contrasts in inherited rank or wealth, no serious conflicts over social or financial policy. It appears that there was almost complete absence of personal quarreling between Edward Bellamy's father and mother. His father was easygoing and good-natured, and his mother, though of far more determined character, was too well-bred and had too much intuitive refinement to cheapen the family relationships in that way. There was no conflict as to which parent he should love best, and the exercise of choice was not diverted into those emotional, primitive alignments which so often are demanded of young children. With no marked superficial differences to detract Edward's attention, his necessity for choosing between contrasting traits was concerned with differences which ran deep, to the very make-up of personality.

In physical constitution Rufus Bellamy was "short and chunky." "He was so fat he could not lean over." The boys of the village used to say that if he should fall down hill he could roll endwise as well as sidewise, being so nearly globular. In contrast, Maria Bellamy, Edward Bellamy's mother, was described as "a thin, almost translucent wisp of a person, immaculately dressed, seeming like a piece of frail Dresden china." At the time of their marriage she was suffering from "consumption," and was not expected to live a year.

One is led to speculate as to what tends to be the effect on the physical or personal characteristics of children of such marked diversity of physical type in the parents. One might state as a tentative theory, which it would be interesting to explore, that extreme likeness of sound, normal parents as to physical and mental type—at least if they are not close relatives—will tend to result in children of compact, harmonious, well-integrated, and sound constitutions, but not of greater originality than their parents. Moderate variation in parents, with the resulting greater necessity for integration and adjustment in the biological development of children, will tend to break up excessive physical and mental stability and will increase the range both of chance and of choice in physical and mental development.

Excessive differences in the physical constitution of parents may, however, result in biological, emotional, and mental stresses too great to be fully mastered by any possible effort; with the result that "growing pains" may be lifelong, indecision may be very difficult to overcome, and physical or temperamental weaknesses may thwart the normal fulfillment of life. Heroic effort for mastery in such case may lead to genius. Less effort, or poorly directed effort, or handicaps which cannot be surmounted, may tend to frustration. Apparently this very idea occurred to Edward Bellamy, for we find it the basis for one of the plots for short stories with which some of his notebooks are filled.

Both in the physical and in the mental structure of Edward Bellamy there was lack of compact, highly integrated organization. Neither he nor his brother Packer, who died young, had a strong constitution. Quite probably the early death of Edward was due in part to lack of good hygienic management, yet a stronger constitution would have rendered defective diet and health habits less serious. Regardless of physical differences between his parents, it is possible that he inherited a frail constitution from his mother, though her weakness may not have been inherited, for her sister seems to have had a good constitution.

In Edward Bellamy's parents there was no less contrast in emotional than in physical traits. Rufus Bellamy was easygoing, comfortably lax in his dress, indulgent, inclined to lack of restraint in eating. Edward Bellamy wrote to his wife on October 21, 1886: "We are much concerned to hear of father's ill turn, which must have been something new for him. I infer from what you say that it was probably the result of overeating, as every one of his bad turns lately have been. That he will in the end kill himself with his knife and fork there is not the slightest doubt, but I hope we may, by constant endeavors, persuade him to postpone his suicide for a few years." This hope was not realized, and he died on November 16, 1886. The record is that he died of Bright's disease.

What a contrast is presented in Edward Bellamy's mother! Her son Frederick wrote of her: "She never had any patience with self-indulgence. Merely that it was a pleasure to do a thing constituted no recommendation or excuse for it, but rather an objection. She regarded the main purpose of life to be discipline of the heart, soul, and mind; and deprivation of sense gratifications she regarded not as a misfortune, but as a blessing and benefit." Was it not a

craving for a synthesis of these divergent traits which led Edward
Bellamy to write in his notebook: "To retain the child's zest for
the pleasures of life, while possessing the ascetic's or stoic's power
of renouncing them without a pang whenever it may be needful—
that is the ideal of philosophy." [10]

N. P. Ames Carter, a neighbor whose family was intimately associated with the Bellamys through two generations, said, "It was
Rufus who had the reputation of being friendly and helpful." He
was everybody's minister. Carter tells of attending the Baptist
Church of which Rufus Bellamy was pastor. As a boy Carter would
sleep through the long, prosy sermon, but wanted to wake up to
hear the prayer which, though long, was sure to be interesting.
Rufus Bellamy had the reputation in Chicopee Falls of being the
best "prayer maker" in town. After the service the boy Carter
would go to the front of the church to speak to the minister. "He
was so jolly and happy; and how he could tell yarns at the supper
table!" He was a favorite pastor of couples wanting to be married. From more than one source come accounts of his habit, when
the groom would hand him a small fee after the wedding ceremony,
of slipping it into the bride's hand, saying, "Just a little pin
money."

Harriet Putnam, sister of Edward Bellamy's mother, married
William Satterlee Packer of Brooklyn. A relative of Harriet Putnam Packer wrote of the Packer and Bellamy families:

> There was always the closest bond between them all, and continual
> interchange of visits. Harriet's husband died in 1850, leaving his large
> fortune to his wife. In 1853 she founded Packer Collegiate Institute in
> Brooklyn. Harriet was a remarkable character, strong, loyal, generous,
> with high ideals of life and its responsibilities.
>
> Rufus Bellamy was devoted to his sister-in-law. He was normal,
> equable, just, and keen; a very lovable, high-minded man, with a fine
> intellect and high integrity. More a brother to Harriet Packer than her
> own brother Joseph, he was a most loyal and able adviser and a strong
> moral support in her many problems. They never considered this as a
> compensation for all her monetary assistance in the education of his
> boys. They were both too whole-souled for such an attitude. Everything

[10] Unpublished papers of Edward Bellamy (B1-2-22, 23).

was freely and eagerly given because of the devoted bond between the two families, and accepted as naturally as it was extended.

Various business letters to his sister-in-law and to his sons disclose Rufus Bellamy as a level-headed person of calm, sound, and shrewd business judgment, but a judgment tempered with a sense of personal as well as economic values. His son Frederick, at about twenty-five, had gone into business with an apparently irresponsible partner. When he was considering whether or not to abandon the venture—of publishing a book financed by advertising—Rufus Bellamy wrote:

It is always good sense not to be swayed by one's mere wishes to have a thing go, or by the opinions of friends whose wishes may be the fathers of their favorable expectations, but by simple truth—welcome or unwelcome though it be. Every man of sense *changes his mind sometimes*. Don't attach too much importance to success in this particular thing. . . . I doubt if I should care to have you associate permanently with Rowe as a business partner. And it may be a kind of providence blocking your way at the outset—to keep you from worse luck in the future. I doubt if he has after all as good or safe a business head as you have. Don't be too anxious to succeed in this book. . . . You will succeed somehow in something . . . keep the reins in your own hands, so that you can dissolve at any time. . . . My idea is not to make you blue, but the contrary.

In cases concerning which correspondence is available his business forecasts were borne out by subsequent developments.

Mrs. Edward Bellamy described her father-in-law as "loved and respected by everyone in the neighborhood, irrespective of race or creed. He was everyone's friend, and spoke to everyone he met, seldom remembering their names." He had a friendly humor, and did not take himself very seriously. "For real work," he would say, "there are few behind me." Edward Bellamy told his wife that the staff members of his paper, the *New Nation*, liked to come to his office and would laugh uproariously at his stories and expressions, and that almost invariably what pleased them most were stories he had heard from his father.

This jovial, dynamic, indulgent personality had a wife who was of vastly different temper. A cousin of the family recalls that

Maria Bellamy was "interesting and clever looking, but she always seemed plaintive to me; inclined to pessimism, I should say, at least prone to look on the dark side of things, though keen in her comments, and no fool, with a dry humor." Ames Carter said of her: "Mrs. Rufus Bellamy had more personality than all the other ministers' wives put together. She was the backbone of the community. She wanted everything done perfectly. She was small, but carried herself wonderfully. She was about the same height as her husband, but had an air that gave her inches." She set standards of propriety in the community. Edward Bellamy's wife wrote of her, "People had to walk a crack with Edward's mother. She was very critical. I was scared to death of her. She would go at things the hardest way and expected others to do the same. She impressed me as an extremely intelligent person."

Though of a cold, intellectual type, she had a keen sense of right and duty, with an austere kindness. She thought of everyone sick or in trouble. She was continually sending her children on errands of neighborliness, as with a bowl of broth or a cup of jelly where there was sickness. "All her life she sacrificed in every conceivable way to make such services possible," Mrs. Edward Bellamy related, and continued, "She was greatly respected in the community, whereas Father Bellamy was greatly loved."

In home manners, also, the contrast of personalities was in evidence. Everything she did was precise, formal, correct. Rufus was informal and easygoing. He would say, "Mother, may I have a spoon for my custard pie?" She would reply, "Why, Father!" That "Why, Rufus!" or "Why, Father!" was a characteristic exclamation when he showed unconcern for the proprieties. She never spoke of her husband to others familiarly as "Rufus," but always as "Father," or "Mr. Bellamy."

In ideas of education and of recreation this contrast continued. Edward Bellamy's brother Frederick wrote:

The father was a great admirer of Dickens and Thackeray, but the mother was wont to look askance at her children if even the best of fiction was often seen in their hands. . . . Her objection to novels was that there were so many more useful books. . . . To sit with folded hands was never palliated. "Get a book," was Mother's never failing suggestion, and it must be an informing book, too. . . . It was largely owing to the father's influence that the boys were brought up to read the daily papers, but the mother thought more of the importance of history.[11]

In religion Rufus Bellamy was tolerant and liberal, too kind-hearted to believe in eternal damnation. His wife was orthodox, but with both there was the quality of sincerity. Edward Bellamy's wife wrote to Rufus Bellamy, "He was far ahead of his time, theologically speaking, and was all but accused of heresy by members of his congregation, because he expressed emphatic doubt as to the existence of hell and the probability of eternal punishment." Mrs. Marion Bellamy Earnshaw, Edward Bellamy's daughter, wrote: "My grandmother was orthodox about everything, even to sewing a seam. Religiously she was orthodox, and deeply spiritual. She read constantly. When Maria Bellamy talked with her son Edward, it was nearly always about religious and spiritual matters." Perhaps we can guess the incentive which led Edward Bellamy, during his early or middle twenties, to write in his journal, "If one has a religion he is in misery until at least the closer circle of friends are in the same particular ark with himself." [12]

Maria Bellamy's religion was no mere dogmatism. Brother Frederick, in describing Edward Bellamy's home life, wrote: "Next to revealed religion the chief consideration of his mother was a high aim in life. . . . Anything like sham or affectation jarred. Nothing ever brought stinging rebuke from her so quickly as the least hint of artificiality. She had no patience, either, for talk without solid worth or meaning, and was ever warning her boys against the folly of talking just to avoid seeming awkward." It was between such sharply contrasting traits that young Edward had to choose during those early years when character and personality were taking their lifetime set.

In view of the personal traits of the parents it is not surprising that the spirit of the mother was dominant in the Bellamy household. One of the most intimate friends of the family said that the four boys valued their mother's opinion more than their father's. Her discipline pervaded the home. Her son Frederick wrote: "She

[11] Green, pp. 12–13.   [12] Unpublished papers (B1-1-17).

did not let her boys out in the evening, but promptly after tea they gathered around a common table, each with his own book or studies, and thus passed the time until going to bed. Yet the mother never used her influence to shorten the needful hours for out-of-door exercise. She wanted her boys to be virile as well as studious and earnest." [13]

So far as the mother's influence was concerned, the Bellamy home was a typical example of an ancient process. Whenever any person has made great effort to achieve mastery of his or her life, and has developed clear purpose, that purpose and discipline come to be held with a strong sense of value. They are of all things most precious, and there is powerful desire to pass them on as an addition to the cultural inheritance. Especially in case of a mother whose life finds chief expression through her children, there is strong hope that what she has won by her life's effort shall be transmitted without loss to her children. Yet the world about her is commonplace. It has no clear-cut convictions, no purposes which it considers worth achieving at a great price, no abhorrence of mediocrity, no habit of excellence. And so she may see the achievement to which she has given her whole life powers begin to be dissolved, diluted, blurred, and debased. She fights against that debasement, and as a technique of strategy she tries to restrict the outside dissipating influences, and to increase and intensify those which seem to add value to personality. That is the eternal process of great parenthood and of great leadership.

Such parents and leaders know that intellectual freedom is not caught from the mass of men. From ordinary contacts men become indoctrinated with the world as it is, and are under servitude to its clumsy, undiscriminating, indulgent ways. That is not freedom. And so, back of nearly every life of great achievement we shall find a parent, a friend, or a teacher who has striven greatly to transmit what he has achieved as the essence of his life.

Notwithstanding this sustained, unremitting effort of the mother, all three of her sons who lived to maturity abandoned the orthodox religious creed to which she was committed. How important these

[13] Green, p. 12.

beliefs were to her may be inferred from a letter she wrote to Edward on his twenty-first birthday:

March 26 [*1871*]

To-day, my dear child, you enter on a new year of your life—one too in some respects of more interest than any that has preceded it, inasmuch as it will introduce you to the responsibilities of manhood. May the best of blessings be yours, and chiefest among them a heart to consecrate yourself a *"living sacrifice"* to your God and Saviour. There surely can never be a more appropriate time to commence a more earnest spiritual life. That the spirit of God may incline you to this, is my most earnest prayer, and will you not add yours?

These little *studs* were long worn by your *dear brother* who left us almost two years ago, and I transfer them to you, knowing that this will give them, to you, a double value.

MOTHER

This concern of Edward's mother did not fade. Seven years later, when he and his brother Fred were on the trip to Hawaii, she wrote to them, "How intense is my longing to have you brought into fellowship with him, Christ."

Not only did the habit of self-direction which Edward Bellamy had developed prevent him from fulfilling his mother's hope, but there is repeated evidence that in his effort to become free from the loving pressure upon him, he came to the point of spiritual rebellion. In one of his early journals we find this short note, "It has come to that now that I don't know how a man can better serve his country than by becoming an infidel." [14] Not that he was unaware of the pain which his doubt caused his mother. We find him writing at the age of twenty-two: "I doubt not that often times in New England where people take their religion so earnestly parents of strong dogmatic convictions have suffered more from the irreligious dispositions of children than any satisfactions of parentage have compensated. Love is most tyrannous." [15] The very sincerity of mind with which Mother Bellamy indoctrinated her boys, together with their father's more liberal views, drove them away from the religious faith to which she was committed and to which she hoped to commit them. Had the son held to his mother's creed

[14] Unpublished papers (B2-4-5).   [15] *Ibid.* (B1-1-17).

he would have been false to her highest hope for him—that he maintain his spiritual integrity.

While Edward disappointed his mother in his religious beliefs, she recognized his sincerity and took satisfaction in his life. It is clear from her letters to him in later years that his departure from her creed had not destroyed her confidence in him. In this her intuitions overrode her intellectual convictions. What she actually believed was finer than the creed which she had been taught to think that she believed. Frederick Bellamy wrote of Edward: "He was a boy after his mother's own heart. His earnestness was hers; his studiousness delighted her; his devotion to the pursuit of knowledge fulfilled her every ambition for him, and his early-budding facility in the use of language satisfied her correct taste and high standards."

The statement of Edward Bellamy's wife, "There never was any quarreling in Rufus Bellamy's family," seems reasonably to represent the actual conditions. The fact that two persons, so divergent in many ways, yet each strongly individualistic, had a long companionship of harmony and co-operation is testimony to the character and culture of both—an illustration of the truth that a successful home is an achievement, and not just a fortunate accident of circumstance. Had there been a lack of tolerance, good will, and persistent determination to make the home a success, it might quickly have disintegrated through incompatibility, with the result that the background and cultural inheritance of the children would have been distorted and greatly impoverished.

The effect on Edward Bellamy of this achievement of an atmosphere of harmony in the presence of great diversity of traits is reflected in the following entry in his journal of some time during his twenties: "Quarrels seem to me somehow impertinent, trivial, however grave. They are such assertions of personalities, which are at best the altogether insignificant side of men's nature. They are irrelevant to the existence of the Soul of Solidarity." [16]

The effect of this good breeding in the home lasted through the years. The freedom and necessity for choice which was innate in

[16] Unpublished papers (B2-4-5).

the family naturally led to diversity in the children. A cousin wrote of the Rufus Bellamy family, "Their four delightful sons were each a personality, all different and lovable in various ways." The strong loyalty and affection between the brothers survived extreme differences of social outlook. When Edward Bellamy, in Denver during his last illness, wished to return to his home, both his surviving brothers made the trip to Colorado to return with him. One of these brothers was an active and prosperous member of the New York bar and of the profession concerning which Edward had written frequently in extreme condemnation.

In this great diversity in the Bellamy home, combined as it was with mutual respect, tolerance, patience, and affection, do we not have one of the major conditions which led to that rare capacity for creative thinking and for independent critical judgment which characterized the life and thought of Edward Bellamy?

III · Boyhood

EDWARD BELLAMY kept diaries from the time he was about ten years old. Apparently they were destroyed in the fire which burned the material collected by Mason Green for writing his biography. As a result, we have little information concerning his boyhood except a few references by Green and some miscellaneous papers.

To a degree we seldom realize, the thinking of our lifetime has its beginning in very early experience. Bellamy's boyhood thinking forecast the major themes of his life. The very earliest record we have of his mind discloses an interest in problems of metaphysics. When he was about three years old, his mother observed that he seemed greatly concerned as he repeated his prayer, with the familiar lines:

> If I should die before I wake,
> I pray Thee, Lord, my soul to take.

For several evenings, after repeating these words, he would turn to his mother and say, "Then I shan't have any soul, shall I?"

The incident of the child's prayer is an early hint of a theme that runs through the life of Edward Bellamy. In one of his journals we find the entry:

It is generally believed that men have a double mode of existence, that of the body and of the soul; the one a material existence by the senses, the other a spiritual existence by the consciousness. However we may claim to be souls, we feel after all that the life of the mind and the body is our most substantial hold on existence, and that the soul is only a little better than nothing when the body perishes.[1]

As the earliest recorded conversation of Edward Bellamy dealt with metaphysics, so his earliest recorded writing presents a plan for the economic organization of a society. The following literary

[1] Unpublished papers (B3B-Miscellaneous Fragments, p. 4).

and sociological achievement is a product of the year 1860, when Edward was ten years old:

A Law for the Republic of San Domingo

I learn from books that the inhabitants of that country are a Idle and Lazy set of people I have thot it over and thought of a remedy for it here it is That the National Assembly or Congress should make a law compeling every person to cultivate a portion of land given them by government let government be willing to buy as much of the produce of the land as the people are willing to sell to them. Begin with a small piece of land and give the people a little more every year till they have quite a farm then cease The people Must and Cannot help in a short time being interested in it

Ed S [2]

The conviction that people could not help but be interested in his plan is a boyhood expression of that optimism which we find many years later in his attitude concerning the prospect for the social changes pictured in *Looking Backward* and promoted by the Nationalist movement. In 1888, shortly after the publication of his great book, he wrote:

Looking Backward, although in form a fanciful romance, is intended, in all seriousness, as a forecast, in accordance with the principles of evolution, of the next stage in the industrial and social development of humanity, especially in this country; and no part of it is believed by the author to be better supported by the indications of probability than the implied prediction that the dawn of the new era is already near at hand, and that the full day will swiftly follow.[3]

Also when he was ten years old, Edward gave expression to another interest which led him to discover what he called "the cornerstone" of his social system, the industrial army. He admired military organization and the career of the soldier. The following is from an entry in a boyhood diary or journal:

What I think ought to be the character of a soldier.

1. Self control. In order to control others.
2. Obedience to orders. In order to help gain victories.

[2] *Ibid.* (B3B).
[3] *Looking Backward,* Postscript, p. 334. All quotations from *Looking Backward* are used by permission of the publisher, Houghton, Mifflin.

3. Love for his profession. So as to have an undivided heart.
4. Some ambition. If you have love for your profession you will have this.
5. Attention. In order to learn and know more, besides it looks better.
6. Quick decision. If you are an officer you will have to practice it.
7. Determination. In order to carry out anything that you begin.
8. Bravery. So as not to feel uncomfortably afraid.

An apology for having left out so many qualities.

These are perhaps but few of the qualities that ought to be possessed by a good soldier, but they are the principal ones that I thought of that moment. They are 8 that I thought I should like to have and 8 that I think will carry me through my Military career. (1860) [4]

A year or two later we find a tabulated list of Napoleon's marshals, with Edward's appraisal of their relative importance. From about the same date there is a long, painstaking discussion of the formation of an army corps, with outlines of the duties of the several officers. During the impressionable years, when he was eleven to fifteen years old, his country was carrying on a war to preserve the Union and to free the slaves. That conflict had less of sordidness than many wars. The idealistic element was strong and evidently made a very deep impression on Edward.

There are several schoolboy compositions written at the ages of eleven to thirteen, each in the field of one of his vital interests of later years.

Before he was twelve years old we find him giving expression to still another of his lifelong concerns, that of self-mastery and character building:

Resolutions

Made by E. S. Bellamy and approved by the same on the 13th of Jan. 1862 A. D.

I, E. S. Bellamy, Affirm that I will as far as possible, Abide by the resolutions.
Added. Not to blackguard nor cheat. I wrote it.
E. S. Bellamie.

1st Not in any way to equivocate or try to convey a wrong impression.
2nd Not to speak before I think.
3rd Not to give up my will in any wrong way.

[4] Green, p. 16.

4th Never to stand by silently and hear others lie or cheat.
5th To try and keep cool.
6th To stand up for those oppressed.
7th Not to use the word Cant.
8th To hate meanness with all my heart and soul.
9th To cultivate determination decision and presence of mind.
10th To obey those who have a Legitimate power over me.
11th Not to ask any more questions than needful.
12th To speak the truth at all times and without reserve.
13th Not to fight unless my cause is good and I first cool.

Signed,
E. S. BELLAMY [5]

At the age of thirteen he wrote, so far as we know, his first treatise in the field of economics. Here again we see the mind of the man foreshadowed in that of the boy. The gist of this brief essay follows:

Does Time Establish a Usurpation?

In the system of politics usually accepted by men it is held that it does, and whosoever or whatsoever endeavors to overthrow usurpation established by time would be by men considered as revolutionary in a vast sense, and ought to be punished. That is, anything whatsoever, however obtained, if held for a few years becomes rightful property. This doctrine is not just, as it appears to my mind. . . . Time cannot change evil to good nor make a rightful inheritance out of a usurpation. . . .

E. S. BELLAMY [6]

To carry out the implications of these paragraphs would indeed be "revolutionary in a vast sense," and might develop into the proposals which took form in *Looking Backward*. Several other of his unusual boyhood concerns are identical with attitudes or interests of his mature years. For instance, his lifelong, intense dislike of flattery was distinctly expressed when he was twelve.

Most of the issues of his life had taken shape in his mind during childhood. In the fragments of his boyhood thinking and writing that have been preserved we find much of the later mental life in embryo. If our data were fuller, that early pattern of thinking doubtless would disclose a more complete forecast of his mature mind. Is that not true of men generally?

---

[5] *Ibid.,* p. 11.   [6] Unpublished papers (B3B-Miscellaneous Fragments).

Of all that Bellamy wrote, nothing so captured the mind of the public as "The Parable of the Water Tank." It has been reprinted again and again, probably to the extent of several million copies. It may be that the inspiration for this little masterpiece was a memory of his boyhood. The following bit of village history was related by his long-time friend and neighbor, Ames Carter.

In the early days of Chicopee Falls a water supply was provided by building a storage tank on the top of a hill, and by laying a pipe line made of hollowed logs, carefully matched, end to end. Connections were made to individual houses by boring holes into the logs and fitting in lead pipes. In time the hollow logs were replaced by iron water pipe and the system was extended, though served by the same tank on the hill. Probably in payment for some service rendered in establishing the line, the Bellamy home and one other had perpetual rights to a water supply without cost.

The tank and pipe line served the well-to-do families near the top of the hill, and then the pipe line extended downhill to the long rows of tenement houses at the bottom. On Monday mornings, when the week's washing was under way in the tenement houses, the tank would be emptied, and the families of the elite near the top of the hill would be without a supply. Such a condition violated their superior status. Therefore, just downhill from the homes of the elite a high loop was made in the pipe, extending up into the air as high as the middle of the tank. The water could not flow down the hill unless it passed over that loop. When this change had been made, if the tank was more than half empty the elite continued to have water, while frequently the people in the tenements at the bottom were entirely deprived of a supply. The observation of such a condition, of which his father's home was a beneficiary, could not but impress the alert, curious mind of young Edward.

Perhaps the best picture of his life at this age is given by Edward Bellamy himself. When he was about twenty-five he began an autobiography, but apparently he never carried his story beyond the age of seventeen. That fragment is written in the third person, the name "Hugh" being used in place of Edward. In other respects it

EDWARD BELLAMY'S HOME IN CHICOPEE

seems to be a true picture. The first part of this fragment, covering his age from about ten to fifteen, is quoted:

"That lad sitting on the floor in the dim-lighted, book-walled library is very busy, and if you look over his shoulder, you will not disturb him."

"What is the book he is so intently poring over?"

"Well, I warrant you it will turn out to be the life of Napoleon, of Mohammed, of Nelson, or very like some Plutarchian demigod of the foreworld. Over such great stories he spends his leisure hours; that is, all the time he can spare from play. It is interesting to watch the expression of his face as he reads. Now surely he is charging over the bridge of Lodi with the Corsican. Before such a look the Austrian gunners quailed. Now pride, now courage, now self-sacrifice, now shame, now admiration transforms the face. It is a peculiarity of his reading that with every hero he measures himself. Every deed of high emprise challenges him with the question 'Would I do likewise?' " [7]

His brother Frederick gives us a picture of Edward in the Bellamy home:

From his earliest childhood, his distaste for the conventionalities of casual or formal society was very characteristic, and was a frequent source of amusement to his entire family. When in the long winter evening in the country home in Chicopee, he settled down to his books, or to his reading, he dreaded the sound of the door bell which might announce the casual caller, as if it forebode an earthquake. He would often say to his mother or his wife, "Pull down the curtains, don't put a light in the front hall, for it might lure someone in to call upon us." [8]

It would be a mistake to regard young Edward as having no usual children's interests. The Reverend R. E. Bisbee, a friend of Bellamy, wrote: "As a youth Edward was fond of boyish sports. He was an expert skater and swimmer, a skillful huntsman, and a remarkably good shot." [9] All his life he enjoyed exercising his marksmanship. As a boy, though he disliked the formal visits of parishioners, "He loved comradeship, and the Bellamy homestead and grounds were a great haunt for the boys of the village." [10] At home

---

[7] Unpublished papers (B3B-Autobiography).   [8] Green, p. 13.

[9] R. E. Bisbee, "Some Characteristics of Edward Bellamy," *Coming Age*, I, No. 2 (February, 1899), 181.

[10] *Ibid.*

he loved the Chicopee River and the Connecticut River, and was a good boatman. Occasionally the family vacationed on the New England coast, especially on Long Island Sound. Edward liked the salt water. He knew the names and characteristics of all types of boats, an interest which never faded.

He liked to tramp over the hills, and made friends with the farmers. It is recorded that he had a very erect posture as he walked. We get a reflection of his boyhood life in his first book, *The Duke of Stockbridge,* in which he says of one of the characters: "Doubtless he was dreaming of the time when, as a boy, he played all day in the shining fields, or went blackberrying in the ardent July sun. For him the river was gleaming again, turning its million glittering facets to the sun, or perhaps his eye was delighting in the still sheen of ponds in Indian summer, as they reflected the red glory of the overhanging maple or the bordering sumach thicket." [11]

Five years later he wrote in the *Springfield Union,* "Nature can be studied in other ways than with a geologist's hammer or a botanist's herbarium." [12] He took to the woods, the meadows, and the hills as a poet rather than as a naturalist. His sense of light and color, of sunset on the river, or of a vista among the hills, runs through his journals, but we find few observations on the specific characteristics of plants or animals, or of interest in minerals or in geological formations.

Religious interests were dominant in the family of the Reverend Rufus Bellamy. The affairs of the church and of its members were the daily occupation. Mason Green tells us that Edward and his brothers "were expected to attend two services on Sunday besides Sunday-school, while during the week family prayers were said once and sometimes twice a day, and then there were their own at the bedside or at their mother's knee." [13]

At the age of fourteen Edward was "converted," and on April 3, 1864, was baptized and became a member of the Baptist Church of which his father was the minister. The short autobiographical sketch, already quoted, gives an intimate account of this period:

[11] *The Duke of Stockbridge,* p. 37. Reprinted by permission.
[12] "Nature and Ourselves," *Springfield Union,* August 20, 1874.
[13] Green, p. 9.

At an early age this aspirant of a grand destiny had not failed to perceive the necessary and utter pettiness of all achievement undertaken in the selfish spirit as contrasted with the infinite scope of unselfish aims. He was therefore greatly troubled in his mind, lest his own lofty aspirations might spring from a selfish love of fame or personal credit. In this desire to escape self he became greatly captivated by the idea of service. He would be the servant of God, of humanity. He would, in fine, shuffle off the responsibility of being selfish upon somebody else, either God or humanity, by devoting himself to them.

. . . .

This period seemed to close with a religious experience. His life as a child had been one of entire conformity to the rules of propriety. The great dreams which dominated his mind had a restraining effect upon his conduct so that even of boyish peccadilloes, he committed scarcely his share. But he had been taught to believe that he was a grievous sinner, accursed from God with whom he must make peace or suffer the most terrible consequences. He had never thought at all upon such subjects but had accepted this state of the case as an undoubted reality. Accordingly, he submitted to the emotional experience of a religious conversion. He came to feel a sense of intimacy and to enjoy an indescribably close and tender communion with what seemed to him a very real and sublime being. The mental and moral revolutions of later years never blotted from his mind the strange and touching experiences of this epoch. In prayer he took a deep and awful pleasure; it was to him a sensation at once of almost sensuous happiness as of ineffable sublimity when at such times his heart seemed to throb with that of deity and his soul seemed fused and melted in perfect union with the divine. A love more tender and passionate than any with which human charms ever moved him seemed then to bind him to the infinite. From school he hastened home to pray, not that he wanted anything, save only to be with God. . . . He saw the world with new eyes. There seemed no other business in it save God's service, no other reward save communion with Him.

He ceased to feel any interest in any reading which did not relate to this subject. It seemed to him that the only bond of brotherhood between men must be their brotherhood in Christ. His earlier ambitions he did not renounce but they were in suspense.

The relation established by Christianity between the believer and Christ makes a woman of the former, tending as it does peculiarly to cultivate the feminine graces of trustfulness and confidence in protection to be repaid by love. It is better adapted to women than men on whose minds it has an effect to degenerate the masculine virtues of self-reliance and valor.

Death, which had always been an unpleasant thought to him, now became a delightful occasion of faith, an ecstatic experience which it were a pity a man could not more than once undergo. Hugh used to go to sleep at night with a feeling of exultation at the thought that he might die before morning. No thought so calmed and prepared his mind for slumber.

In these days so complete seemed his dependence on Christ for support, courage, inspiration, that he naively wondered how he had formerly got along at all, or how the rest of his world managed to exist in their prayerless, godless state. There were now always two to consult on every step, himself and his deity. The effect of these experiences on his conduct was also noteworthy.[14]

What books did Edward peruse when "He ceased to feel any interest in any reading which did not relate to this subject" of religion? It would seem almost certain that among them were the works of his illustrious ancestor, Joseph Bellamy, whose three-volume life and sermons have survived from his father's library. That Joseph Bellamy was not reticent in expressing what to him were the great realities, the following brief extracts from his sermons will indicate:

. . . the guilt of all the damned will be increasing to all eternity; and no doubt their punishment will increase in the same proportion. How inconceivably and infinitely dreadful, therefore, will be their case, who are thus continually sinking deeper and deeper into the bottomless pit of woe and misery![15]

There is nothing more difficult in the whole work preparatory to conversion, than to make the sinner see, and feel, and own, that it is just, quite just, altogether just and fair, for God to damn him.[16]

The ecstasy after conversion recounted in the autobiography was much like that described by Edward's great ancestor:

Marvelous is the change which the poor sinner passes through in that awful hour of inexpressible solemnity, when he first comes into the awful presence of the dread Majesty of heaven and earth, through Jesus Christ, the glorious Mediator, venturing his ALL for ETERNITY upon this sure foundation. And now, from this time forward, he is quite another creature, under quite new circumstances.[17]

[14] Unpublished papers (B3B-Autobiography).
[15] *The Works of the Rev. Joseph Bellamy, D.D.*, I, 109.
[16] *Ibid.*, p. 159.
[17] *Ibid.*, p. 452. That Edward Bellamy was not permanently awed by these terrifying predictions of his ancestor is clear from the following comment in a

It is not surprising that the boy of fourteen was "converted," with the family praying nightly for his soul, and his beloved mother anguishing for his salvation. Emotional pressure upon him at that time must have been extreme, exercised as it was by those whom he most greatly loved and most highly respected. Where was his refuge from such pressure?

For the period when Edward Bellamy was fifteen to twenty years old, we have very little information. A paragraph in the autobiography already quoted relates to these years:

His plans were as definite as they were prodigious. Nor does this mean that the boy was vain. He was simply penetrated through and through by the intoxicating aroma of glory exhaled from the pages, for so many years his daily recourse. His only views of life and action in the world were gathered from them. The men and women whom he saw in the world about him, he regarded with a serene contempt or rather a total indifference. They seemed to him merely the lay figures of the world. From his intercourse with heroes and kings he had gained a royal air in regarding the common herd.[18]

Just why there is almost no record of the years which often constitute the most vitally and tumultuously active time of a man's entire life, I do not know. Quite probably the journals and diaries of the period were burned with the house of Mason Green. The fact (stated by his daughter) that Bellamy read Latin, French, and German with ease, had some knowledge of Italian (his daughter remembers numerous Italian books in his library) and translated Greek reasonably well; the unusual range of information disclosed in his editorials and book reviews for the *Springfield Union* during the early seventies; and the quality of his literary style by the time he was twenty—such evidence indicates that these years were not wasted.

book review written when he was twenty-three: "When D.D.'s disagree it does not become seculars to express any very positive opinion, but we presume to say that the general flux of theological opinion at this epoch is not more marked in any particular than in regard to the state of the dead, especially of sinners, the only class whose numbers are sufficiently large to make their fate of interest. The conclusion is obvious that in this variety and confusion of opinions, it is a far more risky thing to depart this life than formerly, when views were more settled." It is probable that his father chuckled and his mother frowned on reading this in the *Springfield Union*. ("Literary Notices," *Springfield Union*, August 14, 1873.)

18 Unpublished papers (B3B-Autobiography).

Among letters of the family of Edward's Aunt Harriet Packer we find a few references to this period. On December 20 of 1865 or 1866, Edward's mother wrote to her sister Harriet about his education:

With reference to what you say of Ed, we are of course very thankful for your intimation with reference to assisting us &c. As to the time when it is best for him to leave home, I presume you are wise—that it is better for him to be put off as long as may be. The only difficulty is to know what to do with him *in school* in the interval. He has read nearly all the Latin and Greek, and been over more than all in Algebra & Geometry, that they do the Senior year in Easthampton or other preparatory schools. Still I think he is too young, especially not being stronger, to enter College next fall, and doubtless there are ways in which his time can be spent profitably.

Under the date of October, 1867, when he was seventeen and a half, we find a memorandum of study that he set for himself, which indicates that his dominant traits had not changed:

Necessary Self-Education

I. A thorough acquaintance with the history of the world, Social and Political, Ancient and Modern.

II. A thorough acquaintance with Physical and Political Geography.

III. A thorough acquaintance with the Laws of Society in its life and government, which Laws are properly comprehended in the subject of Political Economy.

IV. A thorough acquaintance with the French and Spanish Languages, particularly the latter, with such other of the principal modern languages as may be attainable without the neglect of other branches of study.

V. A thorough acquaintance with the theory of Military Science.

VI. The study of such works of mental science and logical demonstration as shall tend to strengthen and methodize the operations of the mind.

VII. Such practice in public speaking and writing as may be attainable.

VIII. Finally, in addition to this system of study, such acquirements of general knowledge, of mental discipline, of conversational power, of acquaintance with human nature as developed in myself and in others, by the processes of introspection and extraspection, as may altogether make up a man equal to the accomplishment of those purposes in life to which I have appointed myself.

IX. With such moral self-education as shall prevent me from yielding or departing from my high purpose through any temptation of personal reputation or indolent repose, or any other influence whatsoever.

X. And for the physical system, such care and strengthening and discipline as shall prepare it to be the effective instrument of my mind through life.[19]

The one phase of this program which he did not sustain was the care of his physical health. Had he been as conscientious and skillful in that as in the other elements, he might have had a much more complete life.

The emphasis on military life and training, which had continued from his early boyhood, found its climax in his effort in 1867 to be enrolled at the United States Military Academy at West Point. There is a definite tradition that he passed all other examinations with very high ratings, but that he was rejected because of physical inadequacy. Failure to be admitted to West Point probably was the greatest blow to his hopes that Edward Bellamy had experienced up to that time. It came after at least seven years of interest, almost to the point of infatuation, in a military career.

In the fall of 1867 Edward's brother Frederick was entering his senior year at Union College at Schenectady, New York, and Edward, following his failure to enter West Point, joined him there. So far as remaining written records, or even traditions, are concerned, the succeeding year in Edward Bellamy's life is almost a complete blank. Forty-five years later Frederick Bellamy wrote:

During the year 1867, when I was in college in the class of 1868, he was with me for a year, taking a special course in literature which the professor kindly allowed him to select for himself. . . . Edward Bellamy was an extremely reticent man and mingled very little with men of the college, except those of my class whom he met with me.

There is no official record of attendance of Edward Bellamy at Union College. The books of the Philomathean Society show that he paid his initiation fee some time between January 17 and May 18, 1868. According to college officials:

[19] Unpublished papers (B3B-Miscellaneous Fragments).

The fact that he joined this society and also the Delta Kappa Epsilon fraternity establishes a strong presumption that he had regular standing in the College. He apparently took a course in English, whatever else he did at Union.

His teacher of English must have been the Reverend Ransom B. Welch, Professor of Rhetoric and Logic at Union College from 1866 to 1876. He was a Presbyterian minister who had preached in the towns to the south. From 1858 to 1860 he traveled in Europe, Egypt, and Palestine, and sent many letters back to the *New York Herald,* and the *Tribune*. He published a long series of books, as well as articles in various magazines.

A sketch in an unnamed religious publication further describes this teacher, and perhaps reveals the atmosphere of the college:

Three characteristics, as a teacher, stood out prominently in him. First, his earnestness and truth. Out of this came a second characteristic, a conservative caution. Clearly and sharply drawn, in his own thinking, was the line between revealed and speculative thought. In regard to the latter, he was exceedingly careful. Where a sure word of Scripture was not behind him, he was cautiously reticent. Two reasons seem to have shut out the Socratic method from his classroom. He wished to avoid useless discussion and to place before his students a system of truth in its entirety. He was convinced of the ultimate fruitlessness of all merely impulsive discussion. The third point was his progressive and charitable spirit. He was cautiously progressive. He was a gentleman of singular polish and courtesy; a scholar of wide and accurate research; a teacher, whose clearness and frankness won, and whose thoroughness stimulated, every pupil.

Is not this a good description of the "ideal" denominational college teacher of that period? In view of Edward's inquiring and rebellious spirit, such a mental outlook in a teacher or in a college may well have been one of the reasons why he did not return.

Letters from his parents make it clear that he had refrained from taking financial help from them, which indirectly might have come from his Brooklyn aunt. His wife definitely is of the opinion that this was the reason for leaving Union College. An article in the *Springfield Union* records her memory that he "could not bear to have his mother sit up night after night, by the dim oil light, darning stockings for him." [20]

[20] Walter A. Smith, *The Religion of Edward Bellamy.*

When he was twenty-two his mother wrote to him:

I had however a notion of being a little hurt that you scorned my poor little V; it wasn't mine either except as a member of the family, for Father gave it to me & would have sent more but for fear of your being annoyed at it. If we were straightened in any way & had to practice self-denials in pecuniary matters, it would not be strange that you felt sensitive about receiving a little in this way, but as it is I feel it is a pity you have such notions. This is especially out of place when you have had *so much less expended* on you & *your education* than the other boys—in fact hardly anything, directly. We are abundantly able to render you all the assistance you require & have all the requisite seamstresses beside. Father says he was never as well off in this respect as now, & I feel that it is true, because we can *pay all our debts,* and have a very tolerable margin to begin again.

The Reverend R. E. Bisbee, his friend and neighbor, wrote of his return from Union, "He came home, and by himself learned three or four modern languages, read an immense amount of literature and history, and secured much more than the college could give him." [21]

There may have been still another reason why Edward did not return to Union College—the demand, after the death of his brother Packer, that he go to Europe. Packer Bellamy, Edward's oldest brother, was a boy without a rugged constitution, but with an active mind. William Packer said of his cousin that he was an equally good judge of a poem and of a steam engine. The two cousins, Packer Bellamy and William Packer, were traveling in Europe in 1868 when Packer Bellamy died on the second of April in the south of France. William Packer's mother and sister were in Europe at that time, and late in May Edward's parents joined them there. On reaching Europe they decided that since William Packer, who had returned to America with the body of his cousin, was much depressed by his death, Edward should spend the year with him in Europe.

There followed urgent letters from Edward's parents and his aunt, asking him to come to Europe. Edward did not wish to do so;

21 R. E. Bisbee, "Some Characteristics of Edward Bellamy," *Coming Age,* I, No. 2 (February, 1899), 181.

whether because he wanted to return to Union College, or because
he did not want to receive money from his aunt, or because he had
his own program of work and study laid out, we can only guess.

Then, on July 16, 1868, his parents, who were at Neuchatel,
wrote him most peremptorily. His father, in a letter addressed to
all his sons, said, ". . . it will be extremely foolish for Ed not to
come . . . it would seem to them selfish pride not to come." His
mother wrote even more urgently: "Will seemed very sad. Almost
every place, as he told father, reminding him so much of Packer. It
is wonderful to see how much he loved our dear child and brother.
It is for this reason that I do feel that Ed is in duty bound to come
to us and to him." Then, speaking of Edward, she added for final
insistence: "I may forgive his past failures to meet our wishes, but
he need not calculate upon it if he disappoints us here. But he won't
be so perverse I know."

Under this pressure from his parents, with no less insistence from
his Aunt Harriet Packer, Edward gave up whatever plans he had,
and in the fall of 1868 went to Europe to spend part of a year with
his cousin.

Edward's journals and letters of his European trip probably
were among the papers destroyed in the Mason Green fire. Mason
Green wrote:

Shortly after the funeral [of Packer Bellamy] William and Edward
sailed for England and joined Mrs. Packer, who took the two young
men to Dresden and saw them comfortably settled in a German family
before her return. The young men studied in Dresden during the winter of 1868–9, learning to speak and write German and attending lectures.[22]

One surviving sketch for a story seems to indicate that they
spent a few days on the coast of Holland. Absolutely no other direct record of the European trip, not even a letter, has been found,
except brief and general statements of Edward Bellamy himself, of
which the following is typical:

I well remember in those days of European travel how much more
deeply that black background of misery impressed me than the palaces

[22] Green, p. 22.

and cathedrals in relief against it. I distinctly recall the innumerable debates, suggested by the piteous sights about us, which I had with a dear companion of my journey, as to the possibility of finding some great remedy for poverty, some plan for equalizing human conditions. Our discussions usually brought up against the same old stump: who would do the dirty work? We did not realize, as probably few do who lightly dismiss the subject of social reform with the same query, that its logic implies the condonation of all forms of slavery. Not until we all acknowledge the world's "dirty work" as our common and equal responsibility, shall we be in a position intelligently to consider, or have the disposition seriously to seek, a just and reasonable way of distributing and adjusting the burden. So it was that I returned home, for the first time aroused to the existence and urgency of the social problem, but without as yet seeing any way out. Although it had required the sights of Europe to startle me to a vivid realization of the inferno of poverty beneath our civilization, my eyes having once been opened I had now no difficulty in recognizing in America, and even in my own comparatively prosperous village, the same conditions in course of progressive development.[23]

The visit to Dresden of Edward Bellamy and William Packer took place shortly after the war between Prussia and Austria. Saxony, of which Dresden was the capital, had sided with Austria, had been conquered by Prussia, and then had joined the North German Federation. At the time of Bellamy's arrival the Prussian troops had only recently withdrawn from the city.

During the decade from 1860 to 1870 the world, and especially Germany, was seeing stirring times. German science was vigorous, and so were liberal social movements. Max Beer, in his *Social Struggles and Modern Socialism*, sums up the period:

The years 1860 to 1870 marked the era of Liberalism. In great Britain, John Stuart Mill and William E. Gladstone celebrated political triumphs; in the United States of America there raged a civil war (1861–1865) for national unity and slave emancipation, from which the liberal Lincoln emerged as the victor; in France the middle-class-republican opposition raised its head and Napoleon's throne began to shake; in Prussia the liberal middle-class organized itself in the National Union as an opposition to Bismarck, who was eventually compelled by the exigencies of home politics as well as by his warlike policy

<hr>

23 Bellamy, "How I Wrote *Looking Backward*," *Ladies' Home Journal*, XI, No. 5 (April, 1894), 2. Reprinted by permission.

towards Austria (1866) to pursue a liberal policy (manhood suffrage, 1867); in Russia the so-called emancipation of the peasants was begun in 1861, and inaugurated a protracted revolutionary period of alternating advances and setbacks; Japan emerged from her mediaeval seclusion and embarked upon an epoch of enlightenment and modern economic methods.

This wondrous decade (1859–1869), which brought us so many things: Darwin's chief work, the cutting of the Suez Canal, the political emancipation of the negro slaves in North America, the beginning of the Russian transformation, the dissolution of the German Confederation in consequence of the war of 1866, the removal of the ban on combination and manhood suffrage in Prussia (North Germany), the franchise conferred on the urban workers in Great Britain, the fateful beginnings of the national unity of Germany and Italy in addition to the awakening of Japan, also brought us the first national and international attempts of the Continental proletariat to organize as a class and to inaugurate the struggle for a new economic order.[24]

While Bellamy was in Germany, Karl Marx was fighting with Bakunin and Proudhon within the First International over principles of social revolution. Bebel and Liebknecht were active in this contest. In the year during which Bellamy lived in Dresden the German Worker's Party issued a statement of principles and program which indicates the spirit of the liberal movement. The first part consists of a catechism of questions and answers, of which the following are typical:

Question: What do you understand under the interest of the Working
   Class?
Answer: Under the interest of the Working Class I understand that
   every member of this class has the possibility of leading a dignity-of-
   man (*menschenwürdiges*) existence.
Question: What is that: dignity-of-man existence?
Answer: A dignity-of-man existence is a condition of a man in which
   he can freely express all his spiritual and material talents.
Question: What does a man require in order to find himself in this con-
   dition?
Answer: Not merely a comfortable and healthy way of existence, but
   also (1) Freedom and (2) Intellectual (*Geistige*) and (3) Moral
   Cultivation (*Bildung*).[25]

[24] Max Beer, *Social Struggles and Modern Socialism,* pp. 119–21.
[25] *Die Deutsche Arbeiterpartei.*

The program of the party followed along the same lines, and included the following six points:

1. Universal, equal and direct suffrage for all German states, provinces, counties, and communities, with free and secret ballot.
2. Abolition of all indirect taxes and the imposition of a single direct progressive income tax.
3. Abolition of the standing army and establishment of a people's army.
4. Establishing free productive-associations (*productio-associationen*) on a large scale with state credit. Laws for the protection of labor, in particular legal limitations on working time for children and women's work.
5. Energetic measures to advance the education of the masses, in particular thorough and free instruction in folk schools for all.
6. Realization of personal freedom. Especially reform of the press gag law and the establishment of absolute freedom of press.[26]

As a suggestion of a way to organize society in striking contrast to that prevailing in America, Bellamy could see the great state-owned Dresden china works, highly profitable while meeting world competition. In 1868, apparently while he was in Dresden, Saxony borrowed $17,500,000 for railroad building. Perhaps his later conviction that government could administer industry with success was partially based on what he saw at Dresden.

But underneath the tide of liberalism Bellamy saw stark and revolting poverty everywhere, such conditions as made American poverty seem very moderate. This was true both on the Continent and in England. While he mentioned England only briefly in describing his European trip, discussions of conditions there appeared in his writings for years to come, not in vague terms, but with facts and figures. In one of these entitled "English Serfdom" he wrote:

The thing nearest like slavery at present existing in the civilized world is the condition of the English farm laborers. . . . This is the description of an average peasant's hut: Total length, seven yards, height of wall six feet, to ridge pole ten feet, divided into two compartments, each nine feet square, loosely paved with large stones, between which in wet weather ground water oozed up, family consisting of a man, wife, and six children, all sleeping in the "bedroom." This repre-

26 *Ibid.*

sents the manner of life of hundreds of thousands, no, millions of the
English people.

It is very common indeed for the father and mother of a family with
their grown up sons and daughters, together with men lodgers, to be
compelled to share between them one small bedroom. The immorality
is shocking, and crimes of the most abominable descriptions are exceedingly frequent.[27]

In English cities the situation, if possible, was even worse than
in agricultural districts. Thirty years later Jack London in his
People of the Abyss described the hundreds of thousands of men
and women in the East End of London, themselves or their parents
come from the country, who were slipping into hopeless squalor
and actual death by starvation, exposure, and overcrowding. Both
as to agricultural labor and as to city dwellers in the areas he described, it probably would be safe to say that the slaves of the
Southern States of America, before they were freed, were in better
physical and economic and moral condition. This poverty was not
peculiar to England. Jack London quotes Thomas Huxley, who
wrote concerning the slum districts "from the knowledge gained as
a medical officer in the East End of London, and as a scientist pursuing investigations among the most elemental savages":

"Any one who is acquainted with the state of the population of all
great industrial centres, whether in this or other countries, is aware that
amidst a large and increasing body of that population there reigns
supreme . . . that condition which the French call *la misère,* a word
for which I do not think there is any exact English equivalent. It is a
condition in which the food, warmth, and clothing which are necessary
for the mere maintenance of the functions of the body in their normal
state cannot be obtained; in which men, women, and children are forced
to crowd into dens wherein decency is abolished, and the most ordinary
conditions of healthful existence are impossible of attainment; in which
the pleasures within reach are reduced to brutality and drunkenness;
in which the pains accumulate at compound interest in the shape of
starvation, disease, stunted development, and moral degradation; in
which the prospect of even steady and honest industry is a life of unsuccessful battling with hunger, rounded by a pauper's grave."

. . . .

[27] "English Serfdom," *Springfield Union,* May 14, 1874.

"Were the alternative presented to me I would deliberately prefer the life of the savage to that of those people of Christian London." [28]

Jack London writes further: "The Reverend Hugh Price Hughes is authority for the statement that beds are let on the three-relay system—that is, three tenants to a bed, each occupying it eight hours, so that it never grows cold; while the floor space underneath the bed is likewise let on the three-relay system. Health officers are not at all unused to finding such cases as the following: in one room having a cubic capacity of 1000 feet [about ten by twelve feet with an eight foot ceiling], three adult females in the bed, and two adult females under the bed . . ." [29] Again London writes: "Bishop Wilkinson, who has lived in Zululand, recently said, 'No headman of an African village would allow such a promiscuous mixing of young men and women, boys and girls.' " And again, "Nearly fifty per cent of the workers pay from one-fourth to one-half of their earnings for rent." [30]

It was no irresponsible radical, but the venerable Alfred Lord Tennyson, poet laureate of England, nearing four-score years, who wrote:

Is it well that while we range with Science, glorying in the Time,
City children soak and blacken soul and sense in city slime?

There among the glooming alleys Progress halts on palsied feet,
Crime and hunger cast our maidens by the thousand on the street.

There the master scrimps his haggard sempstress of her daily bread,
There a single sordid attic holds the living and the dead.

There the smouldering fire of fever creeps across the rotted floor,
And the crowded couch of incest in the warrens of the poor.[31]

The owners of these crowded tenements, as of the hovels of the agricultural workers, were the nobility or the wealthy classes of England. In contrast with these conditions Bellamy observed that

[28] Jack London, *The People of the Abyss,* pp. 276, 313. Reprinted by permission.
[29] *Ibid.,* pp. 217–18. [30] *Ibid.,* pp. 216, 219.
[31] Tennyson, "Locksley Hall Sixty Years After."

the wealth and leisure of some of the upper classes were extreme. Discussing "the idleness of English youth of property," Bellamy commented in the *Springfield Union* that with them "idleness has probably been more nearly reduced to a science than anywhere else in the world. The lilies of the field are laborious in comparison." [32]

Such were the pictures of European life that so stirred his spirit, and that gave direction to his thinking during later years.

The young Edward Bellamy presented a typical example of *the afflatus of youth,* of a sense of unique worth which denied the finality of failure. When he failed in his physical examination for West Point, there ended the most vivid hopes of his youth. Then he entered college, but dropped out after less than a year. When, after about two years' training for the law and after admission to the bar, he gave up that profession almost at once, he recorded another failure. Yet, although no other opening for a career had appeared, his faith in himself remained. In his journal of September, 1871, we read: "Were the ambition which spurs my labors any of the ordinary ones, as for pelf or fame, I fancy I should be well content to let it go and earn my daily bread in some plodding business such as men ply all about me. But I can not turn my heart from the great work which awaits me. It is a labor none other can perform." [33]

These are the thoughts of a young man of twenty-one, writing for himself alone. Would he have dared to express that faith in public? Probably not. Many boys and girls who have this inner conviction of a great work to do suppose that the feeling is unusual and peculiar to themselves, and to a few others who are either great men or mad men. Commonly such a feeling is carefully hidden as if it were trivial, misleading, and dangerous, a secret deformity or a strain of insanity, and is suppressed and dismissed from the mind. Few young people have enough faith in themselves to give it nurture, and those few sometimes allow it to develop into a feeling of superiority and of contempt for other men, or into a messianic complex which sees its subject as a savior of mankind. When unenlightened and undisciplined it often results in intolerable dictatorship

[32] "Literary Notices," *Springfield Union,* July 23, 1874.
[33] Unpublished papers (B1-1-5).

in business, government, religion, and in family and social relationships.

This feeling of unique worth—the afflatus of youth—needs to be enlightened, educated, and disciplined as surely as does any other human trait. The process of growing up would be much better understood, and the development of personality would be helped, if young people could realize that it is neither the obsession of a disordered mind nor evidence that the one who has it is to be a savior.

Bellamy did not know how to appraise this feeling which so possessed him—how few people do! In a healthy, vigorous young person a strong, intuitive feeling that his life is to be significant is a natural physiological condition, like a feeling of being in sound health. Does not every seedling oak in the woods start life with a sublime intuition that it is to become a monarch of the forest?

But the feeling of worth is not of itself proof of superior worth, and may be quite independent of any valid aim or understanding. Sometimes a man has a tremendous feeling of self-value, with great vital drive, but lacks adequate intelligence, character, or purpose. He may have a prophet's urge without a prophet's message. William Randolph Hearst had a greatly developed sense of significance which seemed to be rudderless and without a unified aim. Conviction of unique worth, sometimes educated, sublimated, and intelligently guided, but sometimes wild and undirected or attached to some capricious or accidental purpose, is a driving power in history as surely as is economic need. It is like burning fuel, which supplies the motive power of a ship, but which of itself does not determine the direction of travel.

Young Bellamy was fortunate in realizing that he had only a more than average development of a natural trait, as when he wrote in his autobiographical sketch, "The child's feeling of unlimited, because untried, powers which makes this sort of reading interesting because it makes it seem probable and rational, was peculiarly developed in him. . . ." [34] At the age of twenty-four he wrote:

The conceit of youth which instantly concludes it would have done the noble thing it hears of, we find laughable. Rather respect and regret it. Growing years disclose to us our weaknesses of character which bring

[34] *Ibid.* (B3B-Autobiography, p. 2).

us into self-contempt. Let us then cherish the testimony of our child-hood's undoubting self-confidence as evidence at least of the nobility of our instincts ere yet our fatal inability to realize their behests has been experienced.[35]

In Bellamy as a youth we see a struggle with a strong feeling of unique worth which he does not fully understand. Without adequate teaching and guidance for that feeling of inherent power, he learned by mistakes, by overreaching himself, by being rebuffed. His description of this process of disillusionment is characteristic:

From his intercourse with heroes and kings he had gained a royal air in regarding the common herd. When he came to go out in the world, it was with profound surprise and bewilderment that he found these common people quite capable of obstructing his course. Thus with his head in the clouds the boy grew up. Thus as utterly out of joint with the world as Don Quixote in his library, he drew near his maturity.[36]

In such untrained condition he took slight rebuffs and necessary discipline as being interference with his destiny. At twenty-one he wrote in his journal, "What angers me most is not that I am put off for a day or a week or a year from wealth and position, but that it is in the power of the foolish men with whom I deal to delay me about a whole life work." In the next entry he discloses that his state of mind "resulted from a supposed disappointment in regard to the acceptance of an article. Supposed, I say, because the article turned out to have been accepted." [37] Sometimes his faith in himself seemed justified, as when he wrote, "There are moments when I get glimpses of grand generalizations that seem to explain the universe and include all mystery." [38]

As a young man of twenty-three he realized that he had found no clear object for his inner drive. In his journal of February, 1874, he wrote: "It is only then the highest sort of ends that deserve to be sought with any zeal whatever. But those to whom especially I address these words are the multitudes of whom, alas, I have been one, whose hearts are gnawed by vague yet poignant ambitions to be accomplishing something, though just what, the fastidious mind cannot choose." [39] Bellamy was far from being alone in this feeling of worth without an objective.

[35] *Ibid.*, p. 1.   [36] *Ibid.*, pp. 3–4.
[37] *Ibid.* (B-1-1-8).   [38] *Ibid.* (B2-4-12).   [39] *Ibid.* (B1-1-31).

In his blind feeling about for a purpose, Edward Bellamy sometimes felt strength, sometimes frustration. At the age of twenty-two we find him already facing the bitter results of his mistakes:

Yes, I am indeed sorely weary and sick at heart. I am not what I counted myself. I had thought myself to be something greater than other men, and find that I am but after all a mediocre person. Well then, I am weary and could wish to die, for good and all and over with it. If I am not more than other men I would be nothing. To achieve ordinary success would be a wearisome attainment. I speak not thus in pride—God knows there is little enough of that left in me—but as one who having strung his theory of life and pitched his mind at a high tone finds himself unable to perform the first notes. I can come no lower and find life worth a farthing. I am unable to play the role I had dreamed of and find it altogether not worth my while to learn another. This mediocre self that I find I am, is a stranger to me; I abhor it, I have no sympathy with it save only a sort of pathetic self-pity. It has been my fate to have a pride above my merit, to have a belief in myself which apparently is not to be justified. My case is like that of one nurtured in the belief that he was a prince and a royal heir, feeding his youth on dreams of war and high council, who should at the threshold of manhood suddenly find himself to have been a mere nurse's changeling, a plebeian. Just so sick at heart and disappointed with an unspeakable disappointment am I. How well fitted would this poor prince plebeian be, think you, to pursue the ambitions of a commoner? What attractions would the rewards of such a career have for him? No, he could only desire to die. How much worse and more bitter his plight a thousand times than if he were howsoe'er persecuted and in flight, being only assured that he was of the true royal lineage. I was formerly proud of my identity: now I would fain swap it off for almost any other trinket. Yes, then what am I? A little greater than the average, nay more, a little, even than that, but so all is said. Not a king of men, not one in whose fingers nations should be as clay and kings as playthings, not one who should concentrate in himself the world's being.[40]

Such writing gives symptoms of the messianic complex, of a psychopathic development of the sense of unique worth; although in a young man of twenty-two, unwilling to give up the best that is in him, it may be but the turbulence of growth. There is an even simpler explanation for the unrestrained tone with which this passage ends. The very next entry in the journal, written five months later, refers to that just quoted:

[40] *Ibid.* (B1-1-24, 26).

Reading the last over now (May 1873) I had a notion to tear it out, but it is better to leave it, I conclude. That mood was a winter megrim. Shut up to oneself in that dead season, who could but feel the smallness of his quarters. . . . Giving up liquors too, as I did in February, was a mighty good thing for my disposition.[41]

Little by little as the years passed Edward Bellamy found his own peculiar work. With a patient thoroughness which to his family and friends seemed unnecessary, he perfected his chief instrument, his literary style, and qualified himself to speak with authority in his field. He learned by bitter experience what might be made a part of the education of everyone at less cost—the wise appraisal, education, and use of the sense of unique worth.

We should not have contempt for a young person's feeling that there is work for him which cannot so well be the labor of anyone else. Turn wheresoever we will, we find that men are only at the beginning of things, that we have as yet only the raw materials of civilization, and that culture of fine quality, with the necessary internal harmony of fine proportion and adjustment, still is to be won. Each element which we prize in the existing human culture is but the residue of the work of some life, or of many lives, that were moved by the conviction of unique worth and, believing in that conviction, added to the heritage of our common life. The concerns of men are so varied, the elements in which harmony must be achieved are so many, that only by the unique achievements of very many men can a good and stable society be won. Numberless jobs, great and small, that never have been well done are waiting for those who dare believe in themselves and in their conviction of worth, and who will pay the hard price of preparation. There is room and need for every person to have a life and work of unique significance. It is essential to democracy that this conviction of unique significance be recognized as a common human quality, and not as something limited to a few inspired leaders. Such recognition might have as much to do with the emergence of a good society as would any change in the structure of government.

Sam Walter Foss, a friend and follower of Edward Bellamy, in

41 *Ibid.* (B1-1-26).

his poem *The Songless Poet* expressed the tragedy of the man who dared not have faith in that urge within himself. The poem ends:

"Ere a bard shall sing as God made thee to sing,
  The earth in grief and tears
Must bide its time," said the Angel of souls,
  "And wait for a thousand years." [42]

We may be thankful that Edward Bellamy was not a songless poet.

[42] Foss, "The Songless Poet," *Whiffs from Wild Meadows,* p. 153.

IV · The Thread of Life

THE significance of Edward Bellamy does not lie in external events in which dates and places are important. The current of his life took its own course, and one can seldom tell from a piece of his writing whether it was done in Chicopee Falls or in Dresden, London, Boston, or Hawaii. The only hint that he ever was in Holland is a story which shows intimate familiarity with a piece of the Dutch coast. There are one or two references to the poverty he observed in England. A first visit to Central America en route to Hawaii would seem a stirring incident, yet the only evidence he has left is a folksong in a notebook, written in German and dated at a town in the interior of Nicaragua. The visit to Hawaii left no record except a few Hawaiian words in a notebook, some items in an expense account, and a two-line mention of Hilo. He made a few visits to the Maine woods, but his writings give no hint of that fact, and his few letters from there are undated. His summer visits to the New England coast are reflected indirectly in a few items in his notebooks and in the setting of his first published book, *Six to One*.

Each of the several lives which Edward Bellamy lived had a unity of its own which would be lost to the reader if a record of that interest should be broken up and scattered through a rigid chronological framework. Yet in following the development of his mind the reader needs a thread of chronology and of location. It seems desirable, therefore, to devote one chapter of this biography to a consecutive account of factual events in his life.

Edward Bellamy was the third of four brothers. They were: Packer, born March 25, 1843; Frederick, born April 14, 1847; Edward, born March 26, 1850; and Charles, born May 7, 1852. Except for Edward and Packer, the parents and brothers reached ages of sixty to about eighty years.

The decade following Edward's birth is almost blank so far as

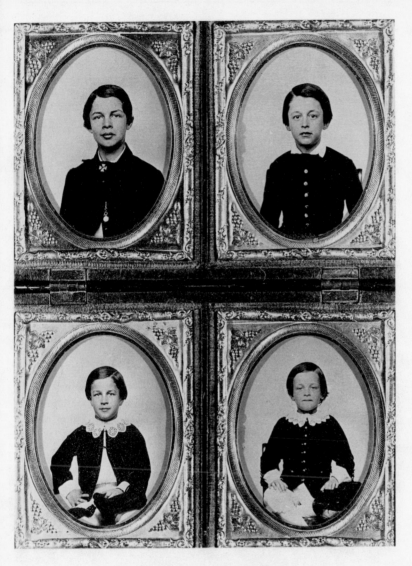

THE FOUR BELLAMY BOYS
(From a daguerreotype taken in 1858)

William Packer, *aged 14*
Edward S., *aged 8*

Frederick Putnam, *aged 13*
Charles Joseph, *aged 6*

records of him or his family are concerned. During that period Rufus Bellamy moved a few blocks to a house he had purchased, recorded as 91 Church Street, Chicopee Falls, where he lived the rest of his years. There, too, with a few brief intermissions, Edward spent his life. In 1861, when the storm of the Civil War was breaking, we find Edward writing a painstaking statement on what should be the character of a soldier. With the years from eleven to fifteen spent in wartime, it is not surprising that military affairs should have made a lasting impression upon him. In 1862 he was writing on prospects for reuniting the warring states.

On April 3, 1864, Edward was baptized and became a member of his father's church. A year later his mother wrote that he had completed nearly all the Greek and Latin and all the algebra and geometry available in the preparatory schools, but that, because of his frail constitution, she hesitated to send him away to college at that age. (His wife relates that when he helped her with her high school Latin he read it almost as easily as he did English.) Two years later, in 1867, he failed in physical requirements for entrance to West Point, and went to Union College with his brother Frederick.

In the summer of 1868 Edward's elder brother, Packer, was in Europe with his cousin William Packer, and died in the south of France. William returned home with the body, and in the fall, at the urgent insistence of his parents, Edward went to Europe with William. They spent part of a year together at Dresden. Returning from Europe some time in 1869, Edward entered the law office of Leonard and Wells in Springfield, and in June, 1871, was admitted to the bar. He opened a law office for himself, took one case, and then abandoned the law as a career.

On September 7, 1871, his cousin William Packer wrote him from New York of a possible opening on the staff of the *New York Evening Post*. He was soon at work there as an editorial contributor, and remained until June, 1872, when he returned to Springfield to be book reviewer and editorial writer on the *Springfield Daily Union*, which had recently changed hands. The first of his characteristic writing appeared in its columns on August 18, 1871. During this year two of his first articles were published in other periodicals. One of these, "A Plea of Insanity," in the *Christian Union* in May, is one of the few things he ever wrote which reflect his legal training. The second, a story entitled "The Cold Snap," appeared in *Scribner's Magazine* in September.

In the winter of 1871 or 1872, before he was twenty-two, he read two or three papers at meetings of the village Lyceum, and in them presented the basis of the social and economic philosophy with which his name has since been associated.

The next five years were spent on the staff of the *Springfield Union*. In 1874, when he was twenty-four years old, he wrote "The Religion of Solidarity," which outlined his general life philosophy. This was not published until 1940.

In September of 1874 his parents took into their home Emma Augusta Sanderson, a girl of thirteen years. While the girl's mother preferred that she should not be formally adopted, she was in all other respects made one of the family. Eight years later she became the wife of Edward Bellamy.

In 1875 an event occurred which, quite aside from any decision on Bellamy's part, was to affect his destiny. The Theosophical Society was organized in New York by Madame Blavatsky. Her later commendation of *Looking Backward* and its author had much to do with the fluctuating fortunes of his movement.

In the fall of 1877 the six-year grind of book reviewing and editorial writing had left Bellamy in poor health. Following family consultations, Edward and his brother Frederick left in November or December on a trip to Hawaii—the "Sandwich Islands." They went by way of Panama and San Francisco. Edward wrote home from San Francisco on January 15 before sailing, and on April 1 on his way back. Had he known of Henry George, living there and at that time working feverishly to put the finishing touches on his *Progress and Poverty*, an interesting meeting might have taken place. Edward returned by way of Reno, Salt Lake City, and Omaha, reaching home about April 23, 1878. The total expense of the trip to Edward, according to a meticulous but untidy notebook, was $690.22.

Almost no mention of this trip is found in his later writings, and the 3½- by 5½-inch notebook of fifty pages which he used on the trip might almost as well have been written at his desk before he started, so far as any information concerning the trip is concerned. His two letters home are no more illuminating. A "Süd Deutsch Volkslied," written in German on the inside cover of his little notebook, and dated "Granada, Jan. 4, 1878," suggests that the brothers visited that Nicaraguan inland town on their way.

Following a familiar theme in his notebooks, that the universal elements in men are important and the personal and particular traits unimportant, he listed the passengers and undertook to classify them by types. The following extract is characteristic:

Cases of resemblance to types with which, without recalling the names, I was familiar: the stylish woman; Coleman Middleton; his wife to Mrs. Varnum Taylor; the mining engineer; Mr. Ellsworth. . . . The consumptive Californian, the ideal 49er whom I have seen on the stage or pictured a hundred times. . . . I am like Mr. Ellsworth's friend. The second officer of the *Acapulco* and the first officer, reproductions of exceedingly common types. . . .

And so all of them are reproductions of people I've seen, so much so that I shouldn't be surprised to see my mother or father next, or find myself puzzled to tell Oil [nickname for Edward's brother Frederick] from half a dozen counterfeits on board. . . . I think a dozen types would include most characters, physical as well as mental.

The important diversities are very few. The deity did not task his ingenuity much in devising personalities. And well too, for the impersonal life which all have in common is the only important part of men or women. They can afford to be as much alike as blades of grass, and so they are. Talk about studying characters as an occupation. Bosh! As well find an occupation in tracing the infinitesimal differences between the leaves on a tree. When you know half a dozen men, you know all, and when you know three women you know all.[1]

He described a love match on shipboard in a spirited and novel style which suggests that the absence of such themes in his published writings was not because of ineptitude.

Throughout the notebook he tells us nothing of his experiences, though sometimes we can guess at them, as in the following:

It is noticeable that a slight sickness, not acute but leaving one languid, brings the soul wonderfully into the impersonal mood and makes it long for absorption into the grand omnipotency of the universe by death, as

[1] Unpublished papers (B2-HI-1, 2).

it does not in times of vigor. Death then is shorn of every terror and the surroundings of the personality become faded and look wearisome and childish.[2]

Evidently he made friends along the way, for he wrote:

Good or interesting qualities in men and women are generally found like the metals in some more or less complex chemical combination with worthless and inconvenient materials. They are rarely found in the pure state, but are mostly ores, sulphates of selfishness, chlorides of boorishness, or found with bigotry, with bad manners, with God knows what of lower elements. The proficiency in moral chemistry which most men have barely suffices to unlock the simplest of these combinations. But I boast that I can get some good or interest out of everybody, that it is rarely that any interesting quality in a person can be kept from me by however complicated a chemical union with the most stubborn and vicious of objectionable elements.[3]

That he reached Hawaii is indicated only by items in the expense account, by a brief list of Hawaiian words with English equivalents, and by the entry, "Commodore bets Admiral that we cast anchor in Hilo before midnight, $1.00."

Watching the sea, he reverts to his favorite theme of the "double life," meaning the personal individual life on the one hand and an impersonal, universal life on the other:

As regards the Double Life, overcast skies, gloomy seas awake the same desire to lose the personal in the universal in nature, as do bright skies and glittering waters, only in the one case it is because the individual feels lonely, isolated and oppressed, and in the other because he is in a lover's rapture and like him would lose himself in absorption with what he loves.[4]

In another entry on the same theme we read:

What a dreary benumbing thought it is how much living there has been done since the beginning, how many times human eyes have been lifted to the same sky, have been baffled by the same horizon, how many times human minds have thought the same thoughts, feared, hoped, loved and hated the same things. Ay, and how many millions are simultaneously doing it. What a wearisome thing and how it makes one long for an all embracing death.

But the double life shows better things.[5]

2 *Ibid.* (p. 4).   3 *Ibid.* (p. 4).
4 *Ibid.* (p. 6).   5 *Ibid.* (pp. 6–7).

The notebook tells us nothing at all of what he saw, but only of ideas that passed through his mind. The following items are characteristic:

Ay oy, he was a deep sea drunkard, none of your timid coasters who, venturing out a little into the ocean of intoxication, put back soon. He hoisted all sail and drove straight out to sea.

Vagaries

Time buying business

A man starts an agency for buying up odds and ends of time cheap and selling them dear. He buys hours before dinners of hungry men, hours of imprisonment from prisoners, and sells to lovers and happy people who have as much interest in having time go slow as the prisoner in having it go fast.

Show how time is made in long strips, variously colored, very elastic in parts and in others tough and thick, etc.

Show how rights look: woman's rights, oblong, yellow; human rights, square, blue.[6]

(David Starr Jordan in his autobiography described similar impressions of ideas as related to colors.)

There are times when sitting alone gazing into the silent sky, I can imagine, can inwardly hear, and faintly follow harmonies so sweet, so ineffably solemn or joyous, so lofty, grand and endless in rise and fall that all human audible music is a vile rattle of tin pans. Whether the faculty could not be cultivated. Certes, to hear such music rests and comforts me mightily.[7]

Such comments make up the contents of this little notebook, the only information we have about the longest trip of his life, save a family tradition that the brothers helped to put down a mutiny of the Chinese crew. Like a gyroscope compass, his mind kept its wonted direction regardless of the direction and circumstances of his travel. This lack of reference to his environment might be attributed to dullness of perception were there not abundant evidence along the way of an alert mind. A key to this curious trait may be found in an entry in his notebook of seven years previous:

6 *Ibid.* (p. 7).   7 *Ibid.* (p. 14).

I don't propose to govern my selection of matters for entry into this book by any rules whatever. The family horse may be very lame and yet no mention thereof be found herein unless perhaps it might be inferred from a dissertation on the disadvantages of pedestrianism. If I should change boarding place for the worse it is very likely that the alteration in my earthly state would be indicated, so far as this book is concerned, only by an increased acerbity of style, cynicism of disposition, and more dyspeptic philosophy.[8]

During 1878 his first book, *Six to One*, a light summer novel, was published, and from December 18 to the following March his *Dr. Heidenhoff's Process* appeared serially in the *Springfield Union*. William Dean Howells reviewed this when it was published by Appleton two years later, expressing the opinion that Edward Bellamy promised to become the literary successor to Hawthorne. The book is almost the first published hint of the sustained and serious thinking which Bellamy was doing on the subject of nemesis.

In the following year *The Duke of Stockbridge*, Bellamy's historical novel dealing with Shays' Rebellion, was published serially in the *Berkshire Courier* at Great Barrington, Massachusetts. His treatment of the theme shows a critical and unbiased historic sense, though his picture of that episode was strikingly in contrast to that which had been presented to Americans by nearly all their historical writers. There is evidence that the story as published in the *Berkshire Courier* was considered by Bellamy to be a rough first draft, which he planned later to rewrite for permanent publication. He never did so, however, and his cousin Francis Bellamy published it in book form two years after his death.

During 1879, also, Edward's brother Charles, then a young lawyer in Springfield, published his novel, *The Breton Mills*. This was a picture of industrial exploitation such as was going on in the mills of their own town, and it presented an advanced standard of economic justice and good will. (In this year also, Henry George completed his *Progress and Poverty*, which he had begun in August, 1877, though the first edition did not appear until January, 1880.)

In February, 1880, Edward and his brother Charles started the

[8] *Ibid.* (B1-1-1).

tri-weekly *Penny News* in Springfield. As the first non-Republican-party and non-conservative paper in the city it was widely received from the first, and it grew rapidly in circulation. Edward was publisher and his brother was business manager. The first few issues show a courageous but responsible spirit of independence and of sympathy for those elements of the population which had no voice in the direction of local affairs. After the first few issues, copies of the paper are missing from the files. When they again appear several months later the paper has become the *Springfield Daily News* (the change was made on May 13, 1880), and the independence of tone is modified. Edward Bellamy's style is less in evidence. On December 8 the printing office and its records were burned. Shortly thereafter Edward Bellamy turned over to his brother his interest in the paper with its debts and its promise. (He had supplied all the money—$1200—invested in the venture.) He became again a free-lance writer.

Just how Edward Bellamy maintained his family from the time he left the *Springfield Daily News*, in 1881, until the publication of *Looking Backward* in 1888, we do not know, except that he had saved and invested some of his previous earnings. His books and magazine articles could not have produced more than a few hundred dollars a year. We do know that he lived abstemiously, and on a narrow margin.

On May 30, 1882, he married Emma Augusta Sanderson, who had been taken into his father's family eight years before. She was born at Whately, Massachusetts, on February 12, 1861, and was thus eleven years younger than her husband.

During this year Rufus Bellamy resigned from his ministry of the Baptist Church under some pressure. Edward had long before ceased to hold to the doctrines of the church, and his father's resignation made it possible for him to withdraw his membership without family embarrassment. This he did by letter on June 29, 1882.

In 1883 John Macnie, under the pseudonym Ismar Thiusen, published his little-known utopia *The Diothas*. *Looking Backward* has such striking similarities to this book in certain details as to give rise to the charge of plagiarism. There is some evidence that Bellamy and Macnie had known each other, perhaps at the summer home of Bellamy's cousin William Packer, fifteen miles from where Macnie lived in Connecticut. There was a tradition among Macnie's friends, too, that the two men had discussed the theme before either of them had written on it. In the following year another book, *The Co-operative Commonwealth*, by Gronlund, was published. Bellamy was charged with plagiarism of this book, also. For reasons stated elsewhere [9] the writer believes that neither of these charges was well founded.

During 1884 Bellamy published his novel *Miss Ludington's Sister*, a continuation of the treatment of the sense of guilt and of nemesis which was begun in *Dr. Heidenhoff's Process*. These two books give fragmentary and immature expression to some original and incisive thinking on an ancient problem of great import.

On December 26, 1884, his first child, Paul, was born. According to Bellamy this event had much to do with changing the whole course of his life. Heretofore, he related, he would think of social problems as an observer, interested, but not spurred to action. When he came to think of the world in which his children would live, these questions began to seem intensely practical to him.

In March of 1885 Bellamy attended a dinner for storytellers given by Charles and Arthur Scribner, and according to a surviving account was the chief center of conversational interest, his theme being substantially that which later found expression in *Looking Backward*. During this year, too, his brother Charles published his book *The Way Out*, which in many respects is as daring and radical in its proposals as is Edward Bellamy's own utopia.

The years 1885 and 1886 were filled with industrial unrest and labor disturbances which came to be known as "the great upheaval." Such conditions naturally gave rise to many suggestions, proposals, and panaceas, of which *Progress and Poverty* and *Looking Backward* are the chief survivors.

On March 4 his daughter Marion was born, adding further point to his interest in the kind of world his children should inherit and

[9] A. E. Morgan, *Plagiarism in Utopia: A Study of the Continuity of the Utopian Tradition, with Special Reference to Edward Bellamy's "Looking Backward."* Published by the author, Yellow Springs, Ohio, 1944.

especially focusing his attention on the status of women. His father, Rufus Bellamy, died on November 16 in his seventy-first year.

The only publication of Bellamy's which appeared during this year was a story in the November *Atlantic Monthly*, "The Blindman's World." This, like many of his short stories, was an effort on Bellamy's part to get a point of view objective to humanity, to see the race as a stranger might. These stories are significant principally as marking his steps in that increasing power of objectivity.

Edward Bellamy has written that it was in the fall or winter of 1886 that he sat down in earnest with the definite purpose of reasoning out a method of economic organization of society. *Looking Backward* was substantially finished in the next six or eight months, was revised and polished during the summer, went to the publishers in August, 1887, and appeared in January, 1888.

On June 17, 1888, Bellamy wrote to William Dean Howells discussing the name "Nationalist" for the movement to grow out of his book. On July 4 he wrote an admirer, Cyrus Willard, approving the organization of a Nationalist Club in Boston. On September 7 two ex-army officers, Bowers and Devereaux, wrote him proposing the organization of a Bellamy Club. Two or three such groups united and after preliminary meetings the First Nationalist Club of Boston was formed on December 1, 1888. Other meetings were held on December 8 and 15, Edward Bellamy being present for the first time on the latter date. A statement of principles, approved on January 8, was generally adopted by Nationalist clubs over the country.

In November, 1888, Bellamy made a contract with Rabbi Solomon Schindler for translating *Looking Backward* into German. By the end of the year sales of his book did not exceed ten thousand copies, but they increased very rapidly thereafter.

Apparently while *Looking Backward* was in process of publication he wrote other short stories, or he may have cleared his desk of those already written in order to give free play to his greater interest. Of the several short stories published in 1888, "To Whom This May Come" is by far the best and is the result of Bellamy's effort to view human habits and affairs as a stranger might. Others were "An Echo of Antietam," which reflects his high regard for military organization; "A Positive Romance"; and "With the Eyes Shut." These were the last expressions of Bellamy's earlier interests to find publication.

Following the formation of the First Nationalist Club of Boston the members of the club began publication of a monthly magazine, the *Nationalist*, the first issue appearing in May, 1888. In March the Theosophical magazine, the *Path*, began commendation of *Looking Backward*, and *Lucifer*, the London Theosophical magazine, followed. When *The Key to Theosophy* was published during the same year, with its approval of *Looking Backward* and of the Nationalist movement, Theosophical clubs at once began organizing Nationalist clubs.

During the year Bellamy wrote numerous articles on Nationalism and its treatment of various issues. On October 24 the Second Nationalist Club of Boston was formed, and soon clubs had been organized in Hartford, New York, Baltimore, Washington, Chicago, and elsewhere. On December 19 the first anniversary of the First Nationalist Club of Boston was observed at Tremont Temple, with Bellamy making an impressive address.

Eighteen-eighty-nine to ninety-one were the most prolific years for Edward Bellamy's pen and for the growth of his movement. The *Overland Monthly* for June, 1890, reported sixty Nationalist Clubs in California. The Nationalist movement was widely discussed in magazines and other periodicals, and Bellamy's services were in constant demand for writing and speaking. He continued to live at Chicopee Falls. Toward the end of 1890, however, Bellamy became convinced that the *Nationalist* magazine lacked the vitality necessary to give effective expression to his ideas, and he decided to publish a weekly newspaper of his own. The first number of the *New Nation* appeared on January 31, 1891. The *Nationalist* expired with the March-April number. With its death the interest of Theosophists in the movement faded and nearly all Nationalist Clubs disappeared. For three years, from January, 1891, to February, 1894, Bellamy supported the *New Nation* from his own resources, editing many of the issues and guiding its destiny. During this period the Populist party had its period of greatest growth, and Bellamy's ideas had widespread distribution.

Finally, however, he approached the end both of his health and of his financial resources. On October 21, 1893, he wrote Green, "I have been wretched in health since I left you, and much discouraged as to the personal outlook, but within the last few days I believe I have turned a corner and am going to be all right again." [10] But a month later (November 20) he was again in bed when he wrote: "I don't wonder my conduct makes you nervous. I am pretty nervous myself, though not too much to appreciate the embarrassment my breakdown causes you. The fact is, I'm sick, more seriously so than in some years, and that on top of a run-down condition." [11] The precarious state of the *New Nation* worried him, but in spite of that incubus and his illness he was not without interests. "My literary work," he wrote on December 15, "engrosses me very happily. I hope to do something in time." [12] He was then writing his *Equality*.

Gradually but surely the *New Nation* reached the end of its resources. On January 31, 1894, Bellamy wrote to Green telling him that there was no hope: "My boy is down with scarlet fever, but I have engaged, I think, a nurse to help my wife out while I am absent, and expect to take the 9:15 train for Boston tomorrow, Thursday. If the paper is to perform *hara kiri* I wish to superintend the operation. I would that I had more in my stocking, but I have got down to the toes." [13] Green adds, "Thus the end came."

After the paper was suspended he wrote a few magazine articles on the Nationalist program, including one in the *Ladies' Home Journal* for April on "How I Wrote *Looking Backward*," one on "Christmas in the Year 2000," and one on "The Programme of the Nationalists." Also he wrote an introduction to the American edition of the *Fabian Essays*. In 1896 the *Dawn*, a Christian Socialist publication, which was the outgrowth of interest aroused by *Looking Backward*, ceased publication.

Mason Green, who on the death of the *New Nation* had become

[10] Green, p. 178.   [11] *Ibid.*, p. 181.
[12] *Ibid.*, p. 182.   [13] *Ibid.*

editor of the *Rutland* (Vermont) *Herald*, "would pay an occasional visit to Chicopee Falls . . . only to find the earnest worker intent on his *Equality* manuscript. . . . He wrote rapidly in a hand that at times almost defied deciphering, and he rewrote frequently. He did not have the appearance of an invalid upon the streets and in the fields where he often wandered, for his bright, grey, penetrating eye and steady step were about as they had always appeared to his neighbors; but he had a perfect knowledge of his impending dissolution . . ." [14]

Of the same period his son Paul writes:

For days on end my father buried himself in his study, frequently declining to come out even for meals. Food, in fact, always seemed to bore him, both on general principles and also, I suspect, because he had constant trouble with his stomach.

Occasionally he found it necessary to have a bit of fresh air and at such times he was wont to stroll about the village. Friends did their best to lure him into conversation as they met him, but I do not recollect that any of these efforts were very successful. He was uniformly courteous but also extremely resourceful in slipping away. Frequently of a Sunday, he used to lead his family on a stroll up to the cemetery where his father and mother and brother Packer lay buried.

Many men under similar circumstances would have spent the ebb of their lives fretting at the ingratitude of the world and striving more and more feebly to regain a position of prominence. Bellamy's experience as a national figure, however, did not give him a craving for the spotlight. He must have been deeply disappointed over the failure of the *New Nation* and the dissolving of the Nationalist movement, yet he was glad to be at home and relieved of public duties.

On September 11, 1892, his mother died. After his early renunciation of her theology she seems to have come gradually to respect his philosophy, and took great satisfaction in his life. She is reported to have said that Edward was the most Christlike man she ever knew. They were intellectual and spiritual companions, and her death moved him deeply. On April 23, 1893, Edward was present in Brooklyn at the death of his cousin William Packer,

---

[14] *Ibid.*, p. 183.

with whom he had spent part of a year in Europe. This cousin was closer to Edward than either of his brothers, and again he keenly felt his loss.

Shortly after his twenty-first birthday Edward Bellamy wrote in his journal:

Even as I sit here in the study gazing out on the gentle summer rain there comes before my dreaming eyes a vision of an old man, who looks like me, holding in shrivelled hands these pages grown yellow with the lapse of many years. Each word traced by a hand that once was his brings back some life-like memory of a far distant youth. Ah, the space of years which lies between! Does he look back upon them with the calm triumph of one who has performed the task whereto he had set himself, or are his dim eyes filling with the bitter tears of unspeakable disappointment, and his poor old heart trembling with impotent repinings and the despairing sorrow which refuses to be comforted over an age which has disgraced his youth, and a life which has broken its promise? Poor old man, in either case I feel tenderly towards him, and in either case I know he will feel lovingly towards me.[15]

No such ripe old age was to be his lot. From his school days his program had been interrupted frequently by poor health. Frail health also was a factor in postponing college. His trip to Hawaii when he was twenty-eight followed a physical breakdown. Ten years later, after *Looking Backward* was published, illness prevented him from being present at the initial meeting of the First Nationalist Club of Boston, and repeatedly prevented trips to Boston. "They say it is my lungs," he once remarked whimsically during the *New Nation* period, "but I've two or three diseases ahead of that." [16] In 1896 he caught the whooping cough from his children and developed a cough which never left him. The end of Bellamy's productiveness came not because his creative imagination was exhausted but because he had not the physical constitution to support the activity of his mind.

Mason Green wrote, "When Edward Bellamy had finished correcting the proof sheets of *Equality*, and before he would admit the approach of a complete physical breakdown, he sketched a

---

[15] Unpublished papers (B1-1-2).   [16] Green, p. 178.

brochure on psychology." [17] So far as Green's notes and other information indicate, this was a summing up and an integration of the ideas expressed in "The Religion of Solidarity," on nemesis, on the economy of happiness, and on the psychological and social implications of *Looking Backward* and *Equality.*

While in Denver in the fall of 1897, a few months before his death, he said to his wife, "If God will spare my life a year longer, I think I can do the best work I have ever done." [18] Mason Green continues his account:

When the last proof sheet of *Equality* was read he spent a few weeks at Blandford in the Berkshire hills of Western Massachusetts [his brother Charles had a cottage there]. Frederick and Charles had a medical specialist visit him at Blandford and it was decided that he had better go to the Rockies. On arriving at Denver he found that a formal reception had been arranged for him by the governor of the state, the mayor of the city and other officials, which he declined.[19]

Readers of the *New Nation* came to see him in Denver, and he was encouraged by proposals to revive the paper there. At least one issue of such a paper was published just after he died.

Contrary to all present-day treatment of tuberculosis, the doctor at Denver prescribed long walks and much exercise, until Bellamy was greatly exhausted. He was dosed with creosote until his stomach was ruined. For years preceding his final breakdown he had eaten almost nothing but raw eggs and milk, with regular use of whisky. Such a diet would have undermined even a good constitution. It would seem very probable that with an intelligent regimen of good diet and hygienic care from his boyhood he might well have lived to a ripe old age and have had a fair supply of strength and energy. Versatile as he was, lack of intelligent hygienic management proved to be the weak link in the chain of his life.

By the spring of 1898 it was apparent that the climate and the treatment at Denver were doing him no good. It is evidence of the strong family bonds that his brothers Frederick and Charles and their cousin Harriet Packer came from the East to bring him back

[17] *Ibid.,* p. 195.   [18] *Ibid.,* p. 205.
[19] *Ibid.*

home. His wife relates: "I shall never forget the light in his face when he decided that the Denver climate had done all it could for him and that he would go home. He was never really happy anywhere else. His joy on arriving home from Denver revivified him to such an extent that he was able to walk from the carriage into the house, where he slumped into a rocking chair and exclaimed, "Thank God, I'm home!" During the following weeks he was able to arrange his short stories for publication, "a work of affection which Frederick later took upon himself to perform," the title of the book being *The Blindman's World, and Other Stories*.

He returned to Chicopee Falls on April 26, 1898, and on May 22 he died. The official diagnosis of the cause of his death was pharyngeal tuberculosis. One doctor reported that his lungs seemed to be healed, but that his throat had the appearance of cancer.

Two years after his death, in 1900, his cousin Francis Bellamy edited and had published *The Duke of Stockbridge*, which had appeared serially in the *Berkshire Courier*. Arrangements were made to have a biography written by Mason Green, and he was given opportunity to take from Edward Bellamy's manuscripts and papers whatever he thought would be useful for that purpose. This project did not make rapid progress, and in 1906 Green's home burned, and with it all of the Bellamy material in his possession. Some portions of his own manuscript, and files of the *New Nation*, were in his desk at the office of the *Rutland Herald*, and were saved. From these and from memory he endeavored to complete the biography. It contains inaccuracies as to dates and facts. It deals more with social theory and with contemporary social and political conditions than with Edward Bellamy's personal life, but goes into greater detail as to current political developments than does this volume. (Copies of this manuscript by Mason Green are being placed in the Harvard College Library and in the Library of Congress, the Huntington Library, and the Antioch College Library, along with other source material used in writing the present biography.)

In 1905 Edward Bellamy's widow, finding it necessary to restrict the family expenditures, disposed of his books and most of his papers and correspondence, sold the family home, and moved to smaller quarters in Springfield, Massachusetts, where she was still living in 1944, at the age of 83. Her assistance in the preparation of this biography has made possible the inclusion of material that otherwise would have been unavailable.

Both of their children also are living. Paul Bellamy attended Harvard University, where he was graduated in 1905. Immediately after graduation he worked as a reporter on the *Springfield* (Massachusetts) *Union*, where his father had worked thirty years before. After a year or more on the *Union* he went to the *Cleveland Plain Dealer*. From 1920 to 1933 he was managing editor, and since then has been editor of that paper. He was president of the American Society of Newspaper Editors in 1933–34, is a director and has been vice-president of the Associated Press, and has received honorary degrees from Oberlin, Ohio Wesleyan, and Kent (Ohio) State University. He has three sons, John Stark, Richard King, and Peter, and a daughter, Joan Marguerite.

Edward Bellamy's daughter, Marion Bellamy Earnshaw, after graduation from Springfield Normal College in 1906 taught school in Chicopee Falls and in Springfield. She moved to Cleveland in 1908, was married there on June 23, 1911, to Ralph Allan Earnshaw of Toungoo, Burma, and lived in Burma for ten years. Their children are Bellamy, born April 23, 1912, and David, born December 28, 1914. For the past ten years she has been active in the Bellamy movement, carrying on a large correspondence with groups all over the world, and lecturing and writing in that interest. She lives with her mother at Springfield.

V · *The Rebel*

THE greater the violation of a man's spirit by the compulsions under which he lives and the more relentless the tyranny over his mind and life, the more extreme will be his reaction when he tries to break free. Where the Inquisition had ruled, giving men no choice but to cower in spirit or to be burned at the stake, violent reaction and rebellion in later times brought about intense anti-religion and dogmatic atheism, but relatively little of that discriminating liberal religion which is determined to "prove all things and hold fast that which is good." Similarly, where extreme political despotism has ruled, moderate reform fails, and extreme rebellion takes control.

As compared with men living under severe forms of repression, Edward Bellamy was favored by a mild and tolerant environment. In such relatively favorable circumstances, many men lacking his alert and sensitive personality accept conditions without being aware of any coercion of their spirits. So far as personal comfort is concerned, such men have a great advantage over Bellamy, as he fully recognized. In one of his notebooks we read:

As the world now wags, a man of not great mental and moral sensitiveness is happiest. I believe the time will come, through more perfect development of our universal sympathies for taking hold on infinite things, when the keenest minds and most sensitive natures will find full compensation for their pains in mighty exhilarations. Then ignorance will first cease to be bliss.[1]

He was keenly aware of the violations of human dignity and fineness all about him, and he rebelled against them. He sought for freedom to find fulfillment for the best that was in himself and in others.

Every man lives his whole life under social compulsions. It is the sum total of those compulsions—many of the milder ones going

[1] Unpublished papers (B1-C-4).

under the name of "influences"—which makes up the fabric of culture and civilization. Only where there is conflict or contrast of influences or compulsions does a man become aware of the possibility of freeing himself from those which tend to thwart his life. Even then, many men allow conflicting forces to play upon and to influence their lives almost unopposed, with resulting internal conflict and lack of unity. As Edward Bellamy wrote in *Equality*, "But while great minds master their circumstances, the mass of minds are mastered by them and formed by them." [2] It is the constant aim of purposeful men and of purposeful society to select and to arrange the influences which bear upon men's lives so that only those shall be active which add to the quality and value of living.

In Edward Bellamy's own case several elements worked together to make him a great rebel. His was a highly organized, sensitive personality. Also, he was possessed of a strong drive of aspiration which did not let him surrender for long. Moreover, the experiences, influences, and compulsions of his own life had been of exceptional variety, contrast, and conflict, so that it constantly was necessary for him to appraise and select. The commonplace life around him was in striking contrast to his home and to his reading. Had he allowed his life to drift, these conflicting compulsions might have torn his spirit asunder, as is the case with so many men today. However, he won for himself a unifying philosophy. In working out a design for his life according to that philosophy he rebelled consciously, deliberately, and vigorously against many of the limiting compulsions of his environment and of his own nature. As a result his rebellions showed a very great range and versatility, and deliberate purpose. They were not haphazard outbursts of the emotions. One of the moods in which he undertook to achieve a deliberate design for his life is well indicated in a passage in a notebook, written when he was twenty-two:

Oh, the jarring multiplicity of creeds, philosophies, and sentimentalities; what then seems to be the part of a man, the thing that must be the right thing so far as it goes, whatever at any time may be superadded by any revelation, inspiration, divination? This is that a man above all things, act out himself, that he be thoroughly and fully a man. If man love an intelligent creator, it is reasonable to suppose that he will please him, if at all, by conscientiously fulfilling his instincts, one and all, while it is certain that only so can he attain any consistent development whatever. Being so he will at least be assured that he is in his right place in the universe and among the orders of being, and will be less likely to be deceived in his conjectures concerning the correlation of the parts of the general plan. This principle then gives us for our rudimentary religion a hearty hatred of shams, conventionalities little and great, all habits whether of thought or action that misrepresent or conceal ourselves from ourselves. Further than this by way of confession of faith I cannot see my way clearly, but so far I tread firmly and know whereof I affirm. By what I have just said I mean no repetition of meaningless jingle of words about doing right whate'er befall, etc. One might as sensibly tell the sailor to steer straight whate'er befall, etc., when the poor devil has no compass nor can make out a star in the sky. I mean not that a man should cut his conduct by any of the manifold patterns which morality-mongers and religionists suggest, but that he should be a law to himself.[3]

It seems probable that Edward Bellamy did not realize—as who in his day did?—the extent to which so-called "instincts" are rather intuitions which are largely determined by social influences, such as family teaching and reading, and that to a large degree "acting out himself" meant acting in accord with early teaching and example. Yet fundamentally he is right. He undertook to use these influences as food, to digest and make them into his own substance according to his own nature, rather than to use them as clothes, to cover up the nakedness and undeveloped condition of his spirit and to give him the appearance of other men.

At the age of twenty-four he comes to the subject again, this time in an editorial in the *Springfield Union* on the choice of a profession:

Whatever profession a young man may choose, let him take heed lest he merge his profession as man in his profession of law, or medicine, or journalism, or whatever it may be. A man's profession should always be incidental and subordinate to himself, never the chief thing to be said about him.[4]

---

[3] Unpublished papers (B1-1-18, 19).
[4] "From College into the World; Choosing a Profession," *Springfield Union*, July 11, 1874.

A person writing at a subsequent time, with Bellamy's note-books, fragments of manuscript, published writings, and the facts of his life as guides, could picture a very orderly and continuous development of life purpose. Such a picture, however, would be inaccurate. What actually did take place was a long succession of attempts, some brave and ambitious, others weak and faltering, with frequent interruptions due to lassitude, discouragement, disgust, and indulgence. Yet the interruptions did not last, and after each the struggle for freedom was renewed. We see increasing clarity of purpose and definition of aim until, even at a fairly early age, there begins to emerge a unity of life purpose. What to the outsider may have seemed to be vacillation and lack of consistent effort in following a career was in fact evidence of Bellamy's determination not to accept the appearance of success on terms he could not respect.

Some men have revolted from religious orthodoxy, others from acquiescence in social injustice; some have sought freedom from the stupid, taxing routine of conventional social intercourse, and some from the crudeness and vulgarity of the times. On rare occasions men try to break the hold of folkways which have societies in firmer grip than do formal laws. A few men try to cure themselves of the itch for fame. Some have determined to avoid dependence on wealth they did not earn. We have seen men fighting against the distortion of their lives by the claims of family affection.

On all these fronts Edward Bellamy fought for freedom for his life, and on most of them he won. Constantly we see the effort not to fight blindly, but to understand. An entry in one of his note-books, written at the age of twenty-four, gives a young man's appraisal of the influences which many men experience, but which few clearly face and define:

The power over him of the opinions on moral questions in the atmosphere of which a man is brought up, is terrible. He may fight against them, he may outrage them, but fearful is their revenge upon him. None but the strongest natures should venture to make a moral law for themselves, to follow the dictates of their reason where they oppose their early prejudices. Even where such prejudices are manifestly mistakes, a weak or a mediocre character is to be advised to submit to them rather than to defy them. For if in moments of mental exaltation that defiance may appear easy, yet these moments do not last always, and when they give place to periods of depression, then fearful is the Nemesis of defied prejudices. In youth and manhood the soul may maintain its independent attitude, but in age the moral convictions of childhood will reassert themselves, no longer as sustaining corroborating influences, but as avenging furies, whose influence will cast a gloom over the evening of life. Self-respect will finally give way before their assaults, and all his pristine stiff-neckedness gone, the old man will grovel in utter self-contempt before the deities so boldly defaced in the days of self-sufficiency. He is sadly mistaken who thinks he can give laws to himself. Every man has laws given to him by his education, inheritance and surroundings, laws which he is permitted but to administer, and defies at his peril, be they never so foolish. The atmosphere of the soul is something that the reason as vainly struggles against as a candle against the overshadowing darkness. At every flicker the darkness rushes in.

A man with difficulty realizes how little he really at best can have to do with the making of himself. It may be doubted if a man has much more power to alter and transform his own nature, than he has to modify the face and course of external nature. This, however, amounts to something, but very little. He is a wise man who, before attempting any reform or transformation of his own nature, sits down and calculates whether he can probably accomplish it.[5]

If nearly all of a man's compulsions have been without contrast and competition and make a single pattern of life there may be small incentive for him to rebel. However, when he has met one sort of indoctrination in the home, another kind in his community, and perhaps still other and varied elements of influence in his reading, a mixed and conflicting pattern is created in his personality, and whatever course he takes is a rebellion against some other element of compulsion. Here enters the necessity for choice, and with it a degree of freedom.

A man may start with full force to rebel against some strong influence to which he feels subjection, but before he has proceeded far he finds that his rebellion is delivering him into the control of some other powerful influence from which also he craves to be free. So the pursuit of freedom ceases to be a grand, soul-satisfying charge upon some one romantic spiritual dragon and becomes a

5 Unpublished papers (B1-2-27, 28).

complex weighing and balancing of efforts. One gradually realizes that freedom must be painstakingly, deliberately, and intelligently designed and created, as a great and complex institution is developed and achieved.

Evidently Bellamy considered himself to be one of "the strongest natures," for, despite the solemn warning to himself which has been quoted, he did "venture to make moral laws for himself." The drab discipline of Puritan Calvinism has roused violent reaction in many a young New Englander, though often with a conscious awkwardness. There are occasional outbursts in Bellamy's notebooks, affirming his rebellion to himself. The following entry, a few months after that just quoted, starts out bravely and blasphemously enough, but shortly comes to a point of diminishing vigor, and settles down to mere sophomoric solipsism:

There are times when a man gets to that state of disgust with himself and things in general that all means of expression fail him. The most shocking blasphemy which he might concoct seems preposterously tame and inexpressive. There is nothing left him but to get drunk or go to bed, the latter of which I proceed to do. To this condition I have been reduced by a day of idleness and what they call a holiday. God damn you, you are the old journal I can confide in. The other is for decorous fancies, sober imaginations, goodish sentiments, which will stand publication, which the Philistines will approve. But you, old boy, are the confidant of wicked moments of careless, reckless, drunken, blasphemous moods when I have creation and creators for my contempt or laughter. I am blasphemously inclined tonight sure enough. I would fain invent me strange oaths. But no, that would help nothing, would in fact be tedious. What I want to know is why in the name of creation should I bow down or be expected to bow down to any thing. I am; I know not that anything else is. If there be anything else, I deduce its existence from myself who am the major premise in all metaphysics. To bow down then to aught I deduce from myself is flat idolatry, and catch me at it. I am, others may be, and shall the real worship the imaginary; the actual, the possible? Good Lord deliver us from such folly.[6]

Since this entry is directly followed by an outburst beginning, "It is cursed folly to talk of liberty of utterance in these days; but one hasn't got it," quite probably our young man was upset because his paper would not use some of his outspoken book reviews.

6 Unpublished papers (B1-1-31, 32).

This occasion is not the first evidence we have of an inclination to leave behind restraints that were associated with the pattern of the family life. Two years earlier, in February, 1872, while on the staff of the *New York Evening Post*, he wrote in one of his notebooks:

After all I do apprehend that more and saner philosophy lies at the bottom of a mug of ale—or say rather two—than ever was skimmed off from moonlight or concocted by dyspepsia. A man feels then—I mean after the beer—master of life, the serene contemner of misfortune, an attitude to which no amount of unspiritualized speculation can exalt him. I am aware that it is the custom to jest at this pot-valor, but in reason's name why? Is it valor? That is the only question. Does it exalt the soul, if so why should beerless philosophy pride itself over beery?

On whatsoever wings we mount to heaven, when once there we can well afford to deride the highest-headed terrestrial, the haughtiest earth-hugger, that ever refused a drink.

All I can say about it is that if the sensual malt has stronger wings wherein to lift and support me above the world's base exaltation, than Divine Philosophy can offer, then vivat malt.

Yet this ostentation of rebellion is not unalloyed, for he adds:

Philosophy must wait till next morning when, having derived an accursed headache and general disturbance from the inevitable tumble over night, I am in need of consolation. In fact, if matter, envious of spirit, had not annexed as consequences to vicious excesses a heavy headache and a belching belly and puking paunch, then indeed terrestrial meads would be entirely absorbed and humanity would be eternally drunk.[7]

Tradition sustains Edward Bellamy's notebooks in picturing a period when he sought freedom from restraint and hoped to find satisfaction in "having a good time." At this time Edward had one brother three years older than himself, and one two years younger. According to accounts given by the younger brother, Charles, to Edward's son Paul, the three brothers for a time had a habit of rather fast living. The livery stable proprietors found it necessary to refuse to rent them "horse and buggy" outfits because they were very fast drivers and brought their horses back in a state of exhaustion. They were free drinkers. According to tradition, Ed-

[7] *Ibid.* (B1-1-11, 12).

ward could carry his liquor better than the others (or did he exercise greater restraint?). On returning home from a wild evening, while the others would be obviously intoxicated, Edward would bear himself with the utmost decorum, and so maintained better relations with his mother.

However, his freedom from the Calvinist restraint tended to throw him into another servitude—that of the time-wasting, spirit-deadening process of physical indulgence which was the conventional habit of some young men among his associates. It seems that Edward began gradually to withdraw himself from this type of good-fellowship, and to find satisfactions in his own way. He did not make any sharp break with his associates, but persisted in making a life of his own.

His mind kept turning over the subject of his rebellious spirit, and again and again he tried to understand his impulses. A little discourse on "the charm of wickedness" touches one phase of the matter as effectively as many a ponderous discourse of psychology:

The charm of wickedness is a subject deserving an essay. To the proper minded person wickedness is unaccountable; alas, common enough, but as it were an inexplicable mystery, a confusing quantity, a disease, an abnormal excrescence, a deformity of human nature and not strictly a natural activity of it. This notion, it seems to me, is a popular fallacy, which has, however, attained the strength of a superstition. . . . In the first place, wickedness pure and simple, that is, wickedness for its own sake, must be distinguished from wickedness induced by the passions. This latter sort is normal and natural as all will admit.

It is the former sort, of wickedness for its own sake, that is considered by some inexplicable. Its true explanation, to my mind, is found in the gratifications of the instinct of liberty, the passion for freedom, which is popularly reckoned a by no means discreditable or undesirable feeling. To break laws without the least regard to their quality, just because they are laws, to defy and overlook restraint just because it is restraint, these are among the most ineradicable instincts of human nature. They gratify that passion for freedom whose active form is a revolt against all restraint. It will be further noted that the revolt is against restraint as restraint, without reference to the wisdom acknowledged by ourselves of the course into which it would force us. We may indeed recognize that course as ideally most desirable, it may be the one we had made up our minds to follow, and yet so soon as we find ourselves guided and constrained thereto we instantly rebel and, leaping the fences, take to the fields. There we taste the sweets of liberty. The pleasure of sin is the sense of freedom; this gives its flavor to stolen fruit, a flavor so wild, racy, penetrating, that no sauce on earth equals it. With it the root and herb of the lawbreaker have a zest that no ragout of virtue can ever possess.

Let not the law-abiding grudge the Ishmaelite this advantage over themselves; they have many to set against it. But their notion that laws have power to bless only when they are kept is most mistaken; they also bless those who break them. Without laws how could any fruit be stolen and where then should its sweetness come from? Given a law, the wise economist of happiness takes his choice not without deliberation whether he can gain more by obeying or by breaking it. Law is a two-faced blessing, blessing him who keeps and him who breaks. If there were no laws it would be the wicked who would first be heard beseeching that some be straightway made, and hard ones, too.

It is to be feared, however, that the tendency of the times is to lessen the possibilities of wickedness, at least as regards all divine lawbreaking, by lessening the faith of the world in divinely revealed statutes generally. Breaking human laws is comparatively poor recreation, especially in a democratic country where a man feels that he makes the laws himself. His only resource is to defy divine sanctions. In this respect the subject of a monarchy has the advantage in that the human law, as being imposed by a master, gives him some satisfaction in breaking it.[8]

It is a very common occurrence for young persons who have lived in great intimacy with their parents, and exceptionally under their influence, to turn strongly against them, sometimes with bitter resentment and a feeling of hatred. This is an expedient provided by nature for intellectual and spiritual weaning. When the child has established himself as an independent, self-reliant personality, then relations of affection usually are re-established, at least where parents have been wise enough to appraise the situation rightly, and to respect the child's impulse to freedom. Where that impulse is recognized and respected soon enough, these temporary alienations may be avoided.

Either consciously or intuitively Edward Bellamy was undertaking to establish himself as an independent personality. Having done so, he tried to reach conclusions without external compulsion.

[8] Unpublished papers (B1-2-13, 14).

The tenor of his life bears out the judgment elsewhere quoted from his journal, written evidently before he was twenty-five:

To retain the child's zest for the pleasures of life while possessing the ascetic's or stoic's power of renouncing them without a pang whenever it may be needful, that is the ideal of philosophy.[9]

While he took part in the informal social life of his community, attended the local Lyceum, and liked hunting, boating, and fishing, he nevertheless refused to lose himself in the social drift. More and more he came to follow his own way of life, rather than that of his friends and associates. Here, again, his course seems to have been determined, not by any feeling of rebellion against society, but rather by the necessity for determining which values he would keep and which he would give up. As he persisted in living his own life and going his own way he came to be looked on as a recluse. Most people would not realize that his solitary way was compelled by a philosophy of life he had achieved, and was not the drifting of a colorless and spiritless personality. Life to him was too important to be frittered away.

To be an attractive and eligible young man of one of the better families in a town where "proper" people all know each other, to belong to a "fast set," and yet to gain control of himself and to save time for living, is an achievement which could result only from a firm rebellion against time- and spirit-consuming social activities. There, Edward Bellamy fought and won.

THE REBEL IN LOVE

Many a man who undertakes to achieve unity for his life makes an exception when it comes to falling in love, and acts without relation to that design. The companion of his life and the mother of his children, through whom he hopes his life may continue, frequently is chosen in an offhand manner. Wisdom would seem to require that this most important relationship should be assumed in such a way as to harmonize as fully as possible with the design of life as a whole.

Edward Bellamy thought over that issue during much of his

[9] Unpublished papers (B1-2-22).

life, and toward its close he roughly formulated an opinion as to the course which it might be well for the relations of men and women to take in a good society. In what appears to be the last of his notebooks he jotted down some brief, unorganized comments:

Love will be without tragic undertone, a cheerful comradeship only of people who suit but do not adore each other. Men and women will be broader and less intense correspondingly in their relations to one another, while a thousandfold more than now occupied with nature and the next steps of the race, i. e., that which is at present called the superhuman.[10]

He strove consciously to discover what place love, home, and family should have in the entire design of his living. He rebelled against the conventional course of love-making and of family life. Yet he craved love and home and family. The course he took, as so often is the case with rebellion, was at first immature and blundering, and sometimes it was so self-conscious as to raise the question as to whether he had strong emotional drives; but in time clear purpose began to emerge. It is worth while to follow the development of that phase of his personality.

When he was twenty-one, during a period of depressed spirits while he was on the *New York Evening Post*, he wrote:

After all, it is a great burden to have to live. To my mind, the heaven of the Christians and of the Mohammedans seem alike wearisome and unprofitable. I cannot conceive myself ever so ardent an admirer of the economy of the universe, particularly of the human part of it, as to lose myself in the praises of God; and as for the houris, although the delights of women are the best antidotes for our misfortunes, yet it were better if, being without life, we needed no such antidote. The Nirvana of the Buddhists is the ideal state on which I pin my faith, though to be sure my faith never did stay where it was pinned.

To love a woman [he wrote in the next entry], to lose one's self in the intensity of passion, must be a fine thing, but the experience is said to be thorny. I fear I am too thoroughly self-conscious, a little too well acquainted with the mechanism of my emotions, to be capable of losing myself, except very temporarily, and then with a perfect knowledge of what I am doing, in any enthusiasm whatever.[11]

10 *Ibid.* (B2-7-11).   11 *Ibid.* (B1-1-6, 7).

A little later, apparently early in 1873, he wrote, "I think that the love of women is the nearest like a gift of all that God has given, the best evidence that the sticklers for Divine benevolence can adduce for their thesis." [12]

That Bellamy found himself in the ranks of those who had determined not to yield to this weakness he implies in another of his notebooks shortly before his twenty-fifth birthday:

The true lover . . . has all his life railed against marriage. With a sublime inconsistency that is so perfect as to be unconscious of itself he straight begins to ruminate on matrimony. He has not cared to stop for overthrowing his old arguments. They are all there, not defeated but simply flanked. Those defences were good against a logical assault but they are flanked by an emotional experience.[13]

At this time he was recognized in his home community as a superior young man, and according to dependable accounts was highly regarded by well-to-do eligible young women. He visited their homes and took them buggy riding, but for some reason never carried his acquaintance far enough to be "mentioned" with any young lady, as the New England saying went. Some of them may have wondered at this, for he probably never expressed to them what he wrote in his notebook, just after his twenty-fifth birthday: "It is the misfortune of women that they are bound up with conservative ideas and the preservation of the status quo. Hence, a man must hate them when he rebels. Then it is that love is a chain." [14]

This is not an isolated expression. At various times in his notebooks and in his unpublished stories, which are largely autobiographical, he debates the question of how to have a wife, home, and children, and yet to maintain that freedom which seemed to him to be a supreme need. Here, for instance, is an early hint for the book "Eliot Carson," which never reached completion:

In hermit story let Carson and Schoolmaster discuss the idea of an order—but not organized—of modern monks, being men answering the purpose of medieval monks in keeping alight in the world the love of study and the religious life. The modern monk, like Carson, to be a testimony against the sordidness of the times and its worship of money and lust of luxury by choosing poverty and eschewing matrimony and

<hr/>

12 *Ibid.* (B1-1-8).　　　　13 *Ibid.* (B1-2-23).　　　　14 *Ibid.* (B1-2-32).

keeping himself unspotted from the world, to study and think and enjoy nature and sense the wonder and mystery of his own life.[15]

Repeatedly young Bellamy returns to this theme, and the mystery of it holds his attention, as in a notebook entry:

Praise God, not your mistress, for the happiness her love gives you and for the good influence, if any, it has over you. For the power she has over you is, in the mystery of sex, as much a work of God and a hiding place of His power as the thunder or the sunrise. It is not by her volition or her might that the power is exercised upon you. It may be against her will for that matter. A woman who is wise marvels and praises God at the influence with which she is gifted over men, and only unspeakably vain and shallow fools think of taking the glory to themselves.[16]

There are repeated evidences that he believes that for a man who is seeking to go his own way, and not the way of the world about him, a wife and family may be an encumbrance. In "Eliot Carson" we find Carson when he has determined to quit his job going to see an old physician friend. The story proceeds:

He was a few years older than Eliot, and by taking a wife, had passed under the yoke of society . . . When Eliot came into his office the evening after he had given notice with a radiant face and told him that he had at last thrown off the yoke, the doctor warmed up and became fairly enthusiastic. "It's too late for me, Old Boy. I can't leave Mary and the babies, or, by Jove, I'd throw up my practice and join you as a chum out at the hermitage." [17]

According to the story, Eliot Carson was engaged to marry a young woman of his home town. She became aware of this conflict in his spirit, and finally broke off the engagement in a letter which includes the following passage:

"I am proud that you see an end of life and a use of time more worthy than the mere accumulation of the means of bodily comfort. But, dear boy, such an ambition is not consistent with matrimony. To one who already finds the burden of self support so irksome, the additional burden of a wife would be intolerable. I cannot consent thus to burden you. . . .

"If ever I must have a husband to draw my carriage, I will take some common man whom nature meant for nothing better." [18]

15 *Ibid.* (B2-1-36).
17 *Ibid.* (B2-EC-15).
16 *Ibid.* (B2-Plots 1-30).
18 *Ibid.* (B2-EC-32, 33).

In the economic order which Bellamy proposed in *Looking Backward* this condition would be greatly changed. In this new society men and women would be economically independent, with separate and equal incomes, derived directly from the state.

He was trying to harmonize two conflicting impulses in his life, a passion to be free from entanglements with the world, and a desire for a home. Both seemed good, though at times it appeared that to act in accord with either one was possible only by thwarting the other. Yet "love found a way."

When Emma Sanderson was taken into the Bellamy family at the age of eleven, it fell to Edward Bellamy to go after his foster sister and bring her to his father's house. She remembers him as a quiet person with tousled hair and a pimply face. In the home this young man, almost twice as old as she, had a way of showing little thoughtful kindnesses toward her. At her request he took her chestnutting, and they were successful in filling a basket with the nuts. By accident she learned later that the season had passed, and the squirrels had gathered all the nuts on the ground. Rather than disappoint her, he had gone to the chestnut grove ahead of time and scattered a basketful of nuts where she would find them. On another occasion she made for a church fair some cloth "holders" for picking up hot dishes. At the close of the sale she went to take home the stock that remained, and was pleased to find that they were sold out. On trying to find who had bought them, she ferreted out the fact that her immature sewing had not found a market, and that Edward had surreptitiously bought the whole supply to save her embarrassment. Many bits of considerateness may never have been discovered, but the spirit which animated them could not be hid.

As the years passed she looked upon him as an older brother, whom she admired and worshipped but who seemed in another world. He had given people to understand that he did not intend to marry. When she was twenty-one years old some young men in the village took great interest in her. As the situation began to look serious, Edward proposed to her himself. He needed only to express his affection for all contenders to be left out of consideration. They were married when she was twenty-one, and he was thirty-two. That the prospect did not come to him suddenly is indicated by the fact that five years earlier he had published a story, "The Stolen March," the theme of which was the elopement and marriage of a young man and his foster sister against the wishes of his mother, but with the father's tolerance or approval. That seemed fairly to represent the parental attitudes in Edward Bellamy's case.

He knew Emma Sanderson thoroughly. There was little danger that she would turn from him for more luxurious living or would become weary of co-operating in the plans for his life work. In this he was not disappointed. Emma Sanderson accepted the simplicity of his life, and did not nag him on with fretful ambition or envy of her neighbors. Thus, in another field, he kept open the way to the life he had designed, and that without cutting himself off from home and family.

THE REBEL AGAINST "SUCCESS"

The rebellion which culminated in *Looking Backward* was not in the interest of the poor alone. Whichever way Edward Bellamy turned he saw men in servitude, the favored and successful young men of his acquaintance as well as factory workers laboring twelve hours a day. One reason why he was uninterested in class warfare was because he saw that the system under which he lived had put every class in bondage, and he sought freedom for them all. Among his writings which have survived are numerous drafts of parts of an unfinished novel, "Eliot Carson," a sort of spiritual autobiography. A quotation from one of those drafts expresses his sense of the servitude under which successful and promising young men lived, though many did not feel it. Eliot Carson is the successful assistant to the manager of the Hilton Woolen Mills. He is slated to succeed his superior in a year or two. (In Hilton and its woolen mills it is easy to see the setting of Chicopee Falls.)

He was now thirty years old and by common agreement looked upon as the most promising young man in Hilton. Of excellent habits, he combined the culture and manners of a gentleman with the steady industry of the man of business. . . . How were the good people of

Hilton to guess that the man among them most of all dissatisfied with himself, most bitterly disgusted with his achievements in life hitherto, and most disheartened and hopeless as to the future, was Eliot Carson?

They said of him: "Here is a young man of thirty, educated, popular, with money saved up, an excellent position, and the prospect of becoming by the time he is gray, one of the richest and most influential men of the county. Why should not he be satisfied?"

He said of himself: "Here is a man of thirty who has not grown morally or intellectually an inch for ten years past, in whom those enthusiasms and sympathies transcending the limits of the individuality, which constitute the soul, are nearly dead, imparting in place of mighty joys, but pain, despair, depression; here is a man who in the ten freshest years of manhood has added to his knowledge of the marvel of his own life nothing more than a store of village gossip and some knowledge of the mechanical processes of the woolen manufacturer; who ceased to read books years ago, finding only time in the engrossment of his daily business for hasty perusal of newspapers. This man after twenty years more of the same process may hope to be able to draw his check for $50,000, and by that time his soul won't trouble him at all. . . ."

As a boy he had had an extraordinary and abiding conception of the strangeness, the wondrous interest of his own life. He had not dreamed it possible that time or custom could ever make it seem common to him as it did to others. He had not dreamed it possible that he should live through seventy years of his life without attaining to something like a solution of himself. The boy had promised himself so much from the fullness of knowledge, the enlargement of experience, the ripening of judgment that should come to him with manhood. It had not occurred to him that life could be anything else, at least till old age, except mental and spiritual growth, or that the man could fail to exceed the boy in knowledge, intellect, and all the finer attributes of the mind as much as in physical stature. Eliot was haunted by the reproachful ghost of this eager-eyed lad. He was humbled and ashamed before his own youth so full of high resolve and splendid enthusiasms only to be so bitterly betrayed. He seemed to stand with bowed head and cheek flushed with shame before a judgment seat, whereon sat a noble boy judging him with the brow of Rhodamanthus (He has a picture of himself as a boy, painted and hung up over his table. It is his inspiration. He will do nothing unworthy of it.), and demanding, "Where are my dreams of learning that ere this should have made you contemporary with all the ancient worlds; where are my dreams of science that should ere this have enabled you to walk among the stars as along lighted streets; where is my dream of a philosophy that ere this should have drawn for you the stings of death and disappointment?" [19]

[19] Unpublished papers (B2-EC-8-10).

In another draft of the same chapter we find a similar expression:

"I ought to take the spoiling of my life more quietly, as others do. It is the general fate, like death. What use to repine? It is a law of society, which the individual finds it as idle to omit as a law of nature, that at the age of twenty-one or thereabouts mental culture shall cease and the mind be thenceforth used merely as a tool, a third hand so to speak, to help the other two work, to weave woolen, to spin cotton, or keep books, or grind off editorials at so much a column. The world press-gang lies in wait at the gate of the college to seize the young man as he passes out and put him into the workhouse. What he then is as regards mental acquirements, he is bound to remain the rest of his life. That is his intellectual climax. Did I say that his mental acquirements would remain at that point? Even that is not true. They will decay and rust out and be forgotten as the years pass by. At forty the accomplishments of twenty will be a shut book. But it is idle to complain. It is such an old story and so quite without remedy." [20]

At about the time Bellamy wrote this he was "grinding off editorials" and book reviews for the *Springfield Union*.

It appears from his notebooks and from drafts of "Eliot Carson" that Bellamy seriously considered undertaking to live alone as a sort of hermit, after the manner of Thoreau, whom he greatly admired. He seemingly had chosen an abandoned farmhouse on a lake shore as his hermitage, and he had carefully estimated the cost of food and clothing on a budget of one hundred and fifty or two hundred dollars a year. Such were the thoughts of Edward Bellamy as he decorously walked the streets of Chicopee Falls and wrote interesting and provocative book reviews.

The memory of this period of his youth remained with him throughout his life. In his last book, *Equality*, he gives a picture of the plight of a young man who tries to live the type of life he has dreamed:

"Youth was as noble in your day as now, and dreamed the same great dreams of life's possibilities. But when the young man went forth into the world of practical life it was to find his dreams mocked and his ideals derided at every turn. He found himself compelled, whether he would or not, to take part in a fight for life, in which the first condition of success was to put his ethics on the shelf and cut the acquaintance of

[20] *Ibid.* (B2-EC-18).

his conscience. You had various terms with which to describe the process whereby the young man, reluctantly laying aside his ideals, accepted the conditions of the sordid struggle. You described it as a 'learning to take the world as it is,' 'getting over romantic notions,' 'becoming practical,' and all that. In fact, it was nothing more nor less than the debauching of a soul." [21]

Yet it was of this same man that William Morris wrote: "Bellamy's . . . temperament may be called the unmixed modern one, unhistoric and unartistic. . . . In short, a machine life is the best which Mr. Bellamy can imagine for us on all sides . . ." [22]

Such misappraisal by so great and fine a personality as William Morris is typical of the inability of the literary and aesthetic world to understand Edward Bellamy. For half a century the reputation of the author of *Looking Backward* has been under a cloud, not in this respect because of limitation on his part, but because he had a fullness and universality of personality which the aesthetic literary man seems constitutionally unable to understand. Bellamy considered the issues which were involved in the exploitation of one class by another. In planning a way to remove that exploitation he faced realities, pleasant and unpleasant, and proposed a sharing of unavoidable burdens as well as of advantages. Many who called themselves liberal or socialist revolted from an actual facing of this issue and turned upon Bellamy as a crude materialist.

We may say that Bellamy lived under two clouds—one, the feeling of so-called "practical" men that he was a dreamer and idealist; and the other, the contempt of literary men who classified him as a materialist. The fact that Bellamy achieved an inclusive view of life gives him high rank among those who loved their fellow men.

Edward Bellamy revolted from insincerity. He referred to "the vast system of lying called Society." In one of the "Eliot Carson" manuscripts there is a passage which excellently reflects his own personality. It describes one of his characters, a young woman from the city who was visiting a simple farm family.

---

[21] *Equality*, pp. 251–52.
[22] "Review of *Looking Backward*," *The Commonweal*, V (June 22, 1889), 194.

Edna had never particularly shone in city society. To do so involved for her quite too much affectation of interest in things that bored her, too much pretension of interest in people . . . too much looking wise when she did not understand, too much smiling at remarks that made her feel sad, too much simulation of agreement when she vehemently disagreed, too much silence when she wanted to cry out. But given these simple, true-hearted people [in the family she was visiting] who laughed when they were amused, and would as soon have told a lie as laughed when they were not amused, who wanted to know when they did not understand, who stated when they disagreed . . .[23]

This trait of open directness was a characteristic of Edward Bellamy which was recognized and commented on by people of every relationship to him.

Bellamy rebelled against labor as a virtue in itself. Settlers in barren Massachusetts had to work hard and long to avoid sheer starvation. From this intense experience labor came to be looked upon as one of the cardinal virtues. The social compulsion which required that one be always at work, even if what he did had no economic value, became a social tyranny. In one of the notebooks we find this stray item:

No man should be a burden on others, but beyond that there is no propriety or duty in work. Nay, it is folly. If one man fails to make an invention, another will make it, if one man fails to do a piece of work, another in the fullness of time will do it, if it is needful.

But the one work that never will be done if each man fails to do it for himself, the one work that can not wait, is the development of his own soul and its enjoyment.[24]

Perhaps this note was the basis for a literary notice in the editorial column of the *Springfield Union* which in more than one respect has the Bellamy quality:

The American has always had a high idea of the value of time. He used to think that time was money; now he is beginning to learn that it is more and better than money, it is opportunity for cultivating the finer susceptibilities of his nature, for opening up new avenues of feeling removed from every sordid strain. To spend an hour looking at a sunset, or admiring the trembling leaves, or listening to the purling brook till

[23] Unpublished papers (B1-3-84).   [24] *Ibid.* (B1-C-3).

"beauty born of murmuring sound" passes into the soul, all these our excellent forefathers, the Yankees of fifty years ago, would have set down as gross breaches of the eleventh commandment, according to Brother Jonathan, "Thou shalt not waste time." But the latter day American views the case rather differently. He is beginning to understand that "Man shall not live by bread alone, but by every word that proceedeth out of the mouth of God," that is, by every revelation, grace, and unity read in sky or earth or any of the innumerable forms and sounds which are the speech of God. The modern American is beginning to use his eyes and ears as well as his hands. Leisure, which was tedium to his grandfather, becomes a precious opportunity to him.[25]

Throughout his life Edward Bellamy refused to follow the American custom of going through the motions of having a vocation for the sake of a feeling of worth in himself or to achieve social respectability. Had he not won that freedom he could not have done his life work.

THE REBEL AGAINST FAME

Young Bellamy observed that an itch for fame tyrannized over the lives of many men, and that often it drove them more ruthlessly than any taskmaster. He rebelled against that servitude. At twenty-four he wrote of his boyhood:

He was therefore greatly troubled in his mind, lest his own lofty aspirations might spring from a selfish love of fame or personal credit. This point he never fairly got over. At times he felt that the service of humanity was his chief motive, and at other times he explained his ambitions, if not on an unselfish, yet on a neutral basis, by ascribing them to the natural passion of the human nature to fully expand, exert, and express itself in great activities.[26]

Apparently at that time the craving for fame had not been fully mastered. In a notebook of his early twenties we find further effort to analyze the appetite for a lasting name:

I am a bit of a fool like the rest and have an eye to the applause of readers. The desire after personal fame is such an unphilosophical, ridiculous idea that it seems to me it is destined to die out of human nature as men progress in culture. I am inclined to think that in some

[25] "Literary Notices," *Springfield Union*, July 7, 1874.
[26] Unpublished papers (B3B-Autobiography).

subtle way it may take hold on some profound instinct of our natures and in this find its justification, but certainly the superficial analysis yields contemptible results. Here am I, A.B., my name being a certain convenience of notation, for distinguishing me among others. I take it into my head that it is a very desirable thing to have this name repeated by a multitude of persons whom I do not know and have never seen and who are to my mind a pure abstraction. . . . Verily, vanity is the least exacting of our pleasure giving attributes; it can make the most of the least. . . .

After all, perhaps we may learn a lesson of philosophy on this point from a class to which we are not wont to look for instruction, to wit, burglars, thieves, and other classes who prey upon the community. The burglar or the footpad has renounced the pursuit of fame in the great world. . . . He has, however, a small circle of intimates, a coterie of fellow craftsmen and their dependents, a circle as large probably as that of the intimates of any person. In their eyes he shines or seeks to shine, but concerning the hatred or contempt of the millions cares not a straw. We would do well to take a leaf out of his book in this respect.[27]

His unpublished treatise on "The Liberty of the Press" refers to fame as "the will o' the wisp that has led astray so many noble minds," and in the same paper he wrote, "In the education of the race we needed thus for once to learn how cheap and vulgar a thing fame essentially is." [28]

This rebellion from a prevailing servitude was successful to a high degree. During his later years he did not renounce fame as Caesar renounced the crown, with an ostentatious flourish, while his fingers itched to grasp it. Rather, he disregarded fame without a pang, as one in a market would pass by cheap, shoddy goods if he were searching for material of the highest quality.

Discussing candidates for office, he wrote in his notebook, "Why should a man pride himself on having done a service to his country which hundreds of other men as able as himself could have done, desired to do, and were bitterly offended that he should have done it?" [29] Such expressions represented his actual way of life. His brother Frederick said of him: "From beginning to end he sought nothing and he had nothing which could properly be called a public life." When Frederick tried to lionize him in his New York home,

27 *Ibid.* (B1-2-6, 7).   28 *Ibid.* (B3B-"Liberty of the Press," p. 11).
29 *Ibid.* (B2-Plots 1-5).

Edward simply did not appear until most of the guests were gone.

This selflessness gave his work some of its peculiar quality. William Dean Howells truly said: "His imagination was intensely democratic, it was inalienably plebeian, even,—that is to say, humane. It did not seek distinction of expression; it never put the simplest and plainest reader to shame by the assumption of those fine-gentleman airs which abash and dishearten more than the mere literary swell can think." [30]

Bellamy's disregard for a conspicuous place was evident to almost everyone. Sylvester Baxter, who knew him intimately during the years of his success, wrote of him, "All opportunities to realize upon the magnificent advertising incidental to a phenomenal literary success were disregarded." [31] Requests for books, magazine articles, and lectures were alike declined. A neighbor said of him, "He never met people as an author, but as a man." [32] Against that servitude with which the itch for fame enslaves a man, the success of his rebellion was well-nigh complete.

THE REBEL AGAINST THE CITY

Edward Bellamy rebelled against the city. He wrote in a notebook, "Cities are always pagan." [33] William Cullen Bryant, under whom he worked on the New York *Evening Post*, had written much about the woods he loved so well, where

> Thou wilt find nothing here
> Of all that pained thee in the haunts of men,
> And made thee loathe thy life.[34]

His heart was with the fringed gentian, the water fowl, and the autumn woods. He longed to escape from the city

> And leave the vain low strife
> That makes men mad—the tug for wealth and power—

[30] "Edward Bellamy," *Atlantic Monthly,* LXXXII (August, 1898), 254. Reprinted by permission of the publisher.

[31] "Edward Bellamy's New Book of the New Democracy," *American Monthly Review of Reviews,* XVI (July, 1897), 63.

[32] R. E. Bisbee, "Some Characteristics of Edward Bellamy," *Coming Age,* I, No. 2 (February, 1899).

[33] Unpublished papers (B2-4-4).

[34] "Inscription for the Entrance to a Wood." Reprinted by permission.

> The passions and the cares that wither life,
> And waste its little hour.[35]

Yet the great poet seemed chained to his desk at the *Post*, and he lived and died there. After less than a year on Bryant's staff, Bellamy did what Bryant wrote of but did not do. He gave up his job and returned to Chicopee Falls, where, even though Springfield was near by, so were the river and the forest. In one of his drafts for a story we find a characteristic dialogue:

"The only thing I can't understand is that Mr. Beecher or any other man with a soul can be satisfied to live in a city of brick and stone, instead of in a country of hills, forests and brooks."

"But," said Edna, "I believe that city people, and certainly most of the clergymen, mean to spend summers in the country. It is only in the winter, when the country is frozen up, that they return to the city."

"The country is never frozen up," replied Mr. Carson. "It is their souls that are frozen up. . . . The forest in winter, the icy river with open spots, the sleeping brook, the thickets against snow, like black lace on a white shoulder, the dark brown of the clinging oak leaves, the brown stubble half covered by the snow, the tree trunks on a wet winter day. Oh, no, the clergymen and the vacationers are all wrong. Let them stay in the city in summer, and go to the country in winter." [36]

Bellamy did not even know his nearby city of Boston. In reviewing *Looking Backward*, Sylvester Baxter wrote of him, "He tells us that it was only by close study of the map of Boston that he secured fidelity to locality, and when he occasionally runs down to see the friends his work had made for him, he still finds the labyrinthine streets of our city a perplexity, and makes his way about successfully only by a free use of cabs." [37] When he was publishing the *New Nation* in Boston he refused to move to that city, but lived at home and spent two or three days in the week at his Boston office. As soon as a man begins to succeed, the city tends to pull him, almost irresistibly. In that respect, too, Bellamy kept his freedom.

[35] Bryant, "Autumn Woods." Reprinted by permission.
[36] Unpublished papers (B1-3-86).
[37] "The Author of *Looking Backward*," *New England Magazine*, n.s. I (September, 1889), 93.

By his neighbors Edward Bellamy commonly was looked upon as a solitary man. But for the opportunity to tramp the Berkshire Hills his spirit might have starved. Leaving New York City was for him not just a whim of circumstance but a major life necessity. Though much alone, he was not lonely, for "a purpose is always a companion."

When Bellamy sought solitude it was largely because his hard-won and clearly defined way of life ran counter to the usual ways of men, with resulting great friction and with weariness to his spirit. He could know what William R. Alger meant in writing, ". . . no one ever attained to supreme excellence in any art without, in the phrase of Pope, 'an inveterate resolution against the stream of mankind.' " [38]

Was it not primarily to keep his spirit whole and to save him from wearing out his life that he stepped aside from the crowded ways to where he could keep his own course with less collision and obstruction? The quality of Bellamy's genius led him to be much alone in order to protect the integrity of his life.

There were, moreover, very practical reasons for his solitude. He wrote in one of his notebooks:

Perhaps the worker desperately resolves that his mind shall not utterly vegetate. He resolutely reads a little in the intervals where he should rest. This merely makes his case pathetic. For the serene atmosphere in which alone reading can breed meditation, he cannot command. A man might as well go to the ballet as read what he cannot think over. Thinking is as necessary to reading as digesting to eating.[39]

Repeatedly in his notebooks and manuscripts we find him turning over the question whether it would not be better for him to give up prospects for home, family, and business success in order to live in his own way. He wrestled with the old, old problem of trying to maintain one pattern for his life in a world that was living by another and a very different pattern; of how to do his work with and among men without spoiling the design for his life. In that undertaking he had no small degree of success.

[38] *The Genius of Solitude*, p. 115.
[39] Unpublished papers (B2-EC-41, 42).

THE REBEL AGAINST MONEY

Edward Bellamy fought against dependence on unearned wealth. His mother's sister, Harriet Packer, came into a large fortune on the death of her husband. Next to her own children, the family of her sister was her chief interest, and she tried in every way possible to smooth their paths. With the others her efforts were fairly successful, but not with Edward. He, of all the Bellamy children, did not go to college on Packer money. The decision to spend a year in Germany with William Packer, at the expense of his aunt, was made only when, after his refusal, his father and mother most insistently demanded that he do so to relieve the grief of William Packer over the death of his cousin and companion, Edward's elder brother.

Thus we find Edward Bellamy consciously and deliberately keeping himself free from that servitude which is created in the spirits and habits of men by access to wealth. He lived on such a simple and modest scale that, except for his books and a plain, old-fashioned house of fourteen rooms which he inherited from his father, many a workman in the mills of Chicopee Falls could have equaled or exceeded him in personal expenditures. Attention is drawn elsewhere to the fact that repeatedly he gave up prospects for economic security in order to hold to the pattern of his life.

THE REBEL AGAINST INJUSTICE

Of all the revolts of Edward Bellamy, that on the social and economic front was longest and hardest fought, and it is by the fruits of that rebellion that he is chiefly known. One of the most persistent and most frequently mentioned traditions concerning him is that previous to the writing of *Looking Backward* he had taken little or no interest in social or economic matters. Shurter, in his thesis on *The Utopian Novel in America, 1865–1900*, said of him, "His whole character [at the time of his marriage in 1882] . . . was that of a dreamer, unskilled in the practical affairs of life and uninterested in mundane speculations." [40]

[40] Robert L. Shurter, *The Utopian Novel in America, 1865–1900*, pp. 119–20.

The facts of Bellamy's life disclose how completely unfounded is this type of appraisal. The social and economic views expressed in *Looking Backward* were no sudden inspiration; they were the mature results of a rebellion against surrender to a social order which in many ways was in conflict with his hard-won convictions.

Rarely does a man arrive at his fundamental economic and social conclusions earlier in life, or follow them more consistently to its close. In the account of his boyhood is a quotation from a composition at the age of thirteen on the subject, "Does Time Establish a Usurpation?" Immature as is that schoolboy expression, it consciously takes hold of one of the fundamental economic issues of society, which many a learned volume on economics fails to recognize. One of the few remaining fragments of his boyhood writing indicates that at seventeen he was reading John Stuart Mill's *Considerations on Representative Government*. Among the earliest of his writings to be preserved after the period of boyhood is an address prepared for the Chicopee Falls Lyceum, which Edward Bellamy identifies as having been delivered in 1871 or 1872. The boyish handwriting, very distinct from that of even a few years afterward, and the paper on which they were written, would indicate that they may have an earlier date. Some extracts from the second of these Lyceum addresses will indicate how far his views had developed at that time:

Several weeks ago, appointed in my turn to address this Lyceum, I called your attention to an element of modern social order which I do not think I qualified too harshly in denominating it a Barbarism. . . . It is because I am so deeply impressed with the importance of the matter that I address you again upon it this evening.

Concerning the existence of a vast inequality in the estates of men consequent upon the institution of property, concerning the general subjection of the poorer to the richer classes, you will easily agree with me . . . We, whose Christ was the son of a carpenter, shall not be likely to consider white hands that witness of idleness a sufficient claim to mastership, a valid pretension to peculiar privileges. And that you are Americans is a sufficient pledge to me that those ringing words of Robbie Burns' will find an echo in your hearts. If

> The rank is but the guinea's stamp,
> The man's the gowd for a' that,

why is it that while confessing the radical injustice of the present order of things, men scout as chimerical every project, the idea itself, of reform? Why has the name Socialist by which is designated a believer in this renovation of society, who denies that the world ought to be administered any longer in the interests of darkness and chaos, become a by-word and a name of reproach? . . . Why is the prejudice so deeply rooted in the popular mind that the integrity of our civilization is so intimately bound up with the maintenance of the grossest perversions of the principle of property? . . . Worse than all this, there are good men who apparently think the preservation of the present social order to be identical with the interests of Christianity . . .

Is it then, as these claim, absurd to dream of the reign of justice on earth, chimerical to anticipate an era when, by equality in the distribution of the fruits of labor, every man at the price of moderate exertion shall be as secure of abundance and comfort, of the means of education and recreation, as he is today secure in his political rights and independence? . . . Undoubtedly man must labor to live, although with his continually new application of the powers of nature, and his continual discoveries of titanic forces waiting his yoke, the amount and severity of this necessary labor is daily decreasing. There is then enough in the world to support all in abundance if it were equally divided. If the burdens as well as the pleasures of life were apportioned equally among all, then should none labor beyond moderation, and none be utterly idle. This is the social condition which justice demands, and to which a reform in the interests of justice will lead us back. . . .   58997

Let us not, shrugging our shoulders, rashly pronounce impracticable a reform so just, so natural, so reasonable, a reform *beside* which all others are insignificant, *without* which they are all crippled and halting: a reform which, banishing the fell power of gold from the earth, will bring back the Golden Age. . . .

I have been at pains to express my meaning in words as simple and in a manner as dispassionate as possible. And this too in treating of a subject whereon my soul could only utterly express itself in an inarticulate cry of perfect abhorrence. Abhorrence that a system so iniquitous could have so strongly intrenched itself in the order of society, so thoroughly have permeated its every relation, its every institution, and most of all, that it could have so familiarized its deformity to the minds of just and liberty-loving men that they can with difficulty be made to see its inconsistency with the plainest principles of equity. . . . No freedom, no happiness of the future can cancel the slavery, the sorrow, already recorded; nor teach us to forget the blood of slaves flows in our veins.

Gentlemen, I do not imagine that I have called your attention to matters new to you . . . No, the facts of the case are sufficiently evident, God knows. . . . Is it nothing to us that not alone the sustenance of the body, but also mental and spiritual food, is bought with gold alone? That the privileges of our academies and the access to our churches are alike venal?

I do not blame particular men, whether rich or poor, for the existence of these things. They are the inevitable result of a social institution which not the men of this or distinctively of any other age have established, but which has been the slow development of many ages. Of this social order the rich as well as the poor are the creatures, not the creators, and all that is to be demanded of them is that, perceiving the utter and cruel absurdity of their claims, they should not hinder reform, should not deem it unjust that they are called upon to renounce their pretensions, and take their place in the ranks of their fellow creatures. . . .

Finding infinite injustice and much to wonder at in this condition, humanity determines to distribute once again, and equally to all these sons of a common father, the goods of their great estate. And in this new division, lest some time again the heavens be horrified with the outrageous spectacle of brothers enslaving each other, will especially provide that in the future no covetous and crafty Jacob shall buy his brother's birthright for a mess of pottage, nor withal take it from him by force, nor finally in any way usurp more to himself than that sufficiency which is his just share in the common wealth.

Gentlemen, if you expect from me this evening a theory of Socialism, if you expect a minute description of the institutions of that new world of whose peace and liberty and happiness I have told you, you will be disappointed. It is an undiscovered country, no community of men ever essayed its Elysian climes, no human foot has ever trod its shores. But I know that it exists—the faith of humanity points to its existence—and we must find it.

For the toiling masses of the world are already fiercely questioning the right to exist of a society which is founded upon their subjection. The atmosphere is rife with revolution. Society in its present form will not long exist. Whether shall succeed it an anarchy, a chaos to which organized slavery were preferable, or an era of a more perfect liberty and happiness than the world has ever known . . . depends on the action or inaction, the folly or the wisdom, of this generation of whose eternal responsibility we must bear a part.[41]

This was written when he was about twenty-one. Except for the element of his "industrial army," it is an epitome of his social

[41] Unpublished papers (B3B-2d Lyceum Talk).

philosophy as expressed in *Looking Backward*. Such deep feeling does not spring suddenly into existence. We can be sure that even this early statement had back of it months, and probably years, of earnest thinking and strong feeling. It follows that the foundation of his economic system was fixed upon very early, for equality in the apportioning of income was to be the primary element of that structure.

His statement that present social conditions "are the inevitable result of a social institution . . . which has been the slow development of many ages" shows a depth of understanding too often lacking in the radical reform movement.

The intense feeling in evidence in this Lyceum talk is not the result of the idealistic dreaming of a boy. Edward Bellamy spoke of what he knew. He had been deeply impressed by the degradation of poverty in Europe. In his own home community the poor were so crowded that, according to a generally laudatory article on "The City of Chicopee" in the *New England Magazine* for May, 1898, families were living in holes dug into the river bank. In one of his editorials quoted later he describes as an eyewitness the mass of gaunt, bedraggled children that worked long hours in the factories of his home town. Part of this squalor was due not so much to the inherently evil social system of America, as to the fact that immigrants from poverty-stricken Europe were crowding into New England towns faster than they could be made part of the community. The failure was somewhat like that of a housewife to have an adequate dinner ready when a dozen unexpected guests are added to her family just at mealtime. Yet, contemporary descriptions of working conditions where there were no immigrants indicate that workers fared little better.

Edward Bellamy's rebellion against submergence in the prevailing economic atmosphere can be followed further in his writings in the *Springfield Union*. He seems to have begun to write for the *Union* during that summer, apparently in August, 1872. With his coming there enters an entirely new zest and flavor into the columns which, even after the paper's reorganization in May, had been used largely to curse Horace Greeley and the Democratic party in standard and hackneyed political fashion.

An editorial of May 29, 1872, just before he joined the staff, announcing the new policy of the paper, states, "The gentlemen who have bought the paper are thorough Republicans, without the smell of Cincinnati or Greeleyism in their garments." Yet within a year Bellamy was paying tribute to the "great heart" of Horace Greeley.[42] His particular columns were called "Literary Notices" and "New Publications." Doubtless he was expected to review poetry and *belles lettres*. Whether partly from pure cussedness, or solely out of interest in practical sociology, almost his first review was of *Healthy Houses,* an English work dealing chiefly with drainage, ventilation, and sanitation. To his literary readers he presented such matters as the following:

The city of Springfield by her untrapped sewer wells and similar abominations, is furnishing a deadly though subtle poison freely and in great abundance, at almost every corner, and the protest is very mild. . . .

Everyone who builds a house, everyone who lives in one, ought to know how to keep sewer gas out of their dwellings. How many who are anxious about the decorations and finish of their residences know or care about the drainage? . . . [There follow rules for installing plumbing.]

The chapter devoted to water closets and their proper arrangements will repay careful perusal. How often does a faulty arrangement of these modern conveniences render futile the best efforts of the modern physician and make one ready to return to the old-fashioned outhouse, which, with all its inconveniences, yet "wasted its sweetness on the desert air."[43]

Within a month or two of the time Bellamy joined the *Union* we find editorials or book reviews in the new column on fiction, poetry, biography, and history; but scattered among them are articles on social and economic subjects. We find comments on education— "there have been but two possible foundations for human governments, bayonets and common schools." He comments on factors influencing longevity; on picnics for poor children; drunkenness as a disease; price fixing and limitation of production in the oil industry; the condition of the Southern Negroes; and a discussion of the enlightened labor policy of the Cambria Steel Company. He

[42] *Springfield Union,* May 29, 1872.

[43] "A New Book about an Important Subject," *Springfield Union,* August 30, 1872.

comments on the effects on public policy of bad health of government officials—"God save the commonwealth of Massachusetts from dyspeptics."

During the following year, 1872–73, we find him discussing the ruthless treatment of French Communists by M. Thiers, and the hopes and follies of the Communists themselves; he has a continuing interest in English agricultural strikes and in the serfdom of English labor. He discusses monopoly in anthracite coal and pleads for public parks. Among so many provocative, witty, and penetrating observations it is difficult to make selection.

During this first year on the *Union* there is a constant succession of book reviews and editorials dealing with social and economic issues. In a discussion of the Welsh coal strike is the comment, "It seems that the coal producers are scaring their recalcitrant hands with threats of 'cheap Chinese labor,' this celestial spectre being apparently the particular bogey on which employers nowadays rely to frighten naughty workmen into good behavior." [44]

A discussion of "fagging" in English public schools in February, 1873, illustrates Bellamy's keen loyalty to the democratic American atmosphere:

The boys of the lower classes are distributed among the upper classes as body-servants, or "fags," as they are called. These fags are compelled to render all manner of menial services to their proprietors . . . Rebellion on the part of the fags is uncommon and always put down with brutal violence. . . . A system more admirably calculated to destroy the self-respect and develop the bullying instincts of boys could not be conceived. . . . Although in late years some voices have been raised against the custom of "fagging," the prevalent opinion of the English press has been in favor of retaining it as one of the guarantees of the British constitution. The moral of the subject, if we mistake not, is that "fagging" is an outgrowth of the system of caste, fundamental to the constitution of English society, and ingrained in the spirit of its people, nor will it be likely to pass away except as our British cousins are converted to the spirit of democracy, which is hostile to the subserviency of class to class, whether boys or men, whether in the mimic world of the school or the real world without it.[45]

[44] Editorial, *Springfield Union*, February 6, 1873.
[45] "A British Custom," *Springfield Union*, February 13, 1873.

Mrs. Bellamy's daughter recalls that when her brother Paul was reading *Tom Brown's School Days*, their father vigorously expressed the opinions indicated in this editorial. His daughter wrote, "I have never forgotten his vehemence."

Yet the inherent vulgarity of the fag system, which was a product of English aristocracy, was no more repellent to him than some of the vulgar expressions of American democracy. A few months after the above editorial appeared came another in which he was critical of democratic taste. In the *Springfield Union* of July 3, 1873, evidently with a persistent unpleasant memory of earlier Fourth of July celebrations, he wrote:

Civilized man is still a barbarian in his celebrations. The cannon, drums, and hurrahs with which we welcome great days and great personages, are but improved forms of the fifty cent muskets, the tom-toms, and miscellaneous yelling, wherewith the central African worships the new moon, or welcomes a returning war chief. . . . A Fourth of July crowd, as to persons perspiring, as to men swearing, as to women fretting, as to babies in full cry, as to linen limp, and as to general aspect a "dem'd, damp, moist, unpleasant, disagreeable body," is at once one of the saddest and most ludicrous spectacles we have ever been called upon to behold.[46]

Bellamy rebelled against lack of refinement, no matter what social or political dress it might wear.

Even at the age of twenty-three Bellamy was not satisfied with satirical or cynical references to lack of fineness, but he sought to understand its cause. In June of 1873 there is a long editorial discussing child labor in the local mills. This is worth quoting from, both because it is a picture of economic and social conditions in America at the time and because it is an example of the kinds of facts which entered into the formation of Mr. Bellamy's views on social questions:

Mrs. Browning has put the pith of volumes of sombre statistics into the lines of "Aurora Leigh":

"A holiday of miserable men
Is sadder than the burial day of kings."

What then shall we say of the children of this misery? We saw them out in crowds on the recent Decoration Day in one of our nearby manu-

[46] Editorial, *Springfield Union*, July 3, 1873.

facturing towns, squalid, bare-headed and bare-footed, ragged and meagre, some of them crippled for life either from birth or accident. . . . We almost felt that it were better to be dead than to be so alive. And where had these boys and girls come from? Out of the mills which had given them a few hours to run about and see the show. Any day at noon you can see them in dingy flocks, hovering along the sidewalks between their boarding place and "the yard." Any morning you can see them piling into the early train to go to the neighboring villages to their tasks. The mere sight of them; so old and worn and miserable to look at, yet so young, is proof enough that a great wrong exists somewhere among us which is inflicting a vast amount of barbarity, a positive cruelty of monstrous proportions upon these children and others like them in New England. This premature labor dwarfs them in size, so that when sixteen or eighteen years old, they have the diminutive, puny aspect of a scant dozen years. It twists them into little knotty deformities out of which coming years will never untwist them. . . . Half-starved and overworked, cuffed and shoved about as though there were no room for them anywhere, they are considerably more in need than the omnibus and car horses of the protection of a society to prevent cruelty to animals. Ten, eleven, twelve hours a day in our mills, and sixteen to eighteen in other countries, is a heavier burden than any such young shoulders should carry.

Ignorance of almost everything useful is an inevitable result of this juvenile imprisonment to hard labor; and vice and crime come along in most natural sequence in numerous instances. Children as young as six years are sometimes put into this daily work, with utterly deplorable results. . . . The plea commonly is the need of their wages to support their impoverished families. Every penny must be harvested for the common stock. But this is a most short-sighted view of the matter. Joseph Arch, an authority on this subject, says that "child labor means pauperism, crime, ignorance, immorality, and every evil." . . . Civilization does not deserve the name in any land, if it cannot run its business enterprises of whatever kind, indoor or outdoor, without such a sacrifice of human rights and well being.[47]

This picture of child labor did not pass from Bellamy's mind. We find it again in *Equality*. This editorial is evidence that in his last book he was relying on his own personal observation of factory workers in his home town of Chicopee Falls, and not on vague rumor, when he wrote:

Picture low rooms roofed with rough and grimy timbers and walled with bare or whitewashed brick. Imagine the floor so crammed with

[47] "Overworked Children in Our Mills," *Springfield Union*, June 5, 1873.

machinery for economy of space as to allow bare room for the workers
to writhe about among the flying arms and jaws of steel, a false motion
meaning death or mutilation. Imagine the air space above filled, instead
of air, with a mixture of stenches of oil and filth, unwashed human
bodies, and foul clothing. Conceive a perpetual clang and clash of
machinery like the screech of a tornado.[48]

Outspoken at the age of twenty-three concerning conditions in
his home community, Edward Bellamy continued to speak his mind
until his death. While his home town in time became proud of having a famous author in its midst, it did not take kindly to his
criticisms, and in his last years he had very few intimate friends
among the people of his own station in his own community. One of
these few loyal friends and frequent visitors was the Reverend
R. E. Bisbee.

In July, 1873, a review by Bellamy of a series of articles in an
English magazine on "Luxury and Extravagance" expresses strong
feeling, but without the clearer analysis which developed later:

A lively debate has been going on for some months past, in the
Contemporary Review, over the question: Whether luxury is culpable.
Goldwin Smith, Mr. Ruskin, and Mr. Greg have thus far given the discussion dignity and vivacity: the first two assailing the plutocrats and
sybarites, and the last and weakest of the three defending them. . . .
Mr. Ruskin makes himself very merry over a paragraph in the report
of the Common Council of New York city upon the commercial crisis of
1857, which affirms that "Every extravagance that a man with $100,000
or $1,000,000 indulges in adds to the means, the support, the wealth
of ten or a hundred who had little or nothing else but their labor,
their intellect or their taste." . . . Thus the New York economists,
and this is probably a common view of the subject. It surely is not,
however, a very moral view. It avowedly licenses a large amount and
variety of conduct which is directly destructive of personal and social
virtue. . . .
Men who have gathered up large estates for themselves generally go
on with some useful enterprise which benefits the community. They are
entitled to a very different consideration than are the others whose only
activity lies in satiating their own costly tastes.
There are social and common interests lying along this path which
deserve patient and impartial study. . . . There is a large margin for

[48] *Equality*, p. 54.

the useful, right, justifiable expenditure of money in making home life and social intercourse comfortable, elegant, rich, where affluence abounds; and proportionately so where there is a less ability. But beyond these rational limits there is a wasteful prodigality and profligacy of luxurious display and self-indulgence which is utterly unseemly, which is both morally and economically bad; which springs from the grosser natures of men; which burglarizes and debauches society; which has had much to do in embittering the poorer classes against the richer and in fanning the fire which is burning so hotly in the hearts of many of our labor reformers and their followers.[49]

In August, 1873, is a review entitled "Sense and Nonsense about Servants."

The servant question is always in order. . . . The fact is that servants . . . are governed by about the same considerations as their masters and mistresses. . . . The parlor sets the fashion for the kitchen. . . . If it were possible to establish a "bureau of registry" for servants on the *Scribner's Monthly* plan, it would be useless unless a "bureau of registry" for employers could be established too.[50]

In the *Springfield Union* of October 26, 1877, in one of his last editorials before leaving the paper, Bellamy wrote:

If American civilization is to pass for anything valuable or original, it is by virtue of its central idea that labor is honorable in all, and that caste pretensions, based on hereditary laziness, are absurd. Therefore, any usages of language which shut up any honest avocation to self-respecting persons by stigmatizing it with a word that hurts sensitive ears, is an offence against the genius of our civilization. . . . It is absurd to argue that the word "Servant" is not a hard one to use about a fellow creature. The very fact that it tickles the ears of snobs shows that it is.[51]

Sixteen years later he discussed the same subject in an article entitled "A Vital Domestic Problem—Household Service Reform."[52]
A woman in Chicopee Falls who had been a "hired girl" in the home of Edward Bellamy carried a feeling of friendship and affection for him. His was the only home in which she ever worked, she

49 "Luxury and Extravagance," *Springfield Union*, July 7, 1873.
50 "Sense and Nonsense about Servants," *Springfield Union*, August 16, 1873.
51 "Shall We Call Them Servants?" *Springfield Union*, October 26, 1877.
52 *Good Housekeeping*, X, No. 4 (December 21, 1889), 74–77.

said, where she was treated entirely as an equal. Edward Bellamy
lived as he wrote.

In November, 1873, is an editorial entitled "Feudalism of Modern Times" which expresses Bellamy's thinking. That this should
appear in a staid Republican party newspaper is quite remarkable;
its appearance is a tribute to the independence and tolerance of the
publisher:

Political feudalism went out of existence some three or four centuries
ago, giving place, first to absolute monarchy, and in later times to a
more or less pronounced democracy. In commerce, however, feudalism
still survives, and in the present age shows signs of rapid development.
. . . As the political was once dominated by a few great nobles, so
now the industrial and commercial world is altogether controlled and
dominated by the princes of merchandise, manufactures, and commerce.
The analogies between the old political and modern commercial feudalism are many and various. . . . In political affairs, which touch the
welfare of the citizen at comparatively few points, we have replaced
feudalism with democracy, but in the affairs of industry, which touch
the welfare of the citizen at all points, feudalism still survives in its
pristine vigor. . . . It is the dream of socialism to introduce democracy
into the industrial world also, but whether it be realizable, experience
only can show.[53]

Bellamy reviews the Brook Farm experiment; proposes a system
of public pawnbroking, after the European custom; gives statistics
of home ownership in Scotland, where most of the land was owned
by a few men, and argues for small land holdings; upholds the right
of labor to organize. In 1876 he discusses the debasing terrors of
Australian and Tasmanian prison camps; reviews a book by Washington Gladden on *Moral Economy and Political Economy;* repeatedly advocates the repeal of "the trustee process," by which
poor men are thrown into bankruptcy while the well-to-do escape.
Two or three brief quotations will illustrate the gradual maturity
of his style and the development of a sense of humor. Following a
bank robbery there is an interesting editorial:

Some clever papers bringing the intellectual department to bear on
the Northampton bank robbery, have hit upon a simple plan by which

the robbers in such cases can always be balked. They propose that the cashier, instead of telling the safe combination or unlocking the safe for the burglars when threatened with death, shall calmly fold his arms and let them kill away. The cashier is assured that probably the burglars won't kill him anyway . . . and if they did kill him, he would die in the confidence that grateful bank directors would make suitable and sufficient provision for his family. We certainly would not say anything to deter cashiers from taking this course. Martyrdom in a good cause is always edifying to the survivors, and would be especially so to the depositors of the bank. The cashier's wife and family might be inclined to view the matter differently, but as interested parties, their opinions would naturally be regarded with suspicion.

Some cashiers of a sordid disposition might urge that they were paid for ciphering, bookkeeping and clerical duties generally; and that guarding the funds of the bank, or of its depositors, and especially getting killed in their defense, was not in the bargain. But such a hair-splitting temper would not, we trust, be general. And, moreover, it is probably true that the burglars would not generally kill the stubborn cashiers. . . . A pair of thumbscrews, or even a candle held under the back of a hand, or a dozen other simple appliances of which Fox's Book of Martyrs contains full descriptions, would have a very persuasive effect on the mind of the average cashier, while at the same time they would not expose the burglars to hanging.

We would suggest to messieurs the gentlemanly bank robbers, that they now give the cashiers a little rest and go for the bank presidents. The latter have a good deal the most to say what property shall be left in the vault, and how it shall be protected, and it would be only fair to give them a chance to show their pluck in defending it. If the burglars would transfer their attention to the presidents for a while we presume we should very shortly see the general introduction of chronometer locks without regard to expense, and of watchmen who don't go home at four o'clock.[54]

Throughout Bellamy's career as a book reviewer and editorial writer, and in his notebooks and manuscripts of the same period, we find him to be a rebel against many elements of the prevailing economic system. Here as elsewhere, he was not moved to rebellion for rebellion's sake. Rather, there was growing in his mind a concept of the way in which men might live in order to retain their self-respect and to realize their possibilities. He simply endeavored to live in that way, even though the result was that frequently he was

[54] Editorial, *Springfield Union,* January 28, 1876.

out of harmony with ruling custom. Yet in this period he was little
more than a knight errant, wandering about and fighting any evil
thing which came into his path, but with no clearly conceived plan
of campaign for effective action.

THE REBEL IN HISTORICAL RESEARCH

After leaving the *Springfield Union* and making his trip to
Hawaii, Bellamy worked at his home as a free-lance writer. And
here his rebellion against prevailing outlooks again appears—this
time in the field of historical research.

Doubtless he had read in his school history—as has every American school child—a brief reference to Shays' Rebellion, to the
effect that just after the American Revolution a number of "malcontents" in western Massachusetts made some kind of disturbance
because of high taxes, or for reasons but vaguely described, and
that the rebellion was put down. Not one person in a hundred has
a much clearer impression of that incident. Few realize that it was
perhaps the first organized revolt in the New World against social
exploitation.

The occurrences of Shays' Rebellion were in Bellamy's own
neighborhood and in the Berkshire Hills just to the west. The
rebellion had to do with the fathers and grandfathers of the farmers
he talked with in the long walks he loved so well. Perhaps it was as
a result of these talks that young Bellamy became skeptical of the
accounts in the histories he read, and made a first-hand study of
Shays' Rebellion. In 1879 his findings were published in the *Berkshire Courier,* a newspaper at Great Barrington. In preparing his
account he personally visited the villages and farm homes where
the tradition still lingered, and also searched the written records.

It must have been a disillusioning experience for a young man
between twenty-five and thirty, on becoming interested in some
phase of his country's history concerning which only one point of
view had been presented in textbooks and historical literature, to
discover upon careful, first-hand investigation that a whole nation for a century had been misled.

Because the preparation for and the writing of this book may
have had a marked influence on the growth of his social views, it is

worth while to review what actually happened in this episode in our country's development, which has been so lightly and deftly treated by the makers of American histories.

Thoroughly typical of the generally accepted view is the following brief paragraph in which John Fiske, in his *History of the United States,* disposes of Shays' Rebellion:

In the Massachusetts legislature the paper money party was defeated. There was a great outcry among the farmers against merchants and lawyers, and some were heard to maintain that the time had come for wiping out all debts. In August 1786, the malcontents arose in rebellion, headed by one Daniel Shays, who had been a captain in the Continental army. They began by trying to prevent the courts from sitting, and went on to burn barns, plunder houses, and attack the arsenal at Springfield. The state troops were called out under General Lincoln, two or three skirmishes were fought, in which a few lives were lost, and at length, in February 1787, the insurrection was suppressed.[55]

Yet General Benjamin Lincoln, who put down Shays' Rebellion, unconsciously implied a case for the rebels when he wrote of the situation: "The proportion of debtors runs high in this state [Massachusetts]. Too many of them are against the government. The men of property and the holders of the public securities are generally supporters of our present constitution." [56]

General Knox, who was sent to Massachusetts by the Congress to end the rebellion, wrote:

Their [the rebels'] creed is, that the property of the United States has been protected from confiscation by the joint exertions of all, and therefore ought to be common to all.

This dreadful situation . . . has alarmed every man of principle and property in New England. . . . We imagined that the mildness of the government, and the virtue of the people were so correspondent, that we were not as other nations, requiring brutal force to support the laws. But we find that we are men, actual men, possessing all the turbulent passions belonging to that animal; and that we must have a government proper and adequate for him.[57]

55 John Fiske, *A History of the United States,* p. 250. Reprinted by permission.

56 Albert Bushnell Hart, ed., *American History Told by Contemporaries,* III, pp. 192–93. Reprinted by permission of the publishers.

57 John Marshall, *The Life of George Washington,* IV, pp. 223, 224. Reprinted by permission of the publishers.

General Lincoln, who put down the rebellion, wrote: "They [the rebels] had no doubt if they could keep up their influence until another choice of the legislature and the executive that matters might be moulded in General Court to their wishes. To avoid this was the duty of government." [58]

The military force which overcame the rebellion, according to Marshall, was not financed directly from public funds, but by men of means in Boston who advanced money at six per cent, the expenditure being made without prior legislative approval. These Boston merchants took it upon themselves to see that the "duties of government" should be determined in accordance with their wishes.

General Washington was confused by the reports brought to him. He wrote from Mount Vernon to Colonel Lee, a member of the Congress:

The picture you have exhibited . . . and the accounts which are published of the commotions and tempers of the numerous bodies in the eastern country present a state of things equally to be lamented and deprecated. They exhibit a melancholy verification of what our transatlantic foes have predicted; and of another thing perhaps which is still more to be regretted, and is yet more unaccountable—that mankind, when left to themselves, are unfit for their own government.[59]

We get a glimpse of the narrow margin by which the "father of his country" was a believer in democracy. On his broad, slave-tilled Virginia acres Washington could little know the bitter lot of men on stony Massachusetts hills; witness his fervent plea, "For God's sake tell me what is the cause of all these commotions." Had he inquired of conditions nearer home he would have found similar exploitation of farmers in the Piedmont of his own Virginia and of North Carolina by the wealthy men of the Tidewater region—that is, by men of his own social and economic class. In Massachusetts the farmers protested with ultimate success, while in Virginia and the Carolinas they only grumbled without organized revolt.

[58] Hart, *American History Told by Contemporaries*, p. 193.
[59] Marshall, *The Life of George Washington*, IV, 227.

Over the rocky hillsides of western Massachusetts, one still sees where these hardy men dug out their farms, stump by stump and stone by stone from the excessively rough land; he observes laboriously built stone fences around the tiny fields, substantial barns and simple and attractive little cottages which this breed of men won for themselves by lifelong, back-breaking toil. Then, when he recalls as well the contributions they have made to American civilization as they moved toward the West, he doubts the suitability of such epithets as "perfidiousness," "malcontents," "disorderly spirit," "lax notions concerning public and private faith," "desperate and unprincipled," "lawless men," "a beginning of anarchy," "treason" (all but the first from Marshall's *Life of Washington*), which smothered these rebels with contempt for a century in the opinion of Americans.

The extreme distress of the farmers of Massachusetts and of the rest of New England was matched by the unequaled spending of the few. The flight of money to Europe was balanced by the import of luxury goods. When the tercentennial of Portsmouth, New Hampshire, was being celebrated a few years ago, as an incident of this celebration the principal houses of the town were labeled as to the original owners and the time of erection. Although nearly a century and a half had elapsed in which wealth might accumulate and houses might be built, a substantial part of the fine homes of this old seaport and merchant town had been built within about ten years of the date of Shays' Rebellion.

Though there was danger of rebellion in the 1780's, it was a harvest time for men of money. Men who had bought bonds at greatly depreciated prices to finance the Revolution were receiving high interest rates which returned the purchase price every few years. In the lack of currency, prices of goods were ruinously low, a comfortable situation for those who had money.

The easy paper money of Revolutionary days, together with the imperative expenses while the head of the family was away with the army, had led to general indebtedness. Then the returning soldiers found their soldier's pay "not worth a continental." Debts incurred with easy money had to be paid with gold, and of that there was almost none. The courts and the lawyers were with the "honest money" party.

One wonders whether Bellamy had observed the same coincidence of hardship and luxury in the fine old colonial homes of Stockbridge and Great Barrington. According to his cousin Francis Bellamy,[60] who edited the book for publication after Edward's death:

> The indescribable poverty of the years after the Revolutionary War, and before the adoption of the Constitution . . . (1783–1789), is indicated by a few facts . . . Our imports were three times greater than our exports. Consequently, the small amount of gold . . . had left the interior for the seaports, and from there it was rapidly sailing away.
>
> During these years the annual tax in Massachusetts amounted to $200 per family—more money than the average farmer or mechanic saw in two years.
>
> The chief industry, therefore, was the law; the courts were concerned in emptying farmers' houses under foreclosures, and in filling the jails with good men who could not pay their debts—unless, indeed, their creditors gave them the privilege of working their debts on account, in virtual serfdom.[61]

The book pictured conditions and events in the western Massachusetts towns of Stockbridge and Great Barrington; the shiftless and hard-drinking loafers, the docile, patient, and simple-minded farmers, the dignified self-assurance of men of position and quality, the wild rumors and half-baked social theories. It described the contempt of men of quality for the common herd, the pathos of farmers being driven from hard-won homes, the inability to pay debts because of the nonexistence of gold, the agitation to make a farm foreclosure a final settlement of debt without the further dread menace of forced servitude or the debtor's jail. We see also the instability and cowardice of the common man who still feels himself half a peasant, the drinking and rowdyism, the cloddish vulgarity, in contrast to the culture, power, dignity, and decision in "the classes." Bellamy's dice are not loaded.

[60] Francis Bellamy was the author of the "Pledge of Allegiance" to the flag, known to every American schoolboy.
[61] *The Duke of Stockbridge,* pp. vii, viii. Reprinted by permission.

His story of the gradual fizzling out of the rebellion, owing to the rigorousness of winter, the leaderlessness of the common people, the love of rum, the decision and superior strategy of men of property, and the power of central government, conveys what seems to be an accurate historical impression.

There was beginning to exist in western Massachusetts a class of gentlemen-farmers, men who lived in the towns in relatively luxurious homes and were gradually accumulating ownership of the lands around them. Had the acquisition of land for debts not been checked, a new feudalism might have developed in New England. Shays' Rebellion failed as a military effort, but at the next election Governor Bowdoin, who had been a chief factor in suppressing it, was overwhelmingly defeated by John Hancock.

Then came the issue of approving the new Federal Constitution. John Hancock was chairman of the convention called to consider ratification, and apparently held the balance of power. Spokesman for the discontented and exploited back-country people, he refused to support ratification except on condition that a series of amendments, which have come to be known as the Bill of Rights, be recommended to the states. By this course, by his action as governor, and by the suitable legislation which he promoted, the plight of the unfortunate farmers was relieved, imprisonment for debt was ended, and a new order was established. In substance then, the aims of those who took part in Shays' Rebellion were achieved, and the Bill of Rights became part of the Federal Constitution.

In his researches in preparation for writing *The Duke of Stockbridge* Bellamy saw all this. He saw how this genuine social revolt against extreme injustice had been presented to the American people as a disturbance caused by a few "malcontents." He may have observed, too, the fate of John Hancock. The wealthiest of New England merchants had turned against his class to support the common people. The result was that this man, who had been president of the Continental Congress, governor of his state, chairman of the Massachusetts convention which ratified the Federal Constitution, who had used his powerful influence to present the Bill of Rights to the country—this man, too, was largely buried in contempt and disparagement. Not until after Bellamy's death was a biography of John Hancock written, and then it represented the point of view of the element of society with which Hancock found himself out of accord.[62]

In this adventure in historical research Bellamy had a chance to observe the power and pervasiveness of class interest. Also in his home town he saw boys and girls crowded in boarding houses and tenements, working twelve hours a day for fifty cents or less, while well-to-do families lived luxuriously.

Had his experience been limited to urban workers he might have thought of exploitation as a result primarily of the machine age, and he might have sought some such solution as a retreat from mechanical civilization, as William Morris did in his *News from Nowhere*. Bellamy's acquaintance with rural New England taught him two things: first, that exploitation preceded large-scale industry; and second, that even for the farmer who is out of debt and who has inherited the houses and barns and the cleared fields won by a century of grinding toil—even for him, life without the help of modern industry is in large part relentless servitude to nature. Against his love of homely simplicity he became committed to amelioration of common life by the full use of modern inventions. Men who talk so glibly against public regimentation generally are among those who have been freed by the hard private regimentation of others. Edward Bellamy's wanderings about New England farms, which resulted in *The Duke of Stockbridge*, provided important elements of preparation for his life work.

THE REBEL IN SEARCH OF A VOCATION

It seems that in his choice of a vocation Edward Bellamy did not have an appetite for rebellion. With great effort he determined upon a way of life for himself, and when the demands of a calling were inconsistent with his course, he adhered to that way, even though in his opinion it required him to give up his chosen field of work.

---

[62] Lorenzo Sears, *John Hancock, the Picturesque Patriot.*

Shortly after he returned from Germany, some time in 1869, he decided to study law, and in October of that year entered the office of Leonard and Wells in Springfield. The only definite record we have of this study period is a thick notebook which consists of a summary of Blackstone, an exemplary review without evidence of originality. From other sources we know that his eyes and ears were open during this period. He began his studies with a high opinion of the law as a profession. It was to provide opportunity to fight the battles of the wronged and the oppressed, and to deal with problems of constitutional law.

An intelligent young man of twenty in his day-by-day work of lawyer's assistant would get a concentrated education in what actually constitutes the work of his firm, and of the other lawyers in his community. Edward's law education was largely a process of disillusionment. He had struggled as few young men do for a philosophy of life and a purpose for living. It would appear that in the law he found neither. Rather, he found a law office to be a place where people came for help in giving effectiveness to their lower motives and their more sordid interests. It is probable that the firm for which he worked was not unrepresentative. Its two partners were among the ablest and most respected members of the Springfield and Hampden County bar. What he found to criticize there he would have found in most, but not all, law offices. There doubtless were many lawyers in his state of Massachusetts of such mold that a young man working for one of them would have found a philosopher and friend, as well as an employer whose personal and professional standards he could respect and admire; where his convictions would have had sympathetic understanding and strengthening support.

On being admitted to the bar, in June, 1871, Edward refused a law partnership and opened an office for himself the following October. After having a single client he closed his office and turned his back finally upon that calling.

A greatly disillusioning experience often shakes and sometimes shatters a man's life philosophy. That Edward Bellamy's life was severely shaken by his brief experience in the law, following his

earlier disappointment in not being accepted at West Point, we
have evidence in his journals. Under date of August, 1871, we
find the following entry:

I have had not a few disappointments in this life, already the bitterness
of hope deferred is with me, already become an old story, and yet I do
not find my self-confidence one whit abated. I am certain indeed that if
under every circumstance of ignominy I should fail in all my earthly
strivings, I should for all that feel the prouder, nor dream of being cast
down before a sneering world. It is very like a kind of mental lunacy but
it is true that were I in Hell I could not feel ashamed or inclined even
to self-reproach. Although no man could appreciate more keenly the
rewards of fame or the ignominy of public contempt, yet neither of these
is essential to my mental ideal; but I have an inner refuge, a citadel of
self, within which, once retired, the whole world, nay the Universe and
the Great God himself seem to be outsiders whose alliance and affection
I would indeed conciliate, but with which I could never be identified,
there existing an eternal gulf between us, a moat impassable. That is to
say, I suppose, the feeling of utterly isolated and necessarily self-
dependent personality is peculiarly developed in my mental constitution. I feel that I have an inexpugnable fortress of self-existence
whereto I may retire invulnerable when e'er my outposts advanced
here in the world among men or among the gods in the realm of
thought are driven in, the eternal integrity of which is the most assured
of all things.[63]

Whether or not we agree with Bellamy's view, we must recognize
that his disapproval of the standards and motives of the law resulted, not from vague imagination, but from about two years of
very intimate contact with legal practice as it actually was carried on. That his action was from courage and not cowardice the
entries in his journal give evidence, and that his spirit recovered
from that bitter experience, his whole life bears witness. It is
to his credit that he clearly appraised the situation, judging
it by such evidence as was available, and gave up this one hold he
had on a vocation, rather than make the sacrifice of his life purposes which he believed that the practice of law would demand.

In the unfinished novel "Eliot Carson," which, as already indicated, is largely autobiographical, there is an account that, aside
from a few minor details, seems to represent Bellamy's own experi-

---

[63] Unpublished papers (B1-1-4).

ence. The hero of the story, like Bellamy, had left college without completing his course. He too had been an irregular student "devoting more time to the college library than to the college text books." Then the story continues:

After he had been at home a couple of years he attained his majority, and the choice of a profession seemed to be incumbent on him. He went into the office of Lawyer Bliss, the Hilton practitioner, and in due course became a lawyer and settled down to practice in the village. It did not take him long to become utterly disgusted with the dirty trade of a local pettifogger. What he had in his mind's eye when taking to the law was the arguing of great constitutional questions, the chivalrous defense of the widow and the orphan against their oppressors, and the vindication of accused and sorely beset innocence. He found in fact that his business was the collection by browbeating or legal duress of the bills of the local grocers and shoemakers against the mill operative and the shophand, the confiscation of the sorely needed and meagre wages of work girls and fathers of families to satisfy claims of whose real equity he most generally for the protection of his own conscience preferred to know nothing at all. . . . Some of his fellow practitioners to whom he confided the questions produced by these experiences admitted, with a shrug of the shoulders, that they had felt so at the beginning of their practice, but assured him that he would, like them, get tough after a while. He did not, however, get tough. . . . The claim collecting side of his business was not the only disagreeable one. He did not relish any better being used as a tool by Johnson, Jones, or Patrick Flaherty to gratify a grudge against some neighbor by the means of legal persecution. It really seemed to this sensitive young man that this setting up in business as a public blood hound whom anybody might hire for a little cash to set on anybody else, either to run down and throttle a debtor or mangle and tear an enemy till called off, was not exactly the ideal trade of a gentleman. He stood it a couple of years and finding that he became no tougher, then took down his shingle and left the law.[64]

In another draft of the same story, Eliot Carson's fiancée suggests that he enter one of the professions, whereupon Carson exclaims:

"The principle of the profession that the lawyer is morally irresponsible for the ends he is employed to further, that his duty is only to his fee, is the survival of the Swiss Musketeer's principle that his

[64] *Ibid.* (B2-EC-6, 7, 8).

loyalty was due only to the keeper of the money chest. In all other professions and occupations this barbarous principle is cut out. In the so-called liberal profession of law alone it is still professed by personally honorable men." [65]

It is evident that Bellamy's rebellion against the law, which grew out of his personal experience, unfortunate and unrepresentative as that may have been, was made necessary by his determination to live in accord with the pattern of life he had adopted for himself.

Next Bellamy tried journalism. In September, 1871, his cousin William S. Packer, with whom he had traveled in Germany, wrote that he had called on Charlton Lewis, his near neighbor in Brooklyn, who recently had been made managing editor of the *New York Evening Post*, suggesting that Edward Bellamy would be a good assistant editor. In reporting his visit, William Packer, who had been Bellamy's most intimate associate, wrote a letter which throws light on himself, on the character of Bellamy's thought and study at the time, on the character of the *Post*, and on the man under whom Bellamy was to work:

I told him what little good I could of you, and slurred over your most glaring defects, and I really succeeded in making out a good case without "drawing a very long bow.". . . Mr. Lewis is rather a young man, about 38, a graduate of Yale, very bright, well read, and solid. He has fitted himself for his position by attempting every profession under the sun. . . . You know the high reputation and general policy of the Paper. Strong Free-trade Republican, eminently respectable, never dealing in personalities, etc., etc. Mr. L. has just taken the principal post in its editorial management on the withdrawal of Mr. Charles Nordhoff, who has gone to the *Times*. I gathered that Mr. L.'s former position was now vacant, and I believe you can obtain it if you try. . . . Your age is regarded as no disadvantage. (I confessed the whole fatal 21 years.) The absence of "Poetry" is regarded as a great advantage. [William Cullen Bryant was the publisher and editor-in-chief.] Your studies in the line of Political Science and Law, your German study, and your habit of thinking out your own political creed, are just the requisite qualifications. [Bellamy was to write an editorial on some political subject and send it to William Packer, who would hand it personally to Lewis.] Don't venture into the N. Y. Ring [The *Post* at that time was attacking the "Tweed Ring."], and be prepared for a good deal of

[65] *Ibid.* (B2-EC-19).

practical knowledge in the *Post* editor. . . . Some of us here have faith in you. . . . You have nothing here to lose and everything to win. Go in!

> Yours very truly,
> WM. S. P.

Bellamy secured some sort of connection with the *New York Evening Post*, and held it for about seven months.

As to all of his reasons for leaving, we cannot be sure. Apparently the place given him was not as important as he had hoped. Though his income was very low for living in New York City he insisted on being independent. His father wrote him in May, 1872:

I was a little hurt at your sending back the little bank note Mother enclosed—I am quite flush at present. . . . I should like to know why you refuse your father's gifts—more than the other boys—especially when you have never received half as much as either of the others.

Then his father wrote him of an opening on the newly reorganized *Springfield Union*. Bellamy secured the position, and served on that paper more than five years as editorial writer and book reviewer. Bellamy's contributions show a freedom of expression seldom given to a staff writer whose social and economic opinions differ so widely from those of his paper. During the last year of his service, however, there seemed to be a marked reduction in unconventional expressions. Was his failing health partly a reflection of a spiritual stress over increasing lack of freedom to express his views? Did he leave the Springfield paper because he could no longer say what he thought? We can only guess. There is evidence, however, that the pattern of life to which he had so fully committed himself made difficult times for him, even in the field of journalism.

As in case of the law, he entered the field of journalism with a high standard for the calling. Among his handwritten manuscripts, under the title of "The Liberty of the Press," is a reasonable and sane expression of those standards, of which the following is representative:

Journalism is a business that requires more conscience than any other by which men make a living. Its powers of injuring are only equalled by its powers of benefiting the community. It is a business whose moral responsibility is at once more onerous and more plausibly to be evaded than that of any other. The journalist has his choice, either to make the public concupiscence his excuse or to correct it by his own sense of fairness and decency. He must either get behind the community as to the matter of responsibility or stand before it. He must either be better or worse than the community, for he must either rise above it in refusing to gratify its morbid tastes or he must sink below it in pandering to them. . . . The freedom of the press in this country is so complete that it has been able perfectly to adapt so that it answers to them as a plaster cast to a face. The mask is not flattering to the subject or pleasing to the admirers of human nature.[66]

In the story "Eliot Carson," Bellamy pays his compliments to journalism as well as to the law:

"Then journalism. If I were a man, I think I'd be an editor. Did you never fancy that?" [said Nelly]

"It is a good trade [replied Eliot Carson]. When a man controls the paper he edits and can say what he will, he has an enviable position. But such editors are growing fewer and fewer as journalism develops— and a paper requires corporate capital. The hireling editor is another sort of fellow, whom one can pity as he can poor lawyers, for the poor devils have their living to make, but cannot respect. I mean the editors and editorial writers who are given their texts from the counting room, paid so much a month and expected to advocate or condemn public measures and enterprises as they are ordered without regard to their own private convictions. They go from paper to paper changing their politics as convalescents change their living. They have advocated in turn so many contradicting principles, have boxed the moral, political, and social compass so many times, that by the time they have got through, the only personal identity left them is a little bundle of personal appetites and necessities for the support of which they have done all this world of lying. Personalities are in danger of adopting the abominable principle of the lawyer that a man may advocate an idea or end if he is regularly employed and paid for doing so, even if he does not approve the idea or end, and yet be an honest man. I say that no device under heaven was ever invented by which any man could or ever did that thing and remained honest. We cannot change the definition of that word to accommodate the experience even of two such important professions as law and journalism." [67]

If confidential confessions of editors, reporters, and correspondents are dependable, the stress which Bellamy felt was not unusual, though his handling of himself was after a rare pattern.

[66] *Ibid.* (B3B-"Liberty of the Press," p. 6).　　[67] *Ibid.* (B2-EC-20, 21).

That Bellamy's concept of the freedom of the press was not capricious or irresponsible is evident in the following extract from his editorial in the *Springfield Union* in May, 1875, "Concerning Newspapers," a condensation and popularization of his manuscript, "The Liberty of the Press":

Newspapers have their weak spots and their besetting sins as much as individuals. They stand flattery no better and run into the excessive culture of self-esteem on slight temptation, clipping out of each other's columns complimentary notices of their own shrewdness and smartness, and carefully shunning, both with eye and scissors, what looks the other way.

. . . .

There is something to be thought of by the conductors of newspapers besides the liberty of the press. That is, of course, essential to its life as a useful agent in the community. When that is really assailed or imperiled, there can be but one feeling among sensible people, whether inside or outside the newspaper world. It is not necessary to go back to John Milton to get materials for a strong argument or an indignant protest against the restriction of printing. Such freedom is the birthright of every American thinker, author and reader. But the possession of this birthright carries with it the obligation of courtesy, not to say decency, in the enjoyment and employment of it. There is among us a good deal of editorial strength which seems scarcely at all to feel this obligation of good manners in exhibiting its mental muscle. It does not cultivate politeness, though it certainly knows that the presence of this is the only thing which can keep even the strongest from now and then dropping into the swagger of the bully. It is a pitiful blunder of a certain kind of smartness that believes it has a prescriptive license to be boorish and insolent whenever it can find no matter how flimsy a pretext . . . It is, in fact, a very loud style of quackery—all the more so with its fondness for advertising itself and parading the wonderful certificates of its admiring patrons.

. . . a daily or other journal has no more liberty in the line of personal defamation than its editor would have on the street in conversation, or on the platform in declamation. No honorable newspaper would desire it. The careless and malodorous license which many have taken to themselves in handling the character and acts of others is as culpable as it has been mischievous . . . Much of it has sprung from the passion of reprisals, in some way, for offenses laid up against the scandalized parties. . . . This needs repression as much as does any sort of assassination. The injury inflicted upon individuals or bodies of men by wrong information, must find its cure in a more effective organization of the journals themselves. This is simply a matter of careful supervision. Perhaps the most careful will never effect a complete exemption from all mistakes. But when the public is satisfied that a newspaper is doing everything which is possible to make its intelligence absolutely correct, and that it is entirely above the temptation of designedly traducing any person or interest, suits for slander or libel will soon become a mere tradition in editorial circles. There is no natural hostility between a daily journal and the public. . . .[68]

Very seldom does a newspaper speak out so plainly against the shortcomings of the press. In the preceding August another expression indicated that his mind was running on the subject. The title of the earlier editorial is "Moral Murder as a Fine Art." Here again, we have substantially an extract from the manuscript referred to:

What gives to the malice of the slanderer its peculiar power for evil in this age and country is the existence of a class of newspapers which take a peculiar pride in putting a slander through in good shape. . . .

Nowadays we have made so much progress in the science of police, that it is made very inconvenient for a man to murder his adversary. The commoner and safer procedure in these days is to slander him. That kills him far more thoroughly and with far less trouble, and if you are vindictive you can comfort yourself with knowing the victim suffers far more in this process of being killed by slander than the unlucky teamster whom the Sioux made a bon-fire of. . . .[69]

For Edward Bellamy, journalism was not just an interesting occupation, or a way to make a living. He had certain standards for his life by which every activity was measured. It is evident from what has been quoted that he gave long and intelligent consideration to journalism as a career. It is possible, especially in view of his dislike of change, that when he gave up his job as book reviewer and editorial writer after more than five years of service, it was because in some vital respect his work there was in conflict with the standards he had set for himself. On the other hand, his reason for leaving may have been no other than an urge for complete freedom to live and do as he chose. He was an artist, and

[68] "Concerning Newspapers," *Springfield Union,* May 18, 1875.
[69] "Moral Murder as a Fine Art," *Springfield Union,* August 20, 1874.

was impelled to do the work of an artist. He fretted at the routine requirements of writing so many columns a week. It must be said of the *Union* during most of this period that seldom is a newspaper more tolerant in making possible the expression of views which it does not approve.

In *Equality* Bellamy gives his mature impression of the newspaper:

"The great nineteenth-century newspaper was a capitalistic enterprise as purely commercial in its principle as a woolen factory, and the editors were no more allowed to write their own opinions than the weavers to choose the patterns they wove. They were employed to advocate the opinions and interests of the capitalists owning the paper and no others. The only respect in which the journalists seem to have differed from the clergy was in the fact that the creeds which the latter were employed to preach were more or less fixed traditions, while those which the editors must preach changed with the ownership of the paper. This, Julian, is the truly exhilarating spectacle of abounding and unfettered originality, of sturdy moral and intellectual independence and rugged individuality, which it was feared by your contemporaries might be endangered by any change in the economic system." [70]

When Bellamy left the *Springfield Union* at the end of 1877, this phase of his career came to a close. The trip to Hawaii which followed seems not to have helped him in the choice of a career, though we cannot tell what contribution leisure and the comparative solitude of travel may have made toward clarifying his purposes. On returning to his home in the spring of 1878 he seems to have settled down for a time to the life of a free-lance writer. In the succeeding year and a half he wrote a few short stories, which appeared first in the *Springfield Union*, and three books. His first book, *Six to One*, was a light story for summer reading, which only occasionally gives a hint of his mind. Next came *The Duke of Stockbridge*, and then *Dr. Heidenhoff's Process*, one of his best pieces of literary work, which ran also as a serial in the *Union*. We have no record of editorials or book reviews during that period, though they may have constituted a considerable part of his work. His next adventure in the field was to be with a paper of which he and his brother Charles were the owners.

[70] *Equality*, p. 401.

That he had turned over in his mind the possibility of other careers is suggested by a passage in the manuscript of "Eliot Carson."

You are plenty good enough for a minister [said Nelly], but I'm afraid your notions about the soul and such things are a little queer."
"I'm not sure that would disqualify me," said Eliot with a laugh. "It is old-fashioned notions nowadays that are unpopular. But I'm afraid I wouldn't like the trade. The only sort of preachers that I ever thought worth their salt were the itinerant monks of the middle ages, who did not depend on their hearers for a stiver, or care a straw for their favor or their worth . . . The essence of any preaching to my mind is the absolute utter independence of preachers upon people, and that essence today is wholly lacking." [71]

As he continued his search for a vocation Bellamy found that he was not dealing with just the limitations of particular callings. There was something in the prevailing customs of men, in the very fabric of society, which seemed to result in similar blemishes in all callings. In the "Eliot Carson" manuscript he comments:

"But why do I waste breath pointing out the drawbacks of the other trades and professions men live by? In the main particular they are all on a par. All alike are states of involuntary servitude; all alike involve the cessation of anything like sustained mental culture or a life of thought at the threshold of manhood. Intellectual development henceforth, though acute and brilliant, is limited to breadmaking expedients." [72]

March 26, 1880, was Edward Bellamy's thirtieth birthday. What had he achieved at that time? He had matured a philosophy which had to do not only with theories about the world and about life, but with a practical program for himself. He had defined his own fundamental aims, and had held to them at great cost to himself in loss of economic status and in denial of a feeling of success. The pattern of life he had achieved had far greater range and depth than was customary among his associates or among men generally. He had educated himself widely in literature, science, history, biography, sociology, and economics. He had read and thought seriously upon many economic problems and had formulated his

[71] Unpublished papers (B2-EC-19, 20).   [72] *Ibid.* (B2-EC-21).

deliberate opinion on not a few. He had matured a style and a literary discrimination that were to be a chief source of effectiveness in his life work.

Since coming of age he had supported himself and had declined to accept financial assistance from well-to-do relatives. He had held himself rigorously to a very modest standard of living, had saved enough money to start himself and his brother modestly in business, and had learned how to keep solvent on a small income. He was on the way to an established name in American letters. He had refused the appearance of success which might be had at the sacrifice of his fundamental aims for his life. These are no negligible achievements for a man of thirty. The success of his later career was not an accident but was built on that foundation.

A PAPER OF HIS OWN

It was on the twenty-fourth of February, 1880, about a month before Edward Bellamy's thirtieth birthday, that he and his brother Charles issued the first number of the *Penny News*, a triweekly newspaper, shortly afterwards changed to the *Springfield Daily News*. At that time Springfield had two Republican newspapers but no liberal or Democratic paper, unless the *Springfield Republican* might be classed as liberal. All "respectable" people in Springfield were solidly and conservatively Republican. The *Penny News*, liberal and friendly to labor, found a welcome among working people.

Edward had put up all the money, $1,200, for the venture. Other money was borrowed from time to time, but no other family money was invested. For a time the financial problem of the rapidly growing paper was difficult. Shortly after Edward Bellamy withdrew it reached the point of showing a profit, and when the property was finally sold after Charles's death in 1910, it netted his family about a third of a million dollars. The *News* is still a prosperous Springfield paper. When Edward Bellamy withdrew he waived his financial interest and did not profit in any way from its later success.

The paper was published at first in an upstairs room. For tables and desks the brothers used boards laid across the tops of dry-goods boxes, with other wooden boxes for chairs. No expense was incurred for the sake of appearance. Edward Bellamy was editor, while Charles was business manager. Charles must have worked effectively, since from the first issue the paper carried a large amount of advertising. Judging from the printed scale of advertising rates, the income must have been about $300 a week from the start. There is considerable evidence of thrift and business acumen. Laundry delivery wagons, which were usually idle in the afternoon, were secured at a low rate to deliver papers to the carriers, and streetcar conductors were used for the same purpose.

The first number was sold out, and of the second 2,500 copies were printed. Less than a month later 3,500 copies were being printed; by September the circulation had increased to 4,400 copies and the triweekly had been turned into a daily. By the next June the circulation was 5,250 copies, while the advertising, which consisted of a large number of half-inch to four-inch one-column notices, had similarly increased.

In its contents the *Penny News*, and later the *Daily News*, was a small replica of the *New York Evening Post*, on which Edward had worked nine years before. A similar proportion of space was given to foreign news and comment, literary reviews, and comment on local and national issues. There seems to have been an effort to adapt the literary style to the working classes who probably would be the chief readers of the paper.

The subjects treated in the early issues of the *Penny News*, and later in the *Daily News*, are so like those in Bellamy's notebooks and the book reviews and editorials in the *Springfield Union* as to be "all of a piece" with them. In the editorial column of the first issue is a remark reminiscent of Bellamy's editorials on journalism in the *Springfield Union:* "We mean to interest our readers, but we shall not seek to do so by spicing our columns with questionable personalities. The *Penny News* means to be a gentleman." [73]

In the first issue there is a letter from "A Working Man" which we suspect was written by the editor, that is, by Edward Bellamy. It concludes: "Don't make it a point to say that the workmen are in the wrong when there is a strike. Don't fill your paper with lies about how terribly easy it is for a poor man to live on $1.00

[73] *The Penny News,* February 24, 1880.

a day. Remember it isn't so very much easier than it would be for you, and don't forget either that there are a hundred poor fellows for one even decently well off. I shall keep my eye on you, and a good many of my sort beside." [74]

In the "Holyoke" column of the first issue there is an article on "A School House for the Poor—Wading through Mud to Their Lessons—More Sickness Than in Any School in City." This is a continuation of the style and temper of Bellamy's writings in his notebooks and in the *Springfield Union*, and later in *Looking Backward*:

Holyoke is more a city of the people than any city of the country. Its population is very largely of foreign birth and poor purses. Yet our reporter was astonished to find the condition of the Chestnut Street Schoolhouse, which is packed with little children who have the same feelings and the same precious health as the offspring of the rich. . . . But our reporter waded deep through the mud on his way to the school house and across the low, damp, soggy school yard. There were side-walks on the opposite side of the highway, but no pretense of any near the school house, nor across the street. . . . With wet feet and damp, draggled clothes the children make their way to their seats and run the risk of colds that perhaps lay them on beds of sickness. There has been more sickness, our sympathetic reporter was informed, in this school than in any school in the city. If the children want to play, as health demands, in recess it must be in the soggy yard, all the place provided for them. Our reporter was astonished that he had not heard of this shocking state of affairs before. The children of course could not make their little voices heard, however, and as for the teachers probably they were afraid that they should lose their meager salaries if they dared to whisper a complaint. . . .[75]

In the "Chicopee" column is the following explanation of a strike:

The recent story about the reason for the strike in the Dwight Mills turned out to be mythical. It was stated that the girls struck because they did not get hot coffee at midnight, like their laboring sisters at Chicopee Falls. Our reporter finds that at the time of the strike there was no night labor in Chicopee—so the natural longing for hot coffee had nothing to do with it. The girls struck for higher wages, and obtained an advance of from five to ten per cent." [76]

[74] *Ibid.*   [75] *Ibid.*   [76] *Ibid.*

In the second number there is a note about a strike in the Harmony Mills at Cohoes, New York. There is also a comment that "the Pope has just received four thousand dollars Peter's pence, contributed by the famine stricken Irish people of Armagh and Kilmore. Most people would have thought this a time when their charity should begin at home." After three items about Russian nihilists there is the comment:

The Czar has had about as many narrow escapes as the public credulity will stand. If he is not killed next time, the opinion already whispered in some quarters, that a good part of the nihilist plots and performances are humbug, got up by the police to make capital against them, will become general. That used to be a favorite trick with the last French emperor.[77]

There is also a comment on working conditions in the village of Chicopee, adjacent to his home community of Chicopee Falls:

To make it easier for somebody, the Chicopee Manufacturing Company are arranging to work the night help differently. It will be twelve hours for five nights in the week and no work on Saturday night. This keeps within the sixty hours a week law, but some people in the village are disposed to think that it is going to be a little too hard for the help. Twelve hours' work is too much for women and girls, such as most of the help is, and harder for nights than it is for days.[78]

Beginning in an early number there is a column entitled "The Strikes," reporting on labor troubles over the nation.

It should not be understood that the *Penny News* at this time dealt chiefly with social and economic issues and with labor troubles. These have been emphasized here to dispose of the frequent assertions of both literary men and European socialists that Edward Bellamy was a writer of fiction who had no concern for economic issues until he wrote *Looking Backward*. The paper in these early days had a remarkably wide range of reading matter. The proportion of space given to foreign news is greater than that, during peace times, in most metropolitan papers today.

Only one file of the *Penny News* could be found, the early numbers in brown and crumbling fragments. The issues between March 20 and September 24, 1880, are missing. When the file recom-

[77] *Ibid.*, February 28, 1880.   [78] *Ibid.*

mences toward autumn the paper is a daily and has changed its name to the *Daily News*. The column on "Strikes" has disappeared, and the outspokenness is much toned down, though there are occasional prolabor editorials for at least five or six years. Edward seems to have disposed of his interest to his brother shortly after the plant burned on December 8, 1880. There are many questions concerning this period for which no answers have been found. Why did the tone of the paper change? Why did Edward Bellamy withdraw his active interest? Did the young men find pressure from advertisers no less insistent than the pressure of the owner upon the editorial writer? Edward Bellamy stated humorously that the paper began to make money as soon as he left it.

Charles Bellamy in his early days was not conservative in his thinking. However, he married a woman, formerly a clerk in the office where Edward Bellamy studied law, who had social aspirations, and thereafter Charles became active in the conventional social life of Springfield. Edward took less and less interest in the *News* until, according to Charles Bellamy's son, a complete separation was concluded by an informal agreement during a friendly game of billiards. Charles took the paper with its promises, its prospects, and its debts. Edward took his freedom, and turned again to that quest in which he had been repeatedly disappointed.

That the way continued to be hard we can guess from a sidelight supplied by a letter from his wife, written in November, 1886, about the time he began to write *Looking Backward*:

I am sorry to speak about money when you are away from home, but I thought you perhaps could send me some, if you thought best. I need some very much for present needs, besides owing the milk man three dollars, and Mary's payday [she was paid three dollars a week] came Thursday . . . In any common circumstances I could borrow what I wanted, but I seem to be entirely unable to do so now.

THE REBEL IN RELIGION

The fight which Edward Bellamy made to hammer out for himself a satisfactory way of life was nowhere more rebellious and determined than in the field of religion. As a boy he had been "converted," had joined his father's Baptist church, and had felt deeply

moving religious experience. Complete consecration was his dominant aim. Yet that very completeness of commitment is so closely
associated with sincerity of mind that often it drives one to a
sincere, open-minded inquiry as to its own basis. That was Bellamy's
experience, and while he was still in his 'teens, it appears, his religious orthodoxy had faded or entirely disappeared. Then there
followed a long period of stress and of apparent drift. In February,
1872, just before he was twenty-two, and while working on the
New York Post, he wrote in his journal:

How often do I feel, at thought of the vast crowd of unsolved, insol-
uble problems of infinite consequence which surround, overpress and
underlie human life, as if encompassed and oppressed by felt darkness.
Every step—and immobility is impossible—must be taken under protest—provisionally. A single hour's reflection—at times when the gross
and sensual atmosphere, which ordinarily surrounds our minds and
prevents their clear vision, is momentarily dissipated—evokes troops of
great questions from the outer darkness, as the strained eye at night
detects high looming outlines of monstrous things. The foundations of
being slip from under and precipitately we turn our aching minds to
rest in viewing the known proportions of petty things.[79]

The months pass. He leaves New York and goes to work on the
Springfield Union, and lives again at his old home. Perhaps it was
only the depression of homesickness and the oppressiveness of the
great city which had upset his health, his spirit, and his mind.
But no. Back in his old familiar room, on the familiar hills, and by
the friendly brooks, the mood stays with him. In October, 1872,
he again communes with his confidential journal:

I do not imagine that my own profound anxiety and longing almost to
sickness for light on the purport of life, is very unusual among young
men. I believe on the contrary that there is a great deal of it going on
always in the hearts of men just upon the threshold of life. Viewed from
this point, existence seems a very potent thing and there arises a profound longing to weave it into some universal eternal woof, to build it
into some universal eternal building. For a while indeed the young
man may remain satisfied with the ideals of truth and duty in which
he was bred. Then seeing or fancying that he sees their insufficiency, he
casts them aside and with soul wide open goes through dry places seeking everywhere to find God. He carries his loyalty in his hand anxious

[79] Unpublished papers (B1-I-12).

only to find some fitting shrine where he may lay it down and be at rest. Then indeed as the hopelessness of his search is borne in upon him come days and nights full of bitterness, of blasphemy, or recklessness, and at last of profound life-weariness. But afterwards as the enthusiasm of youth dies away and his life verges on maturity, the world grows on him, the horizon of the soul becomes contracted till it is coincident with the limitations of sensual life. Then indeed life may be a bit enjoyed, for a man is at least reconciled to it. To this I look forward, but my period of travail of soul and reaching for the meaning of God already has been much prolonged. Of course the prospect of such a life is not exhilarating. But it is better than the chances of suicide, than which last, my present lot is not.[80]

The young man is too introspective, you say. Why should he rack his brain over questions that have puzzled the world for ages? He had better forget them and go about his business of writing reviews and editorials for the *Union*. But he has his own opinion on that matter. In one of the drafts of the "Eliot Carson" story, Bellamy projects his own inclinations into the actions of his hero:

"This life is a mystery, men say, and therefore leave it as such and go about their business. This life is a mystery, I say, and therefore do no other thing until I solve it, in some measure at least. That mystery underlies all things, and therefore until I know what I am doing, I will do nothing. I will not live at random as men do. It is not that I necessarily expect to solve it. Not at all. It is merely that in the presence of that mystery none of the affairs in which men interest themselves seem to have any importance or attraction whatsoever." [81]

A rash and foolish attitude on the part of a young man? This account of Bellamy's religion happens to be written in the springtime, just as the leaves are coming out on the trees. There are wide variations in the habits of different trees and plants. Many of the flowering plants in the forest must do almost the whole year's growing in a few weeks before the trees overhead put forth their leaves and shut out the sun. Likewise the great forest trees, oaks, elms, and maples, make all their new growth within a few weeks. After that the tree must wait for another year, spending the intervening time in maturing its wood, ripening its seeds, and storing food for the short, rapid growth of the succeeding season.

[80] *Ibid.* (B1-1-22, 23).   [81] *Ibid.* (B2-EC-43).

It is the same with many men. The period of growth in a mastery of the fundamental issues of life may be a matter of a very few years, and earlier in life than generally is realized. After that burst of growth, life settles down—to acquire experience and judgment; to follow through the large generalizations to their detailed implications; to check its visions by the facts, and give them effect in action; to feed itself, and to care for the next generation.

No, it is not rash for a young man to neglect temporal affairs and to pour the whole of life's energy into this greatest of all issues—no more rash than it was for his mother to set aside her routine to give him a chance to be born. Had her will and desire been strong enough to suppress the course of nature and go about her affairs, that would have meant death. Were his will and desire strong enough to put aside these great issues of the meaning of life, and to lead him to go about his routine business, that would have meant death to his soul. There are many dead souls in living bodies. There are some processes which will not wait—among them that of a young man or woman searching for a way of life.

Yet, to give that quest first place does not mean years of mere philosophical speculation. An isolated paragraph in one of Bellamy's notebooks reads, "Meditation, introspection, is not alone the avenue to realization of the Solidarity, but rather deeds of generosity and self devotion. These are better than fasting and prayer, or rather, both are equally essential to the perfect work." [82] His mind continually turns to the subject. A stray paragraph in his notebook reads: "What work is after all worth while in this world (save only the indispensable filling of the belly) beside inquiry into the relation of man with the infinite." [83] As his mood changes, so does his expression. Another stray paragraph reads:

Human life is such a clever riddle that its invention certainly reflects credit upon the ingenuity of Divine Providence. . . . As a conundrum it is open to the objection of being too hard to guess. People get discouraged for the most part and give it up, and those who keep on fiddling have their labor for their pains. No Oedipus has come along yet.[84]

There was no smooth uniformity of development in these moods, but rather a series of explosions of spirit. Though this description

[82] *Ibid.* (B2-4-9, 10).   [83] *Ibid.* (B2-4-14).   [84] *Ibid.* (B2-4-23).

of them gives a semblance of a separate and distinct program of thinking, they were in fact mixed in with all the other teeming issues of his life, and with the day-by-day process of making a living. Sometimes a sense of humor enters in: "A man with liver complaint sees the world just as it really must be to a thoughtful man who does not believe in God." [85]

The story of Edward Bellamy's religious pilgrimage deserves more consideration than is feasible within the bounds of this biography. It is further detailed in *The Philosophy of Edward Bellamy*, separately published. It was not an aimless vacillating to and from religious concern, but a determined forging ahead to the achievement of a unity and freedom of mind and spirit on the one hand, and on the other a commitment to the best he knew.

As his religion gradually developed it had two phases: first, a philosophy of the world and of life which appears in some degree to be his own, and not to be borrowed bodily from an existing philosophy, though greatly influenced, it would seem, by Emerson and, perhaps through him, by the Neoplatonists and the religions of India. He called this "The Religion of Solidarity." It furnished an intellectual foundation for the structure of his life and for his social and economic thinking, somewhat in the manner that the dialectic materialism of Karl Marx provided a philosophical basis for his life and work. This "Religion of Solidarity" is the answer he found to the struggle of his mind and spirit for light.

The other phase of Bellamy's religion is the practical working program and the expectations which he worked out for his life and for society. Quotations from *Looking Backward* and *Equality* epitomize that applied religion:

"If I were to give you, in one sentence, a key to what may seem the mysteries of our civilization as compared with that of your age, I should say that it is the fact that the solidarity of the race and the brotherhood of man, which to you were but fine phrases, are, to our thinking and feeling, ties as real and as vital as physical fraternity." [86]

"The great enthusiasm of humanity which overthrew the old order and brought in the fraternal society was not primarily or consciously a

---

[85] *Ibid.* (B2-Plots 1-25).   [86] *Looking Backward*, p. 134.

godward aspiration at all. It was essentially a humane movement. It was a melting and flowing forth of men's hearts toward one another, a rush of contrite, repentant tenderness, an impassioned impulse of mutual love and self-devotion to the common weal. But 'if we love one another God dwelleth in us,' and so men found it." [87]

It is evident that Edward Bellamy had a deep craving for light on the significance of life, that he sought earnestly and persistently for the light, that he had a critical, open mind, and did not hesitate to view religion as it was actually practiced, without turning his eyes from any unpleasantness. In that rebellion from religion as it was commonly practiced, he did not "throw out the baby with the bath," as many of the early socialists had done, and as the communists do today. He avoided that most fatal defect of rebels, the tendency to exchange one extreme for another, the willingness to discard great values which have been associated with some evil. He persisted in seeing life whole and in good proportion.

In that actual difference of attitude he is superior to Karl Marx. The bitter criticisms of Bellamy by the Marxians are as unfair as they are unwise. Mrs. John B. Shipley (Marie A. Brown) in *The True Author of "Looking Backward"* (which apparently was inspired or acquiesced in by the Marxian August Bebel) criticized Bellamy for his religious conformity:

In *Looking Backward,* however, not a word is said about the expiration of religion or of Christianity. This is a phase of the subject that Mr. Bellamy absolutely declines to grapple with, nor will he even trust the strong arm of August Bebel to carry him through this thicket. . . . August Bebel discerns clearly that to overturn the State and leave the Church standing, even if that were possible, were an act of puerile folly. But Edward Bellamy chooses to ignore the inevitable issue of the initial conflict for human independence . . .

No, socialism is not a structure that can be raised on a Christian foundation. Any such attempt will fail almost at the outset, for the objects of the two systems are the most opposite of any schemes for the race ever devised by the human intellect.[88]

That attitude has come down to the present day. V. F. Calverton, in his *Liberation of American Literature,* illustrated the orthodox

[87] *Equality,* p. 269.

[88] Mrs. John B. Shipley, *The True Author of "Looking Backward,"* pp. 20, 47.

Marxian point of view. It is typical in its closed dogmatic position that religion is beneath contempt, and that class conflict is the only way. He wrote:

Bellamy marked one of the earliest departures from the individualistic philosophy of the American petty bourgeoisie, and yet even the spirit of his doctrine, the basis of its appeal, as we stated above, was founded upon logic that was more attractive to the lower middle class than to the uncrystallized proletariat. Bellamy eschewed appeal to class as signifying pettiness of outlook. He wished to appeal to all of society, to be above class concepts and differentiations. Even religion was to have a place in his Utopia which was to be "the realization of God's ideal of . . . [the race]." Bellamy was much closer to the tradition of the Utopian socialists, the Fourierists and the Owenites of the early part of the century, than to the scientific Marxian socialists, who did not make any real headway in America until the twentieth century. In a way too, the doctrines of Bellamy, like the illations of Ramsay Mac-Donald in the twentieth century, obscured the class issues at stake, and tended to confuse rather than to clarify the logic of social progress.[89]

When we search for the reason why the class conflict did not make greater headway in America we find that *Looking Backward* was a strong influence working to keep alive in America a belief in its own genius.

Religious concepts that are long familiar to us come to seem natural and reasonable, even though to an outside view they might seem fantastic. Conversely, ideas that are new seem thereby to be improbable and repelling, though they may be inherently reasonable. Bellamy achieved the rare quality of seeing the inherent reasonableness of ideas, somewhat independently of the prestige with which they were presented. He was a religious man; that is, the major interest of his life was the pursuit of the highest values, both in thought and action. Almost any man who takes that course will become a rebel in religion.

And here we may conclude our account of Edward Bellamy's experiences as a rebel. What was he aiming at in these many fights

[89] V. F. Calverton, *The Liberation of American Literature*, p. 349. Reprinted by permission of the publishers.

for freedom? They were not so many individual and unrelated moves, carried through because of zest for living and for action. He was seeking unity for his life in accord with a design which he had deliberately worked out. Here again his notebooks give us a hint. In an item, apparently written when he was twenty-four, we find: "The common weal of solidarity is not advanced one whit when I thrust another aside whose work I cannot do better." [90] And in another notebook of about the same time we find another expression:

When a rain storm comes up and the first drops fall, how we sympathize with each. We count it a separate organism, we make, if we be deemed poets, a poem about the rain drop. We endow it with the qualities of a distinct being, an individuality. We picture forth its aspirations, its disappointments, its barren or fruitful death as it may fall on a desert or a flower. Yet our better reason teaches us it is but a part of the general frame of nature, whose death counts nothing. So are we, and it is this same foolish tendency to particularization that causes us to separate one man from another and to make so much of individual fates. We are but as the drops of rain, as days in a year, as leaves of a tree. It should be our effort to contemplate the individual from the standpoint of the universal. We should seek to reverse the accustomed order and make the objective subjective, and the subjective objective. That is, we should seek to view ourselves as from without instead of viewing all things from ourselves as from within. Seek a home, a center, a more intimate ego in the universe of things without. Cultivate a habit of regarding the experiences of the individual from that standpoint. It will at once breed a great calm. Let that be the Kingdom of Heaven in which you lay up your treasures beyond the reach of moth or rust. It will be found in this case also that where the treasure is there will the heart be also. So long as men persisted in regarding the universe as circling around the earth astronomy was a sad jumble. It was only when the terrestrial astronomer interpreted the universe from an universal standpoint, regarding the earth objectively, that the science was possible. It is so in the mental world. A corresponding discovery to that of Copernicus is necessary in philosophy. Perhaps these are only words such as another might say. The only difference is the earnestness with which I mean them and the reality for which they stand to my mind. I would have a man so fully realize the idea I have described that the prospect of his own death, however suddenly announced, should have no more disturbing effect than if it had been announced of another man. And this, too, not as the

90 Unpublished papers (B2-4-5).

result of any stoical effort at impressiveness maintained with difficulty and at painful sacrifice of other instincts and feelings; but naturally, easily, simply, and without too low an appreciation of the pleasures of life.[91]

In view of the course of his life, how significant are the lines: "Perhaps these are only words such as another might say. The only difference is the earnestness with which I mean them, and the reality for which they stand to my mind."

Enough has been quoted to indicate that Edward Bellamy began very early to think on social and economic problems, that by the time he was about twenty-one the ideas later expressed in *Looking Backward* already were taking form in his mind, that his interest continued with wide reading, penetrating observation, and active thinking. As we follow on to his later expressions as editor of the *Penny News* and the *Daily News* we see that interest no less active. His notebooks and unpublished manuscripts sustain the temper of his published writing. How completely unrepresentative, then, is the reputation which has followed him through the years as a person who had no economic or social interests until he stumbled on them in writing *Looking Backward*.

[91] *Ibid.* (B1-2-20, 21).

VI · The Personality of Edward Bellamy

A CULTIVATED and reserved young American woman who had become an admirer, almost a worshipper, of Ibsen had the good fortune, while on a visit to Scandinavia, to be invited to a dinner in his honor. When she found him to be a pompous, conceited, unmannerly boor, her disillusionment had lasting reactions.

We have several delineations of the personality and mannerisms of Edward Bellamy at about the time *Looking Backward* was written. There is general agreement in the pictures they present, and they give the impression that there was no general incongruity between what he was and what he wrote. Shortly after *Looking Backward* was published, Frances E. Willard, president of the Woman's Christian Temperance Union, went to Chicopee Falls to interview Bellamy. The resulting article, in the magazine *Our Day*, included the following description:

In figure of medium height, harmonious proportions, and agile movement; in forehead full and broad, with thoughtful dark blue eyes radiating good will; with mobile lips, parenthesized by a dark brown mustache, the cheeks covered by a stubby beard; and the dress a little careless,—this he is to look upon. In manner quiet, yet observant, modest but perfectly self-poised, with mild and gentle tones, yet full of personality, and vibrating with purpose.[1]

Similar impressions are recorded in a contemporary issue of *Current Literature* magazine:

His greyish blue eyes are keen and penetrating. He has a Roman nose and a drooping brown moustache, and a mouth that denotes firmness of character. His hair is dark brown and falls down over his forehead in spite of the obvious attempt of brushing it back. . . . He walked with a steady gait and impressed me with an independence that was decidedly pleasing and not in the least offensive. His voice is musical and his conversation has an easy rhythm in spite of its ofttime emphatic tone. He

[1] Frances Willard, "An Interview with Edward Bellamy," *Our Day*, IV, No. 22 (October 10, 1889), 539.

has a good-natured simplicity of manner that delights the listener, and he makes a most enjoyable companion.[2]

Another glimpse is given us by the editor of *The Literary Weekly*:

Personally Edward Bellamy is a quiet, modest man, is an omnivorous reader, has a fine memory, and is always well posted on the questions of the day. He is an exceedingly interesting conversationalist and talks at the rate of about three hundred words a minute.[3]

Sidney Reeves, author of *The Cost of Competition* and other works, wrote of him: "I remember Edward's personality, as he spoke, always hitting the nail on the head, whereas the others [of the Nationalist Club] rambled terribly."

An appraisal of Bellamy's personality by a personal acquaintance, who wrote as editor of *Good Housekeeping*, has been much quoted. Referring to the period a few years before *Looking Backward*, he wrote:

Among his friends who knew him well, but perhaps not best, the impression was unavoidable that he was strongly infused with cynicism. He had a wonderful facility of sarcasm and half concealed ridicule, and in spite of his almost imperturbable outward good nature, there were those among his friends who felt the effects of the exercise of this faculty so keenly at times that their friendly sensibilities were hurt.[4]

We do not know how much weight to give to this opinion, for its author showed inability to understand Bellamy's mind. Concerning Bellamy's writings before *Looking Backward*, this editor commented, "Heretofore he had been playing with humanity—teasing it, holding up its foibles to ridicule and its mistakes to blame, dissecting it, poking fun at it."[5] Toward a person who could so completely fail to understand *Dr. Heidenhoff's Process, Miss Ludington's Sister*, or the general tone of his editorials and book reviews, the reflective, mild-mannered Bellamy may have adopted a cynical or sarcastic mannerism as self-protection.

The people of his home town had the same impression as those

---

2 "General Gossip," *Current Literature*, IV, No. 3 (March, 1890), 185.

3 "Edward Bellamy," *The Literary Weekly*, V (January 4, 1894), 1.

4 "Edward Bellamy," *Good Housekeeping*, X, No. 4 (December 21, 1889), 95. Reprinted by permission of the publisher.

5 *Ibid.*, p. 96.

who came to see him as a celebrity. Edward Bellamy's daughter, Mrs. Marion Earnshaw, tells of a statement made by a woman to whom she was introduced at a League of Women Voters' meeting:

She and another girl [wrote Mrs. Earnshaw] worked at the *Springfield Union,* where my father had a desk for some years before he wrote *Looking Backward.* She said they both were so sensitive to the charm and grace of my father that they always left home early just for the sake of being in their places to receive his gracious "good morning" as he passed them on his way to his desk. Other than that they never held speech with him.

This impression of friendly courtesy and good will seems to have been almost universal among his neighbors. It is significant that his secretary and the women who worked in the household had both respect and regard for him.

In a book review he wrote when he was twenty-five we find an expression which seems to reflect his temperament, "The fact is, there is a surprising amount of suspicion and caution thrown away in this world." [6]

His neighbor and friend, Ames Carter, said of him:

Edward Bellamy was a perfectly charming conversationalist. He enjoyed being in a party where there was interesting conversation. At literary meetings it was often said they hoped Edward Bellamy would come. The more intellectual liked him. Others liked his brother Charles, who was jolly and a practical joker.

An incident in the life of George D. Munsing, manufacturer of "Munsingwear," who as a boy lived in Springfield, suggests that Bellamy was not unapproachable:

In going around, as boys will, on Sundays and holidays, he [Munsing] met a very scholarly man who helped him pick the more helpful volumes. After that, many was the time that young Munsing stood on tiptoe to reach some coveted book in the second-hand stores of Springfield, and would browse through them for hours.

Finally, young Munsing saved enough from his earnings to buy many of those books, and discussed them with his distinguished friend, who proved to be Edward Bellamy, famous as the author of *Looking Backward* . . .[7]

[6] "Literary Notices," *Springfield Union,* March 20, 1875.

[7] Clowry Chapman, "Learning While Earning," *Munsingwear News,* August, 1919, p. 8.

The clearest pictures we have of his personality during his mature years are those supplied by his wife and children. They indicate how naturally he fitted into his simple home environment, and give us a view of the life of a typical middle-class, small-town American. His daughter, largely from her girlhood memories, tells of his latter days at Chicopee Falls:

I remember sitting oftentimes in his lap and pushing away the heavy hair from his mouth, tracing its beautiful outline with one finger. He used to come up to hear our prayers at night after we were in bed and would tuck us in and turn out the light. He told us the Lord's Prayer, but never would let us say, "For thine is the power and glory, etc." He said God did not need to be praised.

He loved the quiet of a Sunday afternoon. After dinner, if the weather permitted, we used to go for a walk, all of us, around the square, and then would come home to a quiet session of Bible reading at which we always read the New Testament, each one taking turns, while my father explained. After supper there were always hymns around the old melodeon with mother, while he sat apart tipped back in an easy chair. He never sang with us. Occasionally he would ask for some favorite and then appear to relapse into another reverie. Some of his favorites were: "Jesus, Saviour, Pilot Me"; "I'm a Pilgrim, I'm a Stranger"; "Jesus, Lover of my Soul"; "Lead Kindly Light."

In the evening we always used to sit around the center table under the glow of the large table lamp, at our various occupations. My father, as I remember him, was always reading or else leaning back in his chair completely engrossed in his thoughts, coming to consciousness of his surroundings occasionally when spoken to. He told us stories of Helen of Troy and the Greek heroes and other great tales of history. He talked with my brother Paul by the hour on all manner of things from the time he was a baby; and played soldier, plotting campaigns and carrying them out with small lead soldiers and toy guns, telling him meanwhile stories of famous generals and battles of history; and at the same time impressing upon him the horrors and imbecilities of war, of how men went away and never came back. He never punished us physically, but when we were at fault talked to us so earnestly and seriously that I, for one, was completely broken up, and he was always forced to end his lesson by comforting me instead.

I can see him at table in the big chair, carving and serving for the rest of us, then settling back in his chair without helping himself, and calling Mary to bring him a glass of milk and a couple of raw eggs, bolting them down, and getting up from the table and like as not going into the study and pacing back and forth across the floor absorbed in thought. He always walked when he was thus occupied, with his hands behind his back. He would pace for hours in the living room and then sometimes abruptly stop and say out loud to no one in particular, "I've got a thought," and would bolt to the study, slamming the door after him.

He always wrote on one side of a large pad in pencil, then tore it off and threw it on the floor until the floor was covered. The sheets were seldom numbered, yet apparently he was able to find what he wanted when he wanted it. His study was absolute chaos, as no one was ever allowed to disturb anything, even for a cursory dusting. Upon the occasions when my mother required the room, which was the back parlor, for a club meeting of some sort, he very graciously consented to clean house, and the room was thoroughly renovated. The next day chaos began to reign again.

He was patient, tireless in research, in getting what he wanted down on paper, often destroying whole arguments, even chapters, that did not satisfy him, and starting over again. He would often work for days over one paragraph. One particular chapter devoted to "Women" which he wrote for *Equality* he left out completely, as he said the world was not ready for it then.

He was so simple in all his ways and so little given to talking business in the family circle that the first intimation I ever had that he was different from other children's fathers was when I was in the second grade in school. The superintendent of the school appeared in my room with two strangers, and the teacher called me forward, whereupon the men asked me if I was Edward Bellamy's daughter, and shook hands with me. When I told the incident at home that day, my father appeared to be very much annoyed.

I do remember, however, the constant telegrams that were being received and the quantities of letters that cluttered up the tables and desks in father's studies. He had a large correspondence with friends and admirers in Germany, which he was often forced to take down to the village brewer, Mr. Gunther, a native German, as the German script was sometimes beyond him. He rode a saddle horse a great deal up to the time he left the *Daily News,* riding back and forth to work in Springfield when the weather allowed.

Not long ago I came across a nurse who lived in our family for four years taking care of my father's mother. She said of my father, "He was always a gentleman," and went on to say that he was always considerate and courteous, treating everyone in the house in the same kindly fashion, with an eye always to their comfort and well-being. She also said that if she met him on the street he always greeted her with the same exquisite courtesy which he would extend to his friends, that he never in any way made her feel conscious of her position as attendant. That this could be the usual attitude of a man of the house toward the people living in it she most indignantly disputed from the experiences of a lifetime: "I never lived in any house where I was treated like that."

From among the comments of his wife we get a similar picture:

He never turned anyone away from the door, and if there was no one at home to feed a tramp he would go to the pantry himself, as strange a part of the house as it was to him, and rummage around to find something to give to him. Like as not it would be a newly baked cake out of the cake box, which had been planned for supper. He used often to talk with these men at length, trying if possible to get at the nature of their difficulties, oftentimes giving them advice and more often money. I heard him say once that he was sorry his feet were so small because he hadn't any shoes that would fit the tramps, although he was always giving them clothing.

That his interest in military affairs carried over into his later life is evident from his son Paul's remembrances of the period when his father was in his early forties:

When I was a little boy, I found that the one childish game which my father really seemed to enjoy playing with me was soldiers. We used to clear off the dining table, set up the little images and shoot at them in turn with a spring toy gun which discharged a small wooden projectile. The troops were maneuvered in all sorts of interesting ways, amid a running comment about Napoleon, whom he considered by all odds the greatest military genius.

At one time I developed considerable zeal in whittling and sawing out models of ships, and I think that the ship game next to the soldier game roused greatest interest in father.

In fact, as I look back at it, father's chief characteristic in these games was the imagination he brought to them. With a couple of clothes pins, if need be, he could construct so vivid a picture of the battle of Waterloo that the blood of his young son coursed through his veins as though he were verily a cuirassier falling into the sunken road.

I have been greatly puzzled all my life at his military bent, as it runs so counter to all his ideas that go along with socialistic philosophy, and of which the central one certainly is that no war is worth while and that the common people only lose in wars.[8]

His wife relates that in his last illness one of the diversions he most enjoyed was to deploy toy soldiers on his bed.

Shortly before he died he made a list of books for his son's read-

[8] Green.

ing. It is in the form of very rough notes in a notebook, as though written under difficulty:

The following list of books is set down as suitable for Paul's reading (among many others) during the next four or five years. They are jotted down as they occur to me, without order or connection, some fit for immediate reading, others not to be well read for several years. Still a good book does no harm at any time of life. The wind bloweth where it listeth.

Green's Short History Eng. People
Macaulay
Froude's Essays
Charles Fifth—Alison rather heavy. Perhaps something better.
Motley's Dutch War of Independence. Recommend considerable reading on period of 100 years, sometimes called 30 years, war. Germany (cannot give names).
Gustavus Adolphus.
Peasants' War.
Anabaptists. Make study of these early Socialists. Book recently published on subject. .
History of France from Francis I, Louis XI down. Many books bearing on it. Study well.
Stanley Weyman's Romances of Henry IV's Time.
Pardoe's Louis XIV.
Taine's Ancient Regime; and did he write a history of Revolution? If so, probably good.
Carlyle's French Revolution. Carlyle unfortunately no democrat and so a poor historian of Revolution, but must be read.
Froissart's Chronicles.
All that can be got about Russia.
Sartor Resartus.
Returning to ancient history: Rawlinson's Five Monarchies, and Gibbon.
Pizarro—Prescott.
Always with reading have *Atlas open.*
Benton's Forty Years U.S. Senate.
Blaine's 20 Years in Congress. Not till seventeen or eighteen.
Taine's English Literature. Not yet. 17–18–19.
Max Muller's Chips from a German Workshop. (In my room) later.
To learn to read German, French, Spanish, and Italian, and to talk, if possible, German and Spanish.
Voltaire's Charles XII of Sweden.
MacMaster's U.S. History.

Parkman's Colonial Histories. Too diffuse as a rule for importance of subject but no harm to read.[9]

It is to be noted that this list was not proposed for a lifetime of reading, but was given to a boy of thirteen to be read "during the next four or five years."

Paul Bellamy wrote of his father's plans for his reading:

He did not believe much in college, in any college, because, as I have said, he thought most young men wasted precious years there. Had he lived he would never have sent me to college, I believe. He planned for me to read under his direction widely in the whole range of literature, history and the arts, and then he wanted to let me travel in Europe for some time. He said that if I had the will to learn I could learn much more that way than I could ever learn in college. He started me at eleven in Ridpath's *Universal History*. When I finished that, and many were the days I wanted to go out and play baseball or football when I had to do my reading stint, he said that I had been a good boy and would be allowed a little relaxation, so he brought out a set of Plutarch's *Lives*. When I had completed that he remarked that it was time I got back to serious business again, and produced Milman's *Gibbon's Decline and Fall of the Roman Empire,* in seven or eight volumes, as I remember it, with Greek and Latin footnotes. I had little more than finished this colossal work when he died.

Paul was thirteen at the time of his father's death. The contents of the list give strong support to Paul's statement concerning his father: "He always believed that history is the key to knowledge. If you know how the human race has behaved under certain stresses and strains in the past, you can pretty well plot its course in the future."

Some imposing men are romantics who worship idealizations of themselves. Whether such a man writes or talks or walks on the street he is not acting his natural self, but is dramatically impersonating the august and romantic picture of himself which his egoism has created. An intimate view of Edward Bellamy discloses no such attitude. He was a normal-minded human being who did not put his imaginary self on any pedestal. He was essentially genuine.

[9] Unpublished papers (B2—Paul's notebook).

The appraisal of his brother Charles bears out the general impression we get of his personality.

He appeared to make it the rule of his life so to bear himself that nobody's feelings should be hurt by word or deed of his. The quality of intense reserve made him very chary of exhibiting his emotions. Intent on protecting the sacredness of his own inner life, he was ever wont to hide under affectation of coldness or cynicism the workings of an exceptionally poetic and emotional heart and soul. The only insight given into the richness of his emotional nature is to be found through his books. His sense of honor was strict, far beyond that of ordinary men. He would refuse a parley with insincerity or falsehood even in their most subtle disguises.

Seldom has a distinguished man been more of a home-loving person, or lived an externally quieter or more uneventful life than Edward Bellamy. When he was three years old his father moved from the house where Edward had been born to another house two or three blocks away, and there, except for a few brief intermissions, Edward Bellamy lived for the rest of his life.

He attended school across the street, not one minute's walk from his home. For thirty-four years his father was pastor of the Baptist Church just around the corner, and in that church, which was almost a part of the home, he was "converted" and had his church membership and associations.

His only job farther away than Springfield was the period of less than a year on the *New York Evening Post*.

Even in choosing a wife he followed this home-bound pattern, when at the age of thirty-two he married his foster sister, eleven years younger, who had been in the family since she was thirteen years old. After a week's honeymoon in Boston they returned to live with their parents. Before their second child was born they decided to be independent and have a home of their own, so they moved into the adjoining house, ten steps from where they both grew up. Within a year, on the death of Edward's father, they had returned to the old family home.

His period of studying law was in an office in Springfield, four miles from his home, and his very abbreviated practice was there.

When he sought a business partner he turned again to the family, and chose his younger brother, Charles.

In his literary work also Edward Bellamy relied on home and home environment. He wrote of what he knew best. His one historical novel, *The Duke of Stockbridge*, concerned with Shays' Rebellion, had its setting in his home neighborhood and nearby western Massachusetts. In his preparatory research for that book he ventured as far away as Stockbridge, about forty miles from Chicopee Falls.

According to Mrs. Bellamy, the six woman characters of his first novel, *A Nantucket Idyll*, are portraits of close home-town social acquaintances, while its setting is a locality where his father occasionally took his family for a summer holiday. His short stories, so far as they had any locus, for the most part were in a familiar small-town setting, quite obviously the village of Chicopee Falls. *Dr. Heidenhoff's Process*, one of his novels, begins with an account of a prayer meeting so like the type led by his father in the home church that for years the book was a sore point in the family. Otherwise the scenes are laid in a village—resembling Chicopee Falls—and the city of Boston, in which he had spent his honeymoon. Another novel, *Miss Ludington's Sister*, also has for its setting a village like Chicopee Falls, and Long Island and New York City, where one can feel the home environment of his aunt, whom he occasionally visited.

Among Bellamy's short stories and unpublished writings one finds the same tendency to rely on intimate home experiences. One of these stories concerns a man who married his foster sister, as he did. Another follows the mental life of a young man who tried the law and was disgusted with it, as was the case with Bellamy himself. In other respects also the latter story traces the course of his own life. Another of these stories in effect is an account of his own religious experiences. In *Looking Backward* his hero, Julian West, was given the surname of a neighbor who lived directly across the street from his home. The name of the next most important character, Dr. Leete, is that of a physician then practicing at Canaan, New Hampshire.

When Bellamy was in the midst of the Nationalist movement he chose as editor of the *New Nation* a man who had been on the staff of the *Springfield Republican*. He did not move to Boston, which was the center of activity and the publishing headquarters of the *New Nation*, but commuted from Chicopee Falls, spending four nights each week at home. When about twenty-five years old he commented in his journal upon this home-loving trait:

I have a deep-seated aversion to change. . . . The night before taking a journey, however brief, and although one long agreeably looked forward to, is always an uncomfortable time with me. I almost repent the undertaking, and but for the foolishness of the thing would fain draw back. Any unavoidable postponement I feel I should secretly welcome. . . . This . . . disinclination to change my surroundings . . . [is] associated with a faculty of taking root and finding myself at home in the new surroundings with wonderful quickness, when once the change is made.[10]

The only breaks in this nearly half century of quiet village life were part of a year at Union College, several months in Germany, an occasional summer vacation in Maine or on the Massachusetts or Connecticut coast, a brief trip to Hawaii for his health during his twenties, a few months in New York, and the trip to Denver shortly before his death.

According to his wife, the small bundle of letters which she has preserved are all that ever passed between them. He was very punctilious in writing to her, except when he was commuting to Boston. Any failure to keep in touch by letters was made up for by telegrams. Yet the total of these letters and messages is but a score or so, and the greater number of them were written when his wife was away and he at home.

Even in his home village Edward Bellamy was not generally known. Though not embarrassingly diffident, he did not seek society. People remembered him as a friendly, courteous, quiet man of erect, dignified bearing, who did not appear reticent but who seemed to be living in a world of his own and did not court companionship. When fame came to him, he refused to be lionized. He would not go on the lecture platform, would not attend dinners in his honor, skillfully avoided receptions, teas, meetings.

[10] Unpublished papers (B1-2-9).

Bellamy differed from most provincials in that his movements were restricted not by inert purposelessness but by the conscious, deliberate design of his life. Few as were his changes of scene, he felt that they provided an ample basis for his life. The comment from his journals, already quoted, gives the gist of his philosophy on this issue: "A very little scope of variety, judiciously disposed, by a wise economist of happiness, may give far more zest to life than unlimited resources employed without discretion." [11]

Bellamy's course reminds us of the counsel of the great Chinese philosopher, Lao-tze. In his *Tao Teh King* we read: "Induce people to grieve at death, but do not cause them to move to a distance. Although they had ships and carriages they should find no occasion to use them. . . . Induce people . . . to be content with their homes, and to rejoice in their customs; then in a neighboring state within sight, the voices of the cocks and dogs would be within hearing, yet the people might grow old and die before they visited one another." [12]

Commenting on the native American quality of his work, he wrote in a letter to William Dean Howells: "The simple necessity of sticking to the life one knows if one would write intelligently, is reason enough why American authors should write as Americans, for Americans, about America. But this necessity, far from being a limitation, is to my notion the best of all fortunes to those on whom it is incumbent."

Because Bellamy knew of what he wrote, and because the fundamental aspirations and spirit of men are alike the world over, he has been read by more people in other lands than almost any other American writer. This provincial, small-town Baptist minister's son, by his proposals for deep-seated, fundamental changes in the structure of society, probably has started more men on the road of pioneer social thought and action than has any other American and has stirred the hearts and enlarged the visions of men the world around.

Edward Bellamy was a lover of nature. A man of shallow sight

[11] Unpublished papers (B1-2-11).
[12] Paul Carus, *Canon of Reason and Virtue, Being Lao-tze's Tao Teh King*, pp. 129–30.

may travel over many lands to find a few experiences, for always he sees only the surface. As Thoreau believed he could find the essence of the world of nature about Concord and Walden Pond, so Bellamy was forever discovering it in his native village and in the nearby hills.

It is fortunate that Niagaras and Matterhorns exist, so that even those who generally are insensitive to nature may sometimes be moved by her majesty and beauty. But Bellamy needed no such extreme stimulus. He saw beauty and order in many forms, as is indicated in a description of one of his characters:

Columbus had not perhaps much more of the delight of the discoverer than did she when, passing through a belt of trees, she came unexpectedly upon some fair glade in the forest. . . . Often enough, too, there was no special beauty in the spots she discovered. It was enough if they had character of their own, any individuality . . . Somehow she found that she did not care so much for the fine prospects, of winding river and valley and mountains, of which there did not lack an abundance, as for these little glades and open spots in thickets, and odd nooks among low trees. . . . She preferred small, low trees, birches, scrub oaks and pines, and such second growth timber, down even to the little springing trees two feet high, to the majestic hundred foot giants of the forest. They were so much more companionable and lovable than the giants, for her attachment for nature was not one of frigid or eloquent admiration, but a tender and gentle fondness, protecting and nurturing, rather than worshipful.[13]

While he was writing for the *Springfield Union* his daily trips to his office furnished themes for his columns. One wonders how many eyes he opened to the world close at hand. On the twenty-seventh of May, when he was twenty-three, he wrote:

Few persons, we suspect, are aware of the number of shades of green the unfolding leaves of the different trees display, but they are almost infinite, some of them of extreme delicacy at a certain stage of development. A specially fine example of the harmonious mingling of these shades is now to be observed on the east bank of the Connecticut River in South Hadley, and is seen to best advantage from the cars between Holyoke and Smith's Ferry. The dark green of the spruce and hemlock there fades into the pale tints of the poplar and the birch through the intermediate shades of the maple and other common trees.[14]

---

[13] Unpublished papers (B1-3-76).
[14] "A Suggestion to Artists," *Springfield Union,* May 27, 1873.

A foggy morning on his way to the office provided a theme for an editorial, and almost for a philosophy for the enjoyment of the world as we pass through it:

To the mind accustomed to find exhilaration in the beauty of nature, there is no circumstance of calm or storm, of sun or shade, of snow or foliage, rain, mist or clear shining, which does not, like the varied toilets of a woman, reveal or accent some fresh charm. . . . There is a delicacy, a softness of tone, a novelty of suggestion, a fantasy of perspective in foggy landscapes, which is incomparable and never otherwise obtainable . . . At seven or eight o'clock one of these foggy mornings, for instance, when the sun looks like a tarnished silver dollar through the mist, the pedestrian passes from one charming surprise to another. Never has he seen the green of the grass, so strong and garish by sunlight, reveal such softness and delicacy. The trees and hedges, becoming successively visible as he walks along, are relieved against a background of white wool, like the nests of cotton which jewels repose in. At every step a part of the objects in the little visible spot around him fade, and others come into view. At no time does he see clearly more than a hundred yards on every side, and the effect of Nature thus presented in detail is at once new and piquant. Instead of being one great sight, the landscape is divided by rims of fog into innumerable bits of scenery, veritable gems, over each of which he lingers reluctant to lose it, while equally attracted by curiosity to go on to the others. And at last, when the sun, refusing to have the wool pulled over his eyes any longer, bursts forth and scatters the fog, one is almost tempted to revile the big, coarse, common face of Nature, and to wonder where the thousand charming little fog-framed pictures have disappeared to. It is as if the partition of a house had been removed and all the nooks were lost in one big room. One would scarcely believe, until after experiment, how full of new effects it is to study the features of a landscape thus in detail, and how different from observing them all together with a sweeping glance as parts of the entire league-broad view exposed by sunlight. We then make the discovery, so easily revealed to the student of Nature, that there is more in a single tree than in a forest, more in a square rod of lawn and hedge than in a landscape, and that Nature grows richer and more varied as we descend to details, and bare and monotonous as our inspection grows general. Microscopic, not telescopic, is the mode of investigation to which our faculties are adapted, and in which they find their happiest occupation.[15]

Even the commonplace changes of the season gave him vivid experiences. On a day in May, when he was twenty-four, he wrote:

[15] "A Foggy Morning," *Springfield Union*, September 26, 1877.

It seems enough to live, and sports and recreations are impertinent. Such air as we now breathe hung over the isle of the lotus eaters, and reconciled Ulysses and his braves to endless revery and soft forgetfulness.

The shadows of the new foliage flecking the sward and playing in the wind strike the mind with a new sense of beauty. It is seven months since we have seen such shadows, and we begin to appreciate what an immense addition they are to the landscape. The sun is not yet so hot that we have begun to take a gross practical view of their advantages. . . . If our hard-working people, not the boys and their sweethearts only who are thinking too much of each other to have an eye for nature, but the fathers and mothers, would spend more time in the woods, it would be the means of grace and usefulness to their souls scarcely second to the sanctuary. . . . Every wise economist of happiness will make the most of these few perfect spring days.[16]

In an editorial on "The Second Phase of Summer," written in August when he was twenty-six, we find a similar expression: "The sun no longer springs from his bed with the lusty vigor of June or July, but slowly and wearily climbs the sky, and not till midmorning does he seem fairly to get about his business. . . . The crops are not so much growing as ripening, a more genuine exhilarating process, a final laying on of color and tone upon completed rudiments." [17] In an October editorial we read, "The Autumn is a bridge, one end of which rests upon a warm and sunny shore, the other on a snow bank." [18] Again from a notebook:

There is in observation of nature play alike for the intellect and the heart of a God. What keen curiosity at every dawn to see what sort of a day it is going to be, what room for discrimination in the qualities of days, no two since the first of all quite alike, those most similar full of subtle deep differences, each having its peculiar inimitable humor.[19]

Edward Bellamy felt the need for getting away from his home streets, to renew his strength and to recover the peace and sanity of which the busy world is constantly robbing men. The following paragraph from "Eliot Carson" is a typical expression of that longing:

16 "These Spring Days," *Springfield Union,* May 28, 1874.
17 "The Second Phase of Summer," *Springfield Union,* August 9, 1876.
18 "The Melancholy Days Are Come," *Springfield Union,* October 31, 1877.
19 Unpublished papers (B1-3-14).

All day to climb these mighty hills, feeling their strength thrill his own limbs as he trod their springy turf; to happen upon little brooks purling their secrets in hidden glens; to sleep at noon on a sunny sward with their murmurs in his ears; to chance all awed and silent upon those secret places of the woods, those room-like nooks whose air is warm with the sense of something living there, something whose shrine it is; to breathe all day long the forest air laden with the perfume of the great trees so much rarer, more delicate, more intoxicating than the sickish scents of flowers; to lie beneath the pines and listen to the song of eternity in their branches till he forgot what manner of life his was; to sit in a corner of the woods before a fire of little sticks on a cold overcast day, and enjoy that oldest means of comfort that an open fire ministers to the nerve, whose roots reach down to the first experiences of cave-dwelling ancestors . . .[20]

In another one of his notebooks he wrote: "Our sympathy with nature is sweeter, tenderer than with men for there are no equal antagonisms to be propitiated." [21]

For a mature American to admit to a love of nature has been looked upon as effeminate, especially among farmers and working people. Not only was Bellamy willing to save his own respectability by carrying a gun as a conventional hunter, but he sought to stimulate similar incentives in others, as in an editorial, "Go Afishing":

Horace Greeley often expressed a desire to go afishing, but he never found time; and now he is dead and will never have another chance. Had he taken a little pleasant piscatorial exercise every year, he might have been alive still. All work and no play was too much even for his strong constitution, and the great brain has stopped working prematurely, and the great heart that made him friend to all the world has ceased to throb.

Let those who would wish to avoid Mr. Greeley's fate make time to go afishing, if they cannot find it. It will do them a world of good, and probably not hurt the fishes much. It does not make much difference how or where people go afishing, if they will only go.[22]

Some persons will be impatient at finding a description of the tints of green of spring foliage in a book about a man who has been known to the world chiefly as a social reformer. But such matters are not trivial or incidental. It is not possible to appraise

---

[20] *Ibid.* (B2-EC-4).   [21] *Ibid.* (B2-4-10).
[22] "Go Afishing," *Springfield Union*, May 20, 1873.

the social and economic theories of Edward Bellamy except in the setting of his life. His was not a one-track mind that had found a panacea. His was a universal personality, interested in and sensitive to everything that is vital to the human spirit. He craved for all men their fair share of opportunity for full development, and he knew that men did not live by bread alone, nor even by bread and cake.

Edward Bellamy pondered over this matter of the love of nature and its significance, and as a young man of twenty-four expressed himself in an editorial on "Nature and Ourselves":

Whether there is anything more in nature than we ourselves put into it, in the way of beautiful and grand impressions, is very much like the question whether the statue is in the marble before the chisel of the sculptor has formed and revealed it. Both queries involve the relation of mind to matter, the power of the spiritual over the material. . . . All literature is full of the sentiments of the restfulness which there is in this old mother of ours when we take our tired, jaded minds into her quiet recesses, and lie off loosely among her rocks and sea weeds. . . . Softer pillows may be found than earth's motherly bosom, but none more sweetly refreshing. But the refreshing comes, after all, more through a spiritual than a material or mechanical process. It is the new life which we drink in through the conscious accord of our minds and feelings with this mighty life of the world, the absorbing of its full, strong harmonies into our natures, subduing our irritations, restoring our disturbed sensibilities, giving us a sort of general regeneration, difficult to talk about, but exquisite to enjoy. And this is the pith of our little disquisition, that we shall get out of this world of ours pleasure and various good about in the ratio of our power to perceive what the Maker of it all has designed to express through its forms to our minds and hearts, and our quickness and delicacy of response to its suggestions. This, to some extent, is a matter of cultivation.[23]

So far as we can find, even from his most private and intimate notebooks, Edward Bellamy never wrote a line of verse. Yet in essence he was a poet, "who in the love of nature holds communion with her visible forms." Bellamy had a creative sense of beauty. Because he saw with his mind and spirit, as well as with his eyes, the common things which most men look at and do not see were

[23] "Nature and Ourselves," *Springfield Union,* August 20, 1874.

to him a source of joy. Did Shelley or Wordsworth ever put more seeing into their words than did Bellamy when he wrote of "the sunset forever glowing over the rim of the rolling earth."

The validity of Edward Bellamy's love of nature was well expressed by J. Arthur Thomson in his *Outline of Science:*

The poetry of the man of feeling must not contradict the formulations of the man of science, but they are speaking different languages, and we may know by feeling some aspects of reality which elude us in scientific analysis. Our delight in fine scenery is not less real than our knowledge of the geology. Both are pathways to reality.[24]

Though Edward Bellamy was not a trained scientist, he somehow acquired the scientific temper to an unsual degree. We do not know that he had any formal schooling in the spirit and methods of modern science, or whether he had any associates with trained scientific minds.

At the time he wrote, while the scientific method was firmly established in the physical sciences and was winning its way in biology, yet nonscientific methods still were in control in psychology, economics, sociology, and government. It still was customary to reason from so-called general principles or self-evident truths, rather than from carefully observed facts. An obvious illustration of the older methods of nonscientific thinking is seen in the American Declaration of Independence: "We hold these truths to be self-evident, that all men are created equal . . ." The "scientific socialism" of Karl Marx was still permeated with a large amount of unscientific dogma.

In the large degree in which Bellamy broke away from the prescientific method and in the extent to which he sought for and relied upon first-hand evidence, he was a real pioneer in the field of social science. In his published works, in his private notebooks, and in his editorials and book reviews, we find evidence of a spirit of open-minded, critical inquiry, which justly deserves to be classed as scientific.

In *Looking Backward* and in *Equality* there are conclusions on

24 J. Arthur Thomson, *The Outline of Science,* IV, 1176. Reprinted by permission of the publisher.

matters of scientific import, presented with little or no evidence of the process by which they were reached. Bellamy was not writing textbooks in science; he was presenting a picture to stir the heart of the common man for a better organization of society. In so far as that picture stands the test of scientific appraisal, the author is not to be condemned for avoiding diversion of the reader's mind by describing the steps by which he reached his conclusions. A few illustrations will show the quality of his thinking in various scientific fields.

Because Bellamy has been criticized as overlooking the importance of the inborn quality of the human breed and of counting too much on the form of society, it is interesting to observe his treatment of the subject of eugenics. Though a very old issue, in Bellamy's day eugenics was emerging to the active attention of modern science. Galton had aroused interest in England by his book *Hereditary Genius,* published in 1869, though he did not coin the words "eugenic" and "eugenics" until 1883 in his book on *Human Faculty.* Most of Bellamy's references to the subject were before the latter date, and we find him using the older term, "stirpiculture." Mrs. Bellamy relates that the problem of improving the quality of human stocks by intelligent mating was one of sustained interest to her husband.

The first reference for which we have a definite date is an editorial in the *Springfield Union* of September 30, 1873, when Bellamy was twenty-three years old. In the course of an extended discussion he wrote, "There is no question that a very manifest modern tendency is toward the application of theories of stirpiculture to the human family, with a view of breeding up to a higher type of humanity." After quoting from an article by Charles Darwin, suggesting legislation to promote good human breeding, Bellamy continues: "The subject is an exceedingly important one —which no notion of false delicacy should prevent from receiving full attention . . . That legal restrictions on the subject are desirable or practicable we doubt. [Darwin had favored such.] But the moral police of an intelligent public opinion should enforce the dictates of reason and sound morality in the premises." [25]

That a young man of twenty-three should venture to take issue with the great Darwin, whom he admired almost to the point of reverence, seems presumptuous. Yet throughout his life Bellamy maintained the position that the chief reliance for improving the human breed should not be legislative compulsion, but education and a quickened social conscience, and a better social order. After two thirds of a century his conclusions, rather than those of the great Darwin, are generally supported by the judgment of authorities.

Among themes for short stories in some of his private notebooks, we find such outlines as the following:

In stirpiculture story of coming race . . . relate how pessimism had so theorized on the evil condition of the race that suicide was the fashion, and a school of thugs was established. The most cultured of the race also as a solemn duty took life whenever they could out of sheer compassion. A convention called which declares that the pessimists are right as the world stands, but that if men were physically, morally and mentally what they ought to be, life would be enjoyable. They also decide that none of the reforms, political or social, which have been agitated since the beginning as means of ameliorating the race, have any chance of success until men are more moral and intelligent. The experiment of stirpiculture is attempted. Hope is born again among men. They see a future for the race and devote themselves with enthusiasm to the new cult. [26]

Such items are interesting in that they show Bellamy as believing that programs of social reform in order to have enduring success must be accompanied by improvement in genetic quality. In one of Bellamy's notebooks is the outline of a plot entitled "Stirpiculture Fantasy—A story of the future, representing a society in which the state has taken hold of the subject of procreation, and has regulated matrimony on the principle of the improvement of the species." Assuming for that day an understanding of the types which can best mate with each other, the theme proposes that all young people be classified as to type, and as to the types with which

[25] "Who Should Not Marry," *Springfield Union,* September 30, 1873.
[26] Unpublished papers (B1-A-4).

they could mate to best advantage. A badge would indicate the wearer's classification. The memorandum concludes: "Subject to the law that men may marry any case of the [appropriate] temperament, entire freedom given to the selection of lovers. The result is that to any man, not over one in five young women could possibly be of matrimonial interest; and in case of some, not one woman in fifty." [27]

In *Looking Backward* and *Equality* we find Bellamy's eugenics program quite explicitly stated. His conclusions compare favorably with the principles and policies that have since emerged in the field of eugenics as the result of two thirds of a century of study and experience. To begin with, Bellamy would prevent the reproduction of conclusively deficient persons. The following passage from *Equality* pictures his treatment of that class:

"A surprising number of the cases you speak of, who had been given up as failures by your civilization, while in fact they had been proofs of its failure, responded with alacrity to the first fair opportunity to be decent men and women which had ever come to them. There was, of course, a large residuum too hopelessly perverted, too congenitally deformed, to have the power of leading a good life, however assisted. Toward these the new society, strong in the perfect justice of its attitude, proceeded with merciful firmness. The new society was not to tolerate, as the old had done, a criminal class in its midst any more than a destitute class. The old society never had any moral right to forbid stealing or to punish robbers, for the whole economic system was based on the appropriation, by force or fraud on the part of a few, of the earth and its resources and the fruit of the toil of the poor. . . . But the new order, guaranteeing an equality of plenty to all, left no plea for the thief and robber, no excuse for the beggar, no provocation for the violent. By preferring their evil courses to the fair and honorable life offered them, such per-

[27] *Ibid.* (B-2-Plots 1-35). This suggestion is strikingly confirmed by recent knowledge of blood types. In case of the blood types known as "Rh positive" and "Rh negative," if these types mate, and if the unborn child has inherited the blood type of its father, it probably will die before birth, or be born anemic. The mother's body seems to tend to develop "antibodies" against the father's blood type as it would against diphtheria or measles, so that if such unions are not childless they commonly are limited to one child. Of Americans, about 15 per cent have negative Rh blood type, and such persons, on this count alone, would be suitable mates for only one person in seven. It is possible that this knowledge of antagonistic blood types is one of the early findings in a field of great importance. In eugenics, as in so many other fields, Bellamy's intuitions have proved to be sound.

sons would henceforth pronounce sentence on themselves as unfit for human intercourse. With a good conscience, therefore, the new society proceeded to deal with all vicious and criminal persons as morally insane, and to segregate them in places of confinement, there to spend their lives—not, indeed, under punishment, or enduring hardships of any sort beyond enough labor for self-support, but wholly secluded from the world—and absolutely prevented from continuing their kind." [28]

This program would go about as far as most qualified and representative eugenists would go today in controlling the reproduction of the unfit, and no further. But, as is beginning to be generally recognized, Bellamy saw that elimination of the obviously unfit touched only the margin of the problem. It might be the way to mediocre stability, but not to excellence. And Bellamy saw another great truth which students of eugenics have been slow to accept: that the social environment and the individual interact upon each other in such a vital manner that to ignore the need for social change will largely nullify any program for human betterment.

Just as the old-line socialists and communists went astray in seeing human betterment as dependent solely upon improvement in the economic order, so until recently, at the other extreme, eugenists have dealt almost solely with a biological problem, without relation to problems of economic society. In the pioneer period of eugenics, when extreme and partial views were not uncommon, Edward Bellamy saw the whole problem and saw it in good perspective.

In *Looking Backward* he pictures the relation of the social and economic order to a sound eugenics program. Julian West and Dr. Leete have been discussing the status of women in the new society, and the following dialogue takes place:

"It would seem to follow, from what you have said, that wives are in no way dependent on their husbands for maintenance."

"Of course they are not," replied Dr. Leete, "nor children on their parents either, that is, for means of support. . . ."

"One result which must follow from the independence of women I can see for myself," I said. "There can be no marriages now except those of inclination.

". . . the fact you celebrate, that there are nothing but love matches,

[28] *Equality*, pp. 363–64.

means . . . that for the first time in human history the principle of sexual selection, with its tendency to preserve and transmit the better types
of the race, and let the inferior types drop out, has unhindered operation. The necessities of poverty, the need of having a home, no longer
tempt women to accept as the fathers of their children men whom they
neither can love nor respect. Wealth and rank no longer divert attention from personal qualities. . . . The gifts of person, mind, and disposition; beauty, wit, eloquence, kindness, generosity, geniality, courage, are sure of transmission to posterity. Every generation is sifted
through a little finer mesh than the last. The attributes that human nature admires are preserved, those that repel it are left behind.

". . . . To-day this sense of responsibility, practically unrecognized in all previous ages, has become one of the great ethical ideas of
the race, reinforcing, with an intense conviction of duty, the natural impulse to seek in marriage the best and noblest of the other sex. . . .
Our women have risen to the full height of their responsibility as the
wardens of the world to come, to whose keeping the keys of the future
are confided. Their feeling of duty in this respect amounts to a sense of
religious consecration. It is a cult in which they educate their daughters
from childhood." [29]

One of the most effective eugenic elements of Bellamy's program
is the provision for equal maintenance of all persons, regardless
of whether they are working in industry or are studying in preparation for later work. Today many of our more intelligent young
men and women postpone home and children in order to complete
professional training and to become professionally established,
whereas unskilled workers may have maximum incomes in the early
twenties and so can have homes and families much earlier, with
enormous increase in their contribution to the population. Bellamy's policy would largely end that condition.

Considering his eugenics program as a whole, it is more farsee-
ing, saner, and better balanced than many of those presented by
scientific specialists of his day, and in its total outline seems to
be abreast of the latest excellent statements of policy of the American Eugenics Society, and even goes further in indicating ways
and means for recognizing more explicitly the relations between
economic status and race improvement. His treatment of the Mal-

[29] *Looking Backward,* pp. 262, 266, 267, 268, 269.

thusian doctrine in the last pages of *Equality* ranks among the best brief statements on that subject.

The views of Bellamy which have been presented on the subject of eugenics do not represent a mind which by chance had followed a single line of scientific interest. Rather, they are but illustrations of an alert, ranging intelligence which had a marked aptitude for recognizing problems and for taking hold of them in a competent and common-sense manner.

In 1875 Bellamy showed unusual interest in an article in a medical journal. Either he found in that article or inferred from it a forecast of the behavioristic theory of thinking, which was not developed by psychologists until forty years later. According to this theory, thinking involves the entire body, and consists of tendencies of the muscles of the body to act. It was unusual for such an article to be reviewed in a local daily newspaper, and for a young book reviewer of twenty-five to be impressed by its significance. The review by Bellamy begins with the following very pointed comments, which indicate that he caught the significance of the article:

The distinguishing characteristic of the writings of Oliver Wendell Holmes is their suggestiveness. . . . There is hardly a contemporary author in whose writings so many original threads of thought are struck out, so many subtle, unsuspected, yet obvious analogies . . . suggested. It often strikes the critic of Mr. Holmes' writings, that if, instead of rambling fancy free through all the field of literature, instead of sipping merely the honey, the first flavor of ideas, he would sometime take time to follow out the leads he discovers, he might attain a more solid reputation, if at the sacrifice of brilliancy, and might contribute valuable discoveries, duly correlated to the science of human nature, instead of a store of tantalizing truths and apercus.

Similar comments on the mind and work of Holmes were made later by his biographers. The review continues:

One of the most striking suggestions which he has recently made is that upon the physiology of versification in a paper in the Boston Medical and Surgical Journal for January. Dr. Holmes believes that the structure of metrical compositions is conditioned by the law of breathing. The natural rate of respiration is from sixteen to twenty-four breaths a minute, twenty being the average. The popularity of octosyllabic verse is owing to the fact that, in being read it follows more naturally than any other the natural rate of respiration. Experiment with Scott's or Longfellow's or Tennyson's poetry in this measure will show that an average of twenty lines will be read in a minute; that is, one respiration will suffice for each line, giving a chance to take breath at the end of each line. Thus, in reading this sort of verse the breathing takes care of itself, so much so in fact, that the main objection to eight syllable verse is that the ease of articulation causes it to run into a sort of sing-song. . . .

Then we come upon the more pointed hint of "behaviorism." Bellamy's review continues: "It is obviously true, as Dr. Holmes remarks, that the same rule applies to writing verse as to reading it, *as the versifier mentally articulates each line.*" [30] (If instead of "mentally" he had written "sub-vocally," his statement would have been more explicitly a forecast of behaviorism.)

An examination of the article by Holmes discloses that it does not contain any such suggestion. What Holmes did write was, "It may be said that the law of relation here pointed out does not apply to the *writing* of verse, however it may be with regard to reading or declaiming it." [31] Either Bellamy added the pertinent observation on his own account or, what is more probable, he was well acquainted with Holmes' writing, and knew that he had made the suggestion in another essay, "Mechanism in Thought and Morals," in which we find the comment: "*Worded* thought is attended with a distinct impulse towards the organs of speech: in fact, the effort often goes so far, that we 'think aloud'; . . . as we say, 'My heart was in my mouth,' we could almost say, 'My brain is in my mouth.' " [32] In one of Bellamy's undated notebooks we find the line "Hegel said, 'We think in words.' " [33] This would seem to anticipate modern symbolic logic and semantics. Had Bellamy's pointed suggestion concerning the importance of this inquiry been followed up by a competent psychologist, the behavioristic theory of thinking might have appeared several decades sooner. This in-

[30] "The Physiology of Versification," *Springfield Union,* January 26, 1875. (Italics added.)

[31] Oliver Wendell Holmes, "The Physiology of Versification," in *Pages from an Old Volume of Life,* p. 318. (Italics added.)

[32] Holmes, "Mechanism in Thought and Morals," *Pages from an Old Volume of Life,* p. 270.

[33] Unpublished papers (B2-4-21).

stance indicates how Bellamy's mind was alert in various scientific fields.

He included scientific books in his reviews to an extent which makes us wonder whether a large part of his newspaper audience would be interested. Among such were, *The Conservation of Energy* by Balfour Stewart, *The Doctrine of Evolution* by Alexander Winchell, another on the same subject by Richard Proctor, *The Chemistry of Light and Photography* by Dr. Herman Vogel, and a translation of M. F. Cozelles' *Outline of the Evolution Philosophy.*

At the age of twenty-three Bellamy wrote a review of Darwin's *Expressions of the Emotions in Man and the Animals,* in the course of which he said: "Like all of Mr. Darwin's books, this contains a mass of the most interesting and unusual facts, the fruit of years of acute scientific observations, facts profoundly interesting in themselves, without regard to the theories which may be based upon them. Both facts and speculations are withal set in that style of simplicity and lucidity which Darwin as well as Tyndall and Huxley affect, and which takes from the most non-technical of readers all excuse for failing to keep up with the progress of science." [34]

A review three years later of Darwin's *The Movements and Habits of Climbing Plants* is written with understanding and profound respect for the great scientist, and shows evident acquaintance with his mind and work. Bellamy comments, "These more recent of his books develop that part of his great philosophy of life which contemplates the relations of plant life to human life as not different in kind so much as in degree, immense as that difference is." [35]

From time to time Bellamy made acute observations which suggest that he was more than a reader and reviewer, as for instance a brief item on lightning in one of his notebooks: "The shadowless glare of lightning. Peculiar effect which the all-pervading circumambient radiance of lightning has in the absence of shadows. You seem to see all around objects. They look far smaller, more

[34] "Literary Notices," *Springfield Union,* January 7, 1873.
[35] *Ibid.,* January 27, 1876.

slender, as trees, on that account, showing that the eye has attributed something of their shadows to them in judging their
size." [36]

Edward Bellamy's opinions on social questions were not just
vague impressions, but very often were based on accurate quanti-
tative knowledge, either from his own observation or from careful
and discriminating reading. Even in his early writings there are
numerous evidences of this fact.

Commenting on his European trip of a few years before, Bellamy
mentioned the impression made on his mind by poverty in England.
In his several editorials on the English agricultural strike we find
his conclusions based on factual information, and we have a glimpse
of some of the terrible conditions of poverty which influenced the
formation of his social philosophy.

While not trained as a scientist, Edward Bellamy had capacity
for thinking as a scientist, an intuition for scientific significance,
and an acquaintance with the scientific method. His social views
were to a considerable degree an outcome of these traits.

We can get an impression of the creative, speculative quality of
his mind from some of his early notebook entries, in which he specu-
lated with an inquiring scientific imagination beyond the limits
of scientific data. In an undated notebook, along with fragments
of themes for short stories, is this entry:

It is more than the imagination can compass to imagine being, unless
it be seeing, feeling, hearing, thinking being. Necessarily by the nature
of the term it must be impossible for us to imagine a mode of being essentially different from our own, because to imagine it implies the existence of some point of resemblance in our own experience with which
we can compare it, and by the very term of the supposition there is no
such point of resemblance. But while we can not imagine *how* a mode
of existence essentially different from our own can be, we are well able
to imagine *that* it can be. The man born blind has no power to form an
idea as to the nature of the world of vision, but he is able to imagine that
it can be. . . .

Surely, then, our inability to conceive of modes of being essentially

[36] Unpublished papers (B2-1-28).

different from our own mode of thinking beings in no way militates against the reasonableness of the hypothesis that there may be innumerable such essentially different modes. Supposing we were all born blind, had no eyes nor places for them, and the race had always been thus made, should we guess what was lacking? Wretched and imbecile we should then be with only four senses, compared with what we now are with five, even as we now are wretched and imbecile with five senses compared with what we should be if we had a sixth sense, still another mode of apprehending nature and life. But the race with only four senses would no more be able to imagine what other sense could be added to them than we with five senses can imagine where there could be room for another. But while we are unable to guess what could be the function of any additional sense, we have no difficulty in imagining that we might have ten more senses, nay ten thousand, without exhausting the universe of its meaning, or failing to find with the addition of each new sense a field opened to us as vast and gorgeous as that which is opened to the born-blind to whom sight is given. But understand, it is not merely of new senses which are mere feeders of thought that I speak, but of other modes of being which have nothing more to do with thought than sight has to do with hearing, which are different in kind, in describing which the terms of thought would be as meaningless as the terms of smell applied to the description of the sense of touch. . . .[37]

This memorandum is characteristic of a quality of speculation which is frequent in his unpublished writings. Even where it is sheer imagination it seldom violates the principles of scientific speculation. Bellamy had a rare quality of freeing himself from prejudices, of keeping an open mind, and of letting his imagination play upon problems; and of trusting to intuition rather than to the carefully reasoned but treacherous *a priori* logic of the philosophical schools. As a result, in numerous fields, as in eugenics, socialism, economics, and religion, he arrived at conclusions which grow in men's respect as the years pass.

Would that it could be recorded that all the thinking and writing of Edward Bellamy gave evidence of the scientific temper. That, however, was not the case. He lived and worked in a period that was in a twilight zone between the time when men sought truth by revelation, intuition, or logic, and the present age when some of

[37] *Ibid.* (B1-B-2).

them seek it by research, observation, and experiment. Fourier, with his theory of the passions of men as God-given attributes which are an infallible guide to conduct, was one of the last of a long procession of the earlier school of thought. Bellamy made real headway in achieving a scientific temper and freedom from absolutist doctrine, yet it was almost beyond possibility that any man of his times and circumstances should completely succeed. He sometimes supported his argument by reference to supposed absolute, philosophical "rights." He did not base his claims solely on the practical, long-range effects of his policies.

Though his mind continued to be cumbered with vestiges of the pre-Darwinian dogmatic philosophy—as is the case with many moralists, sociologists, economists, and industrialists and with most politicians, even of the present day—yet, without much if any formal training in modern science and without the help of a disciplined scientific environment, such as that which favored Darwin and Galton in the Royal Society and elsewhere, he somehow achieved an open-minded, scientific attitude to a very considerable degree.

Edward Bellamy took a fresh look at life. One of the secrets of his power was the ability he developed for finding novel points of observation outside of the human life and culture that we know. By picturing some other way of life as though from the inside, with all the familiar intimacy of a traveler telling us about a land from which he had just come, he enables us to see that other and very different ways might be just as natural, and perhaps more satisfactory, than those with which we are familiar.

This skill on his part did not come by accident, but was the result of deliberate thought and practice. In a notebook item written during his twenties we find: "It should be our effort to contemplate the individual from the standpoint of the universal. . . . We should seek to view ourselves from without, instead of viewing all things from ourselves as from within. Seek a home, a center, a more intimate ego in the universe of things from without." [38] Not only did he develop outside viewpoints for himself, but for ten years or

[38] *Ibid.* (B1-2-21).

more he practiced the art of presenting them in literary form until he was able to make them seem so natural and real to his readers that they, with him, could look at our everyday life with the fresh curiosity of a visitor from another planet or from another age.

This is a real contribution, for relatively few men have the creative fertility of imagination to look at the world or at themselves as a stranger might. Men are not moved by ideas alone, but only by ideas that are made real and vital to them by some method which appeals to the sense of value. A man may be overwhelmed by propaganda and by emotional assault and in that way be converted, without any clear idea of what is claiming his allegiance; or, on the other hand, a very different way of life may be made to seem natural and good by being presented in such a clear and moving picture that a change from his present life to the other may seem highly desirable, and scarcely more unusual than a trip to another city. Bellamy used the latter method.

An illustration of this habit of taking an outside view is one of his short stories, "The Blindman's World"—that being the name given to the earth and its people by the inhabitants of Mars. By skillful steps, which seem so natural as scarcely to surprise us, we find ourselves on Mars discussing the differences between their life and ours. The most striking contrast is that people on Mars, while they have short and fading memories and so have little interest in what is past, have the ability to see all the future events that will take place during their lives. A few paragraphs from this story will indicate how he helps us to this novel viewpoint:

Suppose your life destined to be blessed by a happy friendship. If you could know it beforehand, it would be a joyous expectation, brightening the intervening years and cheering you as you traversed desolate periods. But no; not till you meet the one who is to be your friend do you know of him. Nor do you guess even then what he is to be to you, that you may embrace him at first sight. Your meeting is cold and indifferent. It is long before the fire is fairly kindled between you, and then it is already time for parting. Now, indeed, the fire burns well, but henceforth it must consume your heart. Not till they are dead or gone do you fully realize how dear your friends were and how sweet was their companionship. But we—we see our friends afar off coming to meet us, smiling already in our eyes, years before our ways meet. We greet them at first meeting, not coldly, not uncertainly, but with exultant kisses, in an ecstasy of joy. They enter at once into the full possession of hearts long warmed and lighted for them. We meet with that delirium of tenderness with which you part. And when to us at last the time of parting comes, it only means that we are to contribute to each other's happiness no longer. We are not doomed, like you, in parting, to take away with us the delight we brought our friends, leaving the ache of bereavement in its place, so that their last state is worse than their first. Parting here is like meeting with you, calm and unimpassioned. The joys of anticipation and possession are the only food of love with us, and therefore Love always wears a smiling face. With you he feeds on dead joys, past happiness, which are likewise the sustenance of sorrow. No wonder love and sorrow are so much alike on Earth.[39]

To Bellamy this was not simply an interesting story. It was one of many steps in a life work he was gradually marking out for himself to the end of leading men to look forward to their possibilities, rather than backward to their mistakes and failures.

In another story, "To Whom This May Come," he pictures a strange people—a colony of Zoroastrians who have lived for two thousand years on an isolated South Sea island—who know each other very intimately because they fully read each other's minds. With marked artistic skill the writer enables us to see what human society might be like if men's minds were entirely open to each other, and we are made to realize that in this respect we may not now be living in "the best of all possible worlds."

The two books *Dr. Heidenhoff's Process* and *Miss Ludington's Sister* are other examples of this kind of skill. Bellamy's notebooks contain many themes and plots for stories he never wrote, and among them, too, we find suggestions for curious outside viewpoints on the affairs of men. What we are dealing with is not merely literary craftsmanship, but an intellectual achievement. No trick of words would have enabled him to stand apart and to view himself and things as they are, as an outsider might view them. A reviewer of his story "To Whom This May Come," in contrasting Bellamy's work with that of "the writer who 'reads up' on the subject," said of him: "Mr. Bellamy has a remarkable faculty—which is that of the scientific thinker in the highest sense; the man who beholds

[39] *The Blindman's World, and Other Stories*, pp. 18–19.

things in the light of imagination held in control by law—of supposing a certain condition of existence, either physical, psychical or spiritual, and then depicting life as it must necessarily be under such conditions. This he does with rare consistency and power of verisimilitude." [40]

Finally in *Looking Backward* and in *Equality* we have his masterpiece of this slowly achieved art which he called "making the objective subjective, and the subjective objective." The ideal conditions of the year 2000 seem to be present and real, and so reasonable to us that through his eyes we look back at the present as on a past age which we can examine almost as a stranger would.

[40] "Theosophical Aspects of Contemporary Thought and Literature," *Path*, March, 1889.

VII · The Writer

To write a book on government and economics which in a few years and in a population less than half of that of ours today would sell half a million copies, which would be translated into nearly every important language, and which half a century later would still be selling at the rate of five thousand copies a year in America alone, with new translations still being made into minor languages —this is a record seldom equaled in the history of writing. Within a few years after *Looking Backward* appeared more than fifty utopias had been published in the United States. Probably all of them together did not have as great distribution as *Looking Backward*. Among their authors were very intelligent men, some of them with far greater reputations than Bellamy. Why, then, the difference in the reception of their books?

Success like that of *Looking Backward* is not due to any one cause, but to a rare combination. It reflects good literary taste, skill in writing, careful economic study and organization of ideas, hard work, humane character, stubborn and daring independence, strong conviction, trained, creative imagination, and timeliness. Although it is evident that many elements entered into his achievement, it seems clear, nevertheless, that had not the book been well written, its success would have been far less. How did the author of *Looking Backward* become possessed of that undoubted skill?

Fortunately Bellamy has not left us in the dark as to how he learned to write. Scattered through his journals, notebooks, and fragments of manuscript, as well as in his published articles, books, and book reviews, he has recorded the growth of his skill and has dropped ideas and comments on the art of writing which, taken all together, give us a remarkable picture of the making of a successful writer. As an aid in understanding his skill and how he achieved it, we have assembled some of these expressions.

There are numerous evidences that the masterful touch seen in *Looking Backward* was not due to luck, to accident, or just to native shrewdness, but represented conscious design and deliberate self-education. Few if any of his notebooks, manuscripts, editorials, or book reviews were written with the expectation that they would be read by the public as a guide to the understanding of his style and methods, but for that very reason they are the more revealing.

Unquestionably, his experience as a newspaperman was an important element in his training. In his journal under the date of November, 1871, about the time he became an editorial writer on the *New York Evening Post,* is an entry: "I have been to New York and met with good success. The ministry of disappointment has, it would seem, ceased for the present. I have now an opportunity to manifest all that may be in me of light for the world." [1]

Although while Bellamy was on the *Post* William Cullen Bryant was its publisher and editor, nowhere in Bellamy's papers do we find mention of that name. During most of the time Bellamy was with the *Post* Bryant was on a trip to the Bahamas, Cuba, and Mexico. Quite probably the twenty-one-year-old member of the staff never met the chief.

The *Post* was then a four-page daily, the pages being nearly double the size of a standard newspaper of today. About half the space was taken by advertisements. Reading matter consisted chiefly of editorials and brief paragraphs on local and foreign news, written somewhat like editorials. The writing was of high literary quality and covered a wide range of foreign and domestic interests. Whereas in the *Springfield Union* Bellamy's writing in general was so superior as to stand out conspicuously, on the *Post* the general level of writing was perhaps equal to Bellamy's best at that time. None of his articles for the *Post* can be identified by their style.

In June, 1872, the *Springfield Union* came under new management, and a position there was opened for him. In the *Union,* and also in the earlier issues of the *Penny News* when Bellamy was writing for it, we see imitation of the *New York Evening Post,* not

[1] Unpublished papers (B1-1-5).

only in literary style, but in the very wide range of subjects treated including world-wide news, science, and literature.

Bellamy seems to have begun work on the *Springfield Union* about the middle of August, 1872, and to have continued his editorials and book reviews until late November, 1877. Because articles in the *Union* were not signed, the assumption that those quoted were written by him requires explanation. He was employed as book reviewer on a small city paper which must have unbalanced its budget to afford even one writer in that capacity. Before Bellamy's employment on the paper book reviews were perfunctory or non-existent. Evidence of literary ability on his level was almost wholly absent. The paper had changed hands and had been reorganized about the first of June, 1872, two and a half months before his first articles appeared, but during that period the quality of writing had not noticeably changed.

With his coming, a distinctly new quality, both in style and content, suddenly appeared in its columns. This was most conspicuous in the literary notices. Sometimes book reviews were taken over into the editorial columns, and other editorials appeared of comparable style and quality. The views expressed in some of these editorials are in striking contrast, sometimes in flat contradiction, to the announced policy of the paper. For instance, in the two and a half months prior to Bellamy's joining the paper it included four strongly anti-labor editorials. During the same period the paper specifically denounced "Greeleyism," whereas Bellamy was shortly praising Greeley in his characteristic literary style. The editorials and reviews quoted in this biography are in Bellamy's style. They generally correspond in subject matter, sometimes in exact wording, to items in his notebooks or other published or unpublished writings. Some were extracts from longer articles in his handwriting found among his papers. Some editorials and reviews are on unusual subjects for newspaper treatment, such as eugenics, or the fagging custom in English schools, concerning which he was known to be personally interested and to have strong opinions.

A few weeks after Bellamy left the *Union* his style and characteristic range of subject matter disappeared from its columns as suddenly as they had appeared when he joined the staff. About six months later, judging from the contents of the paper, a new writer of book reviews was added to the staff, but the resulting quality was different from and inferior to Bellamy's. Here and there an article appears which he might have contributed after his return from Hawaii. The tradition is that during his years of service he was relied upon heavily for editorial writing. In answering a questionnaire as a former member of the Delta Kappa Epsilon fraternity of Union College, he wrote: "Editorial contributor to *New York Evening Post*, 1871–72; editorial writer, *Springfield Daily Union*, 1872–77." When shortly afterward he and his brother founded the *Penny News*, the style and content which had characterized the *Union* during his service there appeared in the columns of the new paper. For these reasons the quotations from the *Springfield Union* are included with a feeling of assurance.

Having endeavored through the years to appraise himself without prejudice and without mercy, and having in some degree paid the price and done the work necessary to achieve excellence, Bellamy did not judge himself by the success or failure which resulted from accidental turns of circumstance. "If I should gain a victory or write a book," he wrote in his journal, "I should not think more of myself, but less of the victory. My opinion of myself is the fixed element in my calculations." [2] Having achieved this temper of mind, it is natural that he should see the success of *Looking Backward* as bringing an increase of responsibility rather than of glory. When the book was spreading like wildfire, he wrote to William Dean Howells: "If I publish a poor book I ought to be stoned. The responsibility upon us who have won the ear of the public, to plead the cause of the voiceless masses, is beyond limit. You have stood up to it nobly in your *Altruria*, but the trouble is the better a man does the better he has got to do. 'There is no discharge in that war.' "

Some men seem to be born with their skill assured and their work predetermined. They look upon themselves as little more than passive tools in the hands of fate. As Sidney Lanier expressed the attitude of such men:

2 *Ibid.* (B1-C-2).

> What the artist doeth,
> The Lord knoweth;
> Knoweth the artist not? [3]

Edward Bellamy was no inert pencil in the hand of destiny. Fate seems to have given him an urge to excellence, but without equipping him to satisfy that craving. Again and again in his journals we find expressions of weakness, of frustration, of ebbing courage and halting purpose. At the age of twenty-two he was moved to make this entry: "To have nothing on earth, no idea, no cause for which to be willing to give up life, little as I prize it, that is my state." [4] Again at about the same time he wrote, "I had thought myself to be something greater than other men, and find that I am after all but a mediocre person." [5]

There are occasional evidences through his journals of a mental habit of daydreaming, such as has wrought havoc upon many active minds and proves to be a difficult weakness to overcome. Sometimes we get the impression of an intellectual aesthete, as when he wrote: "When an idea arises clear, distinct and beautiful in my mind, I do not feel a desire to transcribe it to paper. I do so reluctantly and from a conviction of necessity. I would prefer to contemplate it till it fades." [6] Sometimes he seems to be writing of unrestrained daydreaming which tends to the disintegration of personality, as for instance:

Here at this desk I have sat and idled away in vain revery many an hour that might have been employed in writing for fame or money. Do I regret it? No! I regret nothing, and especially not this. Who knows what is best or most profitable? Let others count gold. Let others number the tongues that echo their names. For me, I prize more the vague and wavering images that visit my soul in hours of revery than any other excitations of the mind. Everyone to his taste. Mine runs rather to dreaming than dollars, rather to fancy than fame. My mind to me a kingdom is, to which none other can bear comparison. If these pleasures be unsubstantial, away with all substance; if they be vague, away with all definitions; if they be unreal, down all reality. [7]

---

[3] Lanier, Sidney, "Individuality," in *Poems*, p. 11. By permission of the publisher.

[4] Unpublished papers. (B1-1-23).   [5] *Ibid.* (B1-1-24).

[6] *Ibid.* (B2-4-19).   [7] *Ibid.* (B1-2-25).

Again we find in a notebook: "A man's writing can never be the expression of himself at his most inspired moments, for at such times it seems a profanation to write down his vision. He is forgetful of all but its enjoyment, nor would curtail a pulse of it for the sake of all the fame its publishing could give." [8] These words, taken by themselves, would imply that the only alternatives Bellamy saw at that moment were fame and money on the one hand, and reverie on the other. That such moods did not control his life, even at that period, there is much evidence. Another entry in the same journal seems to indicate that Bellamy was aware of his weakness:

Dullness sometimes assumes an acute form, paradoxical as it may sound, and becomes a positive pain. . . . The mind is like a dyspeptic stomach; nauseated by its own emptiness, it also loathes food. The only thing it can receive is some sharp spice or stimulating draught. Excitement is longed after as a disordered stomach demands a pickle. This is the condition of a sufferer from ennui. . . . The inducing condition of the disease is chiefly a susceptible mental constitution which is also the vehicle of the most delicate and refined enjoyments. Hard work, rather than the pabulum of excitement which it morbidly craves, is the most promising remedy. . . . It is above all not a thing to be nursed or boasted of.[9]

In another notebook we find a brief fragment: "Might-have-been-land. Let me reach it by a stair between my real and potential self which produces a parting. Having fully calculated upon and expected a thing, I am so justly disappointed by its failure to come to pass that the balance of my nature goes over to the potential world, and I go to Might-have-been-land." [10]

In his efforts to overcome such weakness—if weakness it was—no quick success came to him. About a year later he recorded:

In writing I am plagued infinitely by a sense of the insecurity of foundations. I start on one stratum of thought, say the vulgar. Suddenly that seems to me superficial, and I drop into the philosophical, from that I descend to the metaphysical, and finally, deeming the idea too great for any fitting definition or expression, I relapse into the Indian fakir's

8 *Ibid.* (B1-2-31).   9 *Ibid.* (B1-2-15).
10 *Ibid.* (B2-Plots 1-14).

attitude of pure contemplation. This is the bane of my literary labor; continual refinement of my ideas in search of the ultimate generality. I sometimes think all writing a vanity, all expression but a mockery of ideas; and the beasts' or the dolts' attitude toward the world, that of pure feeling, to be the truest one. Everything in the end reduces itself to metaphysics, and is a question of ontology.[11]

Such expressions may have been due at times to sheer weariness, for, as indicated in the book reviews and editorials columns of the *Springfield Union*, he was doing a prodigious amount of reading, and much writing. In another one of his journals, when at the age of twenty-two or twenty-three he was supplying a considerable part of the reading matter of the daily *Springfield Union*, there is still another expression of the inadequacy he felt in his mental and physical resources:

One of the most desperate mental states into which one can fall is that of dullness that is yet restlessness, a condition of stagnation and yet of sharp discontent; a state, say, like that of Byron or Poe when writing some of their most despairing verses, but utterly without the relief which they found in expression—their liver complaint without their muse. At such times the mind is only to be compared with a harbor when the tide is out, a dreary expanse of mud banks and malarial flats. The tides of thought are out. Such a state as I describe is the result of a coincidence of physical and psychical ebbs. When they will be content to alternate we get along very well.[12]

Bellamy's career as a writer was not just a triumphal procession. Such ability as he had, he strove for.

Bellamy's mind labored not only with what he had to say, but with literary quality in general. Several notebooks, used from about 1870 to about 1875, are filled largely with heterogeneous observations and speculations. An extract from one of the better written and more orderly of these, evidently of his early twenties, gives us a glimpse into his mind that is more intimate and revealing than would be many pages of autobiography. The first entry begins, "If this turns out to be a book, which is possible and not much more, it will possess the so-called merit of originality, in form at least." [13] Then he records the following interesting comments:

[11] *Ibid.* (B1-1-29).   [12] *Ibid.* (B1-2-8).
[13] *Ibid.* (B1-2-1).

In early times the mind of the race was objective to a degree no longer attainable. It was capable of the epic, as it never has been since. It was capable of living out in external or single things, undistracted by the multitudinous stirrings of self-consciousness. On this account literature abounded in those times with works marked by an unity, an objectivity, a perfect absorption in the directly exciting cause that is not observable and probably is not possible for modern minds. The characteristics of the literature of the present age are a variety, a subtlety, a complexity, double meanings, refinements upon refinements, that often produce almost the effect of inarticulateness. . . . the idea of the old literature was a one-sided revelation of the mind in its attitude toward some single object or direction: the idea of the modern literature is a transcript of the mind itself undominated by single motives and marked with the almost infinite variety of the mind's own operations. . . .

In this book it is my intention to write as I think without any reference to unity or consistency of design, concerning whatever theme may be uppermost in the mind at the time; now of things social, now things political, now of things religious, psychological or metaphysical. All writers are fishermen in the sea of their own minds, as it were sitting by the current of their own thoughts and angling therein. Other book-makers, the book-maker in general, is bent on fishing for some special sort of fish—say trout, or perch, or gudgeon. He would fain not have his tackle cumbered with any other kind, and if by accident he capture them promptly casts them back again. This I am not going to do. . . .[14]

With uncanny prescience, he stated the case for the "stream-of-consciousness" writing which captured the literary field a half century later. Without benefit of Freud, he outlined a technique of writing which, initiated by a later generation, produced exclamations of "original," "daring," "unique." Bellamy continues his discussion of this form of writing:

Do not our minds hourly entertain a stranger and more motley company of guests than ever did caravanserai, though set at cross roads of the world? Is not the succession of ideas that in an hour passes the focus of our mental vision—that point where we are self-conscious—a more heterogeneous, and fantastic, procession than ever graced a day of carnival? Solemn, mirthful, gay, and sentimental, grotesque, mournful, sarcastic, earnest, reckless, ascetic, sensual, prudish, prurient, thus they troop along arm in arm, intertwined, hanging to each other, a most ill-assorted, inextricable company. Well, what does Mr. Bookmaker do? He sets him down and makes a note of all the grave fellows as they

14 *Ibid.* (B1-2-2).

come along, or maybe it is all those in some other livery. He makes no note of the connection they come in or of their companions; these his wisdom regards as irrelevant. And having thus ranged them stiffly side by side all in a row, as never they were in nature, he invites us to be interested in his picture of the human mind. No wonder books are dull. They present thoughts in most unnatural distorted arrangement. If our minds were such tedious spectacles, life would be far duller than it is.

Heterogeneity is the law of the mind, unity the law of the book. No wonder the book gives little idea of the mind. For my part I am going for once to follow the law of the mind in making a book. . . . There is no order in the mind, the thoughts are a mob, not an army, and a mob of thoughts this book shall be. As regards consistency, there shall be no pretense of it. A consistent man is a liar, for his outward appearance belies his inner experience. Could there be a more amusing illustration of perverted principle than the notion of a man that he serves the interests of truth by preserving consistency to his past ideas at the expense of being false to his present ones?

The current of thoughts is far broader than their narrow channel will accommodate. Thoughts arise side by side, variously intertwined, with countless relations and correlations, as well as succession. The latter can alone find expression. The thoughts must march in single file from mouth or pen. Lines that I have freshly written seem indistinct to my eye for they are surrounded by a certain haze of unuttered thoughts which were connate with those expressed but unembodied and like unquiet shades haunting the page, and confusing the writer's eye. Thinking of their countless number and subtle variances the thought he has chosen to express seems somehow very thin and poor, most unsatisfactory and incomplete, though to another who knows not the abundance whence the thoughts expressed were culled, and in comparison with which they seem to the writer so mean, they seem admirably full and strong. The writer has thus continually impressed upon him what a mockery of thought expression is. Were we able to write our thoughts as they throng in the mind, what a show of interlineations, erasures, and series of footnotes there would be, what execrable copy for the printer!

What is my motive in writing at all? Surely chiefly to see myself reflected from the page, to know myself. Consciously, or subconsciously, this is the motive that impels men to do work of any sort, to express themselves in speech or written words, or stone or colors or song or empire building. The woman before her mirror is after all the type of all human endeavor. . . . I must write me a fable of man that shall present him under the similitude of a genius doomed to walk the earth in banishment, toil, bitterness, misery, until he learn the secret of his own shape and form, and to this end seeking everywhere a mirror and finding only fragments too small or too blurred to render back a full reflection. Poor genius, I am sorry for thee, even if thou wert not my-self.[15]

Why did he not carry out his revolutionary plan? Was he too much bound by conventional literary patterns? Did he fear that it would lead only to a senseless gibberish? Or was it simply one of those streaks of insight or genius which he, a busy person, never got around to express? James Joyce, Gertrude Stein, Virginia Woolf, and others were left free to win acclaim as originators of a new and daring literary style, as well as much abuse as producers of self-conscious nonsense. They got no help from Bellamy for their pioneering, but in the privacy of his notebooks he anticipated them by decades. What is important here about his speculation is that it reveals a mind searching for methods and techniques of most effec-tive expression.

It was after two or three years of writing book reviews and editorials that, in an undated notebook entry, between an entry of "January 1, 1874," and one of "February, 1874," he confided to himself:

Nothing puzzles and confuses me so much as to have my thoughts take in the writing a more glib and complete form than they have attained in my mind. I mean when, as sometimes will happen, the expression is completer than the conception. When I have difficulty in attaining to adequate expression for my idea, then all is well; but when the expres-sion outruns or runs away with the idea, all is ill, and I lay down the pen for that day. There is most emphatically such a thing as too great facility in expression. The taking garb in which this art enables you to invest your ideas deceives you as to their value, conceals their worthless-ness. You are in danger of degenerating till at last gorgeous rhetoric and epigrammatic brilliancy mask mental bankruptcy, and your mind brings forth only Dead Sea apples. . . . In exalting eloquence it is too often forgotten how after all she is but the humble handmaid of thought, and otherwise an errant harlot.[16]

In an interesting and penetrating discussion of Bulwer Lytton's place in literature, which appeared in the *Springfield Union* on February 12, 1874, we find an expression so similar as to indicate

---

[15] Unpublished papers (B1-2-3, 4, 5).   [16] *Ibid.* (B1-1-28).

that the passage in the notebook and the published comment of about the same date were not unassociated. Commenting on Bulwer Lytton, he wrote: "As a weaver of words he was unrivalled, and the gift was a fatal one. He had a faith that words could beget ideas. There are passages of his which resemble philosophy as much as words can resemble ideas. We think that Lytton himself at last lost the power to distinguish between them." [17]

And here, for instance, is a book review which he wrote in 1873, fourteen years before his masterpiece appeared:

Wilkie Collins' last book, *The New Magdalen,* is likely to attract great attention. . . . On rising from its perusal, our respect for Wilkie Collins as a man equals our admiration for him as a novelist. The moral purpose of this book is so interesting that its artistic execution is in danger of being the less appreciated. But it is in this respect a model. There is not a superfluous stroke in it. If, as Schiller said, the master of style is to be recognized rather by what he left unsaid, than by what he has said, this novel confers that title upon Mr. Collins. No ideas foreign to his purpose are introduced to exalt the writer's ingenuity at the risk of diverting the reader's attention from the main purpose. Everything is strictly subordinated to that. Unity of purpose and treatment, the fundamental axiom of art, is fully illustrated. The reader is convinced that if Mr. Collins had just discovered the true secret of the universe he would not leave the thread of his story to mention it.[18]

Bellamy's appreciation of good proportion in writing is indicated in another review two years later. In commending *The Wit and Humor of Shakespeare,* by John Weiss, he wrote, "The art of compression could not well be carried farther. There is not one word too much, while at the same time it stops short of the ellipses which make many of Emerson's sayings obscure through an excess of affectation of brevity." [19]

In these appraisals of the value of conciseness, he sometimes was specifically analytical, as in a review of Browning's poem, "The Inn Album":

. . . To return to this matter of the use of articles, although Browning often drops his "a," "an," and "the" when they really are needed, yet

[17] "Literary Notices," *Springfield Union,* Febuary 12, 1874.
[18] *Ibid.,* May 29, 1873.
[19] *Ibid.,* November 15, 1876.

no doubt he is often right in rejecting them. English composition could still further improve on its peculiar merit of conciseness by a less profuse use of the articles, both definite and indefinite. They are really only necessary when required to characterize substantives as specific or general. If you go through a piece of composition and strike out the articles where they are not necessary to sense, you will be surprised to see how often they may be dispensed with. . . .[20]

In an editorial on "Word Building"—an unusual subject to be discussed in a daily newspaper editorial column—we have an example of Bellamy's characteristic attitude of refusing loyalty to any arbitrary dogma of composition, and of his habit of arriving at common-sense, discriminating conclusions:

Putting words together in composition is much like building a stone wall. Most of the pieces will necessarily be small; but now and then a good large chunk is desirable. Books in one syllable are not, on the whole, pleasing nor particularly forcible or clear. Lines in poetry and sentences and paragraphs in prose sometimes carry great force by being closely packed with these short words: as in Shakespeare often, though he did not reject longer ones, either in his tragic or comic moods, as a glance down his pages will show. But the language at that date supplied nothing like the quantity of sesquipedalians which now hamper more than enrich it—the importations from foreign tongues, dead and living. There has been a great deal written about this matter, neither wisely nor well. Some critics insist upon the shortness of a word as the test of its admission, as if everything that is short is intelligible. But what idea would most readers attach, for instance, to the word "ictic," if they should run against it in a newspaper? It is brief enough, if that were all, and so are "kerf" and "ket," which mean very common things in everyday life, and are thoroughly innocent of any classical origin . . . But the anticlassicists, who are set against Greek and Latin interlopers, will never have done.[21]

He consciously searched for the source of the excellence he found. In reviewing *Cripps The Carrier* by Blackmore, he wrote:

It is quite a puzzle how the impression of individuality is imparted, and we have several times vainly looked back to find out to what phrase of description or dialogue it might be owing in special cases, without, however, being able to ascertain. Mr. Blackmore certainly possesses in unusual measure this extraordinary knack, the most difficult in novel writ-

20 *Ibid.*, January 8, 1876.
21 "Word Building," *Springfield Union*, July 27, 1876.

ing, of characterizing his actors by touches too perfect and too fine to be traced. The characters have a quite spontaneous way of taking form and growing before your eyes. The chisel by which he fashions them and gives them this and that expression is too fine an instrument to be visible. You only see the effect.[22]

Bellamy had thought very carefully of methods to be used in approaching the minds of his readers. A passage in one of his notebooks is a message of universal value to writers, but especially to those who ponderously use the language of graduate schools of education or psychology: ". . . the best effect of reasoning requires that it proceed from a basis of ideas already in the minds of those addressed, rather than from an artificial basis of definitions, however correct, to which the mind is not accustomed; and that, too, although the pre-existing basis be imperfect or indistinct. This course is the one followed by the mind itself in reasoning from old to new conclusions, and it seems to me should therefore be the model studied in seeking to lead other minds to similar conclusions." [23] A somewhat similar view is expressed in his first book, *The Duke of Stockbridge*, written in his late twenties. "They had thought little and vaguely, but they had felt much and keenly, and it was evident that the man who could voice their feelings, however partially . . . would be master of their actions." [24]

We find Bellamy puzzling over the question of just what traits in a writer count for popularity. In discussing a speaker and writer who had unusual popular appeal, he wrote:

What makes up that much coveted quality which goes by the name of popularity is more easily asked than answered. It certainly is not mere strength of intellect or soundness of character, nor is it simple good nature. That may do for a free and easy companionship, but we are talking about the power which draws and holds the masses of average mind and culture to what a writer or speaker has to say. Such a person can hardly be one of the higher grade of mental organization and cultivation, for either of these will put a barrier across his path by removing him too far from those around him in many ways. Eagles on mountain tops are solitary as well as eminent. Somewhere on the side of the hill,

[22] "Literary Notices," *Springfield Union*, July 29, 1876.
[23] Unpublished papers (B3B "How Many Men Make a Man?" p. 2).
[24] *The Duke of Stockbridge*, p. 70.

not too far up or down, is the best place to look for those popular favorites.[25]

While Bellamy sought earnestly to understand the nature of popularity in a writer, and endeavored to remove all unnecessary barriers between the reader's mind and his own, nevertheless he refused to pander to low tastes or to trivialities for the sake of holding his audience. The period of editorials and book reviews of scholarly quality in the *Springfield Union* was one which must have required the general reader to stretch his mind and to increase the range of his interests. There is evidence that Bellamy's stubbornness in dealing with worth-while subjects, and in a scholarly manner, was not always fully appreciated. In an editorial entitled, "Is There a Popular Road to Learning?" written when he was twenty-four, he discloses an impatience with superficial writing:

. . . What is required of him who writes for the public nowadays is not so much wisdom and knowledge, ample and rich materials, as a certain culinary art as applied to literature, whereby to cook up his treatise in some appetizing style with some new sauce. It is no longer matter, but manner that is essential. Everything must be hashed into spoon-victuals, as if this generation had no more any intellectual molars for straightforward chewing. . . . Our fathers used to expect to bring their minds to their books, and to co-operate by close thought with the writer in getting out the ideas. It was all they asked that the writer should bring the walnuts. They expected to crack them and get out the kernels themselves. That is what they called reading. . . .

. . . Nowadays literature surrounds us like an atmosphere. . . . We acquire more knowledge, but it lies like an undigested mass in our minds; we get more ideas, but we get them only half. We are a generation of smatterers. It is well settled that there is no royal road to learning; this generation is engaged in solving the question whether there is a popular road to learning.[26]

Bellamy would not agree with the attitude of many present-day librarians that any reading is better than none. In a review he wrote: "There is no saving grace in reading in and of itself. Bad reading exercises a positively bad effect on the mind, to which men-

[25] "Literary Notices," *Springfield Union*, December 11, 1875.
[26] "Is There a Popular Road to Learning?" *Springfield Union*, July 2, 1874.

tal vacancy, even if it were the alternative, were far preferable." [27]

His conviction that being faithful to reality was the best way for a writer to be convincing is illustrated in a review of Jules Verne's book *Voyages and Adventures of Capt. Hatteras:*

> As long as Verne takes the trouble to give to his improbabilities a slight air of probability, his most extravagant fictions have a sort of interest; but when his stories are a mere narration of bald impossibilities, without any attempt to impart an appearance of vraisemblance by careful attention to details, they are as uninteresting as any other sort of lying. Therefore, while some of his wonder books have fascinated old and young, others are simply tedious, and this is one of the latter class. [28]

Bellamy was twenty-two years old when this review was written. At twenty-three he wrote: "The rounded periods of historical composition are a medium in which generations and communities lose their individuality and all look alike. A volume of village gossip written down by an idle diarist in some Roman hamlet would help us better to realize the way men lived and thought in Caesar's day than would the recovery of Livy's lost books." [29] When he was twenty-six he reviewed another book which illustrated a quality which he thought Jules Verne sometimes lacked:

> *The Curate in Charge* is a story by Mrs. Oliphant. It is a good illustration of what a charming tale can be constructed out of the most commonplace materials when the author brings to her work a faithful observation of human nature. The perfect truth to life produces the illusion of life which is the secret of a novel's fascination. The greatest intellectual stores and originality of ideas lavished in the construction of a story, without this secret of lifelikeness, leaves the reader strained and wearied. [30]

In a review of Stedman's poems he touched upon the same subject:

> The world is obliged to Mr. Stedman for proving once more that the muses have no scorn for common life, and that the poet in whose heart the sacred fire really burns need have no fear that the sordid necessities of the struggle for existence will ever quench it. . . . Burns rhymed behind the plow, Miller among the Modocs, and Stedman, again, is a poet of the marketplace. Mr. Stedman's business life, constantly bringing him into touch with the realities of existence, is perhaps that to which

[27] Editorial, *Springfield Union*, September 10, 1877.
[28] "Literary Notices," *Springfield Union*, October 21, 1875.
[29] *Ibid.*, July 21, 1873.　　　　[30] *Ibid.*, February 22, 1876.

his poetry owes its utter lack of the morbid or sentimental strains which spoil so much poetry now-a-days. A poet who lives an idle life, even a strictly literary life, becomes too introspective, and becomes so tinged with morbidness as in the end to lose the rare gift of telling true feeling from counterfeit. There are few, even of our finest poets . . . who would not write better and truer poetry if they mixed more with the work-a-day life of the world.[31]

In 1884, three years before *Looking Backward* was completed, in a letter to William Dean Howells he expressed the same conviction at greater length:

Whether I belong to the school of the realists or not I do not know. It is the business of the author to write as the spirit moves, and of the critic to classify him. But my own belief is that while the warp, that is the framework and main lines of the story, should be of the author's own invention, the woof and filling should be supplied from his observations of the real life about him. I think that every writer of fiction, when his fancy seduces him too far from the real life which alone he really knows, has such a sense of weakness and uncertainty as Antaeus might have felt when Hercules lifted him into the air, a weakness to be cured with the novelist as with the giant only by a return to earth. If this be true of the novelist, it is yet more true of the romancer, for it is the undertaking of the latter to give an air of reality even to the unreal. Though he build into the air, he must see to it that he does not seem to build upon the air, for the more airy the pinnacles the more necessary the solidity of the foundation.[32]

How fully this aim was achieved in his own later writing is indicated by a review of *Looking Backward* which appeared in the *New York Tribune* in 1888:

He has succeeded in giving to the unexpected, the improbable, even the impossible, all the outward seeming of the natural and practicable. Strange and momentous as are the changes indicated, they are made to wear the aspect not of fantasies but of possibilities; and no higher praise could be given a work of fiction than this impression implies. . . . The prose writer has here shown a power beyond that of poetry, for he has so clothed his conceptions with the garment of realism that they appear to us no longer distant and unattainable shadows, but practical reforms altogether within the scope of existing capacities.[33]

31 *Ibid., Springfield Union*, November 13, 1873.
32 Letter in Harvard Library Collection of William Dean Howells's correspondence.
33 "A New Utopia," *New York Tribune*, February 5, 1888.

Where could there be a clearer case of the pursuit of a conscious, deliberate aim, and its successful achievement? Where could there be a clearer refutation of the shallow criticism by the literary elite, such as appeared in the *Critic:*

Mr. Bellamy's success as a writer was purely accidental. He was barely known to the public when his story, *Looking Backward,* was published. . . . It attained the largest sale ever reached by any American novel, with the one exception of *Uncle Tom's Cabin.* The story is entirely imaginative and altogether improbable, but it fell in with a popular sentiment. . . . It is very doubtful whether Mr. Bellamy intended the book to be taken as seriously as it was, but there is no doubt but that in the end he himself took it as seriously as his most ardent admirer. . . . A little thought proved to the wiser of his followers that Mr. Bellamy's theories were Utopian, and now they are almost forgotten.[34]

Running through the book reviews in the *Springfield Union* are many hints that the young reviewer not only is passing on the gist of a story to the public, but that he himself is appraising it as a literary creation. Of one author he says, "Instead of stopping at the final denouement of the story and letting the curtain fall, the writer must needs produce a perfect anti-climax by adding a half page of dry facts telling how the parties 'all lived in peace and died in grease,' as the children's stories say. This is a mistake a good many novelists commit. . . . The object of the novelist is to leave a vivid impression on the reader's mind, leaving it, as it were, in a state of tension." [35] In another review he wrote, "Mr. S. R. Crocker, the editor and publisher [of the *Literary World*] . . . writes about the book he has in hand, and does not use its title merely as a signboard on which to display his own wit and learning, as is the way of some critics." [36]

His discussion of literary criticism in the daily press shows a sense of responsibility, both for the public taste and for the author being reviewed:

. . . An affectation for smartness will . . . spoil the critical perception for anything beyond a joke or a fling. So there is danger in dulling the power of tasting the real quality of an author through a habit of

[34] "The Late Mr. Bellamy," *Critic,* XXXII, No. 849 (May 28, 1898), 362.
[35] "Literary Notices," *Springfield Union,* March 5, 1874.
[36] *Ibid.,* February 5, 1873.

dogmatic judging. . . . There is a microscopic criticism that sometimes runs itself, instead of the game it is chasing, into the ground. . . . There is much danger in such attempts of substituting for just canons of criticism some pet notions or literary habits of one's own, forgetting that there is a considerable liberty of usage about many things in the republic of letters. . . . Too much caustic in the delicate and often provoking tasks of the critical art is not wholesome nor just, except to inflict capital punishment upon the self-convicted culprits who really deserve the extremity of the law.[37]

We have various bits of evidence as to how Edward Bellamy went about his own writing. Mrs. Bellamy relates that he worked very painstakingly. His brothers Frederick and Charles would say: "There is no sense in your being so painstaking and spending so much time. Why don't you write it and get it over with?" The Reverend R. E. Bisbee, a neighbor and devoted friend of his later years, has given us an intimate picture of the process:

He was a most laborious, painstaking writer. His style was not an inspiration, but the result of the severest application. His first draft was never satisfactory. His early books were written in his father's study at his father's desk. As he wrote he would drop the finished sheets on the floor. One after another they would rapidly fall until the floor was nearly covered; then on his knees he would gather them up and arrange them. After this followed the sternest criticism. The manuscript was interlined, crossed out, sometimes entirely destroyed, and all done over again. Four, six, eight, and even ten times he revised the work, reversing the order of sentences, rearranging paragraphs, changing words, searching for days for the exact term, until at length he was satisfied . . . This method he continued to the end.[38]

He had no orderly habits in his work, but "wrote all over the house, in parlor, dining room, living room, and in his study." Joseph Orr, a former workman in the plant of the Ames Sword Company, said that while *Equality* was being written, two or three times a week from his window he would see Edward Bellamy walking along a railroad track that went by the plant, with his head down as though in deep thought, and with his hands behind his back holding papers. Sometimes he would stand still for perhaps ten minutes. Then he

[37] "Some Words about Criticism," *Springfield Union*, November 7, 1874.
[38] R. E. Bisbee, "Some Characteristics of Edward Bellamy," pp. 181–82.

would sit down beside the track and write for ten or fifteen minutes.

His notebooks, especially the earlier ones, indicate that he was constantly practicing his art. One bundle of manuscript of the unfinished book, "Eliot Carson," which was preserved from destruction is an illustration of this practice. There are many trial approaches to the theme. Of some portions there are half a dozen versions. For the plot as a whole there are several alternatives. One feels a gradual approach to unity and mastery.

We have referred to the fact that Bellamy wrote chiefly from his personal experience. Many of his stories have their locations in a village like his own, often referred to as "Hilton," and the characters are like the people he knew. His stories are interesting not in spite of this custom but because of it. This trait appears in his notebooks, which contain many notes, commonly from his own range of experience, to be used in writing short stories.

In the letter to William Dean Howells in 1884 he makes it clear that this habit of writing from intimate knowledge is not the result of following the line of least resistance, but was a conscious achievement. He also wrote in the language of his audience. One can read all of his books without meeting such a formidable word as *autochthonous*, yet it had the exact meaning he wished to express and he used it in that letter to Howells.

That Bellamy was enormously versatile in his reading and in his interests there can be no doubt. Yet in *Looking Backward* and *Equality* there is no ostentation of versatility. The few literary references are mostly to well-known sources—Shakespeare, Tennyson, the Bible. Bellamy digested and assimilated what he read, so that his writing does not consist of references or quotations, but of his own views stated directly. This simplicity and directness, together with a literary style so thoroughly mastered that the reader is almost unaware of it, is one reason why *Looking Backward* was very widely read.

Mrs. Bellamy said: "He had a faculty for adapting himself to the mental outlook of every kind of person with whom he came into contact. He never talked down to anyone. To a fireman he would talk shop, apparently interested more than anything else at the moment in the work he was doing."

William Dean Howells wrote of him:

Somehow, whether he *knew* or not, he unerringly *felt* how the average man would feel; and all the webs of fancy that he wove were essentially of one texture through this sympathy. His imagination was intensely democratic, it was inalienably plebeian, even,—that is to say, humane. It did not seek distinction of expression; it never put the simplest and plainest reader to shame by the assumption of those fine-gentleman airs which abash and dishearten more than the mere literary swell can think. He would use a phrase or a word that was common to vulgarity, if it said what he meant; sometimes he sets one's teeth on edge, in his earlier stories, by his public school diction. But the nobility of the heart is never absent from his work; and he has always the distinction of self-forgetfulness in his art.[39]

Little did Howells guess that this "public school diction" was in part an effort to "behave well in society," and that underneath the surface a seething rebellion was under way. The following from one of Bellamy's notebooks is dated April 1, 1874, just after his twenty-fourth birthday:

It is all well enough, by which I mean that it is cursed folly, to talk of the liberty of utterance in these days; but one hasn't got it. In Anglo-Saxon days when morality and tight-lacedness rule the roost there is no such thing as expression for the one half of human thought. The body in these latter straight cut days is covered to the chin and only the seven by nine patch of real skin called the face is left visible. So it is with the soul, so it is in literature. Only a conventional scope of ideas finds utterance. The rest are ignored. The great seething, storming, lusting, blaspheming soul of man is turned back on itself, and scarcely a foam fleck tosses over into the polite and proper world. It is as if the good folks thought that by refusing to see the ugly side of themselves, it would pine for lack of notice and after a while cease to exist. Great is their hooting and crying of shame and fie, fie when some fellow not in the secret of this famous strategy speaks unadvisedly of the truth. One is minded at thought of such contemptible self-hypocrisy, such elaborate self-deception, to give way to that passion for the nude in things of thought which impelled Rabelais, Swift, and in a less degree Carlyle. For God's sake off with these interminable veils and petticoats where-

---

[39] Howells, "Edward Bellamy," *Atlantic Monthly*, LXXXII (August, 1898), 254–55. Reprinted by permission of the publisher.

with ages of prudes have covered the antique strength and ruggedness of man's true nature. Let us for God's sake get at the truth, and have done with our ahs and ohs and qualms and queries.[40]

His mind came more than once to the theme of literary restraint and suppression, as is illustrated by an isolated paragraph in another of his notebooks: "What is this passion for the nude that sometimes overtakes all, and has wholly and permanently perverted some geniuses, as Swift. It leads one to tear off madly every garb of language, every haze of association, every abstraction of idea, burrowing for the boldest, barest, statement of the concrete fact. The study of this tendency opens up a philosophy." [41]

Edward Bellamy had a sincere interest in people, and a sympathy for them. He wanted to have commerce with their minds. In his book reviews he was provocative and sometimes controversial, for his business then was to incite people to think, not to lead them to any predetermined conclusion. In *Looking Backward* and *Equality*, where he desired unobstructed entrance to men's minds so that he could present his ideas in a friendly environment, we find him carefully refraining from the use of words and phrases against which society had deep-seated prejudices which, if aroused, would close the door to his message. He had learned that people come to have all sorts of barriers in their minds which prevent the entrance of ideas. People are not opposed so much to new ideas as to ideas which have acquired a bad reputation. If one can find an unguarded way past these barriers, he may discover an entrance. Edward Bellamy learned how to do this. People liked his ideas. Had they been presented under names currently obnoxious, they would have been abhorred.

In *Looking Backward* he had avoided associating his program with the current opinions of socialism. Shortly after its publication he wrote to William Dean Howells:

Every sensible man will admit that there is a big deal in a name, especially in making first impressions. In the radicalness of the opinions I have expressed I may seem to outsocialize the socialists, yet the word socialist is one I could never well stomach. It smells to the average American of petroleum, suggests the red flag and all manner of sexual

[40] Unpublished papers (B1-1-33).   [41] *Ibid.* (B2-4-9).

novelties, and an abusive tone about God and religion. . . . Whatever German and French reformers may choose to call themselves, socialist is not a good name for a party to succeed with in America.

Yet he was sincere in his approach. If there were some offensive associations in the hated names he discussed, elements to which he owed no allegiance, he felt no need for making them a hindrance to his undertaking.

Having gathered from his journals and newspaper editorials and reviews these fragments of his mind on the subject of writing, it may be interesting to note a few examples of his work of these early years, taken from the columns of the *Springfield Union*.

The books which he selected for review, though unusual and varied, were almost never trivial. They ranged all the way from seed catalogues, postal guides, and government statistics to the best of world literature. His reviews of books on history, economics, and even statistics, clearly show the interest which was to dominate his later life. His description of one author he was reviewing could be applied to himself: "He knows by the touch of it whether he grasps a substance or a shadow." [42] His range was in striking contrast to that of Bret Harte, whom he described by saying, "We know of no instance in literature when a writer of such real power has worked in so narrow a field." [43]

In some of these editorials and reviews the unusual range of this young man's mind and interests is evident:

Ninety-Three is the title of Victor Hugo's last novel. As he is now seventy-three years old, it may well prove to be the last we shall ever receive from his hand. A wonderful old man is he, indeed, who at this age still preserves enough of his old fire of enthusiasm, glow of imagination, and titanic grasp of language to make this child of his old age worthy to rank with the great novels of his youth and maturity. . . . The style of Victor Hugo, at once as intense and tragic as that of Carlyle, and marked by French clearness, is peculiarly adapted to the subject . . .

There is scarcely a reform in the legislation of the nineteenth century that was not suggested in the French convention. This enormous

[42] "Literary Notices," *Springfield Union*, October 12, 1875.
[43] *Ibid.*, November 20, 1875.

fertility and originality of conception can only be understood by realizing that the French mind was, at this time, in such a state of ferment, stimulation and enthusiasm, as is only comparable to the creative frenzy of the poet or the artist. As a single intimation of how complete a misapprehension of the character of the French revolution is that which chiefly regards its excesses is the fact that out of the eleven thousand two hundred and ten decrees which emanated from the French convention, two-thirds had a purely humane aim, and but one-third a purely political aim. . . . Concerning the style of Victor Hugo, we need say little. It is familiar to the reading public. It takes the imagination by storm, piling up pictures, extravagant similes, intense epithets, epigrams. You may condemn his style as exaggerated, contorted, frenzied; no matter, he accomplishes his end, he paints upon your imagination the pictures he desires. His short, sharp sentences like darts, transfix the attention. Does he meet a difficulty of expression, he hurls sentences at it from every side, he redoubles the vivacity of his assaults, he avails himself of every possible simile, every possible trick of language to approximate expression and at last he does it. Perhaps we may better express his peculiar mode by saying that, with him, when the difficulty of expression is greatest his sentences grow shorter, instead of longer, as with other writers. He succeeds not by circumspect and steady effort, but by dint of vivacity and variety of attempts.[44]

This review was written in April, 1874, when Bellamy was twenty-four. Two years later another review appeared which illustrates Bellamy's sustained interest in French life and literature. It is quoted at length because it is fully representative of his work of that period:

One of the most notable books of the season is the *Ancien Régime,* the latest work of the eminent French social and literary critic, Hippolyte Taine. The translator, Mr. John Durand, has performed his work with high excellence . . . The French expression "Ancien Régime" implies not only an old regime, but a special regime, a particular historical epoch; to wit, the state of French society in the centuries preceding the French Revolution. It may be very much doubted if so fascinating a chapter of modern history exists. Beyond question the polite world of France at that period was a unique form of human culture, both in its good and bad aspects, without precedent, and very possibly never to be repeated. At that time the intellect, the wealth, the refinement of a great nation was wholly confined to a circle of some thirty thousand noble families, to whom life was a play, enjoyment the sole end of it,

44 *Ibid.,* April 3, 1874.

and the cultivation of the aesthetics of society the only occupation. At no time before or since has social intercourse, as a source of stimulation and pleasure, been so perfected. At no time, except perhaps among the Luculluses of the declining Roman empire, enormous and concentrated, has wealth so gilded existence for a limited class, and so wholly raised it above all contact with the sordid necessities of existence. Whatever may be our sentiments of horror at the popular tyranny on which this splendid superstructure rested, it is quite impossible for the most zealous philanthropist not to feel admiration at so beautiful, so unique a phase of existence. The ancien régime was indeed a gorgeous and beautiful flower, growing upon a fermenting compost heap of popular degradation, misgovernment, and oppression. Add to this the rare fascination which the picture of a civilization so utterly different from our modern democratic era must possess, by very force of contrast, for modern readers, and it is evident that few themes present finer opportunities than this which M. Taine has essayed. And he has proved equal to it. The wonderful clearness of methodical arrangement, the skill with which the subject is developed, combined with the sustained vigor of treatment and the rich and picturesque language, create a vivid and complete tableau of the manners and morals of the epoch. The careful portraits of the leading men of the age, the chapters of carefully selected and skillfully woven excerpts from contemporary letters, the pages on pages of brief and striking details and statistics illustrative of the times, not less than the broad philosophical grasp of the great tendencies of the period, are among the features of this admirable work that cannot be too highly commended. It may be doubted if M. Taine has, on the whole, written anything so likely to meet universal acceptance from the critics as this book.[45]

Bellamy was not uncritical of French literature. He wrote: "There are two sorts of French novels, the immoral and the moral. In the former the heroine commits adultery, in the latter she comes as near to it as she can and miss it. Victor Cherbuliez writes the latter sort. His heroine often comes pretty near tripping, but generally maintains a precarious perpendicularity."[46] He seemed to have a sensitiveness to good literature, and caught great writers of all lands as they were emerging. We find penetrating appraisals of numerous writers of the day, including Turgenieff, Henry James, Dumas, George Eliot, Browning, and Bulwer Lytton. Some of the reviews rise to the level of real literature. Bellamy's column

---

[45] *Ibid., Springfield Union,* April 29, 1876.
[46] *Ibid.,* May 15, 1875.

was not confined to fiction. Sometimes he drags statistics and sociology into a literary review, as in pursuing his interest in English agricultural labor:

Jonathan is Mrs. Fraser Tytler's last novel. The author's special forte is in the description of English village life among the lowest social grades of the population. She delves for her material in lower strata than any English novelist we know of. For example, in this story the characters are English agricultural laborers, a class which in England is as ignorant and miserable as any peasantry of Europe, the poorest of whom live like cattle, and the best not so well off as the most shiftless of American workmen. Jonathan, the hero of this tale, having a trade, is better off than his fellows, but he earns only fourteen shillings, from three to four dollars a week. And yet he is made the successful rival of a rich brewer for the affections of a young lady of refinement. This is in the highest degree improbable if English human nature is the ordinary article. Not, of course, that a man's worth has necessarily any relation to his wealth, but excessive poverty implies such differences of social habits and mental atmosphere as generally preclude intimacy with those in another grade of life. . . .[47]

The comment in this review, that people hesitate to marry below themselves in the social scale because lack of cultural advantages results in crudeness which it is difficult for a person of culture to endure, is a frequent theme of Bellamy, and one of his arguments for economic equality.

There are frequent light touches to his work:

Chaucer couldn't spell. Shakespeare couldn't spell. Milton couldn't spell. Lord Bacon couldn't spell. Or rather, they were luxuriant spellers. They spelled their words as an apple tree blossoms. The vigor of their spiritual and intellectual life proved itself by their spelling. Happy men! There were no dictionaries in those days. People supposed that ideas were important then—and loved the notions that came by words, not the letters with which the words were made. When they were in a hurry they wrote the words short, and when they had plenty of time they wrote them long. . . .[48]

At the age of twenty-three he wrote, "Bulwer is not naturally a cynic, and never learned to make his characters sneer well."[49] In another review we find the comment: "Curious lights slipping through the windows of diaries and letters—broken and fitful cross-

[47] *Ibid.*, March 2, 1876.   [48] *Ibid.*, July 22, 1875.
[49] *Ibid.*, April 29, 1873.

lights they often are—tell us more about the real characters and habits of notable persons than we can get out of the more formal and high stepping biography. . . ." [50]

Bellamy himself could spell, but he could not punctuate; or he punctuated as the spirit moved him. Sometimes he scattered commas along the way in his sentences with apparent unconcern as to where they might fall. At other times he wrote whole pages with no punctuation whatever. Sometimes, but rarely, he punctuated with precision, as though he had learned from the King James Bible. In quoting him, punctuation has been changed only to supply the rudiments, and when there seemed to be no doubt as to the meaning intended.

The nature of the writings from which quotations have been taken should be kept in mind in judging the literary quality of Edward Bellamy. The notebooks and scraps of manuscript were written mostly as reminders to himself or as first drafts. Many are in a hurried scrawl, intended to be read only by himself, and are almost illegible. In some cases it has been necessary to omit passages because some parts could not be deciphered. (A mass of miscellaneous manuscripts, which never have been deciphered, have been placed in the Harvard College Library, where they are available for further delving.)

Some of his book reviews and editorials seem to be fully representative of his best style, while others are but his "best under the circumstances." He seems to have been the member of the staff on the *Springfield Union* to be called on when the paper was short of copy. Tradition pictures, as a not uncommon state of affairs, a messenger boy standing at Bellamy's office door waiting for a few more sheets of copy, and then rushing with them to the typesetter, where together they would try to decipher Bellamy's hieroglyphics. That they did not always succeed is clearly evident in cases where a word which was printed is similar in spelling but entirely different in meaning from that required by the context. Also there are the usual number of printer's errors, and the obviously improvised punctuation of the typesetter.

That these miscellaneous quotations from such sources have considerable literary quality is testimony to Bellamy's mastery of

[50] "Sidelights," *Springfield Union,* February 18, 1875.

expression. Those who knew him say that in speaking he had sure, unfaltering diction, very seldom needing to interrupt, correct, or revise a sentence after he had begun to speak.

Apparently no small part of the reading matter of the *Springfield Union* came from his pen. Frequently book reviews and literary comments were moved over into the editorial column. So full of philosophy, social theory, economics, and sound comment are Edward Bellamy's reviews that it is with regret one draws the curtain and consigns the remainder to oblivion. We can perform that ceremony no better than by quoting his own words:

There is no help for it, that about all the majority of the people of the next generation will know of past authorships they must get from such samples of it as can be put into . . . "Little Classics" and similar selections. The day of complete editions of voluminous writers seems to be going by. This may be unfortunate, but it appears to be unavoidable. One age cannot wear another's garments. . . . All which can be saved of the past is the kernel of its peculiar power: its law is to perish, therefore transfuse the delicate spirit, so far as this was immortal, into the present. Forward, not backward, is the law of life and work. . . . But whoever undertakes the task of expressing their quintessence and putting it up for modern use, let it be done with the care and skill with which Eastern maidens imprison the attar of roses.[51]

When in the fall of 1877 Edward Bellamy's health failed and he went with his brother Frederick on a four or five months' trip to Hawaii, he resigned his position on the *Springfield Union*. His six years of newspaper writing had not been routine work. He had been giving his best. The conviction is expressed in one of his notebooks, apparently written in his early twenties: ". . . that a man may safely at all times say forth the best that is in him and save nothing through fear he should exhaust the fertility of his soul. For the soul is not comparable to the earth that can be exhausted, but it is joined on to the illimitable, inexhaustible sea of the universal illimitable soul, that fears not exhaustion. Therefore speak forth; every spoken inspiration is a relief that makes room for a new supply." [52] He was, in fact, achieving that mastery of style which led Sylvester Baxter to say of him:

[51] "Literature in Samples," *Springfield Union,* November 26, 1875.
[52] Unpublished papers (B1-2-20).

Bellamy's style is of the kind that makes one forget style: direct and clear; imbued with a crystalline quality that so perfectly transmits the life of the mind as to leave one unconscious of the medium until, perhaps, one chances to come into a position that reveals some rare prismatic effect. It could not be strange, therefore, that the mere literary connoisseur, devoted to the art of verbal kaleidoscopy and occupied with ingenious dispositions of embroidered phraseology, should pronounce his work uninteresting. But regarding words as merely vehicles for thought, and not thought as mainly serving as a string for the display of beaded words, our author's style appears a model one. . . . Nevertheless, his words often have a rare beauty of eloquence, fitly conveying a power of earnestness and lofty spirituality—the true beauty of style, where beauty is imparted by the overshadowing thought.[53]

Bellamy had made his years of writing to be years of training, until, as Baxter continues: "Literary beauty of this kind is as unintentional as that of the wild flowers with which Nature strews her mantle. It is to be found in whatever Bellamy does, however offhand; he does not hoard his gems for literary state display." [54]

His second book was written before he was thirty. William Dean Howells wrote of it:

The first book of Edward Bellamy's which I read was *Dr. Heidenhoff's Process,* and I thought it one of the finest feats in the region of romance which I had known. It seemed to me all the greater because the author's imagination wrought in it on the level of average life, and built the fabric of its dream out of common clay. . . . The art employed to accomplish its effect was the art which Bellamy had in degree so singular that one might call it supremely his.[55]

As to Bellamy's literary characters, Howells wrote, ". . . he never falsifies them or their circumstance . . . you would think at times that he had never known, never seen, any others; but of course this is only the effect of his art. . . . One cannot acquaint one's self with his merely artistic work, and not be sensible that in Edward Bellamy we were rich in a romantic imagination surpassed only by that of Hawthorne." [56]

---

[53] Sylvester Baxter, "The Author of *Looking Backward," New England Magazine,* n.s., I (September, 1889), 94–95. [54] *Ibid.*
[55] William Dean Howells, "Edward Bellamy," *Atlantic Monthly,* LXXXII (August, 1898), 253–54.
[56] *Ibid.,* pp. 255–56.

VIII · The Philosopher

IF an impartial appraisal should be made of the inherent quality of the thinking and writing of Edward Bellamy it is possible that first place would be given, not to his utopia or to his other writings on political economy, but to those which would be classified best under the heading of philosophy. It is here that the greatest vigor and originality of his mind appears. To include these writings in his biography, much as they throw light on the quality of his mind, would be to overburden this volume. They are therefore being published separately,[1] and only a brief résumé can be given here.

Bellamy's most imposing single piece of writing in the field of philosophy is a fragment called "The Religion of Solidarity," written when he was twenty-four years old. In this he attempted to state to himself his concept of the nature of things, of the nature of life, and of man's relation to the whole. He introduces his theme with such expressions as the following:

Continually does the spirit in man betray affinity with nature by vague and seemingly purposeless longings to attain a more perfect sympathy with it. So far as this universal and strongly marked instinct can be distinctly interpreted, it indicates in human nature some element common with external nature, toward which it is attracted, as with the attraction of a part toward a whole. . . . This restless and discontented element is not at home in the personality. . . . It is homesick for a vaster mansion than the personality affords, with an unconquerable yearning, a divine discontent tending elsewhither.

. . . . .

Now who can doubt that the human soul has more in common with that life of all time and all things toward which it so eagerly goes out, than with that narrow, isolated, and incommodious individuality, the thrall of time and space, to which it so reluctantly, and with such a sense of belittlement and degradation, perforce returns?

. . . . .

[1] *The Philosophy of Edward Bellamy*, with comments by Arthur E. Morgan (New York, King's Crown Press, 1944).

What, then, is the view of human nature thus suggested? On the one hand is the personal life, an atom, a grain of sand on a boundless shore, a bubble on a foam-flecked ocean. . . . On the other hand is a certain other life, as it were a spark of the universal life, insatiable in aspiration, greedy of infinity, asserting solidarity with all things and all existence.

. . . .

Such is the estate of man, and such his dual life. . . . This dual life, personal and impersonal, as individual and as universal, goes far to explain the riddle of human nature and of human destiny.

. . . .

Our little wells are filled from this eternal life; our souls are not islands in the void, but peninsulas forming one continent of life within the universe. . . . The dual existence of man is at once infinite, and infinitesimal and particular.

The paper is in pursuit of that theme. The universal and the individual lives may be compared to centripetal and centrifugal forces in celestial mechanics:

The instinct of universal solidarity, of the identity of our life with all lives, is the centripetal force which binds together in certain orbits all orders of beings. . . . The fact of individuality with its tendency to particularizations is the centrifugal force which hinders the universal fusion, and preserves the variety in unity which seems the destined condition of being. Thus these mutually balancing forces play each its necessary part.

Although "The Religion of Solidarity" is immature and unfinished, the theme is developed with a sweep of imagination, a fineness of feeling, and sometimes with a beauty of expression which are marks of a mind of rare quality. His proposals seem to accord with what we feel concerning the nature of things, and to ring true to experience.

Like many world leaders, Edward Bellamy had first to achieve for himself a picture of the whole and of his place in it before he could whole-heartedly commit himself to a particular life program. The result of his quest was a philosophy which served as an adequate basis for his life, a stimulus to great effort, and justification for a sense of human dignity.

In "The Religion of Solidarity" Bellamy dealt with the relation of man to the universe. In another field, that of the relations of a man with himself, his thinking was even more original and no less significant. Growing up in a Calvinist environment, Bellamy became aware of the New England phase of a world-wide and age-old incubus of the human spirit, the excessive sense of guilt.

One of the greatest contributions of Christianity was the partial liberation it provided from the sense of guilt or of nemesis. Those who criticize Christianity in this respect are unaware of the more sinister cast of thought of pre-Christian Greece and Palestine, and of most ancient peoples. Even where people have consciously thrown off the doctrines of Catholicism and Calvinism, the shadow still remains.

Bellamy attacked this problem with a freshness of outlook and with a penetrating observation that are rare. His notebooks and his published writings disclose the gradual emergence of a clear philosophy which, if it should become generally current, might make a greater contribution than did Freud in a somewhat parallel field. Because Bellamy's expressions on this subject were fragmentary, often presented in fiction form, and because the current of public interest was not running in that direction, the public never realized what he was driving at, or the conclusions he had reached. If the full implications of his thinking should become recognized, it is possible that they would be no less significant than his writings in the field of political economy, and the resulting liberation of men's spirits from a sense of dread and fear might be as refreshing as liberation from economic exploitation.

Another related subject which Bellamy touched upon repeatedly is implied in his frequently used phrase, "the economy of happiness." Men have long observed the ephemeral nature of happiness. Bellamy believed that a maximum of the sense of well-being can result only from insight and design in dealing with human nature. He would study the biological nature and the possibilities of happiness as one would study the nature of economic well-being. This theme commanded only fragments of his attention, but some of his comments are very suggestive.

Ralph Waldo Emerson wrote in the American idiom and seemed to smell of the very earth of America. His countrymen took his philosophy and wove it into the texture of the national thinking. No other American philosopher has so deeply influenced his people. Little did Americans realize that through the medium of their homely speech Emerson was transmitting to them the philosophy of ancient India. So, without our realizing what was happening, much of the wisdom of the ancient East became native to us. Emerson was not the only American who thus helped to give his countrymen this great inheritance. Of his townsmen, Henry Thoreau and Bronson Alcott contributed to the process.

The same is true of Edward Bellamy. As to how he possessed himself of the thinking of India we do not know. He seems to have had sources other than Emerson and Thoreau. Be that as it may, there runs through Bellamy's writing a strain of thinking which could seem to have no other source. And he was no mean agent for transmitting the values of the East.

Apparently without any clear definition of such intent, Edward Bellamy's thinking dealt with all the major relationships of his life. In "The Religion of Solidarity" and other writings he was concerned with man's relation to the universe; in treating of the subject of nemesis and of "the economy of happiness" he was considering man's relation with himself; in *Looking Backward*, in *Equality*, and in miscellaneous writings he dealt with men's relations with their fellows. Without any effort to construct these products of his thinking into a "system," as is the old weakness of European philosophers, he did outline the major problems of men and dealt with them in such a way that, taking his writings all together, they form a harmonious and unified whole.

IX · Sources of "Looking Backward"

The Times of Edward Bellamy

The social and economic stresses of the period during which Edward Bellamy lived had two general causes. First was a growing rebellion against the ancient order of society in which those who had power exploited those who had not. From the beginning of feudal society and power politics most men in power had looked upon their fellows, at least upon those not members of the ruling class or group, as tools to use or as obstacles to surmount. The possibility of challenging this old order had been increased by the extension of printing and the general dissemination of information, by the scientific attitude which was shattering old foundations of thinking, by a tendency of religion to escape from dogma and to become a way of life, by discoveries and inventions which were revolutionizing methods of production, and by the increase of opportunity which came with the opening up of new lands.

But in addition to growing rebellion against the old order of master and servant, the troubles of society were due partly to what might be called social indigestion or social immaturity. Also, as Bellamy repeatedly pointed out, a great surge of reform and idealism from 1820 to 1860 was largely damped out and to a great degree extinguished by the American Civil War. The centralization of economic power which developed during and immediately after that conflict was accompanied by the blunting of ethical motives which war usually brings about. As the industrial revolution gained full momentum at the close of the Civil War, it was largely haphazard and planless. Improved machinery and more extensive organization were adopted item by item, with no definite conception of what they implied.

From 1780 to 1880 the population of Europe increased from 110,000,000 to 315,000,000, such an increase as the world seldom if ever saw before. What hope was there of improving social conditions, thought the followers of Malthus, with this expanding horde taking up all the ground that was gained by technical progress and with men being reduced again to the bare margin of subsistence? In Europe steam power increased from 2,240,000 horsepower in 1850 to 22,000,000 in 1880, again such an expansion of mechanical power as the world never had known. World production of steel increased from 6,100,000 tons for the decade 1850–1860 to 68,000,000 tons for the decade 1880–1890.[1] In America the rate of increase of steam power and of steel production was almost as great. This was world revolution indeed. The problems would have been staggering, even with a far greater degree of unselfish public spirit.

Enormous growth of cities contributed to the confusion. Many millions of men on farms or in small communities saw hope for better living in the industrial centers. The economy of large power plants and of centralized administration, and all the convenience of city facilities, increased this movement. Men poured into cities in such overwhelming numbers as to bring general maladjustment. As has always been the case, the number of men who preferred the city had no relation to the number needed to make it operate at its best. They multiplied services in order to get footholds for living. There were many more stores, churches, laundries, undertakers, laborers, lawyers, and politicians than were needed. Instead of coming to the cities as they were needed, or starting new cities with just the necessary services in good proportion, which would have been a wholesome process, they chose the prestige and special advantages of great centers, and blamed the social order if there was no good place for them.

Very few men had any clear concept of the efficient and wholesome organization of society, and those few were not easily distinguished from the host of false prophets. In view of the prevailing ignorance of economics and sociology and of the rapid and enormous changes of conditions, such a concept of a good society could be gained by the public or by its actual leaders only through a long period of years and with much fumbling and error, sometimes on

[1] Max Beer, *Social Struggles and Modern Socialism,* pp. 122–23.

a vast scale. Thus the troubles of this explosively expanding society were partly inherent.

Under the circumstances, the rudimentary and hand-to-mouth economy which actually prevailed was far from the worst of possible courses. Unselfishness, patience, and good will might have very greatly reduced the stresses, but could not quickly have eliminated them. In the general absence of understanding of the vast changes taking place, premature stabilization might have been worse than groping and conflict. Various efforts to make ideal communities, even when inspired by social motives and led by men of unusual ability, sometimes had worse results than the rough-and-tumble of capitalistic enterprise. It was an unprecedented new world, and no one knew well how to handle it in the general public interest.

As is common in such cases, there was widespread effort to put the blame on some class. Much social energy was expended in efforts to locate the culprit. One is reminded of efforts at the close of the World War in 1918 to simplify the centuries-old problem of international relations into a demand to "hang the Kaiser." Folkways or great movements have men in their grip. Reacting with primitive emotions rather than with critical inquiry, men attack each other blindly with rage and hate. The results are inquisitions, wars, class struggles, and numberless other conflicts. These are aggravated in times of great maladjustment.

When *Looking Backward* was written, American life was especially full of such stresses. While there was lack of definiteness in public policy, the special influences of private interests were strong in government. The panic of 1873 had brought widespread hardship and unemployment. Everywhere there were strikes, with disappointment and discontent on the part of much of the population, alongside of hope, ambition, prosperity, pride of workmanship. There was also a large degree of satisfying results of thrift, competence, and hard work, and a sense of success on the part of workers and others who were fortunately placed. Immigrants from Europe poured in at an average rate of more than half a million a year for thirty years from 1880 to 1910, adding about eighty per cent as many persons as the entire population of 1850, and making natural social readjustment more difficult.[2]

Public control of utilities was scarcely begun. Big businesses were giants without a master. Such possible controls as the new Interstate Commerce Commission they denounced as sinister and as infringements on the rights of private capital. The suggestion of "parcel post" was combatted as socialistic. "Radical infringements on the rights of capital and of business," such as those later represented by the Federal Trade Commission, the Federal Power Commission, the Federal Communications Commission, and the Securities and Exchange Commission, would have been certain evidence to bankers and orthodox economists that the country was going to the dogs.

The country was in almost unconscious transition from a decentralized, largely rural economy to a highly complex, industrial economy under increasing government control. Conservatives did not see how the industry of the country could continue to prosper if it were not left "free," and radicals did not see how civilized society could continue with private property, especially in natural monopolies and natural resources. The course which has since been taken in bringing private industry under public control, by which, for instance, the great octopus of the railroad has been made quite tame, was not anticipated by either radicals or conservatives and would have been vehemently rejected by both.

Many railroad companies were exploiting, gambling, plunging. Some with well-intentioned bad judgment were becoming hopelessly involved. For instance, the Northern Pacific Railroad, honestly and substantially built with solid, permanent bridges, good grades, and finely constructed locomotives, had greater investment than its pioneer territory justified, whereupon it went bankrupt and was captured by the Great Northern Railroad, which was built on an almost hand-to-mouth basis with temporary pile bridges, steep grades, and cheap locomotives with babbitt bearings, as contrasted to the fine brass bearings of Northern Pacific locomotives. The Great Northern, built and operated with hard-headed Scotch thrift,

[2] *The World Almanac and Encyclopedia* (1943), pp. 508, 623.

was fitted to its pioneer work, and made money. Years later the honestly administered United States Reclamation Service, by "building solidly for the future," laid such heavy burdens on its settlers that a large part of them failed. As a rule, only after three settlers had failed in succession on a Reclamation project farm did the fourth settler, inheriting the results of his predecessors' bitter toil, make a success. Good intentions and honest work were not enough, in either government or private industry, without accurate judgment as to justifiable expenditures.

But in many business promotions even good intention was often lacking. Some of the railroad systems were promoted with sheer financial irresponsibility, as in case of those controlled by Jay Gould. The railroads had lawyers in every community of any size. They dominated legislatures, maintained corruption funds, controlled courts, and often were quite outside the law. The general investor received small returns on his railroad securities, but some insiders made great fortunes. Industries were discouraged in Western communities so that railroads could have long hauls from the East. Trusts and combinations were multiplying enormously, and their controls were not yet evident.

Meantime labor was becoming organized and industrial strife was rampant. During 1885 and 1886, when Bellamy began writing *Looking Backward*, industrial strife was so frequent and violent that the period has been called "the great upheaval." The Haymarket violence in Chicago, on May 4, 1886, is sometimes referred to as the beginning of conscious class struggle in America. It served to discredit radical movements for years. Iron and steel manufacturers were importing shiploads of cheap labor from Europe, men who had little if any knowledge of or interest in American institutions, and in that way the rising "American standard of living" was partly broken. Personal expenditures of the wealthy were flauntingly ostentatious.

Those who held high place in the industrial system of the country were well pleased with their handiwork. James T. George draws attention to an expression of Andrew Carnegie in the latter's book *Triumphant Democracy*, which was published less than two years before *Looking Backward*. This is somewhat characteristic of what

Americans were being told about themselves by their industrial leaders:

The superlative form of adjectives has been so often applied to America when contrasted with other lands, that many a foreign reader, who now for the first time realizes the magnitude and greatness of the Republic, may not unnaturally begin to feel dubious about it all. He may be inclined to believe that it is not a veritable nation to which such magnificent attributes are ascribed, but some fabled land of Atlantis. Nevertheless it is all real and true. The Republic is surely, as we have already seen, the largest, most populous, wealthiest nation in the world, and also the greatest agricultural, pastoral and manufacturing nation. . . . No party in America desires a change in any of the fundamental laws. If asked what important laws I should change, I must perforce say none; *the laws are perfect.*

. . . .

There is not one shred of privilege to be met with anywhere in all the laws. One man's right is every man's right. The flag is the guarantor and symbol of equality.[3]

The farmers of the West were especially heavily burdened by the high cost of farm machinery and by high freight rates to distant markets. The great expanse of free land afforded to incompetent men one of those opportunities which infrequently come their way for a new, fresh chance along with other men, a chance some will use by making themselves competent, but that many are almost bound to lose as soon as any real test comes. Many of the men who went West to farm had never succeeded at anything, were undisciplined, untrained, and lacked the slowly developed tradition of good farming. Many of their farms became mortgaged and were lost, for which they blamed the government and the trusts. Many others by thrift and good management became well-to-do while their neighbors were failing. Among those who succeeded were occasional city workers, sailors, miners, and forest workers of Europe who knew nothing of farming, but who had stamina and intelligence.

Following the classic paper of Frederick Jackson Turner on *The Significance of the Frontier in American History*, it has become a habit of some American sociologists to see "the end of the fron-

---

[3] Andrew Carnegie, *Triumphant Democracy*, p. 204. Reprinted by permission of the publisher.

tier"—that is, the exhaustion of large areas of free land, which occurred at about the time *Looking Backward* was written—as a substantial reduction of opportunity for the common man. This doctrine sometimes is overworked. Only certain types of men were suited to pioneering. For other types the exhaustion of free land coincided with vast expansion of opportunity in other fields.

Another influence tended to bring pioneering to an end—an increasingly high standard of living which made hard pioneer life seem unacceptable. Before free land was approximately exhausted in the West, there was taking place in the Northeast a widespread abandonment of farms because of the greater opportunity in the West and in industry. Even today there still remain many opportunities for pioneering on the land far more favorable than those under which New England was settled.

The hardness of pioneering may be gauged from the fact that hordes of men who left New England farms to work in factories twelve hours a day for a dollar a day were improving themselves economically. A pioneer Minnesota farmer would work himself and his entire family twelve hours a day or more for a total cash income of $200 a year or less, from which he must pay for taxes and for farm machinery, as well as for clothes, doctor's bills, and incidentals.

The New England or Adirondack farmer had dug out a life for himself by prodigious labor on his rocky hills. Now, in Bellamy's day, those farms were being abandoned by the thousands. With fields cleared, with timber and stones removed by unending heavy muscular work, with well-built houses and barns, with stone fences, wells, apple orchards, and roads already secured, much less effort was required to keep such a farm going than to create it. Manufacturing towns provided a market which did not exist before. Though wheat and corn could not be raised in competition with the West, seasonable crops were feasible and, except as land taxes increased, subsistence farming was no less possible than formerly. Yet larger opportunity and the spirit of the times made such life seem no longer worth while. The frontier partly but not entirely disappeared; partly it became unattractive.

Thus we see that with the far-reaching changes which were taking place, the mass results of individual motives, acting in the lives of millions of individual men, made unexpected social stresses of great intensity which were not understood. In view of these strains due to migration from country to city, immigration from abroad, inventions and technical developments, and the organization of vast industries, and in view of the prevailing economic illiteracy and inexperience of the population as a whole, it is remarkable that the political and economic structures remained as sound and flexible as events proved them to be. With the almost universal unpreparedness for understanding long-range trends and in the lack of any dependable design for society, the course taken by the political common sense of the people and their leaders had much of practical merit. It was as though men feeling their way in the early morning dusk through rough, unknown country were concerned with moving about enough to keep warm, and avoiding falling over a cliff at the next step, more than they were concerned with being sure they were traveling in the right general direction.

Such was the confused and surging national scene. Edward Bellamy's home city of Chicopee and the nearby cities and villages reflected many of these conditions. Chicopee, formed by the union of two villages, was changing from a trim New England community to a busy factory town. In his editorials in the *Springfield Union* Bellamy had discussed the steady drift from farm to factory. Immigrants from Europe were pouring in. An article on "The City of Chicopee" written in 1898 states:

The last considerable addition to our heterogeneous population are the Poles. They form a numerous part of the Babel chorus of tongues one hears on our streets. If their social status generally is not high, they are industrious and thrifty. Many read and write in their own language, and some of them have aspirations. . . . Their tenements are overcrowded. A Polish house is sure to be full. On the north side of the river at the Centre they are burrowing into the side-hills. They are gaining property; they are building homes and churches and establishing parochial schools, and some children are in the public schools.[4]

[4] Collins G. Burnham, "The City of Chicopee," *New England Magazine*, n.s., XVIII (May, 1898), 378.

In his editorials Bellamy wrote of pale-faced, ragged children being herded into the mills for long days of work. During his earlier years he saw mechanics and operatives working in the mills for twelve hours a day at nine cents an hour, and women working at about half that rate of pay. Even those hard lives were an improvement over what had gone before. Describing conditions at about the time of Edward Bellamy's birth, an article on "Old Time Factory Life in New England" in the *New England Magazine* tells of women receiving $1.00 to $2.25 a week and board for 12½ or 13 hours' work a day. The factory bell rang at 4:30 A. M. Work began at 5:00 A. M. and continued until 7:00 P. M., with half an hour each for breakfast and dinner. The writer of the article as a boy received $1.00 a week wages and $1.00 a week for board for 12½ hours' work a day in winter and 13 hours in summer.[5] The manager of an important factory at that time would receive perhaps $2,000 a year. During the seventies Edward Bellamy's father paid his household help the prevailing rate of $1.50 a week and board. In the eighties and nineties Edward Bellamy himself paid $3.00 a week and board. A visit to a woman who once had worked in his home found her to be a competent, vigorous, intelligent Englishwoman, who looked upon service in the Bellamy home as the brightest spot in her working life.

Such was the world which impelled the writing of *Looking Backward*, and the world from which Bellamy hoped to find a way to peace and plenty. He himself recognized that the success of his book was due partly to the active craving of the people of his day to find a way out of their confusion.

Such a compressed and partial description of a period has the effect of distortion. It is like a moving picture which shows a plant sprouting from the seed, growing, budding, blooming, and fading in a minute. That period probably was in less active change than is the present decade, and yet many men even today are unaware of being in the midst of a world revolution. For most men, life in those days went on "as usual," and only when listening to a political speech or reading such a book as *Looking Backward* did the average

[5] A. K. Fiske, "Old Time Factory Life in New England," *New England Magazine*, n.s., XVIII (April, 1898), 251, 252.

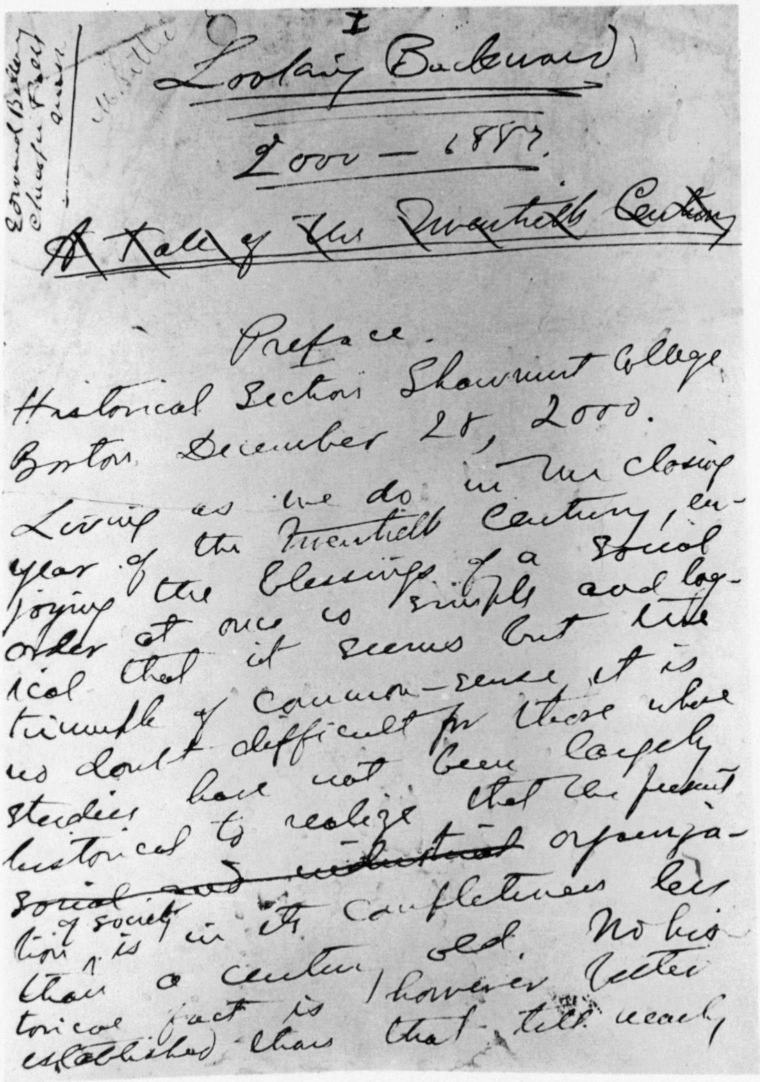
I

Looking Backward

2000 — 1887.

A Tale of the Twentieth Century

Preface.

Historical Section Shawmut College

Boston, December 28, 2000.

Living as we do in the closing year of the Twentieth Century, enjoying the blessings of a social order at once so simple and logical that it seems but the triumph of common-sense, it is no doubt difficult for those whose studies have not been largely historical to realize that the present ~~social and industrial~~ organization of society is in its completeness less than a century old. No historical fact is however better established than that till nearly

Edward Bellamy
Chicopee Falls
Mass.

First Page of the Manuscript of *Looking Backward*

man get outside himself and see himself as in the midst of profound and unprecedented changes.

THE LITERARY BACKGROUND

Millions of men who have read or have listened to the utopian words of Isaiah and the other prophets, describing a day when justice and good will shall rule among men, have been apathetic in the presence of that voice and vision. But on rare occasions one responds to the voice strongly and comes to have in himself the same passion which moved the prophets. Edward Bellamy was such a person, and it is reasonable to expect that the prophets' dreams of a better day which he heard so often as a boy were among the influences that shaped his life.

To most men those ancient forecasts—interesting, perhaps, to listen to at church—were but impractical dreams. What could be more chimerical than Isaiah's saying, "The wolf also shall dwell with the lamb"? It never could happen in fact, for that would require the changing of wolf nature. Yet long, long ago some mute, inglorious Isaiah undertook to do that very thing. He tamed a wolf, or a wild, wolflike animal, and through generations he and his descendants so developed its possibilities that not only did it dwell with the lambs, but became their dependable guardian, ready if necessary to give its life for their protection. Now the same breed of practical men who sneered at the foolishness of the idea accept shepherd dogs as a matter of course.

There gradually developed in the mind of Edward Bellamy the conviction that if human nature could have a great environment it would react nobly; that what men need most is not so much a great change in human nature as better patterns of living and thinking for determining the development of the "natures" they have. In forming that fundamental trait of Edward Bellamy's mind and spirit, the prophetic tradition probably was a major factor.

Among the influences which produced *Looking Backward*, along with the Biblical tradition, I believe we can place Plutarch's *Life of Lycurgus*. Bellamy was one of those writers who, like Shakespeare, almost never mentioned his sources, but read omnivorously, assimilated what he read, and then by a creative process put forth something which bore the mark of his genius. Not a single authority is mentioned in *Looking Backward*, and this is almost as true of *Equality*. However, the fragment of autobiography which he wrote at about the age of twenty-five indicates that Plutarch's *Lives* was one of his favorites.

His high regard for Plutarch continued so unabated that he endeavored to transmit it to his children. While they were still quite young he introduced both his son Paul and his daughter Marion to the unabridged *Lives*, which he urged on them with great enthusiasm.

There are numerous likenesses to the Sparta of Plutarch's *Lycurgus* in the social and political organization outlined in *Looking Backward*. Both provide for a governing group of elders, "appointed from above." Notwithstanding the persistent criticism of Gronlund and others, who held that democratic procedure required selection of officers from below, Bellamy never surrendered his position on this point. From *Lycurgus*, also, Bellamy could have taken his idea of equal division of property, and the practical elimination of money and of trade. One of the most vigorously criticized of Bellamy's policies was the semi-military organization of workers, which is a marked characteristic of the Spartan state as described in *Lycurgus*. Bellamy may have had this source also for the provision of common eating places. Both held to simple living. As in *Looking Backward*, *Lycurgus* pictures a society with but few laws, and dependence for order on the spirit of the people. Both picture an absence of lawsuits, with "neither avarice nor poverty." The central theme in each is that concern for the public good has displaced private business. In view of the wide dissemination of utopian thought and technique, and in the absence of more specific information, we cannot unqualifiedly assert that these common elements are due partly to Bellamy's reading of Plutarch, but there is very strong probability that such is the case.

We have noted that when he was about fourteen years old Edward Bellamy experienced religious "conversion," and he has recorded that for a time all his thoughts and all his reading ran to the theme of his religious life. As he turned to religious reading he had available on his father's bookshelves the sermons of his great-great-grandfather, Joseph Bellamy, who in his day was, next to Jonathan Edwards, the greatest preacher in New England. As the most famous name among Edward's ancestors, Joseph Bellamy was very familiar to him. Now it happens that Joseph Bellamy himself, rock-ribbed Calvinist that he tried to be, nevertheless at times broke loose from that rigorous temper and dreamed his own utopias. Since the book was on his father's shelves (the stamped autograph of Rufus Bellamy is still on the flyleaf), it is probable that Edward Bellamy read the following from the sermon preached on election day, May 13, 1762, by Joseph Bellamy before the General Assembly of the Connecticut Colony:

To view beings and things as they are, and to be affected and act accordingly, is the sum of moral virtue. All moral virtue, is frequently in the sacred writings summed up in one thing, under one comprehensive name. . . . And thus LOVE is the name given to the whole, in that brief summary of the divine law given by our blessed Saviour, "Thou shalt *love* the Lord thy God with all thy heart:" and "Thou shalt *love* thy neighbour as thyself." Love is radically the whole of that duty which God requires of man.

Let us stop here, a few minutes, and think what the consequences would be, should righteousness . . . descend on crowned heads . . . and spread down through every rank . . .

Princes, even the most haughty monarchs of the earth, who, to gratify their pride and ambition, do often now, in the present state of things, summon mighty armies, spread war, devastation, and ruin, through whole countries, would be at once turned into other men . . . and . . . begin to concert measures for a universal, perpetual peace . . . every monarch, from the heart, would soon begin to say to each other, "Take your right, my brother, and let me have mine, and let us live in love and peace, and seek the true happiness of our subjects, and no longer go on sacrificing thousands of precious lives in quarrels which honest men might settle with the utmost ease."

And should righteousness . . . spread through all their royal families . . . from town to town, through all their dominions . . . into what a glorious and happy state would things be immediately brought! Look round upon all ranks and orders of men, and behold the glorious change!

Go to the clergy . . . they love their people . . . And ministers of choice give themselves wholly to their work . . .

Go to the merchants' shop, and you will find not only just weights and just measures, but also piety towards God and love to the human kind, diligence and industry, prudence in their calling . . .

Go to the house, the happy house of the industrious farmer . . . With alacrity and joy they go forth to their labours, and enjoy the delights of heaven in their fields, love and harmony reign within doors . . . hear the wise maxims of the household . . . "Let us be industrious and frugal, that we may be able to render to all men their dues. . . ."

Go into the neighbourhoods; malice and envy are gone; tattling and backbiting are no more heard. Love, undissembled love, and good-will, reign.

Go to courts of justice, and behold, they are unfrequented . . . And while they do as they would be done by, there seldom happens any affair, that needs to be disputed at the bar.

Go to the house of the Governor, who, as he was advanced to his high station merely on account of his merit; so he is the wisest man in the province . . . He is loved, revered, and obeyed by all his people . . . All the influence his high station, superior wisdom and goodness, give him over their hearts, is wholly consecrated to make them a still holier and happier people. . . .

Go to the taverns, and even they are houses of piety and good order . . . At these houses the stranger and the traveller may call, refresh themselves in quiet, or take lodging in peace . . .

Go to the cottages of the poor, if you can find them, for their number will be but small . . . A few, perhaps, you may find rendered poor through some natural infirmity of body or mind, or by some adversity which it was not in their power to foresee and prevent . . . They are beloved by everyone; and their neighbours feel a peculiar pleasure in granting them relief from time to time. So that, in the midst of their poverty, they are really happy, and want none of the necessaries of life, and enjoy many of its conveniences.

Meanwhile peace and plenty, universal love and harmony reign from town to town, through all the province . . . where righteousness thus prevails. . . .

Nor let any think this a description of a fictitious state of things. Rather let everyone know, that all this, and more than all this, shall be accomplished, when once that petition, so oft put up by the true followers of Jesus, by his special direction, "Thy kingdom come, thy will be done, in earth as it is in heaven," is answered . . .[6]

Criticism of the society that is, and concepts of a better society which might be, seem to run in the Bellamy family. For instance,

[6] *The Works of the Rev. Joseph Bellamy, D.D.*, I, 518, 523, 524–26, 527.

there was Captain Charles or Samuel Bellamy, who commanded a pirate fleet off the New England and South Atlantic coast from 1717 to 1726. When a Captain Beer pleaded to have his captured ship returned, Captain Bellamy is said to have responded:

"I am sorry they won't let you have your sloop again, for I scorn to do any one a mischief, when it is not for my advantage; —— the sloop, we must sink her, and she might be of use to you. Though you are a sneaking puppy, and so are all those who will submit to be governed by laws which rich men have made for their own security; for the cowardly whelps have not the courage otherwise to defend what they get by their knavery; but —— ye altogether; —— them for a pack of crafty rascals, and you, who serve them, for a parcel of henhearted numskulls. They villify us, the scoundrels do, when there is only this difference, they rob the poor under cover of law, forsooth, and we plunder the rich under the protection of our own courage. Had you not better make one of us, than sneak after these villains for employment?"

Captain Beer told him that his conscience would not allow him to break through the laws of God and man. "You are a devilish conscience rascal" replied Bellamy; "I am a free prince, and I have as much authority to make war on the whole world, as he who has a hundred sail of ships at sea, and an army of 100,000 men in the field; and this my conscience tells me; but there is no arguing with such snivelling puppies, who allow superiors to kick them about deck at pleasure." [7]

The impression that Edward Bellamy grew up in a utopia-minded family is further strengthened by the fact that another Charles Bellamy, in this case his own brother, thought and wrote in the same field. Charles' novel, *The Breton Mills*, was published almost a decade before *Looking Backward* appeared. Coming from a respectable family in a conservative Massachusetts industrial community, this book must have been almost as breath-taking to the neighbors as the news a century and a half before that one of the name had taken to piracy.

The story deals with the relations of labor and ownership in a large mill, like those which were the chief sources of income for his home town. A few quotations will indicate its fiery spirit:

"Men," he began. Then he stopped speaking a moment. "Yes, men you are, in spite of all the degradation the rich and the powerful can

[7] Thomas Carey, *The History of the Pirates*, pp. 129–30.

put upon you. The time is coming, when the principles of equality vaunted on the pages of so many lying constitutions, and breathed on the lips of so many false-tongued demagogues, shall be fully realized. The time is coming when the work shall not be on one side, and the reward on the other. . . . The gracious favors of ten thousand smiling hills and valleys are gathered only for the few, and those whose arrogance and hardness of heart have least deserved them. And they tell us it must be so; that the few who are more capable and prudent should thus be rewarded for their superiority. They point to six thousand years' oppression of the poor and say what has been must be."

"Great wealth is made up of ten thousand trickling streams, drained from the paltry earnings of as many defrauded workmen. Mere cunning scheming ought not enable a man to turn aside the great river of plenty which flows for all men. . . . These shrewd business men, whom so many praise, have so ingeniously placed their chains on the laborer, that the harder he struggles to escape from poverty, he only turns the faster the wheel that grinds out fortunes for his masters, and draws him in at last to be crushed."

"These corporations are the neatest device of the century for a gagging machine. What the devil's the use of the help grumbling, when there is nobody they can find to blame, only a fiction of law. The overseers and the agent, and each particular stockholder is, oh, awfully sorry, you know, but nobody can help anything, that is unless they want to, . . . There is the shell of a corporation the law provides. A man can creep into it, and even his own conscience cannot logically prick him." [8]

It would almost seem that Charles had received his inspiration from his piratical namesake. After these outbursts he, too, gets occasional glimpses of a better future. The following passage is in the utopian tradition:

"I mean that not one injustice shall ever desecrate these new walls. I mean the new mill shall be a temple of co-operation. I believe the world is just entering on a new epoch, more glorious than any before, because blessings that have been confined to the few, comforts that have comforted only the few, leisure and amusement, even, that has cheered only the few, shall be universal; that each hand that tills the earth shall share in its bountiful harvests which now pack the storehouses of a few in senseless profusion; that each hand that weaves our cloth shall share in its profits according to his worth. It isn't because the world is so poor that you have been poor so long, but because its wealth is wasted. But

[8] Charles J. Bellamy, *The Breton Mills*, pp. 15–16, 75–76, 174. Reprinted by permission of the publisher.

be patient; violence only destroys, it does not build up, and every par-
ticle of wealth destroyed leaves so much less of your heritage . . ." [9]

The Breton Mills was published when Charles was twenty-eight.
We may forgive him his ardor. Four years later, and still four years
before *Looking Backward* appeared, he published another book,
The Way Out, which undertook to be a general solution of the
economic issues of the country. Since this volume was published two
or three years after the two brothers ended their active partnership
which had published the *Penny News* and the *Daily News*, it may
have been thought out while Edward and Charles were working,
living, and talking together.

When we consider that *The Way Out* was the work of a young
man of thirty-two, and that it was written almost sixty years ago,
it is a remarkable production. Instead of being an abstract, philosophical discussion, it presents a limited number of legislative and
social proposals which together constitute a working program for
a national economy. The program which it projected can be guessed
from the titles of the several chapters. Except for the last three or
four they deal with economic issues:

1. The Prosperity and Happiness of the Many should be the End
   Sought in Society
2. The Returns Paid to Capital should Never be Permitted to Exceed
   Market Rates of Interest
3. Increase of Wealth is no Gain to the World, unless its Distribution
   is General
4. The More Even Distribution of Wealth would have the effect of
   Multiplying it in Increased Ratio
5. Concentration of Wealth in a Few Hands, in the Present System,
   Tends to Increase in Enormous Ratio
6. Over-production is not a Fallacy, but One of the Results of a False
   System of Distribution of Profits
7. All Men should Work to Help Forward the Era of Plenty
8. It is Reprehensible for any Class to Spend Money on Extreme
   Luxuries as Long as Necessaries are not Within the Reach of All
9. Equality in the Rewards of Labor is not to be Expected or Desired
10. All Persons who Contribute to the Industry of the World should
    have a Proportionate Share of the Profits

[9] *Ibid.*, pp. 318–19.

11. Legislation, to Effect a Reform in the Distribution of Profits, must also provide Means to Enforce and Superintend such Distribution
12. Eight Hours should Constitute a Legal Day's Work
13. There should be no Individual Property in Land
14. The Amount of Wealth Susceptible of Inheritance should be Limited by Law
15. Government should Grant no Franchise in the Nature of Monopoly for Private Profit
16. The Province of Republican Government should be Greatly Expanded
17. Justice should be Free, Speedy, and Sure
18. Society should Make a more Special Care of the Education of the Young
19. The Sick and Incapable should be Provided for, the Vicious Reformed by Government.[10]

It is interesting that an entire chapter is given to refuting what four years later was to be a central theme of *Looking Backward*— that of economic equality. The harsh expressions in that chapter are suggestive of the hot battles, all in good spirit, around the family table, which, as related by Mrs. Bellamy from her girlhood memories, would lead the father humorously to shout, "Boys! Boys! Let us sing 'Praise God from Whom All Blessings Flow'!"

It would seem to be a safe conclusion that *Looking Backward* is well in the broad stream of the great utopian tradition which we find in existence at the beginning of recorded history, and which reached its highest early forms in Greece and Judea. As may have been the case with Thomas More, Bellamy seems to have enriched that tradition from the remarkable history of ancient Peru. There is evidence that he was well acquainted with the nature of the Inca government. In an article in the *Contemporary Review* for July, 1890, he discussed the ancient Peruvian system at some length, indicating intimate familiarity with the records. In suggesting a limited list of readings for his son Paul, he included Prescott's *Conquest of Peru*, and in his "Talks on Nationalism" he referred to Herbert Spencer's allusion to Peru, and again indicated familiarity

[10] Charles Bellamy, *The Way Out*, p. vii. Reprinted by permission of the publisher.

with the subject. With this indication that Bellamy was familiar with ancient Peruvian history, the very close parallels between *Looking Backward* and the Peruvian regime are the more significant. The author has reached the conclusion that this, more than any other single source, gave form to Bellamy's utopia.

A concept which the old tradition lacked was that of the liberation of man from servitude by mechanical power and the machine. Robert Owen was perhaps the first clearly to have realized that possibility. Then, as his own addition to that great utopian tradition, Bellamy added the humane, tolerant, democratic universality which he got from the atmosphere of America.

One of the most striking proposals in *Looking Backward*, and one which did not follow the historic utopian tradition, was for complete economic independence of women. In her *True Author of "Looking Backward,"* Mrs. John B. Shipley (Marie A. Brown) charged that Bellamy stole this idea from Bebel's *Woman*. But there is a simpler explanation. In 1874, nine years before Bebel's book was first published and while Bellamy was book reviewer for the *Springfield Union*, there appeared an American utopia by Marie Howland, entitled *Papa's Own Girl*. It was written to promote the type of social organization adopted by M. Godin, after the general manner of Fourier, in his remarkable industrial and sociological project at Guise, in France. In her book Mrs. Howland very definitely proposed economic freedom for women. Her attitude may be illustrated by two brief quotations: "Neither sex should be kept by the other. Independence, honest self-support, by honest, productive industry, is the thing for women as well as men." [11] "I see very few really happy women; and they never can be happy, until they are pecuniarily independent." [12]

How similar are Bellamy's expressions:

> The key to the fetters the women wore was the same that locked the shackles of the workers. It was the economic key, the control of the means of subsistence . . .
>
> The economic equalization of men and women for the first time made it possible to establish their relations on a moral basis.
>
> The common and higher code for men and women which the con-

[11] Marie Howland, *Papa's Own Girl,* p. 62. [12] *Ibid.,* pp. 358–59.

science of the race demanded would first become possible . . . when men and women stood over against each other . . . in attitudes of absolute equality and mutual independence.[13]

Elsewhere we have discussed the probable debt of Bellamy to Robert Owen, to ancient Peru as described by Prescott, to John Stuart Mill, and to Fourier through his disciple, Albert Brisbane. Green in his biography of Bellamy wrote, "When asked by the writer whether any one book had influenced him in planning *Looking Backward*, he replied: '*Telemachus*, possibly.' " [14] Fénelon's utopia by that name, written in his effort to educate the heir to the throne of France, had great popularity in its day. Among all the charges of plagiarism by Bellamy which have come to the writer's attention, the charge of stealing from Fénelon's *Telemachus* does not appear. Its similarity to *Looking Backward* is less than that of numerous other utopias.

[13] *Equality,* pp. 132, 139–40, 142.   [14] Green.

X · Looking Backward

THERE has been much discussion concerning why and how Edward Bellamy came to write *Looking Backward*. Elsewhere we have stated that some early book reviews described him as a commonplace writer of popular fiction, who began a popular romance, only to have it unexpectedly turn into an important social and economic treatise which took possession of its author and transformed his life. When *Looking Backward* was published, the editor of *Good Housekeeping*, an old acquaintance, wrote of him: "His active interest in the social problem is of comparatively recent development, and in fact its growth was practically coincident with the growth of the book under his pen, it having been started with a very different purpose, not much out of line with the motives of his former work." [1] At the time of his death a similar view was expressed in the *Philadelphia Bulletin:*

> He sat down to write a fanciful sketch. But behold! The picture was not what he expected. The glare of the light fell upon a wondrous scene of ideal sociology. Instead of a sweet love passage, it illuminated a social study. Bellamy's hero developed as his pen travelled. . . .
> He sat down to his work a novelist, he rose at its completion a social economist—the leader of a new school. He had made ideal surroundings for his fiction characters and then realizing that no such condition actually existed, sought to make it . . .[2]

Having followed the development of his economic views from the time when at the age of twenty-one in a series of Lyceum talks he outlined much of the core of his later plan, we can see that any such explanation is wholly inadequate. In the opinion of such writers his social judgment came in a flash, like a stork bringing a baby. Sophisticated people know that storks do not bring intellectual

[1] "Edward Bellamy," *Good Housekeeping*, X, No. 4 (December 21, 1889). Reprinted by permission.
[2] Walter A. Smith, *The Religion of Edward Bellamy*, quoting from obituary in the *Philadelphia Bulletin*, May 23, 1898.

babies, any more than they do physical ones. Birth is but a critical point in a gradual process of development. Bellamy's social-mindedness was no exception to this rule.

Yet Bellamy himself was partly responsible for that impression. In an article in the *Nationalist* magazine for May, 1889, on "How I Came to Write *Looking Backward*," he stated:

I never had, previous to the publication of the work, any affiliations with any class or sect of industrial or social reformers nor, to make my confession complete, any particular sympathy with undertakings of the sort. It is only just to myself to say, however, that this should not be taken to indicate any indifference to the miserable condition of the mass of humanity, seeing that it resulted rather from a perception all too clear of the depth and breadth of the social problem and a consequent skepticism as to the effectiveness of the proposed solutions which had come to my notice.

In undertaking to write *Looking Backward* I had, at the outset, no idea of attempting a serious contribution to the movement of social reform. The idea was of a mere literary fantasy, a fairy tale of social felicity. There was no thought of contriving a house which practical men might live in, but merely of hanging in mid-air far out of reach of the sordid and material world of the present, a cloud-palace for an ideal humanity.

The idea of committing the duty of maintaining the community to an industrial army, precisely as the duty of protecting it is entrusted to a military army, was directly suggested to me by the grand object lesson of the organization of an entire people for national purposes presented by the military system of universal service for fixed and equal terms, which has been practically adopted by the nations of Europe . . . It was not till I began to work out the details of the scheme . . . that I perceived the full potency of the instrument I was using and recognized in the modern military system not merely a rhetorical analogy for a national industrial service, but its prototype, furnishing at once a complete working model for its organization . . .

Something in this way it was that, no thanks to myself, I stumbled over the destined corner-stone of the new social order. It scarcely needs to be said that having once apprehended it for what it was, it became a matter of pressing importance to me to show it in the same light to other people. This led to a complete recasting, both in form and purpose, of the book I was engaged upon. Instead of a mere fairy tale of social perfection, it became the vehicle of a definite scheme of industrial reorganization.[3]

[3] *Nationalist*, I, No. 1 (May, 1889), 1, 2, 3.

This seems a plain enough statement of how the book came about. Yet, four years later he wrote another article, this time for the *Ladies' Home Journal*, entitled "How I Wrote *Looking Backward*," which gives a very different impression, one more in accord with the actual development of his mind and interests. This latter article throws so much light on the matter, and upon his boyhood interest, that it is quoted at length:

Up to the age of eighteen I had lived almost continuously in a thriving village of New England, where there were no very rich and few very poor, and everybody who was willing to work was sure of a fair living. At that time I visited Europe and spent a year there in travel and study. It was in the great cities of England, Europe, and among the hovels of the peasantry that my eyes were first fully opened to the extent and consequences of man's inhumanity to man.

So it was that I returned home, for the first time aroused to the existence and urgency of the social problem, but without as yet seeing any way out. Although it had required the sight of Europe to startle me to a vivid realization of the inferno of poverty beneath our civilization, my eyes having once been opened I had now no difficulty in recognizing in America, and even in my own comparatively prosperous village, the same conditions in course of progressive development.

The other day rummaging among old papers I was much interested by the discovery of . . . the manuscript of an address which it appears I delivered before the Chicopee Falls Village Lyceum along in 1871 or 1872 [which would suggest that] their youthful author was quite likely to attempt something in the line of *Looking Backward* if he only lived long enough. . . . From numerous equally radical expressions I excerpt these paragraphs: "The great reforms of the world have hitherto been political rather than social. In their progress classes privileged by title have been swept away, but classes privileged by wealth remain. A nominal aristocracy is ceasing to exist, but the actual aristocracy of wealth, the world over, is every day becoming more and more powerful. The idea that men can derive a right from birth or name to dispose of the destinies of their fellows is exploded, but the world thinks not yet of denying that gold confers a power upon its possessors to domineer over their equals and enforce from them a life's painful labors at the price of a bare subsistence. . . . What is the name of an institution by which men control the labor of other men, and out of the abundance created by that labor, having doled out to the laborers such a pittance as may barely support life and sustain strength for added tasks, reserve to themselves the vast surplus for the support of a life of ease and splendor? This, gentlemen, is slavery . . .

"Let not any one falsely reply that I am dreaming of a happiness without toil, of abundance without labor. Labor is the necessary condition, not only of abundance but of existence upon earth. I ask only that none labor beyond measure that others may be idle, that there be no more masters and no more slaves among men. Is this too much? Does any fearful soul exclaim, impossible, that this hope has been the dream of men in all ages, a shadowy and Utopian reverie of a divine fruition which the earth can never bear? That the few must revel and the many toil; the few waste, the many want; the few be masters, the many serve; the toilers of the earth be the poor and the idlers the rich, and that this must go on forever? . . .

"Not so, for nothing that is unjust can be eternal, and nothing that is just can be impossible."

Since I came across this echo of my youth and recalled the half-forgotten exercises of mind it testifies to, I have been wondering, not why I wrote *Looking Backward,* but why I did not write it, or try to, twenty years ago. . . .[4]

What is the significance of these seemingly conflicting accounts? We find in Edward Bellamy's notebooks fragmentary paragraphs and hints of two types of themes for stories. One of these in an undated notebook, the contents of which suggest the years before *Looking Backward,* deals with a utopian theme, as for instance the paragraph:

There were no popular elections in Antononna. No one under the age of forty was eligible for public office. The men most eminent in their several professions . . . constituted a class of eligibles, from whom the governors were chosen by lot in order to avoid all possibility of emulation or self-seeking, and rendering pride in office absurd. . . . No taxes. Everything is the state's. For each high office only those eligible who had served in the lower offices, familiarity with affairs being here required.[5]

This was unquestionably the spirit, and largely the method, presented in *Looking Backward,* though the way of selecting officers differs somewhat from that presented in the published book.

Also, there occur in the notebooks suggestions for one or more fanciful stories which are suggestive of the story plot in *Looking Backward.* For instance, among his plots for stories, we find the

[4] *Ladies' Home Journal,* II, No. 5 (April, 1894).
[5] Unpublished papers (B2-6-4).

following: "How, with a clever physician as an accomplice, a man or woman might escape a complicated situation by simulating death and being buried, and resurrected . . ." [6] This note is followed by a longer plot for a story based on mesmerism, as is the plot of *Looking Backward*, but with only a fanciful theme, and with no suggestion of social and economic interest.

Apparently Bellamy was carrying in his mind these two themes, one a fanciful story and the other a utopian or economic treatise, but for a time with no thought of uniting them. It seems possible that, as indicated in the article in the *Nationalist* on "How I Came to Write *Looking Backward*," it was while working on a fanciful story that the idea occurred to him of incorporating the two themes in a single piece of writing.

In an introduction to *The Fabian Essays* Bellamy wrote:

Nationalists . . . [would make] equal provision for the maintenance of all an incident and an indefeasible condition of citizenship, without any regard whatever to the relative specific services of different citizens. The rendering of such services, on the other hand, instead of being left to the option of the citizen with the alternative of starvation, would be required under a uniform law as a civic duty, precisely like other forms of taxation or military service, levied on the citizen for the furtherance of a common-weal in which each is to share equally. [7]

Thus the two peculiar characteristics of his program were equality of income and universal economic service. While he called the industrial army the "cornerstone" of the new order, he referred to economic equality as "the keystone of the arch." The principle of equal income he had stated in his Lyceum talk more than fifteen years before, at about the age of twenty-one. On the other hand, according to the article in the *Nationalist*, it was while writing a fanciful romance that he came upon the idea of universal economic service. Thus each of the two accounts seems to be an accurate statement of the development of one of the two major elements of his program. The fundamental principle of equality had long been held; the device of military organization was a sudden inspiration.

In the *Ladies' Home Journal* article he states: "For a dozen or

---

6 *Ibid.* (B2-Plots 1-9).

7 Bellamy, "Introduction to the American Edition," G. B. Shaw, ed., *The Fabian Essays in Socialism*, p. xvii.

fifteen years I followed journalism, doing in a desultory way, as opportunity offered, a good deal of magazine and book writing. In none of the writings of this period did I touch on the social question, but none the less all the while it was in mind . . ." This evidently was intended to apply to books and magazine articles, but not to his daily newspaper work, for keen interest in social problems is repeatedly in evidence in his book reviews and editorials both in the *Springfield Union* and in his own paper, the *Daily News*.

In March, 1885, about three years before *Looking Backward* appeared, Bellamy attended a dinner given to story writers by Charles and Arthur Scribner. Edward Page Mitchell, in his *Memoirs of an Editor*, wrote of that occasion:

All who sat at the dinner interested me keenly, but none more than Edward Bellamy. . . . When the party broke up into groups and the conversation became animated, Bellamy was the centre of the largest special audience. He was developing, with the eloquence of sincerity, his philosophy of the insignificance of the individual and the greatness of the commonweal.[8]

Evidently at this time Edward Bellamy's thoughts were on the subject which was to be the major issue of his life.

It seems to have been a habit of Bellamy to try out various approaches to his books and magazine articles. One such suggestion for the theme of a book somewhat along the line of *Looking Backward* is almost identical with his account to William Dean Howells and others as to how he became deeply interested in the social problem. Under a notebook heading, "Title of the Big Book, 'Man, Woman and Child,' " there are various paragraphs, including the following:

Perhaps let Caesar's first appearance be at Debating Society in college on labor questions in which he takes up the cudgels for the poor and oppressed. He is led to talk a good deal about socialistic schemes, but he talked vaguely with strong but vague aspirations for brotherhood and justice.

Afterwards when I meet him at Hawley class supper as hermit, I ask him about Socialism. "Given it all up?" "I see no way out, and I hate to waste words on the inevitable. The various charitable enterprises of

8 Edward Page Mitchell, *Memoirs of an Editor*, pp. 436, 438. Reprinted by permission of the publisher.

the day amount to nothing, and I have no patience with that which is not logical and complete, which does not go to the bottom of things."

Caesar in explaining how he came to be a reformer—"You know I was always interested in those old days as who is not indeed nowadays. But then it was a question which I could play with, could take up or leave. But, by God, I can play with it no longer. I have children; the future America is more to me for their dear sake than the present America. Yes, and not only for my children, for they look ahead to some mysterious tie that makes my life one with my children, makes it one with the race of men, for we are bodies one of another. I was, I admit, dull of mind and slow of heart not to see and understand this before. Quicker men would not have needed the example of the child to teach them, but I have learned now once for all that selfishness is suicide, the only true suicide. Our life is hid in our brethren, in the race, in God, everywhere, but in our petty souls all these ages has man been mangling his own body, oppressing his own members.

"When I came to consider what could be radically done for social reorganization, I was helped by every former disgust with the various socialist schemes." [9]

Apparently this extract is descriptive of the course of his own mind.

There is other evidence that these approaches to his masterpieces may have been made during the course of several years. His brother Frederick wrote:

For at least two years before he began to write *Looking Backward,* in our long travels together and in our constant meetings, he talked much of the ethical and socialistic problems which were ever before him, and in that way I came to suspect his purpose of writing on that subject long before he seriously admitted it.

Since the trip to Hawaii is the only "long travel together" of which we have any record, it would appear that the subject was under discussion as early as 1878, and that *The Duke of Stockbridge,* which appeared shortly afterward, was not an isolated project, but part of a general program which was taking form.

His own description in the *Ladies' Home Journal* of the actual writing of the book is explicit:

According to my best recollection it was in the fall or winter of 1886 that I sat down to my desk with the definite purpose of trying to reason out a method of economic organization by which the republic might guar-

[9] Unpublished papers (B2-7-8).

antee the livelihood and material welfare of its citizens on a basis of equality corresponding to and supplementing their political equality. There was no doubt in my mind that the proposed study should be in the form of a story.

Nothing outside of the exact sciences has to be so logical as the thread of a story if it is to be acceptable. There is no such test of a false and absurd idea as trying to fit it into a story. You may make a sermon or an essay or a philosophical treatise as illogical as you please and no one know the difference, but all the world is a good critic of a story . . .

As I became convinced of the practical availability of the social solution I was studying, it became my aim to sacrifice all other effects to the method which would enable me to explain its features most fully, which was manifestly that of presenting everything from the point of view of the representative of the nineteenth century.[10]

In the same article he tells how the book finally appeared:

As well as I can remember *Looking Backward* began in earnest to be written in the fall or winter of 1886, and was substantially finished in the following six or eight months, although rewriting and revising took up the following spring and summer. It went to the publishers in August or September, 1887, and although promptly accepted did not appear till January, 1888. Although it made a stir among the critics, up to the close of 1888 the sales had not exceeded ten thousand, after which they leaped into the hundred thousands.[11]

The writing of *Looking Backward* crystallized an attitude which was developing for many years, and was ready for expression when the right moment came. The period of gestation of social purposes was fulfilled.

In the Christian Socialist magazine the *Dawn* for September 15, 1889, is an article by Edward Bellamy summarizing the program for the social order which he had described in *Looking Backward*. In this limited space only a bare skeleton of his proposals could be presented, and the adequacy and the characteristics of that program can no more be fully understood from such an outline than the traits of a man could be judged by a rapid pencil portrait of himself. However, in order that the reader may have a view of the program as a whole, that summary is reproduced here.

[10] Bellamy, Edward, "How I Wrote *Looking Backward*," *Ladies' Home Journal*, II, No. 5 (April, 1894). Reprinted by permission.
[11] *Ibid.*

It is probable that this outline was prepared by Bellamy some-what on the spur of the moment, with no expectation that it would become a historical document. Had he expected his proposed system of economy to be judged by a brief outline, he probably would very carefully have appraised and balanced the various elements. For instance, the place of women in the new order, as indicated in *Looking Backward*, probably would have been more carefully stated. However, the outline has the merit of being a product of the author of *Looking Backward*, and not the supposition of someone else as to what elements were most important in his mind. On the whole it is a good summary.

Looking Backward is chiefly devoted, under the form of a romance, to a description of the state of society supposed to exist in the United States in the year 2000.

The labor question, so-called, and all problems growing out of the division of labor and its results, have been solved by the union of the entire nation in a general business partnership, in which every man and woman is an equal partner. The conduct of the industries, commerce and general business of the country is committed by the national firm to a so-called army of industry, which includes all the able-bodied citizens, men and women, between the ages of 21 and 45, the intellectual and professional services being rendered by associated corps. All persons choose their occupations in the army of industry, according to natural tastes and gifts, provided, of course, when there are too many volunteers for the needs of a particular branch that the fittest are taken. In order to equalize the attractiveness of different occupations, the hours of work in those which are more laborious or otherwise unattractive, are shortened as compared with the easier and more attractive trades. The conditions of a trade which does not attract volunteers are lightened until the necessary force is attracted, and on the other hand a persistent excess of volunteers for a particular trade is taken to indicate that its conditions are unfairly easy. The intellectual pursuits are as open to all as the industrial, on the sole condition that the fittest find preference.

In view of the fact that most women marry and become mothers, and in view also of the comparative weakness and uncertainty of their health, the feminine half of the army of industry is organized under exclusively feminine control, and is altogether devoted to the lighter classes of occupations, the discipline being in all ways adapted to feminine conditions.

There is also an invalid corps attached to the industrial army, in which the sickly and feeble who still desire and are able to do something, are enabled to undertake what they safely can for the common wealth.

At the age of 45 both men and women are discharged from further service, and remain absolutely free to occupy themselves as they will for the remainder of life.

That is to say, the industrial duty of citizens has been placed upon the same basis on which their military duty now rests. As it is at present held to be the duty of all citizens to fight for their country, so then it is held their equally obvious duty to work for it, and it is considered self-evident that to be efficient, working requires system and unity of action quite as much as fighting. The nation has, in fine, been organized for peace as at present for war. The people stand shoulder to shoulder, not, as now, to resist the foreign foe (for that peril is no longer known), but against hunger, and cold, and nakedness, and every wrong and every want that human valor can repel; an invincible square of men, with the women and the children, the sick, the aged and the infirm in the centre.

As all the members of a nation of to-day, whether able to fight or not, share equally in the protection of the army and the prosperity it insures, so in the nation of the year 2000, all alike, whether men or women, strong or weak, able-bodied or defective, share in the wealth produced by the industrial army, and the share of all is equal. This share, varying only with the general prosperity of the national business, is the sole income and means of maintenance of all, whether during active industrial service or after discharge from it.

Owing to the method of organizing industry upon the mutual obligation of citizen to nation, and nation to citizen, duty has wholly taken the place of contract, as the basis of industry and the cement of society.

The only exception to the rule of equality of portions is made in the case of the children. While these are regarded as equally partners in the national concern, and are by no means left dependent upon the caprice of parents for any part of their support, the pension allotted them is naturally less than that of adults, their needs being less.

If any question could be supposed to arise as to the comparative claims upon maintenance at the nation's table of the able-bodied and the defective, it would be the latter who would come first, for it is an ethical axiom in the year 2000, that every generation receives the common inheritance of organized society subject to certain liens and charges, and that the first and most sacred of these charges is an ample provision for the care of those who are dependent on account of weakness of mind or body.

But indeed no one in that age would think of demanding an accounting for his personal services, rather than his share as partner, were it only for selfish reasons. It is recognized that ninety-nine one-hundredths of the value of any person's work, and often the very possibility of the work itself, is created by the social organization, which is the joint and indivisible inheritance of all, so that even if any body of metaphysicians and mathematicians were able to determine the element in the value of an individual's work which he had himself absolutely originated and independently created, it would doubtless be a pittance too beggarly to support life. The royalty, that is to say, which society would have to claim from an individual for permission to use the social organization for his personal enrichment would be so large as to be in danger of leaving him in debt.

But while as regards the part each has in the annual product of the nation, it is share and share alike; the honors and distinctions, the offices of rank and authority in the army of industry and in the nation, are allotted to men and women according to their comparative diligence or brilliancy or achievement, to the end that the fittest may lead and rule, and all be encouraged by the hope of honorable distinction to do their best. While for example a man receives no more rations of bread and meat or changes of clothing for doing twice as much work, as the artisan at his side, he does unfailingly win promotion in authority and position, with the social rank such promotion brings in a community in which no other basis of distinction is recognized. As to the rule of equality in the shares of all workers, whether more or less skillful, it is merely the extension to all trades of the rule of uniformity of wages practically enforced in particular trades by the trade unions of to-day.

Owing to the fact that the relation of work and maintenance is directly between the nation and each individual, no man's livelihood is dependent upon the favor or patronage of any other or group of others, nor any woman's upon a man, nor can a child suffer privation. All citizens consequently enjoy moral independence, and are free from social or personal dictation or pressure as to belief, speech or practice, so far as they infringe upon no other's rights. The development of a robust and unfettered individuality, which is rendered so difficult to-day by the partial or complete dependence of nearly everybody upon others for support or business patronage, is thus open to all.

Owing to the fact that all forms of capital are held in trust by the nation for the people, and all commodities produced by the nation, it follows that everything the individual needs can and can only be procured directly from the nation. That is to say, there is no buying or selling, or trade of any sort, among individuals. Therefore there is no use for money and no money. The citizen is credited with his annual dividend of the product of the great partnership, and receives vouchers, upon presentation of which at the public stores he obtains what he wants, at such times and in such quantities as he likes. He expends his share altogether as he pleases, whether his tastes run to renting a fine house, having a fine table, or wearing fine clothes. These vouchers are good only for the year for which they are issued, and cannot be accumulated beyond that, whatever is not taken up being turned over to the public surplus. Spendthrifts becoming public burdens are placed under guardianship as to their expenses. The portions of children are also, of course, expended for them.

While the nation undertakes and controls all public business, smaller groups of citizens co-operate at will, as now, for social, religious, political or other semi-private purposes, and are able, substantially as at the present time, to raise common funds for such ends, by contributions from their private credits.

Crime has shrunken to almost imperceptible proportions. Robbery, theft and fraud of every sort are without a motive in a society where all have abundance, where covetousness is not stimulated by different degrees of luxury, and where equality of resources is annually renewed. Not only fraud, but even falsehood, is almost unknown, owing to the fact that none are dependent for their livelihood or for any advantage upon the favor of their fellows, and having nothing to fear or hope from them, are without temptation to prevaricate. As to crimes of violence, the universal refinement of manners which results from a general high education has tended to reduce them to the same small proportions in which they now occur among the educated classes. As for corruption among public officials, there are no corporate or personal interests opposed to the public interests to create a motive for bribery, neither is there any wealth to bribe with nor poverty to be bribed.

Owing to the equality of wealth, marriages are based always solely upon personal preference, and never upon sordid or prudential calculations. The unhindered operation of the principle of sexual selection in marriage has exerted a marked effect upon the physical, intellectual and moral character of the race.

The general wealth of society is represented as vastly greater in the year 2000 than it is now. This is owing in part to the continuance for another century of the scientific progress which has already so enriched the world of to-day as compared with the world of the eighteenth century. Quite as much, however, it is owing to the vast positive gains and negative savings in the use of labor resulting from the substitution of the scientific methods of an organized and unified industrial system for the wasteful struggle of the present competitive plan with its countless warring and mutually destructive undertakings.

The account of the manner in which the change was made from the industrial system of to-day to that of the year 2000 represents it as resulting from the development to its logical conclusion of the tendency now observable to the consolidation of entire trades under the single management of great corporations, syndicates and trusts. As individual ownership and control of great business enterprises has already almost wholly given place to corporate management, and as corporate management is now before our eyes giving place to the still larger concentrations of the trusts or syndicates, so, it is represented, the syndicates and trusts in due time realized their manifest destiny by absorption in the great trust of the nation, the universal partnership of the people.

The enthusiasm of the people of the United States when they began to foresee the manner in which their salvation was thus to be wrought out, and to realize the greatness of it, is described to have been unparalleled and to have resulted in a popular uprising, peaceful because irresistible, without precedent in history.

While the condition of society in the year 2000 is described as being in all ways vastly improved upon that of the present day, it is represented that the people of that epoch by no means rested satisfied in it or considered it anything more than a single step in the infinite progression of humanity toward the divine. In looking back upon our time their sentiment was chiefly one of amazement that the race should have been so slow to apply to industrial organization principles at once so obviously just, and so economically advantageous.

THE CHARGE OF PLAGIARISM

In his essay on originality, Emerson wrote: "The originals are not original. There is imitation, model, and suggestion, to the very archangels, if we know their history."

Since the first appearance of *Looking Backward*, Edward Bellamy has been charged with plagiarism. It would seem that through the long centuries during which the utopian tradition has been growing in Palestine, in Greece, and in western Europe, nearly every view of society within the range of human conception would have been taken, nearly every type of social organization would have been described, and almost every literary device explored. A reading of many utopias leads toward such an opinion.

The writer of a utopia is in the line of a great tradition. An able man as a rule is familiar with the literature of the field in which he writes. While men of insight tend to reach similar conclusions from similar premises, each is much influenced by his individual social outlook. He undertakes to master and to assimilate what has gone before, making it a part of himself, and then makes his contribution by expressing what is in him. Whatever one creates that is new, or sees more clearly than others, or presents more effectively, generally is the result of that process. The test of a writer is not whether someone else has expressed the same point of view or has used similar literary devices, but whether his own work is masterful and has a quality which makes it a significant contribution to human insight, thought, or feeling. A writer is guilty of plagiarism only if he reproduces, without credit and as his own creation, some significant idea or some organization of ideas which is peculiarly the work of another. Even there he is less often a plagiarist than a chameleon. Unconsciously he takes on the color of thought or style of the author with whom he was last occupied.

In American utopian literature there are numerous productions which seem to be original and which show little or no influence of previous writings in that field, but not one of them will rank among the significant utopias. While some of them have flashes of inspiration, they are on the whole provincial and trivial. The amount of sheer creation with which any man is endowed is very limited. Only those utopian writers who have definitely profited by the great utopian tradition have done great work. A single case will illustrate the fact that common elements run through many utopian plans. There was an outburst of utopian writing in Athens during the last half of the fifth and the first part of the fourth century B. C., culminating in Plato's *Republic*. About 390 B. C., several years before Plato's great work appeared, some of the common elements of this type of writing were satirized in a ribald play by Aristophanes. A brief extract will suggest the theme:

PREXAGORA: . . . The rule which I dare to enact and declare,
Is that all shall be equal, and equally share
All wealth and enjoyments, nor longer endure
That one should be rich, and another be poor,
That one should have acres, far-stretching and wide,
And another not even enough to provide
Himself with a grave: that this at his call
Should have hundreds of servants, and that none at all.
All this I intend to correct and amend:

> Now all of all blessings shall freely partake,
> One life and one system for all men I make.
> BLEPYRUS: And how will you manage it?
> PREXAGORA: First, I'll provide
> That the silver, and land, and whatever beside
> Each man shall possess, shall be common and free,
> One fund for the public; then out of it we
> Will feed and maintain you, like housekeepers true,
> Dispensing, and sparing, and caring for you.[12]

There is no doubt that if this satire had appeared first, not in Athens in 390 B. C., but in Boston A. D. 1890, it would have been taken to be a parody on *Looking Backward*, for every point on which it touches is a part of Bellamy's program.

By its very nature a utopian book deals with man's deepest needs and his highest hopes and aspirations; it pictures the culture, the social organization, and the technology which in the author's opinion will most completely insure their realization. Emerson said: "To believe your own thought, to believe that what is true for you in your private heart is true for all men,—that is genius. Speak your latent conviction, and it shall be the universal sense . . . In every work of genius we recognize our own rejected thoughts . . ." [13] It is partly because the hopes and aspirations of all men have much in common that great utopias have common aims and often present similar solutions.

It is little wonder then that since the visions of Amos and Isaiah and since Plato's *Republic* those men who have dreamed of a better social order have been charged with plagiarism. In the reading of many utopias one meets with constant repetition of purposes, methods, and devices. Some of these likenesses represent simple borrowing or imitation. Others are not so much imitation as conversion and apostleship. Many are but timely paraphrases of the utopian tradition. A few seem to be *sui generis* in some significant elements.

If we take any particular theme and follow it through numerous utopias we shall find a vast amount of likeness. For instance, we find

---

[12] Aristophanes' *The Ecclesiazusae*, Benjamin B. Rogers, trans., pp. 299–300. Reprinted by permission of the publisher.
[13] Ralph Waldo Emerson, *Essays*, I, "Self-Reliance."

equal distribution of wealth as a common element of Plutarch's *Life of Lycurgus*, who lived about the eighth or ninth century B. C., of Phaleas and of Plato in the fourth century B. C., and, during the past five hundred years, of More's *Utopia*, Campanella's *City of the Sun*, Andreae's *Christianopolis*, Berington's *Adventures of di Lucca*, Morelly's *Basiliade*, Ellis's *New Britain*, Owen's *The Book of the New Moral World*, and of numerous others. If we take such definite matters as the elimination of lawyers and a desire for few and simple laws, we find agreement on one, or more generally both, of these points on the part of Plutarch (*Lycurgus*), More (*Utopia*), Campanella (*City of the Sun*), Andreae (*Christianopolis*), Harrington (*Oceana*), Berington (*Adventures of di Lucca*), Macnie (*The Diothas*), Gronlund (*Co-operative Commonwealth*), London (*The Iron Heel*), and Bellamy (*Looking Backward*). If we consider the policy of subordinating the individual to the state we have agreement on the part of Lycurgus, Plato, More, Campanella, Morelly, Bellamy, and many others. Such likenesses might be almost indefinitely extended. Many of them are so striking, and so similarly worked out, that if only two such works were extant it would seem that one must be a plagiarism of the other.

Of those well-nigh universal cravings, from time to time one or another will emerge as of dominant or of critical interest, and during such periods most utopian writers will reflect that current emphasis. For instance, during the long periods when church and state sought to dominate and to regiment men's minds, the deep craving for freedom and for opportunity to inquire into the things of nature found echo in utopian writings, as in Gott's *Nova Solyma*, Andreae's *Christianopolis*, Berington's *Adventures of di Lucca*, Campanella's *City of the Sun*, and Bacon's *New Atlantis*. With this freedom of thought and of inquiry largely achieved for the time being, nineteenth- and twentieth-century utopias express other unfulfilled desires, as for economic and social security and justice, speed of communication and transportation and related mastery of the physical world, and freedom from drudgery.

The literary devices of utopian writing have varied also with the times. For three centuries after Columbus the usual setting was a newly discovered country in some hitherto unexplored part of the world. Many pages have been written on the question of who first introduced his hero into Utopia by the device of shipwreck. Before the middle of the nineteenth century, when explorers were penetrating the last corners of *terra incognita*, Utopia was located in deepest Africa (Hertzka's *Freeland*), or at the South Pole (Bouvé's *Centuries Apart*). Finally, some other resource of plausibility became necessary, and Utopians gradually retreated to Mars or to past or future ages. H. G. Wells with his "time machine" provided another method. Many years before Wells and four years before *Looking Backward*, substantially the same device was used in an obscure utopia by Alfred Denton Cridge, *Utopia, or the History of an Extinct Planet*, published at Oakland, California. Transportation to these new locations of ideal communities presented technical difficulties. In one of the earliest American utopias, *Three Hundred Years Hence*, by Mrs. Mary Griffith, published in Philadelphia in 1836, the hero was overwhelmed by a snowslide, and was thus packed in ice until he was needed again. Obviously, this device is not wholly satisfactory, though it does seem to be original.

In this dilemma, widespread interest in mesmerism or hypnotism came as a lifesaver for utopian writers. The earliest reference to mesmerism in English or American literature was in about 1800, approximately eighty years before *Looking Backward*. The word "hypnotism" was introduced about forty years later.

Now we come to the charges of plagiarism against Edward Bellamy's *Looking Backward*. They are, indeed, numerous. It has been said or implied that he took his theme in whole or in part from Gronlund's *Co-operative Commonwealth* of 1884; from Macnie's *The Diothas*, 1883; from *Mizora, A Tale of Civilization*, by "Vera Zarovitch" (Mary E. Bradley Lane), 1880; from Bebel's *Woman*, 1883; from Cabet's *Voyage en Icarie*, 1840; from Blanc's *L'Organisation du travail*, 1839; from Bacon's *New Atlantis*, 1627; from More's *Utopia*, 1516; from Plutarch's *Life of Lycurgus*, about A. D. 100; from Plato's *Republic*, about 380 B. C.; and from Aristophanes' *Ecclesiazusae*, 390 B. C. Doubtless this list could be much extended by more exhaustive study of contemporaneous book reviews.

Since for several years after its appearance *Looking Backward* had a wider reading than any other utopia has ever had in a similar length of time, the book inevitably drew the attention of critics. For the most part the many charges of plagiarism against the book may be dismissed without specific reference. Most of the similarities between Bellamy and earlier writers which reviewers have cited are such as are general to utopian literature.

I have made a careful and thorough-going study of the charges of plagiarism against Bellamy. The story of that search is intriguing, but too long and too detailed to be included in this biography. (An account of that study is published separately by the author, under the title *Plagiarism in Utopia*.)

Of all these charges of plagiarism, the only two which deserve serious consideration refer to Gronlund's *Co-operative Commonwealth* and a little-known utopia, *The Diothas*, by John Macnie (*pseud*. Ismar Thiusen), published four years before *Looking Backward*. In *The Diothas* the device of hypnotism was used—it had been used by Poe ("The Facts in the Case of M. Valdemar") in 1845. In both *The Diothas* and *Looking Backward* the hero had a sweetheart named Edith. On awaking from the long sleep, in each case the hero fell in love with a distant descendant of "Edith." In each case, too, the father or guardian of the heroine, a man of exceptional intelligence and culture, became interpreter of the new world to the hero who had emerged from the nineteenth century. Each of the works forecast radio, television, automobiles, and other technical developments. In each case the hero awakened to find that his vision of a good world was only a dream, though in *Looking Backward* this awakening itself proved to be only a nightmare. On some points both books have a strong resemblance to *The Adventures of Gaudentio di Lucca*, by Simon Berington (*pseud*. Bishop Berkeley), published first in 1737, and apparently available in English in the New York Public Library when both books were being written. On some points also, all three have striking similarity in plot to *Nova Solyma*, a utopia by Samuel Gott, published in Latin in 1648.

Notwithstanding the similarities between *Looking Backward* and the earlier *Diothas*, it is my opinion that Bellamy was not a plagiarist in this case. That conclusion rests primarily on two points.

First, at the University of North Dakota, where Macnie was long a member of the faculty, there was a tradition that Bellamy and Macnie were personally acquainted and had gone over the themes of their utopias a few years before the earlier one was published. They lived for a time within about fifteen miles of each other in Connecticut and had been in Europe at the same time.

The other point is that in the concluding chapter of *The Diothas*, which is not a part of the plot, but in substance an appendix, Macnie went curiously out of his way to sketch the biography of an imaginary or anonymous friend whom he inferentially credits with having inspired the book. This biography is so remarkably a likeness of Bellamy that it is doubtful whether in all America there was another man who would so nearly exactly fit the description. In this biographical sketch, Macnie wrote:

By a sort of spiritual "transfusion of blood" I find myself permeated, as it were, with many of those peculiar notions of E——'s [Edward?] which I used most vigorously to combat. I can imagine the smile with which, in his distant exile, he will read of the march he stole on me when, in my helpless sleep, he inoculated me with his social and political heresies, which I must get rid of as soon as possible if I am to pursue my profession with any comfort or success.[14]

In an undated notebook of Edward Bellamy's containing preliminary sketches for a utopia similar to *Looking Backward*, we find the following complementary note: "The Idea of Cousin John; one of those anesthetic souls: the row the other soul will have with the working soul on account of his suffering inflicted on it under chloroform." [15]

Where the two authors expressed a similar social philosophy, in the case of Macnie this was a temporary diversion from a conservative bent. He became almost ashamed of his work. With Bellamy the philosophy expressed in *Looking Backward* was the matured outcome of a lifetime of inquiry, and was held throughout life. The writer's conclusion is that Bellamy probably was the inspiration of Macnie's book, notwithstanding the fact that Macnie's was first to be published.

14 John Macnie, *The Diothas, or a Far Look Ahead*, p. 352. Reprinted by permission of the publisher.
15 Unpublished papers (B2-6-7).

That Bellamy was aware of the problem of plagiarism there is no doubt. As a book reviewer for five years he must have met with it frequently. In reviewing *Deirdre*, by Dr. Robert Joyce, he wrote, "Some of the critics of the poem account for its Homeric smack by pointing out many parallelisms between Homer's work and Joyce's, which are so close as to place Homer in an embarrassing position." [16] In one of his notebooks, apparently used about eight years before *Looking Backward*, there are a number of proposed titles for short stories. One of them is, "A story in which is analyzed the peculiar force of covetousness which leads to the stealing of literary fame by the claiming of productions of others." [17] At another place is an entry, "Story of dispute over authorship of story." [18] In another of his journals we find the remark, "Many men ought to be put wholly between quotation marks." [19] Again we find the comment on an unoriginal writer, "He will do well enough as long as the supply of books holds out, but then—" [20]

The evidence we have, especially concerning Gronlund's *Cooperative Commonwealth*, is capable of various interpretations. Under the circumstances, as the only reasonable way to come to a conclusion, I ask myself, "What kind of man was Edward Bellamy? What would such a man do under the circumstances?" Put in that form, from what I know of his life, the answer is clear. Edward Bellamy would not consciously have stolen what belonged to another.

Shurter, after comparison of texts, says of him, "On the basis of this evidence, Edward Bellamy should no longer be acclaimed as the great originator of a movement, as his nationalist followers hail him, but as the most successful popularizer of a modified form of Socialism in America." [21] On the basis of this kind of appraisal, Karl Marx must stand, not as an original thinker, but as a propagandist who impressed his age by ably elaborating, as well as by burying in heavy, technical, philosophical verbiage, the clear intuitive ideas of the Englishman Robert Owen, supplemented in details by John Bellers, and especially by Thomas Hodgskin who gave

16 "Literary Notices," *Springfield Union*, November 23, 1876.
17 Unpublished papers (B1-C-2).   18 *Ibid.* (B1-C-9).
19 *Ibid.* (B2-4-3).   20 *Ibid.* (B2-4-4).
21 Robert L. Shurter, *The Utopian Novel in America, 1865–1900*, p. 193.

him the theory of surplus value. By that same method of appraisal, the man for whom Christianity is named, in view of the fact that much of his message was taken from the prophets, "should no longer be acclaimed as the great originator of a movement . . . but as the most successful popularizer of a modified form of" prophetic message.

Throughout Edward Bellamy's life we have the picture of a straightforward personality, a despiser of pretense, and not a seeker of the limelight. As illustrated by his two versions of how he came to write *Looking Backward*, his statements seem not always wholly consistent. His habitual omission of any mention of books he had read, even in his personal journals and notes, leaves us somewhat in the dark as to his sources. He almost never quoted, but read omnivorously, assimilated, and then expressed himself in his own style and in his own words. In that respect he was like Shakespeare.

Human thought is an endless fabric, to which each adds his own individual elements of design, be it much or little. There can be no pretense that Edward Bellamy created a new world of social thought and plan. However, where Bellamy took other men's ideas it was to use them as bricks to build a house of his own design. When we compare degrees of originality in creation and in synthesis, we shall find Bellamy to stand high, probably superior to Karl Marx. His originality lies partly in the fact that he did not become submerged in technical logic, but relied largely on intuitional processes, with great ability to observe the prevailing mores objectively. He stubbornly refused to give up one region of values—ethical and spiritual—for another region of values—material and political— as had tended to be the case with European socialism. He insisted on achieving a synthesis large enough to include both. He had a mental toughness in keeping to his own path and in not being swept off his feet by the atavistic elements of Marxian socialism. More than any other single person he kept before his country that larger view, which has in it the genius of America.

It is a nearly universal trait of a new and immature culture that it feels inferior before older and firmly established cultures. Even though the new be superior, it commonly has less deep roots and less dominant prestige. America had the beginning of a great social synthesis, yet America felt inferior to Europe. It has inclined strongly in most intellectual fields to cast aside its own pattern as without great worth, and to borrow from Europe. That process can be seen in the planning of American college education. Edward Bellamy performed the incalculable service of believing in what was peculiarly America, and in catching the genius of its spirit. But for him there would have been a more complete surrender in America to class warfare as the way to freedom from class dominance and exploitation, a greater abandonment of the principle that humane means are no less imperative than humane ends. These are not trivial matters. They are more important to enduring social welfare than the differences between capitalism and communism.

XI · The Nationalist Movement

HOW THE NATIONALIST MOVEMENT BEGAN

Looking Backward was published in January, 1888. In writing to his publishers Edward Bellamy had expressed the hope that 50,000 copies would be sold. For nearly a year sales were slow. Then as word of it passed from person to person, the sales increased enormously until it was the best seller of its day. It was not just another story, but inspired hope and expectation of great and beneficial social changes. Many persons were led to ask themselves what they could do to help in the coming of the good age.

Some reviewers were unable to see the inherent merit of the book because of their antagonism toward Bellamy's "radicalism." It is interesting that even a man's literary judgment may not be independent of his social views.

The *Saturday Review* of London said of *Looking Backward:* "Readers of *Dr. Heidenhoff's Process*, a clever book, should prepare themselves for a severe disappointment in *Looking Backward, 2000–1887*, which, to put the matter plainly, is a stupid book. The slender frame of fiction is not interesting; and the solid middle of purpose is about as dull as anything can be." [1]

In contrast, the book reviewer of the *New York Tribune* wrote:

Mr. Bellamy has achieved so brilliant and complete a success in his difficult undertaking that the reader is carried away by the development of the New Utopia, and finds it far more fascinating than any ordinary novel, because the wonderful picture seems not only a faithful representation of what ought to be, but a not too sanguine foreshadowing of what actually might be.

Mr. Bellamy has here succeeded in describing a thorough reorganization of society without demanding the least concession to unpractical fancy. The reader as he proceeds finds no difficulty in conceiving the possibility of the changes narrated, for they are so introduced and accounted for as to seem to flow naturally and inevitably from the whole

[1] *The Saturday Review*, March 24, 1888.

tendencies of modern evolution. To produce such an effect is to rise to the plane of high art. . . . Strange and momentous as are the changes indicated, they are made to wear the aspect not of fantasies but of possibilities; and no higher praise could be given a work of fiction than this impression implies.[2]

Just as literary men lost their sense of literary value in reading of a social organization they did not approve, so the scientific writer sometimes lost his scientific perspective in the same way. A reviewer in the magazine *Science* wrote of *Looking Backward:*

The social order here exhibited assumes such an increase of wealth as could not possibly take place without mechanical or other inventions such as have not yet been even dreamed of, and which Mr. Bellamy does not even hint at. For, not only are all men to be rich under the coming régime [Bellamy assumed an average annual income of about $4,000], but they are not to work more than five or six hours a day, and are to cease work entirely at the age of forty-five. The idea advanced by the author, that such a vast increase in the production of wealth will result from a mere change in the mode of distribution, is preposterous.[3]

Another hostile reviewer took an exactly opposite viewpoint, holding that the productiveness foretold by Bellamy was no greater than could be expected in the ordinary course of events under the existing social order, and without any such social change as he described. Fifty years after this was written the potential productive capacity of America is so great that Bellamy's forecasts seem not out of reason. Bellamy did count moderately on scientific inventions.

Huntington Smith, translator of Tolstoy's works, said of the book, "The crowning tribute to the merit of Mr. Bellamy's noble book is that we put it down with the question on our lips, 'Why not today?' "[4]

The *New Orleans Times-Democrat* gave an equally favorable judgment: "The marked feature of Mr. Bellamy's book is that it contains little of mere fancy, or vagary, but is, on the contrary, so practical that it might almost be used as an economic and industrial manual."[5]

   [2] "A New Utopia," *New York Tribune,* February 5, 1888.
   [3] Review of *Looking Backward, Science,* July 20, 1888.
   [4] Quoted in the *American* (Nashville, Tennessee), June 19, 1888.
   [5] Review of *Looking Backward, New Orleans Times-Democrat,* February 5, 1888.

Practically all the letters Bellamy received have been destroyed, so that we must depend mainly on published reviews for information concerning the reception of *Looking Backward*. Because of the powerful appeal of the book, some reviewers feared it. The Atlanta, Georgia, *Constitution*, with the Civil War and its effects still sharply in memory, reminded its readers: "*Uncle Tom's Cabin* led to the downfall of our property in slaves," and expressed the fear that *Looking Backward* would result in "a new crusade against property and property rights in general." [6]

The publishers' statement announcing the popularity of the book, coupled as it was with a review disavowing Bellamy's philosophy, indicates some of the mixed feelings with which its popularity was viewed by its publishers:

Looking Backward holds in American literature an almost unique place in character and in popularity. Of only one other book (*Uncle Tom's Cabin*) have three hundred thousand copies been printed within two years of its publication. The story of its remarkable popularity and influence will hereafter form a very interesting chapter in the history of American literature and sociology.

Mr. Bellamy's views have been sharply criticized by some, though received by a multitude as equally profound and timely. Granting all that should be conceded to the critics, the following paragraph from *The Churchman* well states a truth that should be recognized:—

"Yet the vision of Mr. Bellamy may not wholly fail. Every successive step of real progress has been lighted with 'a light that never was on sea or land'; and students of social science in the present age, grappling as they are with mournful evils, and seeking to avert momentous dangers, may gain from their impossible ideals something of the loftiness of inspiration. Mr. Bellamy's vision may be—in its broad aspect, and in many details we believe it is—erroneous and utterly impracticable; but none the less we admire and sympathize with the seer of such visions." [7]

THE NATIONALIST CLUB

Shortly after the appearance of the book, Cyrus Field Willard, a Boston newspaperman, wrote Bellamy suggesting steps to promote his ideas. Bellamy replied that this was the first such suggestion he had received, and that it was "like a ray of light." After an

[6] Quoted in the *Nationalist*, I, No. 2 (June, 1889), p. 58.
[7] *Literary Bulletin of Houghton, Mifflin & Co.*, March, 1890.

exchange of several letters, Bellamy wrote Willard on July 4, 1888:

You suggest forming an association to support and propagate the Nationalist ideas of the book as offering the best solutions of the problems of the day. Go ahead by all means and do it if you can find anybody to associate with. No doubt eventually the formation of such Nationalist Clubs or associations among our sympathizers all over the country will be a proper measure, and it is fitting that Boston should lead off in this movement. I have just received a letter from Mr. Sylvester Baxter in which he expresses enthusiastic agreement with *Looking Backward,* and suggests like yourself that it would be a good thing if those of one mind on this subject could work together.[8]

William Dean Howells also had written Bellamy on the same subject, and on June 17, 1888, Bellamy had replied, "What you say about 'nationalist' having occurred to yourself also as a good designation for a party aiming at a national control of industry with its resulting social changes, strongly corroborates my belief that the name is a good one and will take." [9]

Willard and Baxter began to work out an organization, but owing to a trip to Europe by Baxter and to a temporary diversion by Willard, their activities were retarded. While they were laying their groundwork, another group became interested. In Boston there was a reading club of retired army officers. According to Cyrus Willard's account: "The military regimentation [pictured in *Looking Backward*] made a great impression on the retired army officers who composed the reading club. They had pensions to spend and time to kill, and a light airy reading room on Boylston Street opposite the Common." Captain Charles E. Bowers was chairman of the club. Other members were Colonel Thomas Wentworth Higginson, writer, poet, noted abolitionist orator, colonel of a regiment during the Civil War; Captain E. S. Huntington, a retired regular army captain; and General Arthur F. Devereaux, "the hero of Gettysburg."

[8] Cyrus Field Willard, "The Nationalist Club of Boston (a Chapter of History)," *Nationalist,* I, No. 1 (May, 1889), 17.
[9] The reader will of course note that the term "nationalism" had not at that time the specialized meaning which today would make it a poor name for such a movement as Bellamy's.

On September 7, 1888, Captain Bowers and General Devereaux wrote Bellamy suggesting an organization. They at once formed a "Boston Bellamy Club." In the meantime Willard was gathering a list of interested persons, and when Bellamy sent him Captain Bowers' name, Cyrus Willard, Henry Willard Austin, Sylvester Baxter, and Miss Alzire A. Chevaillier called on Captain Bowers, and the two groups thereafter worked together. After preliminary meetings the First Nationalist Club of Boston was informally organized on December first. In a letter to the author of this biography Cyrus Willard gave an interesting picture of the meeting:

I called the meeting in the Merchant's Exchange on State Street, in the heart of Boston's financial district. Captain Bowers and others of the reading club were there in full force. Captain Bowers was elected as presiding officer, and I, being a newspaper man, was elected secretary. I moved that we appoint a committee to bring in a constitution and by-laws. Edward Everett Hale got up, and in his peculiar hollow voice said, "I had hoped that once before I died I might be a member of a body that had no by-laws to squabble over." William Dean Howells was sitting on an empty wood box in the corner, back of a tall stove about six feet high in the center of the room. He kicked his heels vigorously against the wood box in applause. That made us all laugh, and I knew it was no use to press my motion. The permanent organization was formed and the declaration of principles adopted later.

Other meetings were held on December 8 and 15. At the latter meeting Edward Bellamy was present for the first time, and officers were elected to hold office until May of that year. Captain Charles E. Bowers was elected president; Edward Bellamy, first vice-president; Arthur F. Devereaux, second vice-president; Cyrus Field Willard, secretary; and Sylvester Baxter, treasurer. On January 9, 1889, the statement of principles was adopted. In May the first number of the *Nationalist* appeared, and the Nationalist movement was on its way.

Bellamy had written to Willard:

I heartily wish you and Mr. Baxter success in organizing in Boston the first Nationalist Club or association. . . . I thoroughly approve what you say as to directing your efforts more particularly to the conversion of the cultured and conservative class. That was precisely the special end for which *Looking Backward* was written.

In commenting on Bellamy's suggestion, Willard, who was a Theosophist, wrote: "In the Bhagavad-Gita is a statement, 'That which is done by the most excellent of men in time is done by all the others.' We were following Bellamy's own idea that we should be sure to appeal to the highest class of the citizens. . . . Our tactics were successful." The membership of the First Nationalist Club included a number of interesting people. Willard attended Edward Everett Hale's (Unitarian) church and served on an "anti-tenement house" board with him; he interested him in the movement. Hale brought in William Dean Howells and Colonel Higginson, and they brought in Hamlin Garland. Colonel Higginson and Austin interested Julia Ward Howe, already famous for "The Battle Hymn of the Republic," and her daughter.

Frances E. Willard, president of the Woman's Christian Temperance Union, through members of the Harvard faculty had met Laurence Gronlund, author of *The Co-operative Commonwealth*, and he had suggested that she read *Looking Backward*. She was much impressed with the book and went to see Edward Bellamy at Chicopee Falls. The Woman's Christian Temperance Union had worked with the single aim of eliminating intemperance. Miss Willard entered into correspondence with Cyrus Willard, who was her second cousin, both of them of an old and highly respected Boston family. Cyrus Willard writes:

I had a pile of correspondence with her four inches tall, and converted her to the proposition that poverty caused as much intemperance as intemperance caused poverty.

Miss Willard departed from the former policy of the W.C.T.U. and made it into an organization interested in all-round development of a good society. She called *Looking Backward* "a new evangel," and publicized it.

Another of the charter members of the Nationalist Club was Henry Willard Austin, a cousin of Cyrus and Frances Willard. A Harvard graduate and poet, he was later to be the amiable but irresponsible editor of the *Nationalist*. Cyrus Willard writes of his two cousins: "He represented one extreme on the liquor question and she the other, while I was in the center. He was always a hard drinker." Willard's friends took delight in emphasizing the disparity of habits of his two cousins.

Miss Willard brought into the club Mary A. Livermore, the noted woman's rights advocate; and Miss Chevaillier brought in many more women. According to Cyrus Willard, among the twenty-five women members were Anna Whitney, the sculptress; Abby Morton Diaz, president of the Boston Woman's Christian Temperance Union and head of the Woman's Exchange; Constance Howell, an English writer; Lucy Stone, editor of the *Woman's Journal;* Helen Campbell, author of *Prisoners of Poverty,* and Maude Howe Eliot, daughter of Julia Ward Howe. Willard recalls that among the members were Sam Walter Foss, the poet, then editor of the *Yankee Blade;* Thaddeus B. Wakeman, publicist, precursor of Adler and his Ethical Culture Society; Michael Lynch, author of *A Workingman's View of Nationalism,* a talented plasterer of Boston; Arthur Hildreth, a painter; Solomon Schindler, a Jewish rabbi; Laurence Gronlund, author of *The Co-operative Commonwealth;* and John Boyle O'Reilly, editor of *The Pilot,* organ of the Roman Catholic Archbishop Williams of Boston. On the whole the club members made an imposing group of men and women.

The first year of the Nationalist Club of Boston brought a very encouraging growth. In a letter to Bellamy dated April 17, 1889, Cyrus Willard wrote:

I wish you could see the letters I receive so full of the most glowing and lofty enthusiasm. My time is rather taken up in answering them, sometimes to the detriment of my business. . . . New clubs are springing up all over the country. Our magazine will be out April 25, I think, and will be a dandy.

During the year the membership of the Boston Club increased from thirty to about 200. Members were carefully chosen, and a limit of 250 was set. This restriction was made, "in order to pick our members and indirectly to encourage the formation of other clubs in different sections of the city," Cyrus Willard reported in the *Nationalist* for December, 1889.[10] Then he added:

[10] Cyrus F. Willard, "A Retrospect," *The Nationalist,* II, No. 1 (December, 1889), 38.

We desired to pick the best material for effective work and not admit any and every person who came along with a burning desire to reform the world or to join a club. . . . As has been truly said by Henry A. Ford of Detroit, "The Nationalist Club is not a cave of Adullam for the debtor and the malcontent." . . . In fact, one prominent paper accused them of being the Brahmin caste of New England. . . . The dynamic force of this new and small organization, by the variety of its components was calculated to influence every walk of life. . . . The new club went on with quiet persistence . . . until the topic of Nationalism became what it is to-day, the most widely discussed and absorbing topic of the times. The men and women in the new club commanded respect. With the prestige of their social position and the force of their intellect they shattered the "conspiracy of silence." These questions must be discussed henceforth, until they are settled.[11]

The claim to a high quality of membership was questioned by Nicholas P. Gilman in the *Quarterly Journal of Economics* for October, 1889. When the club had 107 members he found but one he could recognize as a business man. He reported the others to include 26 women, 13 clergymen, 6 physicians, 3 or more journalists, and 2 or 3 lawyers.

A second Boston club was organized on October 24, 1889, by Henry R. Legate, who was to play a prominent part in the fortunes and misfortunes of the movement. This second club was to some extent a reaction from the exclusiveness and the theoretical and literary detachment of the original club.

Clubs began to be formed in other cities, first in Washington, D.C., then in Chicago, then in Hartford, and next in New York. In California, with a burst of enthusiasm, seventeen clubs were organized in a few months. Willard estimated that there were over 6,000 members, and the movement claimed 500,000 "believers." He wrote in his report of the first year, "We have fifty or more papers and magazines unreservedly advocating Nationalism." [12] *Looking Backward* had sold 200,000 copies. In the December, 1889, *Nationalist* the Secretary wrote of "The tide of correspondence from every State and Territory in the Union, as well as from nearly every English-speaking corner of the globe . . . If, in the past few months, it had had the quarters and the money, it could have

11 *Ibid.*   12 *Ibid.*, p. 39.

done an amount of work scarcely exceeded by the National Committee of one of the great political parties during an active campaign." [13]

A celebration of the first anniversary of the Nationalist Club, held on December 19, 1889, was a notable affair. It was decided to hold later anniversary meetings in May, to coincide with traditional annual May meetings in Boston. In the following May there were two sessions, each attended by audiences of 2,000 or more. Edward Bellamy was the principal speaker at both the December and the May meetings. Mason Green gives us an impression of him as he appeared at a similar occasion in 1891:

The scene in Tremont Temple that evening was a striking one. The audience—made up as it was of people from the very best circles of Boston, with a generous sprinkling of wage-workers and of those who belonged to no organization, religious or secular . . . Men who were social strangers sat side by side at the Tremont Temple meeting and applauded Bellamy and his earnest declarations concerning the new faith. He stood with manuscript in hand, one elbow resting upon the preacher's desk, and spoke with dignity and force, the deep chest tones of his pleasing voice slightly raised above conversational pitch giving character and culture to an impressive and emphatic delivery.[14]

To Edward Bellamy the prospects seemed very good. In the *Nationalist* for December, 1889, he wrote, "The 'Ship of State' is already being borne onward by a current which it is only needful to utilize in order to reach the desired haven." [15]

PRINCIPLES OF THE NATIONALIST MOVEMENT

To appraise the spirit and the principles of Nationalism we do well to find what Edward Bellamy conceived them to be. In an article in the *Nationalist* for December, 1889, he wrote:

The progressive nationalization and municipalization of industries by substituting public control for the public advantage, in place of already highly centralized forms of corporate control for corporate advantage, is at once the logical and the inevitable policy of Nationalism.

[13] *Ibid.,* p. 36.   [14] Green.

[15] "Looking Forward," *Nationalist,* II, No. 1 (December, 1889), 1.

. . . more, after all, will depend upon its spirit than its method. . . . In offering some suggestions as to the spirit which should animate the Nationalist movement I do but describe what seems to me the characteristics of its present spirit and of the men and women engaged in it.

The first of these characteristics is unselfishness.

The sentiment of human brotherhood which is the animating principle of Nationalism is a religion in itself, and to understand it in its full significance implies a sense of consecration on the part of those who devote themselves to it. Nationalism is, indeed, based also upon the soundest of economic laws; the principle of fraternal co-operation is as certainly the only true science of wealth-production, as it is the only moral basis for society; but the latter is so much more the important consideration that even if a brotherly relation with our fellowmen could only be attained by the sacrifice of wealth, not the less would the true Nationalist seek it. The ultimate triumph of Nationalism demands as its first condition that it be kept upon the high moral ground it now occupies, and retain as its chief motive that pure and uncompromising enthusiasm of humanity which now animates it.

The second of the characteristics essential to the spirit of Nationalism, if it is to succeed speedily, is a tolerant and charitable attitude toward the critical and the indifferent—toward our opponents. If it be true, as the tone of some reformers toward the rest of the world seems to indicate, that they are hopelessly better than the general mass of men, what expectation can they have of the success of their reform, since it can only succeed by converting these bad people? Until we call a man names, there is always a chance that we may convert him but, afterwards, none at all. And not only that, but we are not helping our case with the by-standers. It would seem plain that only reformers who have all the converts they need can afford to call their opponents names. There is especially one form of denunciation which Nationalists have thus far left to other sorts of social reformers, and it is hoped we may continue to. This is the denunciation of the wealthy in the supposed interests of the poor. Nothing could be more unjust and senseless. The rich could not, however disposed, abolish or greatly lessen poverty so long as the present industrial system remains. It is the system that is to be attacked and not individuals whose condition, whether of riches or poverty, merely illustrates its results. Of course, there are many rich men who have become so by vicious methods and these merit personal condemnation, but there are probably more to whose enterprise and leadership the community owes much of the little wealth and comfort it has. It is a very barbarous and wasteful sort of leadership, to be sure, and one for which we hope to substitute a mode of organizing industry infinitely more humane and efficient. But meanwhile let us not fall into the mistake of those who rant against capitalists in general, as if, pending the introduction of a better system, they were not,—no doubt selfishly, but yet in fact—performing a necessary function to keep the present system going.

. . . Nationalism . . . places the whole subject of industrial and social reform upon a broad National basis, viewing it not from the position or with the prejudices of any one group of men, but from the ground of a common citizenship, humanity and morality. Nationalism is not a class movement; it is a citizens' movement. It represents peculiarly neither men nor women, North nor South, black nor white, poor nor rich, educated nor ignorant, employers nor employed, but all equally; holding that all of us alike, whatever our label may be, are victims in body, mind or soul, in one way or another, of the present barbarous industrial and social arrangements, and that we are all equally interested, if not for our physical, yet for our moral advantage, if not for ourselves, yet for our children, in breaking the meshes which entangle us . . .

The third of the characteristics essential to the spirit of Nationalism is patriotism.

There are social reformers who believe, the less one's devotion to his own country and countrymen, the better he will love other countries and humanity at large, as if a man were usually found to be a better neighbor in proportion as he neglects his own family. This is a belief which Nationalists utterly repudiate. The very word Nationalism is an appeal to love of country. Patriotism, though so often misdirected, is the grandest and most potent form under which the enthusiasm of humanity has yet shown itself capable of moving great masses, and in its spirit is contained the promise and potency of the world-embracing love in which it shall some day merge. Social reforms must follow National lines and will succeed as they are able to adapt themselves to National conditions and sentiments and identify themselves with National traditions and aspirations.

The fourth characteristic of the Nationalist movement which it must retain as a condition of success is its present spirit of conservatism as to methods, combined with uncompromising fidelity to ends.

Evolution, not revolution, orderly and progressive development, not precipitate and hazardous experiment, is our true policy. . . . The success of the great reform to which we have set our hands depends not so much upon winning the applause of fellow-enthusiasts, welcome as this may be, as upon gaining and keeping the confidence of the law-abiding masses of the American people. To this end we have need to be careful that no party or policy of disorder or riot finds any countenance from us . . . prudence and conservatism are called for on the part of those identified with it. Our mistakes alone can hinder our cause.[16]

16 *Ibid.*, pp. 1, 2, 3, 4.

This certainly is a moderate and restrained statement. Bellamy was here addressing readers of the *Nationalist*, many of them men and women whose positions would be at the left of the political alignment of the day, and who might well have cheered if he had taken a more extreme position. To assume that it implied any hesitancy to speak out in the presence of wealthy supporters would be a mistake. Only a few weeks after this article was published, in his talk at the first anniversary of the Boston Nationalist Club, on December 19, 1889, he addressed to the elite of Boston one of his most severe condemnations of the abuse of wealth. It is significant that in each case his words were what he thought his audience needed, not what he thought they would applaud. The gist of this speech, in its contrast to that just quoted, will give a fairly balanced impression of his manner of expression, and of his views on the Nationalist movement:

Wealth is power in its most concentrated, most efficient and most universally applicable form. In the presence of great disparities of wealth, social equality is at an end, industrial independence is destroyed, while mere constitutional stipulations as to the equal rights of citizens politically or before the law, become ridiculous.

The great corporations and combinations of capital dwarf our municipalities, overtop our States and are able to dictate to our National Legislature. The extent to which intimidation and bribery are employed to influence popular election taints with the suspicion of fraud nearly all verdicts of the ballot when the majority is not large. Even in the grand appeal to the Nation the money power, by judicious concentration of corruption funds upon close States, is able to set at naught the will of the people. The titles of the Presidents of the Republic are no longer clear. What money cannot effect at the polls, by intimidation or by bribery, it does not hesitate to attempt by the corruption of individual legislators. Our municipal Council chambers are too often mere auction rooms, where public franchises are sold to the highest briber. The Legislatures of some of our greatest States are commonly said to be owned by particular corporations. The United States Senate is known as a "rich men's club," and in the lower House of Congress the schemes of capital have only to meet the sham opposition of the demagogue.

Socially, the vast disparities of wealth afford on every side inhuman contrasts of cruel want and inordinate luxury. The dazzling illustrations of pomp and power, which are the prizes of wealth, have lent to the pursuit of gain, at all times sufficiently keen, a feverish intensity and

desperation never seen before in this or any other country. The moderate rewards of persistent industry seem contemptible in the midst of a
universal speculative fever. In all directions the old ways of legitimate
business and steady application are being abandoned for speculative
projects, gambling operations, and all manner of brigandage under
forms of law . . . Possession of property, though it may have a legal
title, is very commonly without a moral one. This is the deplorable explanation of the cynical tolerance of fraud by public opinion. Property
will not, in the long run, be respected which is without some reasonable
basis in industry or desert, and it is justly believed that much of the
wealth of today could not stand inquiry into the means of its getting.

If you would learn how republics perish, shut up your musty histories of Greece and Rome and look about you.

In time the money power is bound to seek protection from the rising
discontent of the masses in a stronger form of government, and then
the republic, long before dead, will be put out of sight. Then it will be
too late to resist. Now it is not too late.

In order, under the changed conditions, to make good the original
pledge of the republic to its citizens, it has become necessary to re-
establish and maintain by some deliberate plan that economic equality,
the basis of all other sorts of equality which, when the republic was
established, existed in a substantial degree by nature. . . . We are the
true conservative party, because we are devoted to the maintenance of
republican institutions against the revolution now being effected by
the money power. We propose no revolution, but that the people shall
resist a revolution.

. . . we hold the economic equality of all men a principal of universal application, having for its goal the eventual establishment of a
brotherhood of humanity as wide as the world and as numerous as mankind.

The plan of industrial reorganization which Nationalism proposes is
the very simple and obvious one of placing the industrial duty of citizens
on the ground on which their military duty already rests. All able-
bodied citizens are held bound to fight for the nation, and, on the other
hand, the nation is bound to protect all citizens, whether they are able
to fight or not. Why not extend this accepted principle to industry, and
hold every able-bodied citizen bound to work for the nation, whether
with mind or muscle, and, on the other hand, hold the nation bound to
guarantee the livelihood of every citizen, whether able to work or not.
As in military matters the duty to fight is conditioned upon physical
ability, while the right of protection is conditioned only upon citizenship, so would we condition the obligation to work upon the strength
to work, but the right to support upon citizenship only.

The realization of the proposed plan of industry requires as the preliminary step the acquisition by the nation through its government, national and municipal, of the present industrial machinery of the country. It follows, therefore, that the Nationalists' programme must begin with the progressive nationalization of the industries of the United States. In proposing this cause we are animated by no sentiment of bitterness toward individuals or classes. In antagonizing the money power we antagonize not men but a system. We advocate no rash or violent measures, or such as will produce derangement of business or undue hardship to individuals. We aim to change the law by the law, and the Constitution, if necessary, by constitutional methods. As to the order in which industries should be nationalized, priority should naturally be given to those the great wealth of which renders them perilous to legislative independence, to those which deal extortionately with the public or oppressively with employees, to those which are highly systematized and centralized and to those which can be readily assimilated by existing departments of government.[17]

The policy proposed by the Nationalists was the successive nationalization or municipalizing of public services and branches of industry and the simultaneous organization of the employees upon a basis of guaranteed rights, as branches of the civil service of the country. The Nationalist policy was first to nationalize the telegraph and telephone and to establish a parcel post service:

Congress fails to discharge its constitutional duty to maintain a post office so long as it neglects to complete its facilities in accordance with modern standards.[18]

Next would follow the nationalization of the railroads:

The purchase of the roads outright would be uncalled for and unwise, and . . . the best course would be the assumption of a permanent government control of the system. An analogy for such a control, although of course not a close one, may be found in that already exercised with such admirable success over bankrupt roads by United States receivers. The present security-holders would continue to receive such reasonable dividends, on a just valuation of the plants, as might be earned.[19]

[17] "Nationalism—Principles, Purposes"; address of Edward Bellamy at Tremont Temple, Boston, on the Nationalist Club Anniversary, December 19, 1889, quoted from *Edward Bellamy Speaks Again,* pp. 53, 54, 55, 56, 58, 59, 60, 61, 62, 64, 65.

[18] Bellamy, "First Steps Toward Nationalism," *Forum* (October, 1890), quoted from *Edward Bellamy Speaks Again,* p. 106.

[19] *Ibid.,* p. 113.

Then the Nationalists would nationalize the coal mines. Along the way would be the assumption and conduct by municipalities of local public services, such as transit, lighting, heating, and the water supply.

No doubt the comment upon the foregoing statement of Nationalist propositions will be that they are all measures called for by considerations of general public expediency, without reference to Nationalism as an ulterior end. Precisely so, and just this, I hope, may be truly said of every subsequent step which Nationalists shall advocate. They propose no revolutionary methods, no hasty or ill-considered methods provocative of reaction, no letting go of the old before securing a hold on the new . . .[20]

. . . Nationalism does not propose to put an end to private incomes or to private property. It proposes only that the means of production, with the connected functions of transportation, etc., should be owned by the people in common and conducted for their benefit, the people meanwhile working as employees of the national concern, and living on their income as equal partners in the produce.[21]

There is, indeed, nothing in the National plan which does not already exist as a germ of vigorous shoot in the present order, and this is so simply because Nationalism is evolution.[22]

Great revolutions, however peaceful they may be, do not follow prearranged plans, but make channels for themselves of which we may at best predict the general direction and outcome. Meanwhile Nationalists would prepare the way by a step-by-step extension of the public conduct of business, which shall go as fast or as slow as public opinion may determine.[23]

The interweaving lockstitching of a man in conscious mutual interdependence and service with all his fellow members, and its effect to furnish an assimilating power, overcome antagonisms of race and religion which have been so dangerous and always might be. Some such influence is essential in a polyglot nation like ours. Out of it, and the intermarriage of all classes which will follow, will quickly be evolved the American, the heir and offspring, the consummate product of all the races. There will then no longer be either Jew or Greek, Irishman, German, Swede or Frenchman, but Americans only.[24]

[20] *Ibid.*, pp. 117–18.
[21] Editorial, *New Nation*, I, No. 7 (March 14, 1891), 110.
[22] Bellamy, *"Looking Backward* Again," *North American Review*, CL (March, 1890), 354.
[23] Bellamy, "The Programme of the Nationalists," *Forum* (March, 1894), quoted from *Edward Bellamy Speaks Again*, p. 159.
[24] Unpublished papers (B2-7-13).

He would eliminate political corruption by civil service; he would promote woman suffrage; he would limit child labor. In his infrequent talks, and more especially in his magazine articles, and in the columns of the *Nationalist* and the *New Nation*, Bellamy continued to outline his program step by step.

THEOSOPHY AND THE NATIONALIST MOVEMENT

There has been complete absence of recognition of one of the chief influences in the sudden origin of the Nationalist movement, its spectacular growth, and its equally rapid decline. No description of Nationalism can be adequate which does not take into account its relation to the Theosophical Society.

In the unpublished autobiography of Cyrus Willard is the following brief summary:

The Theosophical Society is essentially an American institution. Theosophy was brought to America by . . . Helen P. Blavatsky, who landed in New York in 1873 and founded the Theosophical Society in 1875, with Colonel H. S. Olcott, William Q. Judge and others. She published *Isis Unveiled* in 1877, became an American citizen in 1878, and in December of that year left America with Colonel Olcott, never to return, but leaving William Q. Judge, a young lawyer of Irish birth, to hold the fort . . .

In 1886 the American Section of the Theosophical Society was formed, with Mr. Judge as secretary and later as president. In the course of time the society in America split into three or more groups, which, however, have been substantially independent of the organization in other countries. The major emphasis of the society has seemed to be upon a study of Hindu and other Asiatic philosophy and upon an effort to bring about a synthesis of Asiatic and Christian philosophy and ethics. Since the writer's acquaintance with the society is limited almost to the brief inquiry involved in assembling data for this chapter, he does not presume to give an authoritative statement of its work or purposes.

Among the first men to propose to Edward Bellamy that steps be taken for promoting his ideas were two Theosophists. One of them, Cyrus Field Willard, has described the situation: "Sylvester

Baxter was editorial writer on the *Boston Herald*. I was across the street in the *Boston Globe*. He was a member of the Malden Theosophical Society, and yet we had never met. The only obvious element other than chance in this coincidence is the fact that the members of the new society were full of zeal for the doctrine of universal brotherhood, a dominant element of Theosophy, which seemed also to be the pervading spirit of *Looking Backward*."

Willard, son of an old, aristocratic Boston family, had alienated his people by his sympathy with labor and by his nonaristocratic interests. He had been assistant manager of a telegraph company (predecessor of the Western Union), had represented a telephone syndicate in France for three years, and had traveled over Europe. He learned German, studied Marxian socialism, was editor of a Haverhill, Massachusetts, labor paper, and from there went to the *Boston Globe* as "labor editor" on a capitalist-owned paper that catered to labor interests. He was a member of the American Economic and Statistical Association, secretary and legislative agent of the Boston Central Labor Union, member of a German socialist club, a director of the Anti-Tenement League; and, though an active Theosophist, he attended Edward Everett Hale's Unitarian church. As member of the reception committee of the Press Club he met many notables who came to Boston.

Sylvester Baxter, editorial writer on the rival paper, the *Boston Herald*, possessed exceptional literary ability and discriminating taste. He was author of the first long review of *Looking Backward*, one of the best ever written. He became an able supporter of the Nationalist program and was the most intelligent interpreter of Edward Bellamy.

When the Nationalist Club was formed, the officers were divided between army men and Theosophists. A committee of seven appointed to draft a statement of principles for the club consisted of Willard as chairman, with Bellamy, Henry Willard Austin, Arthur B. Griggs (president of the Boston branch of the Theosophical Society), George D. Ayers (president of the Malden branch), and Sylvester Baxter. With the exception of Edward Bellamy, all were Theosophists. According to Willard, and contrary to published accounts, Bellamy did not draft the statement, but approved it as it was prepared by the others. This statement of principles is idealistic and abstract:

Declaration of Principles

The principle of the Brotherhood of Humanity is one of the eternal truths that govern the world's progress on lines which distinguish human nature from brute nature.

The principle of competition is simply the application of the brutal law of the survival of the strongest and most cunning.

Therefore, so long as competition continues to be the ruling factor in our industrial system, the highest development of the individual cannot be reached, the loftiest aims of humanity cannot be realized.

No truth can avail unless practically applied. Therefore those who seek the welfare of man must endeavor to suppress the system founded on the brute principle of competition and put in its place another based on the nobler principle of association.

But in striving to apply this nobler and wiser principle to the complex conditions of modern life, we advocate no sudden or ill considered changes; we make no war upon individuals; we do not censure those who have accumulated immense fortunes simply by carrying to a logical end the false principle on which business is now based.

The combinations, trusts and syndicates of which the people at present complain demonstrate the practicability of our basic principle of association. We merely seek to push this principle a little further and have all industries operated in the interest of all by the nation—the people organized—the organic unity of the whole people.

The present industrial system proves itself wrong by the immense wrongs it produces: it proves itself absurd by the immense waste of energy and material which is admitted to be its concomitant. Against this system we raise our protest: for the abolition of the slavery it has wrought and would perpetuate, we pledge our best efforts.[25]

In February, 1889, Bellamy received a letter from William Q. Judge, editor of a Theosophist periodical, the *Path*. "Nationalism," Judge wrote, ". . . is, as you know, founded on the principle of Universal Brotherhood. I thus conceive of it as closely linked to Theosophy, and a desirable means whereby Theosophists may assist in the ethical advancement of the race, substituting brotherhood and co-operation for competition, and do good work

[25] *Nationalist*, I, No. 1 (May, 1889).

on the practical plane. Hence I desire to popularize Nationalism, showing it in the above fraternal light. . . . I hope you will be able to let me have a story on the above lines for the April *Path*." No such article by Bellamy appeared in the *Path*.

The first officers of the Nationalist Club were recognized as temporary. At the second election in May, 1889, Captain Bowers declined re-election and George Ayers was elected in his place; while John Ransom Bridge, another Theosophist, replaced Willard, who also declined re-election, as secretary. Thereafter we hear little of the army officers. Captain Bowers remained business manager of the *Nationalist* until he made a trip to Europe a year later, and General Devereaux continued his interest. Colonel Higginson, who in the first number of the *Nationalist* had inscribed a stirring poem, *Heirs of Time*, to Bellamy, within about a year was criticizing his theories in a public address.

When the first number of the *Nationalist*, for May, 1889, appeared, Theosophical influence was dominant. Of the eight contributors named on the front cover of the magazine, four were Theosophists, and they wrote a majority of the articles. Austin, a Theosophist, was the first editor, selected by Willard; but, according to Willard, his bibulous habits and his laziness, unusual traits in a Theosophist, made him so ineffective that Willard had to do most of the work. In August, 1890, John Storer Cobb became editor. He, like Ayers and Baxter, was one of the founders of the Theosophical Society. He was a man of means, and while the *Nationalist* expenses were in general paid by informal "chipping in" of the members of the club, Willard was of the opinion that he met the deficits. Willard had a column, "News of the Movement," and Theosophists continued to provide a large part of the articles. Katherine Tingley, who succeeded Judge as head of the Theosophical Society, a position she held until her death in 1929, was a member of the woman's auxiliary of the Nationalist Club of Boston.

The leaders of the First Nationalist Club, which was thus largely in Theosophist hands, saw it as the head of the Nationalist movement. Clubs all over the country, as well as the one in London, adopted its statement of principles as their own. In reviewing the first year's work of the movement Willard wrote that until half the states had Nationalist Clubs to justify a national league, ". . . . it has been thought advisable that the Boston Club should continue, as in the past, to act as the national organization." [26]

By June, 1890, Willard stated in the *Nationalist:*

At the time the first number of the *Nationalist* was issued there were just seven clubs in existence. To-day it is an impossibility to state just how many there are. We have received information at this office of the organization of one hundred and twenty-seven. These are located in twenty-seven states. It had been determined to wait until the majority of the states had organized before organizing a National League of Nationalist Clubs; but we have now virtually two-thirds of that number and the formation of the league cannot long be delayed. [27]

However, no national organization was formed.

Bellamy did not own the *Nationalist.* It was owned by the Nationalist Educational Association, of which he was made president. He was offered and he accepted the editorship of the *Nationalist,* but withdrew before beginning to serve, on the grounds of poor health. In Willard's unpublished autobiography we find:

Bellamy lived at Chicopee Falls. . . . After the Nationalist Club was formed he would occasionally come to Boston and meet with the Nationalists who were also Theosophists and believed with me that Nationalism was but the working out of the doctrines of human brotherhood as taught by Madam Blavatsky and the whole Theosophical Society. [28]

According to Willard, Theosophist principles were frequently discussed with Bellamy, and he was sympathetic with them, though it seems he never became a member of the society. His brother Charles was listed as a member.

In 1889 there was published *The Key to Theosophy,* which, more than any other document except *The Secret Doctrine,* is the "Bible" of the society. In it appears a definite approval of the Nationalist principles and program in the form of a dialogue between "Enquirer" and "Theosophist." This statement had such marked historical results that it is quoted:

[26] Cyrus F. Willard, "A Retrospect," *Nationalist,* II, No. 1 (December, 1889), 40.

[27] Willard, "News of the Movement," *Nationalist,* II, No. 7 (June, 1890), 274.

[28] Cyrus Willard's unpublished autobiography.

THEO. . . . The organization of Society, depicted by Edward Bellamy, in his magnificent work *Looking Backward,* admirably represents the Theosophical idea of what should be the first great step towards the full realization of universal brotherhood. The state of things he depicts falls short of perfection, because selfishness still exists and operates in the hearts of men. But in the main, selfishness and individualism have been overcome by the feeling of solidarity and mutual brotherhood; and the scheme of life there described reduces the causes tending to create and foster selfishness to a minimum.

ENQ. Then as a Theosophist you will take part in an effort to realize such an ideal?

THEO. Certainly; and we have proved it by action. Have not you heard of the Nationalist clubs and party which have sprung up in America since the publication of Bellamy's book? They are now coming prominently to the front, and will do so more and more as time goes on. Well, these clubs and this party were started in the first instance by Theosophists. One of the first, the Nationalist Club of Boston, Mass., has Theosophists for President and Secretary, and the majority of its executive belong to the T.S. In the constitution of all their clubs, and of the party they are forming, the influence of Theosophy and of the Society is plain, for they all take as their basis, their first and fundamental principle, the Brotherhood of Humanity as taught by Theosophy. In their declaration of Principles they state:—"The principle of the Brotherhood of Humanity is one of the eternal truths that govern the world's progress on lines which distinguish human nature from brute nature." What can be more Theosophical than this? [29]

The American Theosophist magazine, the *Path,* in its issue of March, 1889, and the English Theosophical magazine *Lucifer,* edited by H. P. Blavatsky, expressed equally strong approval. Such endorsements as these, from the very fountainhead of the Theosophist movement, provided a strong incentive to the members.

Theosophists were active in the New York and Chicago Clubs, and probably elsewhere, but California was the most active field of Theosophist development and of Theosophist participation in the Nationalist movement. More than a third of all the Nationalist Clubs reported in the *Nationalist* and the *New Nation* appeared in that state. An article on "Nationalism in California," in the *Overland Monthly* for June, 1890, states that at the time the

[29] H. P. Blavatsky, *The Key to Theosophy,* pp. 44–45. By permission of the publisher, the Theosophical University Press.

article was written there were more than sixty clubs in California,[30] with a total of 3,000 to 3,500 members, and adds: "The class of the people from which the strength of the Nationalist movement has been drawn is its most striking feature. Socialistic movements . . . have found their supporters [heretofore] among the manual laborers and the professional agitators, but the strength of this movement is among the middle classes. For the most part, they are people connected with . . . the professions." [31] The lively interest in Nationalism throughout California may be inferred from a note in a San Francisco paper of the time, which reported, "The tenth public reception of the San Francisco Nationalist Club at Metropolitan Hall last night was attended by nearly 2000 persons."

From Mr. Abbott B. Clark, the sole surviving California Theosophist of those days, the following explanation of that development was secured: "The cities in which there were Lodges of the Theosophical Society were: San Francisco, Los Angeles (2 lodges), East Los Angeles, San Diego (3 lodges), Santa Cruz, San Jose, Oakland, Stockton, Gilroy, Alameda, Sacramento, all in California." Nationalist Clubs appeared in every one of these cities. The *Overland Monthly* article reported five clubs in San Francisco and seven in Los Angeles. Mr. Clark wrote further:

All the Nationalist clubs in the West traced their origin, the first definite cause for their existence, to the kindly mention and praise of Edward Bellamy's *Looking Backward* in *The Key to Theosophy.* . . . This first drew our attention to the book *Looking Backward,* which we purchased and widely circulated.

With such laudatory references to Mr. Bellamy by our leader, H. P. Blavatsky, and in our magazine, it is no wonder that many socially minded and public spirited Theosophists all over America wrote immediately, as we in San Diego did, to the First Nationalist Club of Boston for directions for organizing clubs, and made extensive purchases of the book *Looking Backward,* and we all loaned and circulated our copies as widely as possible. . . . From the beautiful spirit and range of knowledge manifest in his writings we counted Mr. Bellamy as one of us.

The Nationalist Clubs in California sprang up all at once in towns

[30] There were eleven clubs in Massachusetts, nine in New York, and seven in Ohio.

[31] F. I. Vassault, "Nationalism in California," *Overland Monthly,* XV (Second Series), No. 90 (June, 1890), 660.

and cities where there were branches, as we called them, of the Theosophical Society. We all knew that it was a spontaneous action of Fellows of the Theosophical Society that organized the Nationalist Clubs.

Four Theosophists formed the nucleus and obtained directions from Boston for the formation of a Nationalist Club [in San Diego]. Twenty or thirty members of the Theosophical Society invited their friends, and we formed a club which met weekly. Judge Sidney Thomas was elected president and I secretary. We were also respectively president and secretary of the Theosophical Society. Within two or three months we had over 600 members, including the elite of the intellectuals of the city.

Thus it would seem that the Theosophists felt that they had found a suitable channel for giving practical expression to their faith, while Bellamy had unexpectedly found a considerable number of sincere, ardent workers for his cause.

Yet it seems that the relationship proved to be unsatisfactory both to Bellamy and to the Theosophists. Edward Bellamy saw Nationalism as an active political force, entering into the determination of current public issues. The Theosophist view was different. A few quotations from *The Key to Theosophy* will illustrate:

ENQ. Do you take any part in politics?
THEO. As a Society, we carefully avoid them . . . To seek to achieve political reforms before we have effected a reform in *human nature, is like putting new wine into old bottles*. Make men feel and recognize in their innermost hearts what is their real, true duty to all men, and every old abuse of power, every iniquitous law in the national policy, based on human, social or political selfishness, will disappear of itself. . . . No lasting political reform can be ever achieved with the same selfish men at the head of affairs as of old.
ENQ. The Theosophical Society is not, then, a political organization?
THEO. Certainly not. It is international in the highest sense in that its members comprise men and women of all races, creeds, and forms of thought, who work together for one object, the improvement of humanity; but as a society it takes absolutely no part in any national or party politics.[32]

These contrasting approaches to the social problem were exemplified by the First and the Second Nationalist Clubs of Boston. The actual character of the *Nationalist* magazine, sponsored by the First Club, and the *New Nation*, which more nearly reflected

[32] Blavatsky, *The Key to Theosophy*, pp. 231–32. Reprinted by permission.

the attitude of the Second Club (though the *New Nation* under-took to recognize both approaches), tend to confirm the statement in Green's biography as to their different characteristics:

> These two Boston clubs were prototypes of movements in other cities. The First Nationalist was strong on theory and doctrine, and the Second Nationalist was more particularly identified with "first steps." At the meetings of the first club one would hear much about "Evolution" and "environment," the "solidarity of the race," the "Enthusiasm of humanity," and so on; while at the second club government ownership of railroads and telegraphs and municipal tenement houses and the public conduct of the liquor traffic were the sort of subjects that held the boards.

We may believe that Bellamy could have great sympathy for the Theosophist attitude and yet feel that his own movement de-manded greater immediacy in its aims. Moreover, in contrast to the Theosophist doctrine, he was becoming committed to the belief that men are largely the creatures of the conditions in which they live, and to a great degree could be made over by improving their environment.

That the non-political principle was actively maintained by Theosophists is indicated by the following excerpts from letters from Mr. Clark:

> The Nationalist Clubs were strictly non-political and adhered to the spirit of Mr. Bellamy's *Looking Backward* in not allowing class antago-nisms in their discussions. The treasurer of our [San Diego] Club, E. W. Morse, was one of the wealthy retired merchants of the city. He said, "This scheme I can fully endorse because it is as fair to myself as to my employees, and as fair to them as to me." Our principal speakers were city and county officials, judges, school-board members, etc., all elected on the Republican ticket and naturally opposed to radicalisms. The avowed Socialists, except Anna F. Smith, took no part in our meetings. Any claim which the Socialists may make to having organized the Nationalist Club movement is certainly only an after-thought.
>
> It is of particular importance that the Theosophical Society should in no way be connected with any political party or with anything that promotes class or sectarian distinctions.
>
> The charm, the universal drawing power, of Edward Bellamy's *Look-ing Backward* was the absence of "class consciousness." The emphasis was placed upon the transition from the nineteenth-century condition

to the ideal state without class conflict, hate or injustice. It seems to me that this point cannot be overemphasized.

When an attempt was made to lead the Club into politics people stopped coming. The Treasurer and myself were left to pay the bills. The Club dissolved.

In January, 1891, Bellamy started his own paper, the *New Nation,* with himself as editor, Mason Green as managing editor, and Henry R. Legate, president of the Second Nationalist Club of Boston, as assistant editor. It was established in spite of the fact that the *Nationalist,* according to Cyrus Willard, was being published by members of the First Nationalist Club without expense to Bellamy, and with no more tax on his time and strength than he could afford. The new paper, on the other hand, had to be started and maintained by his own personal drive and resources. According to Cyrus Willard, Mason Green domineered over and "hypnotized" the mild-mannered Bellamy. Willard wrote in a letter to the author: "Green was hard, insistent, with a little black mustache like Hitler's; and Bellamy, pale-faced, thin, and fragile, was no match for his stronger and more purposeful companion." Although in authority as headquarters of the Nationalist movement, with the the *Nationalist* the First Nationalist Club had definitely assumed publishing of the *New Nation* the new paper assumed that leadership.

The parting of the ways evidently was reached in the autumn of 1890. Henry Willard Austin, Theosophist and first editor of the *Nationalist,* in an obituary article on Bellamy gave one picture of what took place:

I remember, as it were but yesterday, his almost rustic air of amaze at the manner in which a group of earnest and rather brilliant men, representing a dozen callings, hailed his book as a gospel and himself as an inspired apostle.

There were in that gathering some worldly-wise, who felt that the author's head might be turned by an enthusiasm which promised to become personal very rapidly and feared that "the cause" might be wrecked by one-man-power.

Against this they took precautions and in justice it must be said that for a year and a half there was little or no sign that Bellamy wished to play a star part in the political drama which had been planned.

That he did yield finally to a foolish desire of having a personal organ, and that against the counsels of his truest friends he permitted himself to quit his proper sphere, essay editorship, and play at politics, merely shows that he was human and that the immense adulation he had endured from weak-minded followers at last achieved a temporary victory over his native shrewdness and good sense.[33]

Cyrus Willard has commented on the situation:

With all the writers in the Nationalist Clubs, it was only natural for us to have a magazine. This was issued in the beginning by the Nationalist Educational Association and, as long as it remained an educational movement, it prospered; but when the movement entered politics, we soon found that our legislative committee at the State House had sold out to the, then, Bay State Gas Company, whose trail of corruption is so picturesquely told by Tom Lawson in his book *Frenzied Finance.* And then I found, as secretary and editor of the department "News of the Movement," that corrupt politicians were getting control. The Theosophists all over the country who had been induced by Madam Blavatsky's endorsement to join this movement, seeing the evidences of political corruption, withdrew. And this passing of the spiritual side of the movement meant the passing of its soul, and the movement died some years later.

After the cessation of our magazine, I induced our director to merge with Bellamy's weekly which he wished to start, urged to it by a man named Mason Green, who was its managing editor until it folded up with some financial loss to Bellamy, who put so much of his royalties into it. He asked my opinion before he started his weekly, and I advised him strongly against it, as I had seen the failure of so many labor papers. But my advice was of no avail.[34]

Willard summed up the situation:

The Theosophists were obliged to drop the Nationalist movement when Bellamy alienated the members of the Nationalist Educational

[33] Henry Willard Austin, "Edward Bellamy," *National Magazine,* I (October, 1898).

[34] Cyrus Willard's unpublished autobiography. Henry R. Legate, president of the Second Nationalist Club of Boston, the legislative agent who, in Mr. Willard's opinion, had sold out to the Bay State Gas Company, for the next quarter of a century lived in Boston and had a good reputation among liberals. On the decline of the Nationalist movement he joined the Socialist party and continued to promote public ownership of utilities. Since the campaign which he directed in Massachusetts for the right of the public to own its gas and electric properties was successful, it seems possible that Mr. Willard's opinion, that he "sold out," may have been in error. Mason Green, while not a strong character, and with an uncontrolled appetite for drink, seemed in the thirty years of his remaining life never to waver in his loyalty to Bellamy's ideas.

Association and started his own paper under the influence of Mason Green and such corrupt politicians as I knew Legate to be. I never had any words with him or with Green. I just dropped them, and began to devote my energies to the Theosophical movement; as did Baxter, Ayers, and other Theosophists. . . . The others would not have followed my example so universally had they not concurred in my judgment of Legate and Green.

The *raison d'etre* of the Nationalist Education Association ceased to be, and Bellamy was not strong enough physically to carry it on. That caused all of us who saw how weak he was to be opposed to his destroying the fine spirit of co-operative effort that started the Nationalist Club.

Looking back on those days, Willard wrote: "I felt that it was Theosophy that gave a philosophy that ensouled the [Nationalist] movement." And again, "I looked on the Nationalist movement as the working out of Theosophy on the physical plane, and I was more interested in the Theosophical movement."

What would have been Bellamy's role under these circumstances if he had continued to see the First Nationalist Club and the *Nationalist* as the principal channels for advancing his ideas? The leading editorial in the issue of the Theosophist-controlled *Nationalist* magazine for December, 1889, had dealt with that issue very directly:

Edward Bellamy is one of the most high-minded, kind-hearted and companionable of men. Indeed, it is his real crown, a crown more real than any ever worn by monarch, that those who know him esteem the man even more highly than the genius.

But right here a word of caution to the rapidly gathering army of his admirers—the industrial army in embryo—the Nationalists throughout the country! There is always danger in hero-worship, as in many other pleasant things, under the present social system. Not so much danger, perhaps, to the recipient of the worship, though it is a melancholy fact that again and again in history the heads of great men have been turned by the flatteries of smaller men, even in some cases, to the detriment of nations, by the adulations of contemptibly small men. But the chief danger lies in confusing a person, however great and heroic and worthy of esteem, with a Cause which is at once the composite spirituality and most important practical business of the many—of Man, the Mass, in contradistinction from man, the unit.

This confusion some opponents of the grand and ennobling, yet simple and commonsensible, doctrines of Nationalism have already attempted to bring about. Realizing that in this age any reform, which can be juggled into even the semblance of a mere one-man following, can thus be side-tracked, some of our opponents have tried to make out that Nationalism and Bellamyism are identical . . .

Nor, though great honor is due to Edward Bellamy, should it ever be forgotten that many others have worked and suffered and died young to bring about that clarity in the general intellectual atmosphere which to-day is enabling us to see the full beauty—and, seeing, to help toward realizing an approximate practical loveliness in human relations—of the glorious picture painted by Bellamy with the heartful hand of genius.

Nor, yet further, does Bellamy wish to pose, or be posed, as a guide or leader, like Henry George, for instance. Bellamy recognizes that this movement is too vast to be led or guided by any one man: he knows that to ensure a speedy and permanent success it needs the patient focalization of many earnest hearts and subtle minds . . . the best way to hasten the day of the Reign of Humanity is to avoid in the management of our Nationalist affairs both the show and the substance of the rule of One-man-ity. This can be done by taking counsel together early and often, and there must be just such practical co-operation on the mental plane, were it only by way of training, to bring about finally in its full effect a practical co-operation on the material plane—a co-operation not of paternalism, but of Fraternity, with the widest possible Equality and the truest possible Liberty.[35]

The expressions "mental plane" and "material plane" have frequent use and specific meaning in Theosophical writing. The editorial evidently was written by a Theosophist. Thus it would seem that Bellamy faced the prospect of seeing the Nationalist movement become a phase of the Theosophist movement, with himself perhaps as a figurehead.

Apparently there were elements in the situation which are not fully covered by the statements of Austin and of Willard. A letter of December 26, 1890, from Bellamy to Thomas Wentworth Higginson, throws further light on the situation:

Chicopee Falls, Mass.
December 26, 1890

The *Nationalist* magazine is, I fear, moribund. We have raised, a few of us, some $2000 within the year to keep it along, and it owes money besides. The January number will appear, but from present prospects

35 "Editorial Notes," *Nationalist*, II, No. 1 (December, 1889), 33, 34, 35.

scarcely another. Now the magazine has never amounted to very much, but it has amounted to something, and its decease without substitute or successor, would, I think, be regarded by the Adversary of Souls with a complacency which I am just mean enough to grudge him.

Under these circumstances I feel that the time has come to carry out a project which I have long been maturing, that is, to establish a weekly paper to be conducted by myself and devoted to the discussion of the industrial and social situation from the moral and economic point of view indicated by my book and subsequent work. Of course any paper which I should edit would be devoted to Nationalism, but I should not intend it to be in any narrow sense a merely Nationalist organ. . . .

Were this the only time Edward Bellamy had burned his bridges behind him in order to hold to his purpose, we might assume that he acted from some weakness of vanity or ambition. But when we see him repeatedly setting his course against the prevailing current, giving up college, the law, an editorial career, and a publishing business, always deliberately and consciously holding to his course, though at great danger to his security and prestige, and when we see him largely withdrawing from his most intimate social associates when their ways were not his, shall we not assume similar incentives in this case? The action must have been all the harder because he seems to have had respect and affection for the men who had so unselfishly and loyally supported him, and for the Theosophical movement to which they were committed.

When he started his own paper, in January, 1891, events moved rapidly among Theosophists. Willard writes: "I tried hard to persuade Bellamy not to start the *New Nation*, as I knew how hard it is to make an impression on the mind of the people. But when he said he felt he must do it, I persuaded our Board of Directors of the Nationalist Club to agree to merge the *Nationalist* magazine with Bellamy's weekly paper."

The farewell notice in the final issue of the *Nationalist*, that of March–April, 1891, does not mention a merger or the *New Nation*, which had begun publication as a weekly on January 31, 1891, but states, "An endeavor will be made to place outstanding subscriptions with some other periodical." The *Nationalist* apparently did not transfer its good-will assets to the *New Nation*, though previously it had given notice of the first issue.

Since Cyrus Willard was secretary of the First Nationalist Club, and later correspondent with Theosophists over the country, the increase or decrease of mutual interests was somewhat in his hands. He writes of his own course during this period: "Men like Abbott Clark looked to me to keep them advised by mail, and I did. I sized up Mason Green quickly and felt sorry for Bellamy, and it turned out just as I knew it would. The People's party politicians were no better."

It was in 1889 and 1890 that the great development of Nationalist Clubs occurred under the stimulus of the Theosophists. With the discontinuance of the Theosophist-controlled *Nationalist* magazine, and the starting of the *New Nation* under Bellamy's personal direction, these clubs disappeared almost as suddenly as they had arisen. Concerning their disappearance Mr. Abbott Clark wrote:

In 1892 I spent the summer in Los Angeles in newspaper and Theosophical work. There was no Nationalist Club in Los Angeles at that time.

In 1892, in the fall, I went to San Francisco where were located at that time the headquarters of the Theosophical Society on the Pacific coast. Here I was associate editor of the *Pacific Theosophist* and traveling lecturer, frequently visiting all the cities in that part of California. There were no Nationalist Clubs to be found. In some places there were Socialist societies, but the mention or insistence upon *Universal* Brotherhood brought hisses and sometimes denunciation. The whole spirit of their meetings was different, usually very different, from that in the Nationalist Clubs. During the time from 1888 to 1900 I became acquainted with most of the leading Socialists on the Pacific coast. Some of them became my personal friends, but the character of their work was so different from that of the Nationalist Clubs that I have put off finishing this letter all these weeks lest I seem to be prejudiced or unkind. . . .

I am told that the Socialists now claim the Nationalist Clubs. Such a claim would have been indignantly repudiated by more than nine-tenths of our Nationalist Club membership. The Socialists were advocating "Class Consciousness" (of the working classes), as against the Plutocrats and all of the Bourgeoisie who did not actually sympathize with the Proletarians. The Nationalist Clubs were Universal Brotherhood clubs. Please emphasize this. All "classes" (a taboo word) were well represented in our Club.

The Nationalist Clubs, during their short existence, were more numerous and very many times larger in membership, appealing as they did to all classes equally.

Thus faded away the active co-operative movement between Theosophy and Nationalism. The frail, tired Bellamy picked up the load again to carry it by himself.

As the later years gave evidence, only a few members of the First Nationalist Club had that degree of commitment which led them to great personal sacrifices for the way of life which Bellamy had pictured. It is probable that in most cases the price of such commitment would have been great. Mason Green observed, "It took William Dean Howells some years to recover his literary status after publishing his socialistic novels." Bellamy might have been the saint and the hero of a company of men who eased their consciences by pious hopes and cautious steps toward a better society, while they continued their comfortable ways of life. He undertook actual achievement with such fallible and unskillful help as was available. In that effort he largely failed of immediate effectiveness. As it is, his vision and faith remain, perhaps to be the incentive of men or movements in cases where purpose and opportunity shall coincide.

By isolating this discussion of Theosophy and the Nationalist movement an exaggerated impression of the importance of that association may be created. Theosophy was only one of numerous factors involved. Specific treatment has been given to the relations of Theosophy and Nationalism because heretofore they have been wholly ignored.

THE COURSE OF THE NATIONALIST MOVEMENT

For a time the Nationalist movement seemed to be taking the country. The word "Nationalism," as descriptive of Bellamy's movement, was commonly used in current literature, on a par with "socialism" and "capitalism." About 140 Nationalist clubs were formed. Reform papers sprang up everywhere, their number being variously estimated at from 350 to 1,000. The new People's party, after a first weak effort at the Cincinnati convention, took for its platform most of the "first steps" of the Nationalist program. In Massachusetts especially the platform of the party was dominated by the Nationalists. Interest in Nationalism was country wide.

In 1890 the *North American Review* commented: "After the tariff and the speakership, what are the two subjects uppermost in the public mind?" Its reply was, "Probably Nationalism and electric lighting." [36] In 1891 Daniel De Leon reported that in Kansas "The name of Bellamy brought forth prolonged cheers." In the national election of 1892 the People's party polled more than a million votes for President, and elected several Congressmen and Senators. The *New Nation* quoted a conservative newspaper as saying, "The Omaha platform [People's party, 1892] was a Nationalist one—nothing more—nothing less." [37]

In May or June of 1891 the Nationalists secured the enactment of a law in the Massachusetts General Court (the state legislature) giving cities and villages the right to own and operate their own electric and gas utility systems. In 1892 a similar law was passed giving municipalities the right to own and operate their own coal yards. This latter was declared unconstitutional by the Massachusetts Supreme Court in a decision highly colored by the dislike of the judges for public ownership.

Mason Green, who lived through this period with Edward Bellamy, has given an account of the political currents of the day. The following is quoted from his unpublished biography of Bellamy.

The political skies in the early nineties afforded a succession of storm signals alarming to old-party leaders. In Kansas, and indeed, throughout the West the old guard greenbackers and the rising free silver men were both anxious to step from state campaigns into the national arena. The labor organizations were crowded with men who were getting nervous at the hope so long deferred and the temporizing of their officials. The farmers were ready for almost any revolt that could be peacefully taken to get relief from a currency that was taking from them the legitimate fruits of their labors. Oratory never reached a higher point in numbers and noise or leadership a lower one. In March, 1891, the placing of a [Nationalist] state ticket in the field in Rhode Island on a platform advocating government and municipal ownership, initiative, refer-

---

[36] J. Foster Biscoe, "Attitude of the Press," *Nationalist,* II, No. 4 (March, 1890), 143.

[37] Editorial, *New Nation,* III, No. 18 (April 8, 1893), 182. To tell the full story of Populism would considerably expand the dimensions of this biography. It has been told many times and is readily available.

endum and minority representation gave occasion for Editor Bellamy
to say: "The time has come when the political republic can only be
preserved by making it an industrial republic also. In proportion as
people shall come to recognize this truth, they will see that the Nationalist party is the legitimate heir to the principles and spirit of the patri-
ots of 1776."

This word from the chief was passed along, and nationalists the
country over strove to reach a political formula for the divers remedies
proposed to relieve a suffering people.

. . . .

The Nationalists and Socialists of Cleveland, Ohio, nominated a
ticket and adopted the platform of the Rhode Island Nationalists in
1891.

The Nationalist Club of Chicago came out for the municipal ticket
put up by the Socialists, headed by Thomas J. Morgan.

In 1890 the Nationalists of the Sixth District of California had nominated Mr. Wilshire for Congress, who polled 1,000 votes. Michigan furnished that year another candidate for Congress, and in many places
Nationalist candidates for state legislatures appeared.

It was in the spring of 1891 that the third party mutterings in the
various states drifted toward a demand for a national organization.
Peffer had been sent to the United States Senate by the Kansas farmers, and several Farmer's Alliance Congressmen, notably Jerry Simp-
son, were in the House. These men made trips to the East and, while they
found an industrial rather than an agrarian sentiment in New England,
they returned home realizing that a national party must broaden somewhat the demands of their farm neighbors of the Alliance.

A call was issued for a national conference of the reform third party
elements to be held at Cincinnati, May 19, 1891. This call was addressed
to the Independent party, the People's party, the Union Labor party,
the late federal and confederate soldiers, the Farmer's Alliance, North
and South, the Farmer's Mutual Benefit Association, the Citizens' Alliance, the Knights of Labor, the Colored Farmers' Alliance, and "all
other industrial organizations that support the principles of the St.
Louis agreement of December, 1889, which reflected farm, labor and
free silver sentiments."

The Citizens' Alliance of Kansas issued a supplemental call adding
to this list of organizations invited to attend the Cincinnati conference
the American Federation of Labor, the trade unions and trades assem-
blies, the Federation of Railway Employees, the Nationalists and editors and business managers of the papers which belonged to the Reform
Press Association.

The conference met at Cincinnati and continued in session two days.

There were something like seventeen hundred delegates present from nearly every state in the union, the western states dominating in numbers.

. . . .

The Massachusetts delegates to the Cincinnati conference had little need of credentials, for they were largely Nationalists, and the members of the conference, generally speaking, were familiar with the economics which gave birth to *Looking Backward,* and the amiable yet firm literary methods of its author. When the writer and his associates appeared in the platform committee room as representatives from the Edward Bellamy group, Ignatius Donnelly, the chairman, observed: "Edward Bellamy—whom not to know is to argue one's self unknown."

. . . .

There were five Nationalists upon the committee of resolutions and eight members on the national committee. The money element predominated and their planks made a curiosity in platform literature, for they contained greenback, free silver and multiple standard specifics for regulating the volume of the currency. The one solace to the Bellamy men was the platform demand for "the most rigid, honest and just national control and supervision of public communication and transportation; and, if this control and supervision do not remove the abuses now existing, we demand the government ownership of such means of communication and transportation."

The Cincinnati conference which resolved itself into a third party organization, acted like a premium upon the genius of reform. Congressman Otis, of Kansas, spoke at Topeka in June, advocating the nationalization of the whole liquor traffic and the sale of spirituous beverages at cost, thus taking it out of politics.

The Kentucky Populists polled 25,000 in August and the vote in other states was significant. General Francis A. Walker told the American Economic Association that the Nationalist upheaval was making "every man and every woman an economist.". . .

D. R. Antony, in a political speech at Wyandotte, Kansas, had this word of reproof: "You, my republican brother, and democratic friends, are to blame for the strength of the people's party, because you permitted the publication and reading of Bellamy's book.". . .

After weeks of discussion among the various people's party leaders of the Bay State, an agreement was reached and a platform adopted at a dinner at the United States Hotel, Boston, August 24, 1891. At this dinner among others were Major Henry Winn, whose writings and speeches on taxation and the multiple standard as the true basis of the national currency had given him a name not confined to the state; Henry

R. Legate, president of the Second Nationalist Club and the legislative agent of the Boston Nationalists; George F. Washburn, president of the Industrial Alliance; Henry Lemon, representing the Knights of Labor; E. Gerry Brown, representing the free silver faction; Mason A. Green and Edward Bellamy.

Among the planks in the platform adopted that had an economic bearing as affected by public control or ownership were these:

"We hold that the right to make and issue money is a sovereign power to be maintained by the people for the common benefit. Hence we demand that United States treasury notes be issued in sufficient volume to transact the business of the country on a cash basis, such notes to be a legal tender in payment of all debts public and private, and to be kept at par by being increased or decreased, in volume, by a commission according to a fixed rule in proportion to the population and the average market price of a given number of commodities.

"We favor the establishment of postal savings banks, which could be also used as banks of deposit and exchange, thus affording absolute security. Postal facilities, including frequent mails, free delivery and a cheaper parcel post, should be enjoyed as far as practicable, by the country and farming districts.

"We favor government ownership of all means of transportation and communication; and, in general, when in the course of business consolidations in the form of trusts or private syndicates, it becomes evident that any branch of commerce is used for the profit of a few men at the expense of the general public, we believe that the people should assume control of such commerce through their national, state or municipal administrations. We therefore favor a general statute under which cities or towns in this commonwealth may acquire or establish local transit systems, or substitute public ownership for private monopoly when demanded by the people, such as the opening by cities or towns of public coal yards to furnish coal and fuel at cost.

"We believe that the solution of the liquor problem lies in abolishing the element of profit, which is a source of constant temptation and evil; and we therefore demand that the exclusive importation, manufacture and sale of all spirituous liquors shall be conducted by the government or state at cost through agencies and salaried officials in such towns and cities as shall apply for such agencies.

"We demand that a system of industrial training in connection with the public schools be made general throughout the state; that equal pay for equal work, without regard to sex, color or condition, be recognized by law.

"We hold that no citizen of the United States should be deprived of the electoral franchise on account of sex."

The Massachusetts Populists perfected their organization in 1890 by placing this ticket in the field:

Governor	Henry Winn of Malden
Lieutenant Governor . . .	William J. Shields of Boston
Secretary of State	Joseph D. Cadle of Westfield
Treasurer	Thomas A. Watson of Braintree
Auditor	William O. Wakefield of Lynn
Attorney General . . .	Herbert McIntosh of Worcester

Major Winn was a Yale graduate, a lawyer and a writer on economic subjects. He had served in the Massachusetts House and Senate and had much experience in drafting bills for the legislature, a large proportion of which were enacted into law. He had been Senator Sumner's private secretary.

The press of the country commented widely on the platform of the Massachusetts People's Party, varying according to temperament and partisan basis. Thus the St. Louis *Post-Dispatch* observed:—

"The Nationalists of Massachusetts, who claim great strength in that state, have announced their purpose to support the People's party ticket in the coming election. This was to be expected in view of the Bellamy-ites at the Cincinnati convention, and so far as the principles of the two organizations are concerned they are nearly as identical as they well can be. Mr. Bellamy has perhaps given the subject of socialism, or nationalism as he calls it, more systematic thought than have the farmers of the country, but their conclusions are the same. This is asserted again and again in Mr. Bellamy's own paper, and an examination of both programmes reveals their identity. This is not wholly the result of accidental parallelism of thought. It is largely due to the study of Bellamy's *Looking Backward* by the farmers. He has sown the seeds of socialism in the rich soil of discontent, and the first practical manifestation of the socialistic spirit is the platform of the People's party."

. . . .

Every new party in Massachusetts has to submit to the Faneuil Hall test if it has any hope of a future. The People's party went through this ordeal on the evening of October 7, 1891. . . .

The main speech was delivered by the honorable Henry Winn, the candidate for governor. He reviewed the specific demands of the party and was frank enough to say:

"When in a period of unrest men, just awakened to unjust conditions, are seeking a remedy, numerous plans will arise. Many, being new, will be faulty. Some even if good will not command assent until after debate. And so in the People's party have appeared some to which I cannot subscribe. It will take time and discussion for the truth to crystallize.

My own suggestions are merely tentative. But in the main I assent, and with the great underlying purpose I am in earnest accord. Some can say they agree, but only those can completely agree whose parties present no issues on which to differ, and whose followers are led by the force of habit, the spoils, and the commissariat. My friend (Bellamy) who will follow, has his path, and with him for a certain distance we can walk. Into his mind, like a vision of apocalyptic splendor, came a picture of redeemed humanity, and, like St. Paul, he has turned his life to its accomplishment. All honor to such men. . . ."

Mr. Bellamy was next introduced and entered directly into a discussion of many phases of the platform. While he did not lose that intense zeal which gave him such an influence over those about him, he was much more popular in his treatment of his theme than usual. He said in closing:

"It has been said by our critics that the People's party is demagogical because it appeals so directly to the self-interest of the people. I am afraid that we must admit that there is some color to this accusation. I confess that after careful examination I am unable to find a single proposition in the platform which is not grossly, flagrantly and unblushingly beneficial to the people of the state.

"The general principle which should govern the conversion of private monopolies into public ones is stated by the platform as follows: 'And whenever any branch of commerce is used for the profit of a few men at the expense of the general public, we believe that the people should assume control of such commerce through their national, state and municipal administration.' While I yield to none in my hearty support of the other propositions of this admirable platform, I believe that it will owe its distinction as an historical document to the clear and uncompromising manner in which it declares the application of popular government to industry, to be the proper means of meeting the aggressions of private monopolies. In this declaration is sounded the key-note of the impending industrial transformation. It is the republicanizing of commerce.

"Jesus Christ said: 'A house divided against itself cannot stand.' America today is imperiled because it is a house divided against itself. Oil will not mix with water, however you may stir them. No more will the spirit of republican equality dwell together in the same body with the spirit of mastership. Unless we shall carry the republican idea into industry, we must soon abandon it in politics."

．　．　．　．

A representative meeting of industrial bodies in Indianapolis in November, and the meeting of the national control committee of the People's party at St. Louis, February 22, 1892, when a broader platform was matured and where Miss Willard's national prohibition resolution was voted down, developed enough harmony among the third party groups to unite upon a national convention at Omaha, on July 4, 1892.

Nearly all the Massachusetts delegation were Bellamy Nationalists. He himself accompanied the Boston delegates to the North Station, bidding them Godspeed, but not thinking it wise to add his personality as a delegate to a movement which was assimilating his principles to so great a degree.

The Omaha convention and platform remain as fixed in our political annals as the free soil convention at Pittsburg which foreshadowed the advent of the Republican party. Every state in the Union except Vermont was represented among the 1654 delegates. There were in that gathering white and black, native and naturalized, lettered and unlettered, professors, farmers, artisans, doctors, newspaper men, women, and a millionaire.

At Omaha, the saloon-keepers, who increased their stock of liquors in anticipation of a convention trade, reckoned without their host. The delegates were not a saloon crowd.

Gen. James B. Weaver of Iowa and United States Senator James K. Kyle of South Dakota were the final candidates ballotted for, and Weaver won the nomination by a vote of 995 to 265.

.   .   .   .

The platform made this confession of faith:

"We believe that the powers of government—in other words, of the people—should be expanded (as in the case of the postal service) as rapidly and as far as the good sense of an intelligent people and the teachings of experience shall justify, to the end that oppression, injustice and poverty shall eventually cease in the land. . . .

"We believe that the time has come when the railroad corporations will either own the people or the people must own the railroads, and should the government enter upon the work of owning and managing any or all railroads, we should favor an amendment to the constitution by which all persons engaged in the government service shall be placed under a civil service regulation of the most rigid character, so as to prevent the increase of the power of the national administration by the use of such additional employees.

"We demand that postal savings banks be established by the government for the safe deposit of the earnings of the people, and to facilitate exchange.

"Transportation being a means of exchange and a public necessity, the government should own and operate the railroads in the interest of the people.

"The telegraph and telephone, like the postoffice system, being a necessity for transmission of news, should be owned and operated by the government in the interests of the people."

. . . .

The writer, who was a member of the committee on resolutions, received a telegram from a New York daily asking for an account of the convention, adding, "Put in plenty of hayseed."

To anticipate events let it be said, parenthetically, that "hayseed" convention demanded the popular election of United States Senators, now a constitutional provision.

That "hayseed" convention demanded that Congress shall have power to tax incomes without apportionment among the several states, which is also now a constitutional provision.

That "hayseed" convention demanded the extension of the powers of the government as in the case of the postal service, to which Congress responded by establishing a parcel post and a postal savings service, and has since repeatedly extended federal regulation over activities that benefit the public.

Both of the old parties foraged about the Omaha platform, pulling out plank after plank until they considered the movement comparatively harmless.

. . . .

While the Omaha convention was at work upon its platform, Mr. Bellamy was at his desk in the *New Nation* office at Boston, an eager listener to every echo from Nebraska.

. . . .

The moment the Populists had fought their way to a commanding position, certain of their leaders began a brisk traffic in principles, by bartering away their ammunition. The new-party exploit of breaking into the electoral college to the tune of twenty-two votes as the result of a little over a million votes at the polls, thus defeating Harrison, the Republican candidate for president, and electing Cleveland, Democrat, convinced some of the new-party leaders that their pathway was little short of a promenade to power. Small men in the Populist camp, with large visions of conquest, began trading with rounders in both of the old parties, picking out free silver as a paramount issue, and retiring the Bellamy economic propositions, which had operated during the campaign, as a solvent for the various phases of reform represented at Omaha.

. . . .

Western farmers who supported the Omaha convention yielded to free silver pleas and ran immediately into the panic of 1893.[38]

[38] Green, pp. 145–58.

Bellamy had outlined a program of significant and far-reaching changes in the economic order and had secured for his ideas a wide following in many parts of the country. Green notes that William Jennings Bryan, by taking the dramatic expression in *Looking Backward*, "I have seen humanity hanging on the cross," and turning it into his famous "cross of gold" speech, won the Democratic nomination for President. Then instead of comprehending and adopting the penetrating economic thinking of Bellamy, he used his great oratorical powers to divert Bellamy's following into the sterile desert of free silver, and to futility.

How much the course of history has been influenced by personalities! Had Moses been followed by an emotional but unintelligent Bryan to capture the people's imagination, the children of Israel might never have crossed the Red Sea. In 1892, had Bryan's place been taken by a man of high intelligence as well as of emotional power, progress might have been made toward economic democracy.

Bellamy was not interested in free silver. At home he tried to salvage something by proposing specific next steps. Green has described his course:

The financial upheavals caused by the industrial disorders of 1893 gave Mr. Bellamy an opportunity to indicate a practical scheme for the employment of the unemployed, whose maintenance was taxing the resources of the charitable without opening their minds. Mr. Bellamy talked continually with his friends on this matter. He was distressed at the scenes that he was compelled to confront in Boston, daily, and he realized how misery will compel people to think, while personal comfort only turns the key on the chambers of the mind. How often on those dismal days—for they were doubly dismal to him as he saw the panic clearing away the meager resources of his paper—did he resort to his habit of pacing Boston Common to dream out plans for bringing about industrial peace.

. . . .

After Bellamy had considered the problem for some time he sketched for the *New Nation* an emergency plan for the employment of the unemployed.

He argued that the recognized function of the state is just this business of organizing and directing those interests of the people to which private initiative is not equal, such as the public defense, administration of justice and protection of persons and property, building of highways, and other services once left to private initiative. He argued that the vast army of unemployed in Massachusetts was a crisis calling for a public organization of industry which should at least supplement the defects of the present system, pending its complete substitution for it. A fixed principle of any sound method of providing employment by the state, he contended, is that the employed should be so put to work as to support one another by consuming one another's product, the system being altogether separate from the outside business system and costing the state nothing.[39]

Parallel to Nationalism, and largely growing out of interest in *Looking Backward*, was the Christian Socialist movement. Whereas Marxian socialism, as commonly presented in America at the time, assumed that individual defects of character were chiefly the result of faulty environment, and particularly of the political and economic system, while orthodox Christianity placed almost the entire responsibility for the sorry condition of humanity on the individual; the Christian Socialists took an intermediate position. They held personal character and social organization equally necessary for maintaining balance and for moving forward.

The organizers of the Christian Socialist movement were the Reverend W. D. P. Bliss, long a worker in religious and labor movements, and Francis Bellamy, a cousin of Edward.[40] Francis Bellamy was later known as author of the familiar pledge of allegiance to the flag. After Edward Bellamy's death he published *The Duke of Stockbridge*, Edward Bellamy's study of Shays' Rebellion. Both were charter members of the First Nationalist Club of Boston. The Society of Christian Socialists published a magazine, the *Dawn*, of which Edward Bellamy was one of the editors, and an occasional contributor.

The *Dawn* published a list of 672 ministers interested in Christian socialism or in the labor movement, and the *Nation* of New York, then a relatively conservative paper, was quoted as regretting that "practically the whole church had gone over to a general Christian Socialism." Yet, by and large, the church did not receive the movement in a friendly spirit. American Protestantism was a

[39] Green, pp. 164–66.
[40] A detailed account of the movement is given by James Dombrowski, in *The Early Days of Christian Socialism in America.*

democratic folk institution, representing the average American temper and outlook. A very moderate liberalism would have been welcomed, but any more radical change had to wait for the slow growth of the American outlook. The Christian Socialist movement faded away, and the *Dawn*, after various vicissitudes, ceased publication in 1896.

With the death of the *New Nation* and the waning of Populism, Edward Bellamy was again back at Chicopee Falls, somewhat disillusioned; and his hopes of immediate success disappeared. However, he did not entirely give up the prospect for political activity. In December, 1896, just after the Bryan-McKinley campaign, he wrote to Henry Demarest Lloyd:

DEAR MR. LLOYD:
While we are left practically without a party, it is a good riddance, seeing that the organization has fallen in bad hands. . . . Meanwhile, the past campaign has, unless I greatly err, done much to break up the political soil, cause discontent and prepare the people for the radical doctrines. . . . Would it not be a good idea to put this conference off which you speak of till next summer (unless events otherwise indicate) and spend the intervening time in securing the attendance or endorsement of a sufficient number of persons of large reputation, to command public attention and respect for its action? . . . A manifesto put forth by such a conference stating our full doctrine—keeping nothing back— and advancing a complete set of propositions as first steps, would, I believe, strongly impress the country and furnish the basis for any political organization that might then or later be decided on. . . . the only thing needful is that this manifesto should explicitly declare for full nationalization of the productive and distributive machinery of our government. We do not want any more fooling; and the country is ready for plain talk.

> Fraternally,
> EDWARD BELLAMY

However, he had not physical strength for the necessary leadership.

Bellamy had found himself being backed by an idealistic religious society. He decided that its support of his program was not adequate. He had counted on the best of the elite to support his cause, but they had tired of the hardship and discipline his program demanded. He had tried to find common ground with practical reformers and to start a new political party. As his Theosophical friends had predicted, it was soon "in bad hands." Bellamy was learning, one by one, some of the real reasons why Utopia does not sooner arrive. Had his strength been greater and his life longer, he might have learned still other reasons.

With failing strength, apparently well aware that his days were numbered, he gave himself to "completing the record." He would fill in the gaps in his plan as outlined in *Looking Backward*. Perhaps he would answer his critics, but that seemed less important to him than to leave an adequate statement of his thoughts. This he did in his last book, *Equality*.

WHY THE NATIONALIST MOVEMENT FAILED

In 1890 it seemed that Edward Bellamy had given form to a movement which might soon usher in a new social and economic order and actually fulfill the promise of *Looking Backward*. Yet five years later the entire movement had so faded away that it no longer was a factor in the national interest. Whatever vitality remained for immediate effectiveness had been absorbed by other movements. What is the explanation of this curious phenomenon? At the time of Bellamy's death, the *New York Evening Post* made a typical appraisal in its editorial columns:

The death of Edward Bellamy serves to show the suddenness and the evanescence of the reputation which may be achieved by the dreamer who periodically appears in literature with his patent scheme for reforming the universe. It is just ten years since *Looking Backward* was published, and began leaping into a popularity which carried it all over Europe as well as this country, and made its purchasers numbered by the hundred thousands. Five years ago a great many people took the romance seriously, and were organizing movements, starting newspapers, and holding conventions to nationalize society on a fantastic basis. To-day the newspapers are dead, the organizations have vanished, and even the wildest of the visionaries who once hailed Bellamyism as a revelation are ready to drop it for—what will be the next in the long succession of impossible projects for introducing the millennium by the convenient device of leaving human nature out of the account? [41]

[41] *New York Evening Post,* May, 1898.

The growing respect for Bellamy and his ideas during the succeeding decades is evidence that such an appraisal is inadequate.

The program presented in *Looking Backward*, which became the platform of the Nationalists, was distinctly the creation of Edward Bellamy. Even though each single element of his plan, or several elements in combination, had existed in the minds of others, and most of them at some time had been included in practical working programs in actual societies, yet never had all the major factors been integrated into a unified design for a social order. Although his plan was informally stated, it had the nature of a carefully designed constitution for a commonwealth. The parts were inter-related, and together constituted an organic whole.

A favorable impression of that program might result from a casual reading of the book, but an intelligent, thoroughgoing comprehension of it could be gained only by thorough study and by critical education in its principles. Relatively few people took the time and trouble to acquire that mastery, and the very rapidity of growth of the movement resulted in lack of unification of opinion, even in fundamentals. An illustration of this is the wide divergence of opinion as to the cause of social progress. Edward Bellamy held that character is profoundly affected by environment, and that until decent, wholesome, and encouraging environment is provided we cannot guess what innate nobility in man is seeking for expression. Yet he keenly appreciated the importance of strong spiritual and ethical motives. Many of his Christian and Theosophist friends felt that, while change of environment is necessary, there must be a long period of changing the motives of men before political reform can be more than the exchange of one set of corrupt political masters for another.

At the other extreme were self-styled Marxian "scientific" socialists who held extreme views on economic determinism and on class conflict. A speaker before the New York Section of the Socialist Labor party, as reported in the *Workmen's Advocate* of September 28, 1889, speaking of Nationalism said, "We know that it is as a class movement only that Socialism can accomplish the emancipation of labor." A Socialist Labor party member, in refusing lists of names to the Nationalists wrote, "A Socialist organization directing its efforts 'especially to the conversion of the cultured and conservative classes' is a rather novel affair." A speech in the Washington Socialist Club, as reported in the *Craftsman*, ran: "The Nationalists rather shrink from this class war, but the wage worker is driven to it by necessity. It has been the experience that if the worker is not in a position to compel the employer, the latter would not move an inch." Some of these men looked upon Bellamy as a well-intentioned, naïve middle-class reformer, whose accidental popularity could be used as a steppingstone to real Marxism. Mr. Max Georgii, a charter member of the Washington, D.C., Nationalist Club, who apparently was a thorough-going Marxist, seemed to be such a person and undertook to restate the doctrine of Nationalism after the Marxian pattern. He wrote in the *Nationalist*:

We Nationalists believe, supported by a vast array of facts, that man tends to develop into more exalted conceptions and practices of morality as his environments become more just and tolerable, and that, therefore, it is necessary to ameliorate these before the former can effectually be improved. We have made it a policy, therefore, that no purely ethical, religious, or, least of all, sumptuary discussions should be entertained by us as Nationalists.

If universal sobriety prevailed among workingmen, the consequence, under the present absurd system, would be that the employer would get more work out of him and that, his wants being reduced, his wages would sink; the share he would get in the product of his labor would be decreased not only by the amount formerly expended in drink but also by the additional work the employer would be able to extract from him until the overworked and underfed human machine collapsed.[42]

Bellamy's social philosophy was a synthesis of these seeming opposites. He held that the Nationalist movement was primarily religious and spiritual, an inner urge to human brotherhood; but that the prevailing economic system penalized unselfishness and put a premium on greed and inconsiderateness of others, and that therefore the spiritual impulse to be effective must be active in bringing about a change in the economic organization of society. When Nationalism and the People's party were working together, he

[42] Max Georgii, "Nationalism Versus Prohibition," *Nationalist*, II, No. 6 (May, 1890), 194, 195.

wrote: "The formation of the People's party is welcomed, but we do not believe that the Nationalist Clubs should turn themselves into campaign clubs. The clubs stand for more advanced principles than any party is likely at once to take up . . ."

For Bellamy's design to emerge quickly as a practical working program of an effective social movement would have required a very high order of leadership. That quality Bellamy did not possess. His physical constitution was frail, and fatal disease pursued him. Naturally a retiring, contemplative person of keen sensibility, he was not suited temperamentally to the rough and tumble of public conflict or for dominant leadership.

To a remarkable degree *Looking Backward* had flanked or avoided the barriers of social prejudice in men's minds. By its simple, direct manner, suspicion and fear had been overcome for the time being. Many young men and women had been given a vision and a hope that were to transform their social thinking. At that moment such a public interest, if well led, might have had a profound influence on American history. The Nationalist movement had no such disciplined leadership, no such organization. For the most part he had to let the movement run itself. In 1892, when public interest was near its height, Bellamy wrote, apparently without realizing the fatal significance of his statement: "There never was perhaps, a reform movement that got along with less management than that of the Nationalists. There never has been any central organization and little if any mutual organization of the clubs." [43]

Bellamy did not accurately appraise the wave of approval of his book which swept over the country. He took popular and friendly interest to be evidence of solid achievement, whereas it was evidence only of an unusual opportunity for achievement. The public which most uncritically and unreservedly approves, unless it is persistently educated, may also quickly forget or be similarly impressed with an appeal of opposite import. A good workman who is favored with quick public approval should have a

[43] "Progress of Nationalism in the United States," *North American Review,* CLIV (June, 1892), 743.

suspicion that his public acclaim may have little relation to his merit.

Some of the men who supported Bellamy and the Nationalist movement did so with full expectation that progress would be gradual. Edward Everett Hale expressed this view in the second issue of the *Nationalist*. He wrote: "The American people is a very sensible people, and they will carry forward the business of entrusting different manufactures to the governments, the local governments, the state governments, or the national government, just about as fast and as far as it will pay." [44]

Some of those who at first were enthusiastic about the Nationalist movement later reacted strongly in the other direction, or took an independent course. Among such were William Dean Howells, Daniel De Leon, Laurence Gronlund, Sylvester Baxter, and Cyrus Willard. As they came to look at Bellamy's program in the cold light of reason they came to believe that after all it was not the only good way to organize society, but one of various possible ways. Men are so adaptable that society might be successfully organized in any one of a score of systems, each with its peculiar advantages. Bellamy simply had pointed out one good way. He led people out of the Egypt of hopelessness about things-as-they-are, but they found the wilderness rather tolerable, with several promised lands to choose from, and with much division of counsel as to the respective merits. Therefore, the forty-years-in-the-wilderness may be much extended, and many other counsels will be listened to. However, regardless of the influences which act on the American mind in the future, that of Bellamy, though it be blended and absorbed and thereby lost to view, will continue to be potent.

It was a period of feeling about for a good social order. Henry George favored a continuance of capitalism, modified by a single-tax program. The Populists were concerned with bimetallism, public ownership of railroads, and other immediate issues, with no clear, unifying social philosophy. The socialists were divided, and included such extremes as the individualism of Oscar Wilde

[44] Hale, "The Best Government," *Nationalist,* I, No. 2 (June, 1889), 40.

and William Morris, and the regimentation of the lock-step communists. During that period of education it was fortunate that the public did not decide on any system to the exclusion of others. It is interesting to note that the Bellamy clubs which have survived half a century were not in Boston or New York City, but in the farming regions of Colorado and in similarly rural situations.

The times were against quick realization of the Nationalist program. Quick revolutions almost never occur. A tornado or a French Revolution may blow down what is standing, with the present appearance of great change, but the forest which grows after the tornado generally will be much like that which fell. Great changes represent the completion of a process. When development is matured within the egg the shell may suddenly crack and disclose evidence of new life, but to break the shell of a new-laid egg when the process of incubation has not yet taken place will not produce a chicken. The change in human society pictured by Bellamy is so fundamental that the necessary period of incubation was longer than he thought.

Together with popular approval of *Looking Backward* there was a hardening of resistance. Editors over the country endeavored to smother the book with scorn and ridicule. Those in power frowned on departures from custom. The churches as a whole were not friendly. At first ministers and editors spoke favorably of *Looking Backward*, but quiet, tactful pressure by "responsible, solid citizens" tended soon to correct such departure from regularity. Reform papers which had sprung up by the hundreds disappeared like those early spring annuals which get their growth and die by the time the trees are in leaf.

The Nationalists did not realize how deep in human society are the roots of things-as-they-are. For two hundred years the economic life of America had been built on economic dictatorship, with ideas of class distinction inherited from feudalism.

As American economic life expanded it did not follow the direction of political democracy, but rather that of a modified feudalism, though the political and economic orders greatly influence each other. In the more than two centuries of industrial development, the ownership and management of business had assumed practically all responsibility for business policy, and generally had not encouraged steady development of capacity for democratic participation in industry. At the time Bellamy wrote, the worker had but little to say about his working conditions.

On this basis of economic feudalism a great industrial structure had developed. There has been interminable dispute as to whether political democracy has made possible our great economic development; whether unlimited political suffrage without regard to education or ability might have been disastrous except as it was counterbalanced by free play of natural aristocracy in the industrial world; or whether our great development has been due to a combination of the two, each tempering the other. Certain it is that in any effort at transition from industrial feudalism to industrial democracy we shall pay dearly for failure through two centuries gradually to encourage democratic participation. Any belief that a quick and successful transition can be made without a protracted period of preparation would indicate the lack of a realistic approach. An undefined but strong realization of this condition has led most Americans to be intuitively skeptical of rapid change, and so puts a damper on the quick development of such a program as that of the Nationalists, while the Nationalist repudiation of violent revolution tended to alienate those who were less responsible and more emotional.

Another reason for failure was the fact that Americans had become so accustomed to individual freedom of action that they could not visualize Bellamy's picture of society as an organism in which men would give up some independence of action for the sake of social well-being or freedom. Only a breakdown of the economy within—which break was postponed by the incalculable natural wealth and vigorous energy of America—or by pressure from without by nations which had subordinated personal independence to centralized group action, could bring Americans to make that choice. Bellamy's philosophy of impending social change was to be largely justified by the inexorable long-time course of events, rather than by his arguments. Notwithstanding his friendly reception, he was like Cassandra, to whom it was given to see the truth but not to have people believe her.

Another reason for the failure of Nationalism was its popularity, and the popularity of the People's party with which it was associated. At all times there are in the population many would-be politicians, promoters, adventurers, and unsuccessful men, who quickly see the prospect of personal profit from taking part in any new movement which promises to be successful. Men of this type have sunk many a promising movement by overloading it with their useless weight. Apparently such men flocked to the People's party and helped to discredit it. Then, during the next presidential campaign, in 1896, the Democratic party under William Jennings Bryan drew most of the liberal and discontented vote, and the People's party faded into oblivion.

When to unite and what to unite is always a problem of the reformer and the practical politician. Many a promising movement has died because through compromise it has lost its very soul. On the other hand, many an issue has been lost because those who promoted it lacked genius for moving with the currents of the times, and could not subordinate non-essentials to the main issues for the sake of unity.

Edward Bellamy constantly faced this dilemma. No other group was committed to the particular integration of elements which constituted the essence of Nationalism. From the very first there were reasons why that movement would profit in some respects by being identified, or at least associated, with others—with Theosophy, with Marxian Socialism, with Christian Socialism, with Populism. We can trace step by step Bellamy's efforts to solve that problem. Repeatedly Bellamy discusses the issue of unity. Constantly he insists that the Nationalist aims be held without compromise, but that there should be unity as to common ground.

His disappointment at the weak and vague first People's party platform—that adopted at Cincinnati—was expressed in the remark that it was just about large enough for a party to be born on. The St. Louis program which followed went much further in the direction of Nationalism and was encouraging, and for a time he associated himself and the Nationalist movement wholeheartedly with the People's party. Yet the forewarning of the Christian Socialist, as well as of Annie Besant when she turned her major attention from Nationalism and socialism to Theosophy—that as soon as a movement should become promising it would be captured by selfish men, and that change in men's motives must precede effective reform in government and society—proved to be true to events. Bellamy's comment in December, 1896, "While we are left practically without a party, it is a good riddance, seeing that the organization has fallen in bad hands," is evidence of that fact.

He finally was compelled to leave his ideas and his spirit, as expressed in his books, to work their own way in the lives of men and of peoples. In the end this may not prove to be a misfortune. It seems probable that the difficulty he faced was inherent in the nature of the situation, and that, given his physical limitations, nothing could greatly have changed the result except the good fortune of a dynamic follower to serve as the St. Paul or the Engels of his movement.

Had a great leader followed or accompanied Edward Bellamy, the Nationalist movement might have maintained itself and might have contributed more obviously to the evolution of social thinking in America. Quite conceivably, however, such lack of leadership was a blessing. Very commonly when a man makes a marked contribution or acquires a considerable following, there are men who will strive to capture whatever there is of a movement or a following, and to turn it to their own ends, or will give it an interpretation quite foreign to that of its creator. When St. Francis of Assisi had founded the order of Franciscans, one of his "followers," Brother Elias, selfish, cynical, and ambitious, captured control and turned the brotherhood into channels very different from those desired by its founder. Brother Elias set a type for all such men by having someone follow St. Francis about during his last days in the hope of getting his bones as relics when he died, to use for increasing his own prestige. St. Paul largely captured the Christian following and gave it a theology and temper very different from that of its originator. The memory of Abraham Lincoln became the chief capital of the conservative Republican party; and has not Stalin in a similar manner used the memory, even the mummy, of his enemy, Lenin? Fortunately for the ideas of Edward Bellamy, he had no "Brother Elias," though, according to Cyrus Willard, Mason Green aspired to such a status. His ideas are free from demand for their dogmatic acceptance and forced interpretation, and continue as a source of suggestion and inspiration.

What effective work did the Nationalist movement accomplish as distinct from the general influence on men's minds of *Looking Backward* and *Equality?* One of the first undertakings of the Nationalist Clubs of Boston resulted in a practical achievement. It was admittedly their effort which secured legislation in Massachusetts permitting municipalities to own their own gas and electric systems. Today in suburban Massachusetts towns one finds "sound," conservative business men who are averse to expansion of government functions, but who take great pride in the competent management of their local publicly owned power systems. The Massachusetts law to permit municipal coal yards also was a Nationalist achievement. The state Supreme Court decision declaring it unconstitutional illustrated the supremacy of dominant interests over written constitutions.

When we examine a list of reforms demanded by the Nationalists, we find almost a catalogue of social legislation of the past half century. Proposed reforms which have been wholly or partially adopted included establishment of the right of cities to own gas and electric systems, direct election of Senators, the merit system in civil service, taxation of inheritances, income tax, parcel post, woman suffrage, the initiative and referendum, increasing the school year beyond twenty weeks, free school books and lunches for those in need, raising the age limit for child labor from ten or thirteen years to sixteen years, recognition of the right of labor to organize, minimum wages and maximum hours, recognition of the right of every man to a chance to work, protection of workers from the hazards of industry, prohibition of private industrial armies and spies, public ownership of irrigation systems, soil conservation, and removal of submarginal lands from cultivation.

The surprisingly large part of its "first steps" that already has been achieved includes much of the advanced "New Deal" legislation and policy which has been accepted by both major political parties. Some of the men directly responsible for that legislation are in direct line of descent from the First Nationalist Club of Boston, or received their first social stimulus from *Looking Backward*. Other elements of social legislation now looming on the horizon were substantially parts of the Nationalist program.

Some of these steps are being taken, not freely, but under the stress of war. The nations which initiated the war had adopted large elements of policy similar to those proposed by Bellamy, but without the self-restraint, the refinement of purpose, and the respect for human dignity and freedom which characterize his vision and which it was his passion to preserve. Perhaps it may come to be said of Nationalism, as a result of pressure from within and from without, that "the stone which the builders rejected is become the head of the corner." In that case let us hope that the self-restraint, the tolerance, the spirit of fairness and reasonableness, which he exemplified, may guide and control the tremendous power of a centralized state.

Society is inevitably destined to increased discipline and control. The question is, whether such discipline shall be arbitrarily capricious, and based on favoritism, intrigue, and force, or whether it can evolve the controls of freedom, justice, and good will.

When a specific movement blends into the total culture of a people as did Nationalism, there is no way to quantitatively measure its influence. However, it was that movement more than any other which first brought most of these issues clearly to public attention as a unified program and philosophy, and put them on the agenda of reform. Nationalism largely gave its program to the People's party, except for the item of free silver, which Bellamy held to be essentially a false issue.

The greatest achievement of Bellamy and the Nationalist movement was not in promoting specific reforms, but in an attitude toward social change. At the time Bellamy wrote *Looking Backward*, the Marxians were invading America with their theory of irreconcilable class conflict, with reliance on force rather than on law and orderly process, and with the doctrine that moral principles were the fruit of exploitation, and should give way to the needs of the revolution.

In many fields of thought European standards have swept over the immature mind of America, and have taken the field. Through *Looking Backward, Equality*, and the Nationalist movement, Bellamy repudiated those three elements of Marxism. He believed in America and set up American standards for social change. Qualified Marxians and non-Marxians alike are agreed that it was largely the influence of Bellamy and Nationalism that set another picture in the public mind so firmly that not until half a century had passed and a generation rose up which knew not Bellamy did these atavistic elements of orthodox Marxism begin to get a foothold in America, and then only with difficulty and against the resistance of those who have Bellamy's attitude.

While the Nationalist movement was not destined to succeed quickly, perhaps it was like the tumbleweed on the western prairies, which breaks off from its roots and rolls across country, scattering its seed as it goes.

XII · The Political Economist

In *The Almost Perfect State* Don Marquis commented, "Economic problems that cannot be otherwise solved should be abolished." If we take such a statement not facetiously, as Don Marquis meant it, but as sound, practical advice, we may come to some interesting conclusions.

In complimenting an author on a book, Bellamy once wrote, "Its production has vastly more than justified the expenditure of bread, meat and clothing which you have cost the world, and in general has vindicated your progenitors most amply." To such elemental realities was he wont to reduce the issues of life. When we compare the picture presented in *Looking Backward* and *Equality* with that presented by Marx in *Das Kapital* and that of Henry George in *Progress and Poverty*, and with the dissertations of Adam Smith, Ricardo, and the other classical economists, we find one great generic difference. These distinguished economists discuss capital, interest, rent, wages, surplus value, and a dozen other concepts, each a variable itself, and each influencing all the others. Under such conditions, with unlimited combinations of theories and facts on which one may focus his attention, each can build his own "sound" structure, markedly different from any other, and agreement is arrived at, if at all, only very slowly and with great difficulty. Any one of these economists, after viewing the "principles" and problems in his own way, and with his own emphasis, might feel inclined to claim for major elements of his own system what Henry George claimed for his: "Its conclusions [of my inquiry] completely change the character of political economy, give it the coherence and certitude of a true science, and bring it into full sympathy with the aspirations of the masses of men, from which it has long been estranged." [1] So long as all these variable and inter-

---

[1] Henry George, *Progress and Poverty*, p. xvi. By permission of the publisher, the Robert Schalkenbach Foundation.

acting factors are dealt with, every creative-minded economist may feel that he, in some respect at least, is the true founder of the science. Certain general truths do tend to emerge, such as the doctrine of surplus value, and the importance of economic factors in history; but even then, the *relative emphasis* given to a few factors may vary so as to change the entire picture.

It is possible for a skillful, trained economist, who works within the prevailing economic framework of competitive buying and selling, to describe those customary activities with reasonable accuracy, and even to point the way to their more efficient functioning. Because of the complexity of the prevailing economic order such descriptive analysis is an exacting task, and the economist may be excused if he becomes completely immersed in it and finds no time or inclination for getting an outside view of the whole existing system.

Yet such an economist should not cry "utopian" derisively at a more adventurous spirit who explores the territory outside the framework of prevailing economic society and who looks back upon the existing order from an outside viewpoint. All that the conventional economist should ask of the adventurer is that he observe accurately, describe honestly, and think clearly.

Edward Bellamy's technique for critical thinking, consciously stated to himself and adopted when he was a young man, included the habit of getting entirely outside the way of life which he would study, and looking back on the familiar scene as a stranger might from the vantage point of some other and different system. That is a sound and intelligent, though unusual, technique.

Although Bellamy made penetrating analyses of the existing order, he was not primarily concerned with reforming it. He outlined a comprehensive and pervasive plan for a new kind of economic society. He discarded money, rent, wages, interest, debt; in short, he freed himself from the framework within which conventional economic thought must revolve. He directly faced the fundamental economic problem—of how the goods and services people need and desire can be provided. The blunt, elemental simplicity with which he stated that problem, and his solution, was a helpful service, for in the complexity of finance and trading, and in evolving theories about them, the basic economic issue sometimes is lost from view.

Bellamy's solution essentially was this: We are not bound to a complicated machinery of wages, interest, rents, taxes, and money. The organized community can directly produce what it needs and distribute that production equally among all of its members. There would then be needed no money, no borrowing, no wages, no interest, no rents, no taxes, no private investment capital.

Suppose a society of nineteenth- and twentieth-century economists had been translated on a magic carpet to the Peru of 1500. There they would have found just such an economy, which had lasted for centuries, operating over a greater territory and greater population than any European nation of the time, and producing under very adverse natural conditions a higher degree of economic security than history records for any other people. They probably would have been greatly puzzled to apply their economic theories to the situation. If then they could have been translated to Peru and neighboring countries of the year 1900, they might have been still further puzzled to observe the disintegration, poverty, exploitation, and shrinkage of population which followed four hundred years of European economy. It would have been necessary for them to reconsider their axioms that the earlier system is "impossible" and "contrary to human nature."

Bellamy's economy was substantially that of ancient Peru. The concerns of such an economy would not be so much with abstract theory as with practical administration and social engineering. Are the surplus stores large enough to bridge a year of low water? Are the statistical records accurate? Is the budgeting intelligently administered, especially as between allocation of work and goods for immediate consumption and for supplying greater production capacity? Are the people working in good spirit? Are there simple inequalities to be remedied? Is there needless shipping of goods back and forth? It is to such questions that economics is finally reduced, and a regime may have great advantages which makes that fact clearly evident and which deals directly with these basic realities rather than with symbols or processes several steps removed from the physical realities.

The problems would be the practical everyday ones of the business administrator more than those of the theoretical economist. In such a society many of the more theoretical present-day treatises on economic theory would be about as useful and interesting as the vast accumulations of theological discussions which two centuries ago were considered well worth their fine sheepskin bindings and today are held to have almost no value.

What is the possibility of such a simplified economy as that of ancient Peru, of Thomas More's *Utopia*, and of Bellamy's *Looking Backward?* If we assume the "economic man" of the classical economists, the individual who at each point considers only his immediate individual interest, a regime of that kind is impossible. Only if such an economy is the expression of a religion, of a complete and social way of life, can it be feasible. Henry George saw this and decided against its possibility. In *Progress and Poverty* he wrote:

I will not say that such a state as this [in ancient Peru] is not a better social state than that to which we now seem to be tending, for in ancient Peru, though production went on under the greatest disadvantages, from the want of iron and the domestic animals, yet there was no such thing as want, and the people went to their work with songs. But this it is unnecessary to discuss. Socialism in anything approaching such a form, modern society cannot successfully attempt. The only force that has ever proved competent for it—a strong and definite religious faith —is wanting and is daily growing less.[2]

What Henry George failed to realize is that any vital social program is possible only if it is the expression of a religion which calls on the whole loyalty of men. Communism can thrive only as it takes on the character of a religion, and the same principle applied to the National Socialism of Germany. Even the single taxers have maintained their position by erecting the theories of Henry George into a cult, which is as close to a religion as so limited a philosophy of life can attain. The more adequate the interpretation of life which is provided by a political or economic

[2] Page 320. Reprinted by permission.

philosophy, the better foundation does it constitute for a social and economic program.

Edward Bellamy was of the same opinion as Henry George concerning the need for a religious motive to vitalize the program he proposed, but he differed from Henry George regarding its possibility. In *Equality* he wrote:

A great revolution, you must remember, which is to profoundly change a form of society, must accumulate a tremendous moral force, an overwhelming weight of justification, so to speak, behind it before it can start.

. . . .

By the light of the new teaching the people began to recognize that the strait place into which the republic had come was the narrow and frowning portal of a future of universal welfare and happiness such as only the Hebrew prophets had colors strong enough to paint.

. . . .

Then, to cap the climax . . . came "The Great Revival," touching this enthusiasm with religious emotion.

. . . .

The Great Revival was a tide of enthusiasm for the social, not the personal, salvation, and for the establishment in brotherly love of the kingdom of God on earth which Christ bade men hope and work for. It was the general awakening of the people . . . in the closing years of the last century to the profoundly ethical and truly religious character and claims of the movement for an industrial system which should guarantee the economic equality of all the people.

It contemplated nothing less than a literal fulfillment, on a complete social scale, of Christ's inculcation that all should feel the same solicitude and make the same effort for the welfare of others as for their own. . . .

For many ages—almost, indeed, from the beginning of the Christian era—the churches had turned their backs on Christ's ideal of a kingdom of God to be realized on earth by the adoption of the law of mutual helpfulness and fraternal love. . . . The clergy, in the name of the author of the Lord's Prayer, had taught the people not to expect God's will to be done on earth. . . . They had made themselves the bulwarks and defenses of existing social and political institutions . . . When royalty, in the act of abdication, had passed the scepter behind its back to capitalism, the ecclesiastical bodies had transferred their allegiance to the money power . . .

. . . .

"The Great Revival" followed, when, in the course of this process of education, the masses of the nation reached the conviction that the revolution against which the clergy had warned them as unchristian was, in fact, the most essentially and intensely Christian movement that had ever appealed to men since Christ called his disciples . . .

When the people came to recognize that the ideal of a world of equal welfare, which had been represented to them by the clergy as a dangerous delusion, was no other than the very dream of Christ . . . it is not to be wondered at that the impulse which the revolutionary movement received should have been overwhelming.[3]

Recent history tends to support this view. The New Deal has poured many, many millions of dollars into settlement and cooperative relief projects, with a tragic record of waste and failure, even though it has included some very successful undertakings under the direction of men to whom their work was a veritable expression of religious conviction. In contrast, the welfare program of the Mormon church, which so far as it goes is substantially like that of ancient Peru and like the program of *Looking Backward*, has succeeded remarkably, and on a large scale. It is not an isolated project, but an integral part of a way of life. For instance, church authorities report that when there are not enough unemployed to operate the church canneries at the peak of a vegetable or fruit crop, the wives of merchants, doctors, bankers, and teachers supply the needed help, working side by side with the relief employees in the canneries.

Conventional economists have inclined to hold that concern for religion and ethics is none of their business. Bellamy was inclined to hold that it is their first business, that without the inner incentive, external economic prosperity will be fleeting. He saw that political economy is not an isolated science, but an integral part of the single fabric of human life. He wrote in *Equality*, "Nothing can be in the long run or on a large scale sound economics which is not sound ethics." [4] Because his program enabled him to eliminate and to short-cut many of the economic arguments of his day and to deal directly with the relatively simple processes of food, clothing, and transportation, he has been ignored or scorned by some of those with whom skill in describing and analyzing a particular,

[3] *Equality*, pp. 329, 334, 340, 341, 343.   [4] *Ibid.*, p. 195.

and not necessarily immortal, economic order is the true measure of economic wisdom.

Although Edward Bellamy was a man of universal interests, who saw that many elements must enter into the design of a good society, there are a few controlling policies on which his entire structure must stand or fall. We can get a better understanding of the significance of the organization of society which he proposed if we examine some of these essential elements.

THE KEYSTONE OF THE ARCH—ECONOMIC EQUALITY

Roger Williams, founder of Rhode Island, expressed the essence of Bellamy's doctrine of economic equality when he wrote: "There goes many a ship to sea with many hundred souls in one ship, whose weal and woe is common, and is a true picture of a commonwealth." Bellamy called economic equality the keystone of the arch of his new society. That this conclusion had not been arrived at blindly, and that he was in the habit of examining and criticizing his own viewpoints, is indicated by a contrasting entry which appears twice in his notebooks, the first written in 1878 on his trip to Hawaii:

Equality is the one thing which God will not have, and of which he has refused to furnish one single example in the whole realm of nature. No two leaves are alike; everything is superior to all others in some things, inferior in others, equal in none.[5]

Even at that time the issue had long been in his mind. In a village Lyceum address at the age of twenty-one he said:

There is then enough in the world to support all in abundance if it were equally divided. If the burdens as well as the pleasures of life were apportioned equally among all, then should none labor beyond moderation, and none be utterly idle. This is the social condition which justice demands, and to which a reform in the interests of justice will lead us back.[6]

Such a clearly formulated statement as the latter probably had already a considerable background of thinking. We know that at the age of seventeen Bellamy was reading John Stuart Mill. Some

[5] Unpublished papers (B2-HI-15).   [6] *Ibid.* (B3b-2nd Lyceum Address).

of Bellamy's arguments for economic equality are so similar to those presented by Mill in the fourth and later editions of his *Principles of Political Economy* as to suggest that young Bellamy's interest in the subject may have had that source of origin. Mill wrote:

The objection ordinarily made to a system of community of property and equal distribution of the produce, that each person would be incessantly occupied in evading his fair share of the work, points, undoubtedly, to a real difficulty. But those who urge this objection forget to how great an extent the same difficulty exists under the system on which nine-tenths of the business of society is now conducted.[7]

Mill drew attention to the fact that from hodcarriers to chief justices most Englishmen worked for wages or salaries which were standardized by custom and which did not depend on how much was produced. He said that wage earners generally see less connection between the quality of their work and their income than would the members of a communal society. Economic equality might result in less vigorous work than that of a peasant proprietor, but probably in better work than that of hired laborers. "The neglect by the uneducated classes of labourers for hire of the duties which they engage to perform, is in the present state of society most flagrant." [8] Under economic equality, he held, public opinion would be a strong compulsion to good workmanship. "Mankind," he wrote, "are capable of a far greater amount of public spirit than the present age is accustomed to suppose possible." [9] Point by point Mill mustered his arguments in favor of economic equality, finally concluding with the statement, "And the worst and most unjust arrangement which could be made of these points, under a system aiming at equality, would be so far short of the inequality and injustice with which labour (not to speak of remuneration) is now apportioned, as to be scarcely worth counting in the comparison." [10] For a boy of seventeen, eagerly searching for light on

[7] John Stuart Mill, *Principles of Political Economy,* 4th and later editions, Book II, Chapter I, 3. Reprinted in Jevons, *Economic Equality in the Co-operative Commonwealth,* Appendix I, p. 331.
[8] *Ibid.* (Jevons, p. 332).   [9] *Ibid.*
[10] *Ibid.* (Jevons, p. 334).

the ills of society, to come across such a statement might supply the key to the thinking of a lifetime.

Bellamy greatly admired Matthew Arnold and referred to him in book reviews. It was at about the time Bellamy was acting as book reviewer and literary editor of the *Springfield Union* that Arnold's great address on "Equality" appeared, and it may have been a factor in crystallizing Bellamy's views. Matthew Arnold drew attention to the fact that Paul's comment recorded in the First Epistle to the Corinthians, "Evil communications corrupt good manners," was a quotation from the Greek poet Menander, and he adds: "The same profound observer, who laid down the maxim so universally accepted by us that it has become commonplace, the maxim that evil communications corrupt good manners, laid down also, as a no less sure result of the accurate study of human life, this other maxim as well: 'Choose equality and flee greed.' " [11]

In this essay Arnold makes the pronouncement: ". . . inequality materialises our upper class, vulgarises our middle class, brutalises our lower. And the greater the inequality the more marked is its bad action upon the middle and lower classes." [12] And again he adds, ". . . our love of inequality is really the vulgarity in us, and the brutality, admiring and worshipping the splendid materiality." [13] Arnold also quotes George Sand, another person whom Bellamy admired and frequently referred to, as saying, "The human ideal, as well as the social ideal, is to achieve equality." [14] Thus there were various sources familiar to Edward Bellamy from which he might have become impregnated with the concept which became the central doctrine of his social philosophy.

We have referred to the evidence that for years before *Looking Backward* was written the theory of economic equality must have been a subject of animated discussion in the Bellamy family. The following are some of the blows which his brother Charles, in his book *The Way Out*, showered upon Edward's theory:

Equality is a sweet sounding word, and its seductive intonations have led more seekers after truth astray than many a word a hundred times

[11] Arnold, Matthew, *Prose and Poetry*, p. 329.
[12] *Ibid.*, p. 360.   [13] *Ibid.*, p. 362.   [14] *Ibid.*, p. 331.

more dangerous, so far as spelling goes. [Charles lacked his elder brother's literary skill.]

. . . .

So far . . . as the principle of equality in rights applies to the question of the rewards of labor, it means that each workman, whether he be manager or weaver . . . has an equal right to what he earns,—a right upon which much of this dissertation is based,—but certainly no right to what another co-laborer earns.[15]

One by one, Charles took up and endeavored to demolish the exact arguments in favor of economic equality which his brother presented three years later in *Looking Backward*. First among such arguments was that economic equality is an absolute human right. On this point Charles wrote:

One set of would-be reformers say that it makes no difference whether a man be of superior capacity or not, whether he be born weak or strong . . . that whatever sort of man he is, he is entitled, as a human being, to the same share in the comforts and pleasures of this world.

Now when we attempt to discuss the comparative rights of men, as human beings, to happiness, irrespective of their earnings, merely by virtue of their humanity, we have taken hold of a great subject, too great I think for our data.

Whether the lazy or the inefficient man is to blame for his contemptible qualities or not, the world is certainly cheated and defrauded by his very existence, and must protect itself against him.[16]

Edward based his argument not only on theoretical human rights, but also on the advantages of expediency. Charles also discussed that argument. Finally he summed up the whole matter:

The equalization of the rewards of labor would necessarily destroy personal ambition, the very life and motive power of industry. If it were only by lifting the load of the inferiority of all his shopmates that a mechanic could see any profit follow his greater industry or training, his industry would flag, and the motive for improved capacity be reduced almost to a point.[17]

That Charles' criticism is not motivated by any cowardice before great wealth is clear from the entire tone of his book, as well as from the conclusion of this chapter:

---

15 Charles J. Bellamy, *The Way Out*, pp. 85, 87. Reprinted by permission.
16 *Ibid.*, pp. 88, 89, 90. Reprinted by permission.
17 *Ibid.*, p. 92. Reprinted by permission.

But still it is not wholly strange that men are plunged into despair at the spectacle of so much injustice and wholesale robbery, the wrongful distribution of profits, the disproportion between the worth of labor and its returns . . . It is not wholly strange that in a sort of spasm of impotent wrath some men cry out for an even distribution of the good things of the earth.[18]

It is interesting to note that neither brother ever mentions the other in his writing. There is not a word in *Looking Backward* to suggest that this attack had been made.

For at least sixteen years before *Looking Backward* appeared, this central theme of economic equality had been undergoing vigorous questioning in Edward Bellamy's own mind or in discussion with his brother. At the end of that process we find him with a firm conviction that no other principle is more important or essential to a good society. He never gave up the idea, and in the last significant work of his life, the book to which he gave the name *Equality*, he reiterated the doctrine.

The strength of his conviction is indicated in a letter from him quoted in the first issue of the *Nationalist* magazine, that for May, 1889:

I am profoundly anxious to impress upon everybody that the principle of *equality* in the provision made for the physical wants of all, *must* be urged in any new social order which is to be free from the characteristic vices and defects of the present system. Once consent, on whatever specious grounds, that the principle of *inequality* in the rate of maintenance for citizens shall be retained, and you retain the root and germs of all the evils we are trying to get rid of, and it is only a question of time when they would be flourishing again. Certainly, *Looking Backward* and the whole system of society which it proposes is based upon equality in the material condition of citizens, and stands or falls with that idea. Compromise on this point is impossible without giving up all our organization stands for distinctively.[19]

Since the doctrine is at the heart of Bellamy's philosophy, it is worth while to try to discover just what he means by economic equality. He touched upon the subject so frequently that we are not left in doubt either as to the particular kind of social organiza-

18 *Ibid.*, p. 93. Reprinted by permission.
19 Sylvester Baxter, "What Is Nationalism?" *Nationalist*, I, No. 1 (May, 1889), 11.

tion he had in mind, or as to the spirit which should animate it.

Fundamentally he sees all men as indissolubly associated as neighbors, brothers—fellow travelers in the quest of the ages—with a common interest which makes all differences shrink into insignificance. In an article, *"Looking Backward* Again," he wrote:

With this plan [of economic equality], which counts all human beings equal partners in a business carried on from generation to generation, from the beginning of humanity to the end of the world, and indefinitely further, the practice of Saturday-night settlements between the members of the firm, with mutual handwashings as to further responsibilities for one another, would scarcely be consistent.[20]

Over and over again Bellamy endeavored to support the policy of economic equality by some broad principle or social "law," as in another of his "Talks on Nationalism" in the *New Nation:*

A law awarding to each the value of his deeds or work, as a matter of absolute right, would be fraudulent, because it would assume that an individual owns himself and has a valid title to the full usufruct of his powers, without encumbrance or obligation on account of his debt to the past and his duties toward the social organism of which he is a part, and by virtue of which only he is able to work more effectually than a savage. This assumption is wholly false. "No man liveth to himself." The powers he has inherited from the common ancestry of the race measure his debt to his contemporaries, not his claims upon them. The strong are the rightful servants and debtors of the weak, not their masters.[21]

In the *New Nation* Bellamy quoted a criticism in *The Congregationalist:*

If everybody could be endowed to-morrow morning with an amount of property equal to that possessed by everybody else, and in itself sufficient for his comfortable support, by to-morrow night some would have become rich again and many would have become poor.

Then he made a reply which summed up his position:

So far are nationalists from proposing to divide up the world's capital, that their chief complaint against the present industrial system is that it permits such a division. For their part they propose to make it forever indivisible,—the estate in common of the nation,—dividing only

20 Bellamy, *"Looking Backward* Again," *North American Review,* CL, No. 400 (March, 1890), 361.

21 Bellamy, *Talks on Nationalism,* pp. 27–28.

the usufruct from year to year, precisely as the members of a business partnership divide annually or semi-annually, not the principal, but the profits of the business.[22]

He held that initial equality of opportunity is not enough. "What difference does it make to you," he wrote in one of his notebooks, "that your oppressor is a self-made man risen from the ranks? His rod is even heavier than the born rich man's." [23] At another time he made the statement, previously quoted: "Wealth is power in its most concentrated, most efficient and most universally applicable form. In the presence of great disparities of wealth, social equality is at an end, industrial independence is destroyed, while mere constitutional stipulations as to the equal rights of citizens politically or before the law, become ridiculous." [24]

Here is a great social fact which has been ignored, denied, slurred over, or enveloped in a haze throughout American history. Clean-cut, honest recognition of this obvious fact would go far toward clearing the air.

INCONGRUITIES IN BELLAMY'S THINKING ON ECONOMIC EQUALITY

In his intense desire to promote a social theory which seemed to him to be fundamental, Bellamy supported a promising expedient with some very bad reasoning. First of all, he seemingly claimed for it the authority of an absolute principle of eternal right, instead of presenting it only as a useful social method. Some of his efforts to defend economic equality by giving it such an absolute status are among the most unscientific of his writings. He seemed to feel that in this doctrine he had a revelation of truth which he could not trust the judgment and experience of men to maintain, and he endeavored not only to support the idea as a highly significant social policy which would be worth much more to society than its cost, but to entrench it as an absolute principle to be adopted almost uncritically.

[22] "The Congregationalist on Nationalism," *New Nation,* I, No. 40 (October 31, 1891).

[23] Unpublished papers (B2-7-4).

[24] "Nationalism—Principles, Purposes," in *Edward Bellamy Speaks Again,* p. 53.

Various statements in his writings may be interpreted as evidence of such an attitude. In *Equality* he affirms "the supreme right of all to live, and consequently to insist that society shall be so organized as to secure that right." [25] Does society know any such "supreme right"? Repeatedly he held that the fact of being human was in itself clear title to economic equality. In *Looking Backward* he wrote: "The only coin current is the image of God, and that is good for all we have." [26] And again: "All men who do their best, do the same. A man's endowments, however godlike, merely fix the measure of his duty." [27] In *Looking Backward* he seems to claim the status of absolute right of every man to economic equality by stating: "His title . . . is his humanity. The basis of his claim is the fact that he is a man." [28]

A dialogue in *Looking Backward* emphasizes the same attitude. Dr. Leete is describing the new society to Julian West:

"The right of a man to maintenance at the nation's table depends on the fact that he is a man, and not on the amount of health and strength he may have, so long as he does his best."

"You said so," I answered, "but I supposed the rule applied only to workers of different ability. Does it also hold of those who can do nothing at all?"

"Are they not also men?" [29]

Yet this fundamental, philosophical, absolute principle, as Bellamy apparently saw it to be, while in his mind it applies rigorously to economic participation, does not apply to emotional participation, for a great variety of emotional incentives are provided through inequality of honors and position. Better work gets recognition in honors, badges, first choice of opportunities, in the special regard of fellow citizens, and in other preferences which men so strongly crave.

He would even capitalize non-economic inequality, and arouse non-economic competition to a higher pitch. In the article "*Looking Backward* Again," he wrote:

The rewards of authority, of social rank and public prominence, are held out to workers [in the new society] as the prizes of diligence, in

---

[25] *Equality*, p. 74. [26] *Looking Backward*, p. 135.
[27] *Ibid.*, p. 94. [28] *Ibid.*, p. 93.
[29] *Ibid.*, p. 133.

a manner in which they never have been brought to bear upon human nature under any social or industrial system before, since the world began. The only incentives which are eliminated under the National plan are the desire of inordinate wealth and the fear of poverty.[30]

His approval of such incentives is expressed in a letter quoted in the first issue of the *Nationalist:*

Even under the present brutal system, which leaves the means of livelihood to be fought for by men, half the energies of men are called forth by emulation for non-sordid honors and distinctions. All the good work of the world has always been prompted by this sort of emulation, or by the sense of duty and the natural demand of human faculties for expression in achievement.[31]

His high regard for honors and distinctions seems not altogether consistent with his contempt for moneyed prominence. In Browning's bitter lines:

> Just for a handful of silver he left us,
> Just for a riband to stick in his coat,[32]

was the riband any less sordid than the silver?

Again Bellamy writes, "Excellence receives distinction corresponding with the penalties that negligence incurs." [33] And also:

"When you come to analyze the love of money which was the general impulse to effort in your day, you find that the dread of want and desire of luxury was but one of several motives which the pursuit of money represented; the others, and with many the more influential, being desire of power, of social position, and reputation for ability and success. So you see that though we have abolished poverty and the fear of it, and inordinate luxury with the hope of it, we have not touched the greater part of the motives which underlay the love of money in former times, or any of those which prompted the supremer sorts of effort." [34]

Are not these "supremer sorts of effort" which are not touched by a regime of economic equality, also good and bad, and subject to misuse?

H. Stanley Jevons touches on this point:

[30] *"Looking Backward* Again," *North American Review,* CL, No. 400 (March, 1890), 356.

[31] Sylvester Baxter, "What Is Nationalism?" *Nationalist,* I, No. 1 (May, 1889), 12.

[32] "The Lost Leader," ll. 1, 2.   [33] *Looking Backward,* p. 124.

[34] *Ibid.,* p. 97.

Love of distinction might be used to a certain extent. Bellamy thought so; and Wells, by postulating a class of *samurai* wearing distinctive clothes, is using this incentive in a general way. I am inclined to think, however, that a society so far advanced as to accept economic equality will regard distinguishing marks, whether in clothing, titles or university degrees as a crude appeal to a low instinct; and that public opinion will ban all distinctions.[35]

This conclusion seems reasonable. A society in which honors and titles are sought will find men tipping the scales of judgment to get them—a sordid process.[36] A significant feature of the American Constitution is its provision that the government should not grant, nor any officer accept, a title of nobility. It thus enforced a basic social equality as a protection to other equality.

So, this supposed absolute principle, if we are right in interpreting Bellamy's mind, which required that men be equal in economic income, did not require equality in other fields. According to him, the natural right of equality of all men is not a right to equality in general, but only to economic equality. It is strange that with all his keen thinking he fell into this obvious inconsistency.

In view of such statements, Bellamy's program of economic equality would seem not to rest on any fundamental principle of human equality, but to be a practical expedient for promoting human well-being. It must stand or fall not on any claim to absolute human rights but upon its success in practice.

In promoting economic equality he realized that he was attacking an age-old and deeply entrenched habit of men. Even if his proposals should have friendly reception, a thousand good reasons would be advanced for setting them aside. He seems to have taken the course of many leaders throughout the centuries in striving to promote the survival and spread of his idea by every device of reasoning in his power. A more objective and democratic method would be to present the issue candidly, disclosing both advantages

---

[35] H. Stanley Jevons, *Economic Equality in the Co-operative Commonwealth*, p. 123. Reprinted by permission.

[36] A modern Chinese utopia—*The United States of the World*, by K'ang Yeou-Wei, who held high office under the last emperor—takes exactly the opposite course from Bellamy. It would prohibit all honorary distinctions, and would reward excellence with money, luxurious lodgings, etc.

and disadvantages, and to trust to the judgment and good will of men to come to conclusions in accord with the general good. Democracy will trust the future to the judgment of the future, instead of trying to imprison the minds of men in dogmas or dynasties.

Bellamy's appearance of dogmatism may have been a reaction from a contrary dogmatism on the part of the English (and New England) Utilitarians, whose attitude was described by Tawney as being that "the individual enters the world equipped with rights to the free disposal of his property and the pursuit of his economic self-interest, and that these rights are anterior to, and independent of, any service which he may render." [37]

There probably would be great waste in the administration of the program of *Looking Backward*, at least for a considerable period, due to indolence and to lack of the incentive of private interest. Yet there is also great waste in the present economic order. Several years ago a somewhat detailed estimate convinced the writer that of the total productive resources of our country, probably not less than eighty per cent, and perhaps considerably more than that, is wasted in the process of production, distribution, sales, etc., and by internal friction and mismanagement. Much of this waste, such as advertising for prestige, duplication of investment and services, the direct cost of excessive competition, and the sabotage which goes with class hatreds, is not unrelated to the nature of the present economic order. So much of this would be saved under Bellamy's program that the purely economic gains might very greatly exceed such economic losses as might be inherent in his system. It is probable that man-hour production in America today is at least twenty times as great as in ancient Peru, five hundred years ago, yet the security of food, clothing, and shelter probably is not as great. True, living standards are much higher, and what was seen as economic security in Peru would be considered dire poverty in the United States today.

To assert that economic equality is not an absolute human right does not necessarily question its great significance as a practical

[37] R. H. Tawney, *The Acquisitive Society*, p. 20.

social device. When we come to present substitutes for economic equality in the design of a non-competitive economy we meet with very formidable difficulties. We may smile at Bellamy's proposal until we try to find some other practicable device that is equally effective. If we undertake honestly to appraise the difficulties of alternative methods we come to have increasing respect for the process of Bellamy's mind. He evidently went over the same ground, and was driven to accept economic equality as the only practical course for a non-competitive, publicly administered economy.

THE INDUSTRIAL ARMY

No Working World, any more than a Fighting World, can be led on without a noble Chivalry of Work, and laws and fixed rules which follow out of that,—far nobler than any Chivalry of Fighting was. As an anarchic multitude on mere Supply-and-demand, it is becoming inevitable that we dwindle in horrid suicidal convulsion. . . . Will not one French Revolution and Reign of Terror suffice us, but must there be two? There will be two if needed; there will be twenty if needed; there will be precisely as many as are needed.

Your gallant battle-hosts, and work-hosts . . . will need to be made loyally yours; they must and will be regulated, methodically secured in their just share of conquest under you;—joined with you in veritable brotherhood, sonhood, by quite other and deeper ties than those of temporary day's wages!

—CARLYLE

The two key principles of Edward Bellamy's plan for a new social order are equality of income and nationalized production of all economic goods and services with the use of an "industrial army." These two, also, are the elements of his program most generally criticized both by "scientific" socialists and by conservatives. According to Bellamy's plan, at the age of twenty-one all men and women would be drafted into this army, to serve until forty-five, and be subject to service for ten years longer if needed, though such calls would rarely be made. Each person would choose the field of work which would most appeal to him. If an occupation should be overcrowded, the period of work in each day or year would be lengthened. If there should not be enough volunteers in any field, the periods of work would be shortened to make it more attractive. In this way a balance would be maintained between supply and demand.

"The principle is [Bellamy wrote] that no man's work ought to be, on the whole, harder for him than any other man's for him, the workers themselves to be the judges. . . .

"Preference is given to those who have acquired the most knowledge of the trade they wish to follow. . . . The administration, while depending on the voluntary system for filling up the trades as a rule, holds always in reserve the power to call for special volunteers, or to draft any force needed from any quarter." [38]

Each person on entering the labor army must work at unskilled labor for three years. "This grade is a sort of school, and a very strict one, in which the young men are taught habits of obedience, subordination, and devotion to duty." [39] "These three years of stringent discipline none are exempt from, and very glad our young men are to pass from this severe school into the comparative liberty of the trades." [40] Such a program, if well administered, would put stamina and vigor into the young men of the nation. A reasonable degree of change of occupation would be allowed. When a young person had chosen a vocation, a period of apprenticeship would begin, its length depending on the nature of the calling and the qualifications of the person in training. On graduation from this course one would become a full-fledged workman, of the first, second, or third grade, depending on his merits. Honors, promotions, rank, and a spirit of public service would be relied on as incentives.

There would be periodical regradings to insure recognition of ability and to prevent persons from resting on past achievements. The higher the rating the greater would be the freedom in choice of work. There would be a sort of invalid corps for defective or disabled persons. Ratings would be published and badges worn, so that the public could know the standing of every person. The higher ranking men would have special privileges and immunities. "A man

---

[38] *Looking Backward,* pp. 68, 69. The extent to which the course of events has carried the nation toward Bellamy's pattern is illustrated by the widespread support for the idea of drafting all men and women into the national service. If this should be initiated as a war policy it might continue in time of peace.

[39] *Ibid.,* p. 124.   [40] *Ibid.,* p. 70.

able to do duty, and persistently refusing, is sentenced to solitary imprisonment on bread and water till he consents." [41]

Officers would be appointed from men of the highest grade, and they would be of various ranks, not unlike those in an army. Above the generals of divisions were the chiefs of ten great departments, who formed the council of the general-in-chief, who was President of the United States. The general-in-chief must have passed through all the grades below him.

At the end of the three-year term at common labor any person could enter training for the professions, but the courses would be so exacting that only persons of marked capacity would choose to follow them. Since all incomes would be equal, there would be no financial advantage in undergoing such discipline. No students would be received to begin professional training after the age of thirty, "as there would remain too brief a period before the age of discharge in which to serve the nation in their professions." [42]

Bellamy has been charged with borrowing the idea of the industrial army from other utopian writers. We have mentioned Plutarch's description of such a system in ancient Sparta, and, more pointedly, the ancient Peruvian order. French reformers and utopians in the eighteenth and nineteenth centuries had adopted the policy and had made some efforts to put it into practice. It had been a recurring element in utopias from early times until the period just preceding *Looking Backward*.

From his early youth Bellamy had had an absorbing interest in military affairs, which continued throughout his life. It is illustrated in such writing as the following from his published story "An Echo of Antietam:

Presently there is a burst of martial music, and the regiment comes wheeling round the corner into view and fills the wide street from curb to curb with its broad front. As the blue river sweeps along, the rows of polished bayonets, rising and falling with the swinging tread of the men, are like interminable ranks of foam-crested waves rolling in upon the shore. The imposing mass, with its rhythmic movement, gives the impression of a single organism. One forgets to look for the individuals in it, forgets that there are individuals. Even those who have brothers, sons, lovers there, for a moment almost forget them in the impression of

[41] *Ibid.*, p. 128.   [42] *Ibid.*, p. 73.

a mighty whole. The mind is slow to realize that this great dragon, so terrible in its beauty, emitting light as it moves from a thousand burnished scales, with flaming crest proudly waving in the van, is but an aggregation of men singly so feeble . . .[43]

This interest in military affairs doubtless made him unusually quick to see the advantages of a military type of organization in the economic world.

For many years Bellamy's preoccupation with military affairs was an interest without an object. It had no real part in his pattern of life. Then suddenly it dropped into its place in his scheme of things like a piece in a jig-saw puzzle, in such a way, he believed, that all the good qualities of military life were preserved and all the evils of war omitted. He described that process in a paragraph previously quoted.

The idea of committing the duty of maintaining the community to an industrial army, precisely as the duty of protecting it is entrusted to a military army, was directly suggested to me by the grand object lesson of the organization of an entire people for national purposes presented by the military system of universal service for fixed and equal terms, which has been practically adopted by the nations of Europe . . . What inference could possibly be more obvious and more unquestionable than the advisability of trying to see if a plan which was found to work so well for purposes of destruction might not be profitably applied to the business of production now in such shocking confusion. . . . It was not till I began to work out the details of the scheme . . . that I perceived the full potency of the instrument I was using and recognized in the modern military system not merely a rhetorical analogy for a national industrial service, but its prototype, furnishing at once a complete working model for its organization. . .[44]

In replying to a criticism of his proposals in the *Contemporary Review*, he wrote:

M. de Laveleye is kind enough to say that a system, "very similar to that of Mr. Bellamy," has been known to work very well—for instance, in Peru under the Incas . . . He includes . . . the slave-based military system of Sparta . . .

I find it a quite unaccountable oversight on M. de Laveleye's part,

[43] Bellamy, *The Blindman's World and Other Stories*, p. 42.
[44] Bellamy, "How I Came to Write *Looking Backward*," *Nationalist*, I, No. 1 (May, 1889), 1, 2, 3.

that, while ransacking ancient history back to Lycurgus [Sparta] and Manco Capac [ancient Peru] for intimations of Nationalism, he should fail to take notice of the gigantic contemporary illustrations of the possibility of elaborately organising vast populations for united action to a common end, which are afforded by the military systems of the great European States. To fail to see, in these wonderful examples of what method and order may accomplish in the concentration and direction of national forces, prototypes of the industrial system of the future is, in my opinion, wholly to fail of rightly interpreting one of the most significant of contemporary phenomena. . . . The fundamental principle of the modern military system . . . is that every man able to do military duty is bound to render it, without respect of persons, on fixed and equal terms. . . . The duty to serve depends on the ability to serve, but the right to protection depends solely and merely on citizenship. . . . These two principles are the basic principles of Nationalism as set forth in *Looking Backward,* and Nationalism, therefore, merely involves the application to the business of national maintenance of the principles already freely acknowledged and applied in the business of national protection.

It appears to me that but two questions are left. First: Is maintenance as important as protection, or, in other words, is industry as important to a nation's welfare as war? Second: Are system, harmony, and concert of action likely to be as advantageous in industry as in war? [45]

Over and over he returned to this theme, but the quotations given fairly represent his position. When he did take hold of the idea he worked it out with a thoroughness and intelligence not equaled in any other such program, real or imaginary.

Inevitably Bellamy was accused of militarism. In the sense that militarism is desire for aggressive military preparedness, and inclination to promote national fortunes by means of war, this criticism is unjust. It is not primarily a form of organization which constitutes militarism, but the purposes and motives for which such organization is developed and used. We do not outlaw high explosives in mining and quarrying because they are commonly associated with war. Why should we any more eliminate efficient organization of large numbers of men? Bellamy discusses this issue in replying to a criticism of General Walker, president of the Massachusetts Institute of Technology:

[45] Bellamy, "What Nationalism Means," *Contemporary Review,* LVIII (July, 1890), 8, 9, 11.

General Walker accuses me of militarism. I confess an admiration of the soldier's business as the only one in which, from the start, men throw away the purse and reject every sordid standard of merit and achievement. The very conditions which Nationalism promises—that is to say, security as to livelihood, with duty and the love of honor as motives—are the actual conditions of military life. Is it a wonder that war has a glamour? That glamour we would give to the peaceful pursuits of industry by making them, like the duty of the soldier, public service.[46]

To Bellamy's mind military organization was effectiveness exemplified. Here, for instance, is an expression from *Looking Backward:*

I recall a glimpse of myself standing on the steps of a building in Tremont Street, looking at a military parade. A regiment was passing. . . . Here at last were order and reason, an exhibition of what intelligent co-operation can accomplish. The people . . . stood looking on . . . Could they fail to see that it was their perfect concert of action, their organization under one control, which made these men the tremendous engine they were, able to vanquish a mob ten times as numerous? . . . Could they fail to compare the scientific manner in which the nation went to war with the unscientific manner in which it went to work? [47]

Was not his mind over-impressed by the superficial and obvious order of a military parade? Is not this passage a classic example of this type of delusion, by means of which the unthinking masses so often have been awed? Mass formation may be the best organization of power when it undertakes to destroy, but for creating, building, initiating, and pioneering, that type of organization has not a brilliant record. The expression "I do not think, I obey" well describes such a military exhibition as he saw on Tremont Street. In working out the application of his industrial army he is, in fact, departing from the lock step of army routine, but retaining some of its elements.

Bellamy recognized that the creation of a vast industrial army would mean the end of small industrial units in which a few men work together. This he makes clear in *Looking Backward:*

"Of course such a system of grading as I have described would have been impracticable applied to the small industrial concerns of your day, in

46 Bellamy, *"Looking Backward* Again," *North American Review*, CL, No. 400 (March, 1890), 357.

47 *Looking Backward*, p. 322.

some of which there were hardly enough employees to have left one apiece for the classes. You must remember that, under the national organization of labor, all industries are carried on by great bodies of men, many of your farms or shops being combined as one. It is also owing solely to the vast scale on which each industry is organized, with co-ordinate establishments in every part of the country, that we are able by exchanges and transfers to fit every man so nearly with the sort of work he can do best." [48]

The world owes much to men who, like the Wright brothers working in their little bicycle shop, or Thomas Edison in his little beginner's laboratory, have undertaken jobs which no hard-headed political or industrial committee would recognize as within the realms of reasonableness. The amount of creative work which has occurred in military-type organizations always has been small.

Bellamy himself was not wholly unaware of the limitations and dangers of military organization. Along with his admiration of military life ran an abhorrence of war. At the age of twenty-three in a Memorial Day editorial he wrote:

It is a striking fact that the only great anniversary by which we commemorate war should thus be an anniversary of mourning. . . . The reason for this fact is, partly at least, because this is not naturally a warlike nation. Our people were ready indeed to pour out their lives without stint for the nation's weal . . . but with a deep consciousness of the sacrifice they were making. . . . The glitter and pomp of war did not avail to blind their eyes to its horror. And so it is in fitting accordance with the national disposition that the anniversary of that war should rather represent the pathos than the triumph of victory.[49]

Two years later, criticizing the reporting of the Crimean War, he wrote:

A man might as well give us the journals of a month in a New York or Paris slaughter house, as to linger, with this microscopic detail, over the Black Sea or any similar duel. Wars, past or future, will have their value as historical material, more or less, for their help to a philosophical study of what causes and what comes out of these national cataclysms, and not for any theatrical interest which may be thrown by skillful hands around their incidents.[50]

[48] *Ibid.*, p. 129.
[49] "Decoration Day," *Springfield Union*, May 30, 1873.
[50] "History in the Future," *Springfield Union*, June 15, 1875.

In one of his notebooks we find an outline for a story in a similar vein:

> No real picture of a battle ever yet was presented. . . . The picture should be on this wise: Let there be two lines of battle advancing on each other, each belching fire, these figures to be in full color. Then add in spectral tints the spirit forms of innumerable women and little children, clinging about the advancing soldiers, trying to shelter them with their own bared bosoms. . . . The soldiers' faces set, lit with the fierce joy of battle, unconscious of these yielding spectral forms, which represent the mothers, sisters, sweethearts, wives, daughters of the combatants, who are praying and weeping at home. What soldier would fight if he could see these invisible companions encircling in impotent anguish . . .[51]

We may well assume that Bellamy's interest in military organizations was an expression of his craving for a religion of solidarity, and for an efficient method for doing the public business. Yet he had misgivings. He realized that the military form of organization was subject to abuse. Among plots for stories in his notebooks, apparently of about the date of *Looking Backward*, is one concerned with this theme:

A private soldier is in love with an officer's daughter. The captain, meeting the two, abuses, offends, and humiliates the soldier before his lady love, taking advantage of the absolute power he has as an officer. He makes the soldier do duty as a servant. (Here bring in the cases, many of them cited, of oppression practiced by officers upon privates.)[52]

This simple theme gives a hint of one of the chief criticisms of the entire plan. It would have to be administered by men who would be actuated by ordinary human motives. With industry in private hands and with labor free, a man often can quit his job if he chooses, though economic necessity may largely nullify that freedom. In the industrial army of *Looking Backward* he would be dependent on the officer who had the power to command him and, directly or indirectly, to determine his rating. Since the industrial army is one of the two main features of Bellamy's system, it is worth noting a typical criticism of that element.

About two years after *Looking Backward* was published, an

---

[51] Unpublished papers (B2-Plots 1-31).   [52] *Ibid.* (B2-Plots 1-3).

"answer" was written by Richard Michaelis, editor of the Chicago *Freie Presse*. The story is told as though by a man who got behind the scenes described in *Looking Backward*, and revealed the true state of affairs:

> Officers may give their young friends, who enter the industrial army as apprentices, easy jobs and good records, and enable their friends on the strength of their records, as soon as they have passed the first three years of service, to enter the first class of the first grade of a trade. And such a favorite, who, backed by influential friends, has passed an easy time as an apprentice, and who has received at once the first class of the first grade of his trade, is immediately appointable to a lieutenantship, and he can run up to the higher honors in a few years. . . .
>
> On the other hand, the young men who are not the sons or friends of our leaders are fortunate if they can secure a second grade position, with a record that does not exclude all hopes of further promotion. Relatives of outspoken opponents of the administration can be placed in . . . the third grade . . . and their record can be so kept that they can never hope to secure a higher position. . . . The sons and relatives of men who are known as opponents of the administration have practically to live worse than slaves, and are sometimes treated like footballs. . . .
>
> The men appointed by the President are of course trustworthy friends of the administration, and not expected to decide in such cases against the officers of the government and in favor of the "Kickers." . . . On the contrary, such an officer has a first-class chance to "get even" with his dissatisfied subordinate . . .
>
> So . . . members of the industrial army are for twenty-four years absolutely at the mercy of their superiors. If they desire to have a good time they must blindly obey orders and seek favor by all means in their power. They must influence their friends who have votes not only to stand by the administration, but to do it in a demonstrative manner.[53]

Michaelis continues at length to indicate the kinds of abuse which might characterize such a system. Fifty years after his book was written these identical faults, carried to the point of wholesale assassination, were present in similar systems in Europe.

Men are highly adaptable, and can go far toward working out their dominant purposes in almost any kind of political framework. The test of any method of government is not how it would operate in good hands, but how it will work with the kind of people who will

53 Richard Michaelis, *Looking Further Forward*, pp. 40, 41, 42, 43.

actually have to administer it. The most ideal system, in appearance, may be most wide open to abuse if it has not grown up through a long period of actual adjustment to reality.

But while the system of an industrial army would not work with the flawless perfection which Bellamy pictures, on the other hand it probably would not fall to the degenerate state pictured by the critic just quoted. In general the average character of the people tends to find expression in its government. The American Constitution worked one way in the United States, and another way in certain Spanish-American "republics," which adopted it but which had been and continued to be military despotisms.

There are still other weaknesses of an economy based on Bellamy's proposal for military organization, though we may assume that in working out the program of an industrial army, experience would lead to correcting details. With fear of exploitation past, arbitrary rules concerning child labor would be less necessary. Children doubtless would be taught to work at an early age, when the habits of life are being fixed. As a rule, only early experience becomes second nature. If work during the early years should be a process of education, and not of economic exploitation, there might be recovered a joy in work which can be achieved only with difficulty, if at all, when the first working experience comes after physical maturity.

On the other hand, life attitudes are matured early. Three years of implicit obedience in a military organization would tend to atrophy original thinking and self-respecting, courageous independence of mind and to result in standardized personalities, making men servile in spirit. It might not be possible to eliminate a controlling amount of official propaganda, and therefore the prevailing regime might deeply intrench itself. Exceptional men would survive such experience, but they might be relatively few. With the nation's working manpower in an industrial army, there might not be leadership enough to go round, and the result might be a settling down into an uninspired bureaucracy.

Vocational trial and exploration should take place during the early years. To postpone them until the age of twenty-four would be serious in many cases, and to close the door at thirty would be unwise. Edward Bellamy's own life would illustrate the undesirableness of either course. Among creative men some of the best work of a lifetime has been done in the early twenties.

One of the strongest statements in favor of an industrial army is that by William James in his essay on "The Moral Equivalent of War":

If . . . there were, instead of military conscription a conscription of the whole youthful population to form for a certain number of years a part of the army enlisted against *Nature*, the injustice would tend to be evened out, and numerous other goods to the commonwealth would follow. The military ideals of hardihood and discipline would be wrought into the growing fiber of the people; no one would remain blind as the luxurious classes are now blind, to man's real relations to the globe he lives on, and to the permanently sour and hard foundations of his higher life. To coal and iron mines, to freight trains, to fishing fleets in December, to dishwashing . . . would our gilded youths be drafted off, according to their choice, to get the childishness knocked out of them, and to come back into society with healthier sympathies and soberer ideas.[54]

Economic democracy, either through the development of labor union participation in industrial control, or through co-operatives, may be an alternative to capitalism or socialism. Both union control and co-operative management have disadvantages. Under union control a man cannot work in his field unless he belongs to a union; if he is disrespectful or antagonistic to the union powers-that-be he may be dismissed from membership, and with that dismissal his right to work in his field disappears. Therefore subservience to the union leaders may become a virtue. No road to economic security is without thorns.

The most serious criticism of Bellamy's program is its tendency to emerge as totalitarian regimentation. In that respect his proposals are so in line with modern tendencies that a discussion of the issue of regimentation and freedom seems pertinent.

REGIMENTATION OR FREEDOM

Love of men cannot be bought by cash-payment; and without love, men cannot endure to be together. You cannot lead a Fighting World without having it regimented, chivalried: the thing in a day becomes impos-

[54] Reprinted in *Representative Essays in Modern Thought*, pp. 530–31. By permission of Henry James and Longmans, Green and Co.

sible; all men in it, the highest at first, the very lowest at last, discern consciously, or by a noble instinct, this necessity. And can you any more continue to lead a Working World unregimented, anarchic? I answer, and the Heavens and Earth are now answering, No!

Despotism is essential in most enterprises . . . And yet observe there too: Freedom, not nomad's or ape's Freedom, but man's Freedom; this is indispensable . . . To reconcile Despotism with Freedom:—Well, is that such a mystery? Do you not already know the way? It is to make your despotism *just*. Rigorous as Destiny; but just too, as Destiny and its Laws: The Laws of God: all men obey these, and have no "Freedom" at all but in obeying them.   —CARLYLE

The essential doctrine of democracy is that each man, as a free human soul, lives of his free will in the service of the whole people.
                                        —GILBERT MURRAY

Regimentation differs from planning in general in that it implies compulsory uniformity. The question never is the simple one of choice between regimentation and freedom. Always we have some of each. The persistent problem is as to the best practical harmony or balance between the two.

In some respects rural areas in southeastern Europe still retain a degree of personal freedom and individual initiative that has almost disappeared in America. The writer has observed this in the use of rural highways in parts of the Balkans. A team of buffaloes drawing a farm wagon exercises personal initiative in determining the side of the road on which it will travel. In case two such teams meet, neither the buffaloes nor their drivers surrender their dignity or their self-respect to the demands of social regimentation. There is a process of unforced and unhurried negotiation over which shall pass on the right and which on the left. The infrequent American tourist, in his hurried impatience, is irritated by this freedom. He is inclined to sacrifice the dignity of self-determination to the crass utilitarian efficiency and speed which can be achieved only by such regimentation as uniform turning to the right in passing.

William Morris, with that homesickness of his spirit for the life of the fourteenth century which is a dominant note in his charming utopia, *News from Nowhere*, would have found himself delightfully at home on a Rumanian buffalo cart. The spirit of Edward Bellamy traveled by fast automobiles, airplanes, and broadcasting networks (none of which had yet been invented, but which he prophesied for his utopia) ; and that high-speed life absolutely required regimentation. William Morris would maintain the dignity of freedom by living in a leisurely way in a primitive world.[55] Edward Bellamy would win leisure by an equality of regimentation to achieve the highest possible degree of material efficiency, with enormous increase of production, and of leisure for freedom.

The entire pattern of his individual life showed Edward Bellamy's abhorrence of regimentation. How then can we explain his commitment to the regimentation of the industrial army, and to a state which would absorb to itself all economic as well as political functions? It might be held that Bellamy became enamored of his own invention, and gave up his loyalty to his earlier appraisals of values. Such a weakness may have been an influence. More important was his consciousness of the prevailing oppression of the common man, and his conviction that until all men could have reasonable security and fair conditions of life, no one should claim that simple freedom which he craved so much for himself.

Mumford in his *Story of Utopias* said of Bellamy, "He has invented a high-powered engine of repression, and he does not fool us when he conceals the safety-valve." [56] Much depends on whether one looks at Bellamy's plan from the standpoint of a free-lance writer like Mumford, who can go and come somewhat as he pleases, or from that of the average American workman. For a vast number of workers Bellamy's regime would not create regimentation. The majority of working men in peacetime have been in an industrial army, with life about as regimented as Bellamy pictures it—or more so—but without the degree of economic security he would provide. As corporate organization and mass production have absorbed a constantly greater proportion of our productive resources, free economic initiative on the part of the average man

[55] In an article on "The Society of the Future," in the *Commonweal* for April 6, 1889, Morris wrote, ". . . if we want to go on a journey we shall not be compelled to go by railway as we are now, in the interests of property, but may indulge our personal inclinations and travel in a tilted waggon or on the hind-quarters of a donkey."

[56] Lewis Mumford, *The Story of Utopias,* p. 167.

has grown less and economic self-reliance has decreased. Public and private economic governments do rule men. Bellamy, realizing this seemingly irreversible trend, hoped to humanize regimentation, to equalize its burdens and rewards, and to protect it from irresponsible power.

It is a common weakness of the human temper to refuse to see unpleasant necessities or prepare adequately for them until they have been forced upon us. With the question constantly in his mind from boyhood, "Who will do the dirty work?" Bellamy faced this issue. He believed that a considerable amount of regimentation is inevitable. After struggling with the problem realistically for years he reached the conclusion expressed in *Looking Backward:* that the greatest and best total of leisure and of freedom will result from a policy of sharing the necessary drudgery and regimentation. He wrote in the *New Nation:* "Not to require a man to work is to permit and invite him to live on those who do. To object to the word 'required' is to contend for the privilege of riding on other people's backs." [57]

Americans like the fruits of regimentation. We want our trains to run on time; we want our business services to be prompt and reliable; we want the telephone to serve us unfailingly, even when fishing is good and employees catch the smell of spring. All this dependability means regimentation for those who serve us. Almost alone among those who denounce industrial regimentation, Gandhi, with his loin cloth and his spinning wheel, is consistent. And intimate friends say that he favors machines in native ownership. Few institutions in the world are so uniformly and so mechanically regimented as our common schools—putting children in straitjacket programs at the time of life when most of all they crave freedom. Yet the public approves its school system.

At any particular moment we want to keep about the amount of regimentation we are accustomed to, but are horrified at the thought of any increase. In 1929 all good conservative writers were agreed that the dole was not for America—that it was a totally un-American policy. Yet within five years it was upon us, not as a theory but as a condition. The question then was not whether

[57] *New Nation,* I, No. 7 (March 14, 1891), 110.

the American people like the institution of public relief, but how to administer it.

Society does better to see its problems in advance and to prepare for them, than to be pushed into them blindly and to extemporize madly. Bellamy's contemporary critics, usually writers who kept such hours as they pleased, or well-to-do persons with servants at their call, pointed with contempt or horror at the regimentation he pictured, as though regimentation were something new to America.

Many people today believe that, regardless of the outcome of present military operations, the social pattern of the near future will have much of integration and unification, but also much of regimentation and less of that absence of control from without which has gone by the name of liberty. Bellamy realized that probability half a century ago.

Among those who assume that the national government will continue more and more to absorb our total political and economic life, Bellamy must be ranked very high for his creative ability and practical ingenuity in working out methods to save as much of freedom as possible. He was not a totalitarian. While his plan called for all economic production to be public, he would limit government control largely to the political and economic realms, but among economic interests he would include health and all activities vital to normal life. He would jealously guard from government interference freedom of speech, of the press, and of broadcasting (which he foretold). In many respects he would correct the ills of society by more freedom, rather than less. He opposed prohibition. In *Equality*, describing the society of the year 2000, he wrote: " 'Our spirit of personal sovereignty and the rightful independence of the individual in all matters mainly self-regarding would indeed not tolerate any of the interferences with the private practices of individuals so common in your day.' " 58

While providing equal income for all, he would leave men to spend that income as they chose. Production would be determined by actual demand, not by any form of compulsion. The methods he worked out for insuring freedom of speech and press, of religion,

58 *Equality*, p. 134.

and of personal taste, as described in *Looking Backward* and in *Equality,* are so reasonable and practicable as to amount to genius.

It is worth while to follow the course of Bellamy's mind on this issue, and to observe the strength and the weakness of his position. With the present trend toward increase of governmental powers the world over, the time may come, and that soon, when the well-considered, carefully controlled regimentation of Bellamy under the existing circumstances may point the way to the greatest possible conservation of the best there is in individualism.

Nevertheless, Bellamy's program would result in actual regimentation. With good administration it might be no more distasteful than some of the striking regimentations of present-day American life. However, such far-flung regimentation as Bellamy proposes might be a terrible incubus on society if it should be administered by stupid, corrupt, perfunctory, or biased officials.

He leaves us in no doubt as to the inexorableness of the requirements of his proposed regime. In *Looking Backward* Dr. Leete describes the industrial army of the year 2000:

"To speak of service being compulsory would be a weak way to state its absolute inevitableness. Our entire social order is so wholly based upon and deduced from it that if it were conceivable that a man could escape it, he would be left with no possible way to provide for his existence. He would have excluded himself from the world, cut himself off from his kind, in a word, committed suicide." [59]

In the winter of 1932–33 the Russian regime used the same method. In time of famine its enforcement staff went from village to village, eliminating from the public-controlled economy those who were recalcitrant. The number who starved to death, many of them under that process of selection, is variously estimated at from two to five million. Regimentation in Germany has been even more ruthless. Even in administering an American relief program, political considerations have not been wholly absent.

That Bellamy's regime, if administered by the types of men who commonly achieve public office in all countries, might not be immune

[59] *Looking Backward,* p. 63.

to the arbitrary use of power is suggested by some of his own expressions. Describing the way in which the descendants of liberated slaves were treated in his utopia, he wrote: " 'The centralized discipline of the national industrial army, depending for its enforcement not so much on force as on the inability of anyone to subsist outside of the system of which it was a part, furnished just the sort of control—gentle yet resistless—which was needed by the recently emancipated bondsman.' " [60] Today, even in some Northern states, race prejudice is so strong that it is difficult for a Negro to secure automobile liability insurance, because insurance companies have learned that juries generally decide against colored men. With such widespread class and race feeling as exists, how would the gentleness of that "resistless" control be assured? And might not the same difficulty arise in many other cases of the crude exercise of power, especially where that power extends, as Bellamy proposes, to the drafting of labor recruits, and to putting men on bread and water and imposing "a severer sort of work" if they are not co-operative?

Suppose the administration of such a program to fall frequently into the hands of unimaginative "practical" men, controlled by a narrow, rigid orthodoxy. Might not independent, creative men be at a disadvantage? As an example of the extreme to which a totalitarian government can go, it is worth while to repeat the comment of Prescott on the economy of ancient Peru:

The extraordinary regulations respecting marriage under the Incas are eminently characteristic of the genius of the government; which, far from limiting itself to matters of public concern, penetrated into the most private recesses of domestic life, allowing no man, however humble, to act for himself, even in those personal matters in which none but himself, or his family at most, might be supposed to be interested. No Peruvian was too low for the fostering vigilance of government. None was so high that he was not made to feel his dependence upon it in every act of his life. His very existence as an individual was absorbed in that of the community. His hopes and his fears, his joys and his sorrows, the tenderest sympathies of his nature, which would most naturally shrink from observation, were all to be regulated by law. He was not allowed

[60] *Equality,* pp. 364–65.

even to be happy in his own way. The government of the Incas was the mildest, but the most searching, of despotisms.[61]

An intelligent man's rebellion against regimentation does not imply unwillingness to be part of an organic society, but rather reflects a belief that crudely enforced unity can develop only a very low type of social organism, that it may unnecessarily infringe on freedom and initiative and can make but poor use of the best of human possibilities. Skepticism of a planned society is in reality doubt whether quick planning by political compulsion can recognize and use the finest, the unique, and the fully developed powers of individuals who make up society.

A seeming lack of enforced order, with liberty for the individual to move about freely until he finds the place in society where he can live and work best, in reality may represent a higher quality of genuine social organization than the lock step of arbitrarily enforced order. A spirit and an attitude of working for social ends is necessary to the success of any social and economic order. If this is present, other economic methods may serve better than the state socialism which Bellamy proposed. A mixed economy, including co-operatives, publicly regulated private industry, public ownership in such fields as public utilities, and a residuum of subsistence industry might gain most of what his system would secure, and yet retain a large degree of freedom. There is very much to be said for a maximum use of automatic economic functions, themselves controlled and guided by public policy; rather than to assume their elimination and the substitution of a synthetic economic order.

Those who rebel against the existing organization of society and advocate totalitarianism are largely men and women who are at an economic disadvantage. Because they have now neither freedom nor security, regimentation by the state seems to them not too high a price to pay for the liberation from economic want and insecurity which is promised by promoters of totalitarian programs. The

---

[61] *The Complete Works of William Hickling Prescott,* edited by John Foster Kirk, Vol. V, *The History of the Conquest of Peru,* I, 108.

French Revolution promised liberty, equality, and fraternity. Many of the underprivileged have come to the conclusion that if they can get equality and fraternity, they will consent to forego liberty. Long-time values, such as freedom, will be highly prized only by people who are not suffering grievously from the lack of immediate values, such as security.

Regimentation is historically old, and freedom, in some respects at least, is historically new. Most old utopias breathe regimentation, as do most of the older social institutions, civil and religious. At the period of the recent canonization of Thomas More this fact became clearly evident. W. R. Chambers, a good Catholic and great admirer of the utopian, wrote in his biography of More: "He is regarded as a hero alike by the Communist and by the Catholic. . . . Now Communism and Catholicism have one thing in common. They compel a man to think of himself as a member of a corporate body, under the strictest discipline." [62] As illustration of the discipline proposed by More in *Utopia*, which is quoted by this author with evident full approval, and with no hint of criticism, we read:

Even in the discussion of such opinions as the State allows, any violent or seditious speech is punished in Utopia by banishment or bondage. And, in Utopia, if a man condemned to bondage jibs at his punishment, he is slain out of hand like a wild beast. Suppose that two sceptics, who did not believe the soul of man to be immortal, had discussed, in private, in Utopia, how they could get the law repealed which silenced and disfranchised them. They would have incurred the penalty imposed on those who plot against the fundamental laws of Utopia. And, even for the highest magistrates, that penalty is death.[63]

The road to freedom has been a long and a hard one, and the goal is yet far off.

Being an American and not a totalitarian, Bellamy was anxious that equality and fraternity should not part company with liberty. His effort to combine them was expressed in his "Talks on Nationalism" in the *New Nation:*

No man has a right to loaf, if it is meant by that a right to refuse a reasonable amount of service, because such refusal will necessarily make him a burden on the community, and the community has a right to pro-

62 R. W. Chambers, *Thomas More*, p. 395. By permission of the publisher.
63 *Ibid.*, p. 130. Reprinted by permission.

vide against that. The complexity of the present system of industrial relations may prevent it from being always obvious that the man who does not work, lives upon other people's work, but under nationalism the fact will be always plain, and the would-be loafer will be regarded as a would-be thief. Always excepting this precious liberty of loafing, I am quite unable to understand what liberties the nationalist plan of industrial organization curtails. Assuming that it is right to require a man to work, is it a loss of liberty to guarantee him the opportunity to work at what he likes best and can do best? Is it tyranny to insure him promotion, leadership and honor in precise proportion to his achievement? Is it a curtailment of his liberty to make him absolutely free of dependence upon the favor of any individual or community for his livelihood by giving him the constitutional pledge of the nation for it? Is it oppressive to guarantee him against loss of income in old age, and absolute security as to the welfare of his wife and children after he is gone? [64]

Bellamy's reasoning stumbles in this reference to promotion and honor "in precise proportion to his achievement," for it is one of his chief and soundest points, frequently expressed in his writings, that in a complex organic society the measurement of a man's individual achievement is impossible.

Bellamy did not simply throw freedom overboard and commit himself to regimentation. He endeavored to hedge that regimentation about with many limitations and conditions, so as to save as much of freedom as possible. As to the press, the government would act as printer, but as to what should be written or published, the government would have nothing to say. Somewhat similar administration would be available for religious or cultural associations. A man could win freedom from compulsory service to whatever extent others would contribute to his support by buying his books or articles, or by listening to his sermons or lectures and contributing from their income to release his own time, though his total personal net income could not be increased. Also, as Bellamy stated in one of his discussions, "The National plan is even so elastic that it will permit a man to loaf the rest of his life, after a very brief service, if he shall consent to accept a quarter or half the rate of support of other citizens." [65]

[64] Bellamy, *Talks on Nationalism,* pp. 46–47.
[65] Bellamy, *"Looking Backward* Again," *North American Review,* CL, No. 400 (March, 1890), 354.

By doing unpopular or disagreeable work for which the hours of service were short, a man could gain more free time. Within the limits of his ability, he could largely make his own choice of the work he wanted to do. Even his character "Eliot Carson" in his hermitage might have found life tolerable under Bellamy's program, assuming it to be fairly administered.

Bellamy assumed that the feeling of being regimented would disappear because men would tend to work according to prevailing standards until doing their best work would become second nature. In this he reminds us of Stefansson's Eskimos, who never had the "moral courage" to be lazy or shirk their work. Among Eskimos, as among many primitive peoples, a man would not think of stealing from a member of his community, though stealing from strangers (foreigners) is commendable. Bellamy pointed out that today a man who loafs is in effect stealing from his employer, who seems to him to live in another world. With universal equality of income any man who should loaf would be stealing from his neighbor and from all men. Public opinion might condemn such action.

Had Bellamy lived for thirty years more, and had his ideas continued to mature, the craving so frequently expressed in his unpublished writings—for freedom to find his own place in life in his own way, without external compulsion—might have found even more adequate expression in his plans; so that a Thoreau, a Gandhi, or a Galilean carpenter who was wont to go alone into the desert, would not be an outlaw in Bellamy's social or economic system. He probably would have further used his great creative imagination to get the value of both freedom and integration.

In an article on "A Great American Prophet" John Dewey gives his opinion of the charge of regimentation in Bellamy's program:

I wish that those who conceive that the abolition of private capital and of energy expended for profit signify complete regimentating of life and the abolition also of all personal choice and all emulation, would read with an open mind Bellamy's picture of a socialized economy. It is not merely that he exposes with extraordinary vigor and clarity the restriction upon liberty that the present system imposes but that he pictures how socialized industry and finance would release and further all those personal and private types of choice of occupation and use of leisure that men and women actually most prize today. His picture of a reign of brotherly love may be overdrawn. But the same cannot be said of his account of freedom in personal life outside of the imperative demand for the amount of work necessary to provide for the upkeep of social capital. In an incidental chapter on the present servility to fashion he brings out the underlying principle. "Equality creates an atmosphere which kills imitation, and is pregnant with originality, for everyone acts out himself, having nothing to gain by imitating anyone else." It is the present system that promotes uniformity, standardization and regimentation.[66]

But also it was John Dewey who wrote in his *Freedom and Culture:* "Social movements that have a new direction are accompanied by simplifications. . . . Later on, the things that were left out of the reckoning are noted. They are then seen to be involved in the failure to realize the original program." [67] Castles in Spain have no leaks in the plumbing. Only when those dreams are embodied in reality do their limitations appear. Until then it may seem like treason to idealism to suggest that limitations could be serious.

Yet new social movements not only show up weaknesses; they also disclose unsuspected values and possibilities. Cynical disbelief in the motives and capacities of men many times has been discredited by daring trust in the potential fineness of humanity.

A good state will realize that its appraisals of values are fallible, and that its control should not be all-inclusive. It will protect its citizens in that freedom which will enable men to explore for values, and to live by their own—if they are not definitely antisocial— even if those values do not conform to the prevailing pattern. Bellamy had a conscious desire to design this combination of security and freedom. That is a distinction between his program and totalitarianism.

Bellamy failed to see that there is not *a* good life or *a* good state. Among the endless possibilities of existence, there may be many different kinds of life that are good, and many kinds of state, each of which would make life good for its citizens. Some good lives may be better than other good lives, and some good societies may

---

[66] John Dewey, "A Great American Prophet," *Common Sense,* III, No. 4 (April, 1934), 7. By permission of the publisher.

[67] John Dewey, *Freedom and Culture,* p. 74. Reprinted by permission of the publisher.

be better than others, but a variety of good lives and a variety of good societies will be better than a uniformity of any one kind. Also, Bellamy failed to appreciate that government should be modest; that it should exercise great restraint in seizing or using power within its reach; that it should zealously guard the freedom of its members, and their right to create societies of greatly varied character.

If we look facts in the face as Bellamy did we shall see that with wise and good administration, his program would not create regimentation for the average man, but might relax it, ennoble it, and give it intelligent design and harmony. For writers, inventors, and others who must work by impulse, he leaves a way out in his plan, and if the regime should be honestly and intelligently administered, this or a similar way out could be provided for almost anyone with the initiative and the energy to use it.

Yet, contrary to his expectation, it is possible that after a period of trial most people would be found settling down to the comfort of security, doing their routine work well, and planning for Saturday picnics and auto trips on vacations. The public libraries, the graduate schools, and the cellar and garret laboratories where geniuses work out their ideas, would not at once be overcrowded.

With the passage of time, such a program as that of *Looking Backward* in the actual course of operation would acquire checks and balances, as well as color and variety, by the range of circumstances and of personality involved in its operation. The working out of the program might gradually decrease its vulnerability to abuse until it should actually express the common character. Such is the usual experience with government. On a scrap of paper among Bellamy's manuscripts we find this comment: "Is there a bottom to badness? Yes, not far down. Is there a ceiling to virtue? Yes, not far up." Extreme violence and extreme virtue do not long control society.

One of Bellamy's weaknesses was his assumption that there are but two alternatives in social organization—complete nationalization of production and distribution, or a laissez-faire economy of "each for himself and the devil take the hindmost," which so largely prevailed in the America of his day. He did not realize that there can be many types of social organism. An aristocracy is a social organism; so is a dictatorship; so is a democracy; so can be a mixed economy. Acknowledgment that society is an organism is only the beginning of the problem. Of those which are possible, which kinds of social organism will result in the greatest total value? Is not the problem one of selection, design, creation; not just the discovery of a pre-existing type?

In summing up the advantages and disadvantages of such regimentation as Bellamy proposes, shall we approve or condemn? The writer refuses to do either, not from any hesitancy about committing himself on a delicate subject, but from a conviction that no simple conclusion is adequate.

Along with a hunger for freedom there is needed recognition of the fact that a higher economic level, and perhaps greater actual freedom of action, may result from effective social organization. How can these conflicting needs be harmonized, or which should displace the other? Is it necessary to surrender either? Both are so valuable that it may be good policy to temporize and improvise until gradually the way becomes clear by which we can hold to both. A larger synthesis must emerge which will include both freedom and the advantages of social integration. To gain either one at the expense of the other would be a cheap victory, with more in it of failure than of success. Bellamy saw this, and wrote in *Equality:*

"By the road by which every republic had toiled upward from the barren lowlands of early hardship and poverty, just at the point where the steepness of the hill had been overcome and a prospect opened of pleasant uplands of wealth and prosperity, a sphinx had ever stood, propounding the riddle 'How shall a state combine the preservation of democratic equality with the increase of wealth?' Simple indeed had been the answer, for it was only needful that the people should so order their system of economy that wealth should be equally shared as it increased, in order that, however great the increase, it should in no way interfere with the equalities of the people; for the great justice of equality is the well of political life everlasting for peoples, whereof if a nation drink it may live forever. Nevertheless, no republic before had been able to answer the riddle, and therefore their bones whitened the hilltop, and not one had ever survived to enter on the pleasant land in view. But the time had now come in the evolution of human intelligence when the riddle so often asked and never answered was to be answered aright, the sphinx made an end of, and the road freed forever for all the nations." [68]

THE GREAT DILEMMA—CENTRALIZATION OR AUTONOMY

The course of social evolution may be indicated by the sayings, "Nature is unhurried, but persistent, and not to be diverted from her ends"; "though the mills of God grind slowly, yet they grind exceeding small." Nature seems to say to men: "Take your time, take your time. Make all the mistakes you like. I am in no hurry." And nature seems to add with a grim humor, "Build provincial civilizations if you will, and I shall smash them; oversimplify your social orders, making them neat and imposing by excluding human values, and I shall dissolve them." And nature seems to sum up her temper with the dictum, "No social order that man builds shall stand unless he sees life whole, and includes in his design every important element of human value."

Sometimes essential values seem to be in conflict with each other, and it may seem necessary to choose between them. Yet if these values are vital to human life, the problem is not to choose between them, but to harmonize them and to possess them all. In one very important respect Edward Bellamy failed to realize this great truth, and his failure results in a serious, and perhaps fatal, defect in his system.

There are two great principles which must be recognized if society is to be both strong and stable. First, there must be integration and unity. Bellamy clearly realized that fact, and was constantly declaring that society is an organism, that we are all members one of another. He saw that for the first time in all human history men had come into possession of the developments necessary for a true social organism on a vast scale. Today, far more than in Bellamy's time, society has a digestive system: factories which turn raw materials into what men need to live on. It has a system of muscles in its steam engines, its electric and internal combustion

[68] *Equality,* p. 334.

power, and all its multifarious machinery. It has a circulatory system: its railroads, highways, ships, electric transmission lines and pipe lines; and a nervous system: its postal service, newspapers, telegraph, telephone, radio, movies, and television. It has its memory in books and records. It has its system of glandular controls in the banking system and in many business, legal, and social regulations. It even has the beginnings of a social brain. The organs which in animals were hundreds of millions of years in development have been given to society suddenly, almost as in a lightning flash, most of them in a century and a half.

And now comes the unprecedented job of organizing and adapting them into a synthesis which will be a brotherhood of man, a federation of the world. That is the great need which impressed itself on Bellamy's mind and spirit, and which is the burden of his social message.

But there is another principle of human society which, though very often overlooked and neglected, is no less vital. Man is a small community animal, craving intimate face-to-face associations. During the millions of years of his existence as a human being he has been characteristically neither a hermit dweller nor one of great masses of men, but a member of a small community, in intimate personal relation with all the other members. Nearly every social characteristic that men prize, except perhaps individual freedom of thought and opinion, is the product of that intimate association in small communities.

Character and outlook are determined for the most part during the early years, when imitation and the contagion of example of members of the family, and of the immediate neighborhood, are the chief character-forming influences. The finest traits are transmitted chiefly in small friendly environments, where immature children may dare to exercise generosity, fair play, mutual confidence, and a degree of unselfishness, because they can safely count on having those characteristics exercised toward them in return. The underlying fineness of Edward Bellamy was largely a product of the family circle.

In the contacts and business of the broad general currents of life there is no equal assurance of friendly reciprocation, and among the traits which tend to be stimulated are self-seeking, aggression, suspicion, and sharp dealing. Bellamy's regime, with its greatly increased reliance on central administration alone for economic security and with greatly increased specialization of effort, would tend to dissolve the intimate community groups in which civilized traits are best preserved and transmitted. Unless that tendency should be consciously and vigorously overcome, the result might be a more impersonal society than he contemplated. Men can live together agreeably, not chiefly because of logical agreement, but because of emotional attraction for each other. Weaken that attraction by dissolving or by greatly reducing occasions for community life, and the results may be very serious. Such weakening of intimate human relations is now taking place, and probably is one of the primary causes of such social disintegration as is in evidence. As has happened many times, the solution of some seemingly controlling problem of social life may bring into increased prominence other factors which in themselves become issues of great importance—perhaps even of life and death.

Bellamy would incline to dissolve intermediate organization, so far as major functions are concerned, and would have the individual deal directly with the central government. In *Looking Backward* he wrote:

Had the organization of the nation as an industrial unit done away with the states? I asked.

"Necessarily," he replied. "The State governments would have interfered with the control and discipline of the industrial army, which, of course, required to be central and uniform." [69]

There is the same bent of mind in an earlier expression in the same book:

"It had come to be recognized as an axiom that the larger the business the simpler the principles that can be applied to it; that, as the machine is truer than the hand, so the system, which in a great concern does the work of the master's eye in a small business, turns out more accurate results. Thus it came about that, thanks to the corporations themselves,

[69] *Looking Backward,* p. 207.

when it was proposed that the nation should assume their functions, the suggestion implied nothing which seemed impracticable even to the timid . . . the very fact that the nation would be the sole corporation in the field would, it was seen, relieve the undertaking of many difficulties with which the partial monopolies had contended." [70]

In *Equality* Bellamy speaks of the central government as " 'at once the august representative of all in general concerns, and everybody's agent, errand boy, and factotum for all private ends. Nothing is too high or too low, too great or too little, for it to do for us.' " [71] In a notebook, in discussing the effects of Nationalism, he wrote: "The innumerable petty manufactories will also be brought together." [72]

This picture of an American society in which the individual states had disappeared, with all political and economic life centered in one organization, probably had deep roots in his thinking. In one of his notebooks, probably dating before *Looking Backward*, is this entry:

The democratic and cosmopolitan movement of modern times is favorable to the development of the religion of solidarity. The former destroys in order castes and traditional corporations of all sorts, reduces society to individuals, thus preparing the way for the conception of all existence under the sole aspect of the one universal and the many individuals. [73]

The comparison of human society to a biological organism, so frequently made by Bellamy and other collectivists, does not necessarily lead to the conclusion that the larger and more inclusive the organism, the better. The evolutionary process has not produced a single giant organism, sprawling over the earth, but a million different species, with numberless individuals, no two exactly alike. More than once the evolutionary process has run to extremes of size, as with the great saurians and the giant mammals of a later age, only to return to more moderate dimensions. Just as nature found it better to produce many men, loosely bound together in society, rather than to combine all human flesh into one great giant; so human society has proved to be at its best when it is

[70] *Ibid.,* p. 58.   [71] *Equality,* p. 58.
[72] Unpublished papers (B2-7-14).   [73] *Ibid.* (B2-4-14, 15).

composed of many smaller societies, each having a high degree of autonomy.

The very simplicity which Bellamy saw in his great, centralized, nation-wide organization could exist only by applying uniform treatment to un-uniform conditions. In *Looking Backward* we are told of the great industrial organization of the new state: "The machine which they direct is indeed a vast one, but so logical in its principles and direct and simple in its workings, that it all but runs itself." [74] Such a statement is unsound because the enormous variety of local conditions over the country, with continual necessity for adjusting production and distribution to varied and varying taste and need, would lead to the development of a complex and varied structure. The problem, in noncompetitive production, of determining whether the greatest feasible production is being realized, is a nut which never has been cracked, and in a vast, far-flung, centralized organization the achievement of the optimum degree of economic production would be very difficult.

In a social system where the government is the sole industrial organization, the alternative to an extremely varied and complex organization would be a rigid regimentation, imposing uniform rules and methods for conditions that vary greatly. It is because there is not enough intelligence and character and experience to go round that bureaucracy tends to this latter course, with all the inefficiency and detailed injustice and hardship which that entails.

Bellamy did not see this. As a matter of fact, his system would call for the ablest executive ability of the country. Quite probably, with no private careers available, men of such ability would work just as hard and would take just as much interest as they do now in their private affairs. The management set-up he provides (by selection from above) probably would tend to efficiency.

The arts and skills and qualities of life must be learned in the small before they can find expression in the large. Local initiative and local responsibility are the bedrock of nationality. Local autonomy is the only sound foundation for nationality, the best school for competence. At a time of war or great social stress, the de-

[74] *Looking Backward*, p. 181.

pendence of the central organization upon effective local voluntary co-operation may be of paramount importance. But if community initiative and responsibility have had no chance to develop naturally in normal times, it may be impossible to improvise them in time of crisis, and disaster may result. Bellamy seemed not aware of the critical nature of that issue.

There is an inconsistency in Bellamy's thinking, in that while he strongly emphasized national patriotism as essential preparation for loyalty to mankind, he did not seem to realize that loyalty to smaller units, down to family loyalty, is the absolutely essential school for national patriotism. How can a man love the state, which he hath not seen, if he does not love his neighbor, whom he hath seen?

This inconsistency is not just a superficial contradiction. He faced a genuine difficulty. How could a social order avoid the evils of centralization and yet achieve large-scale integration? As another example of the fact that most of the problems Edward Bellamy struggled with throughout his mature life were stated to himself in his early years, the following is quoted from an address, apparently prepared for his village Lyceum shortly before his twenty-first birthday:

The centralized government of a modern military monarchy is of all others that system least calculated to advance human felicity, or even material prosperity. So long as the iron rule of a centralized government appeared the only feasible principle for the control and protection of society it was with reason that men considered the extension of such a scheme over the whole earth an event as undesirable as it was impossible. It would be to make the earth one prison house, and to leave no corner of the earth a refuge for the victims of tyranny.

But since the dark days when this was the only outlook of humanity, God has smiled upon the earth and taught men two things . . . These are the principle of government of the people by themselves, and the system of federal administration—the one the leaven of the world's redemption; the other, the principle of applying it, without which it would be useless as the lightning which no man can harness. The federal principle may, I think, be defined as that system where local affairs are managed by the people of the localities directly interested in them, while those matters which are of common importance to all sections are directed by a central government.[75]

That young Bellamy saw the unity of the entire problem, from the family up to international government, is indicated by a further comment:

In considering those prerogatives which the nations must give up to constitute a federal union we perceive that they are precisely those which the individuals of the human family were obliged to surrender before the institution of society could be established.[76]

It is possible that had Bellamy maintained health and vigor, his great creative imagination would have contributed further to the solution of this enigma of society.

The conflict of autonomy versus centralization, symbolized by the crisis of the second world war, has been excellently appraised by Denis de Rougemont in the magazine *Common Sense:*

The war will have the fatal result of destroying the very bases of so-called liberal economy, and the very frameworks of nationalism. The theoretical possibility of a federation of peoples will thus be presented, and at the same time, federalism will appear as the unique and genuine alternative to totalitarianism. To the individualism and nationalism of the democracies, it will oppose an ideal of cooperation; to the uniformity and enforced collectivism of the totalitarians, it will oppose an ideal of union in diversity, of organic community.

Federalism is never born out of theoretical projects. On the contrary, in those places where it exists—Switzerland, the United States, the British Commonwealth—one observes that it has always and instinctively cast aside every systematic solution, proposed or imposed from a central point. The existing federations were born out of empirical adjustments, out of compromise effected with difficulty, through struggle and often through war. . . . Every true federalism must start from a basis of existing and legitimate differences, and these must be organized slowly, not into a geometric edifice—the totalitarian procedure—but into a living body wherein each organ preserves its originality and its distinct function.

The clash between the Reich and France was a clash between two unequally centralized tactics, one offensive, the other defensive. On the German side, the central authority prepared minutely organized mechanical raids, preceded by waves of uniform propaganda. On the

[75] Unpublished papers (B3B-Miscellaneous Fragments).
[76] *Ibid.*

French side, the only preparation had been a line of rigid defenses hugging the frontier. This line once pierced, the interior lay open and yielding: there were only gendarmes and a shapeless mass of fugitives. This corresponded to the political schema of France: a centralized administration and customs barriers, but no living regional strongholds. On the other hand, Finland and Greece resisted the tactic of mechanized raids in exact proportion as they had prepared for *local* defenses, in the depths of the country. And Switzerland . . . in keeping with her federalist structure . . . has not relied upon fortified lines for defense, but rightly upon local nests of resistance scattered throughout her territory. Each village, each mountain, is a fortress, defended by troops recruited within the region and therefore so constituted that every man knows what he is defending, without having to be told: his land, his factory, his home, which he can see from his post of duty.

The great military lesson of this war is that the federalist tactic is the only one capable of opposing the totalitarian tactic. And this lesson admirably illustrates the political reality of our times. It is not the centralized pseudo-democracies which will be able to resist the fascist menace, but the federalist democracies. That is the one exact antithesis, and the only one truly possible today: *federalism* (and not democracy in general) *against totalitarianism*. The fact that this antithesis has revealed itself in brute material fact, in the decisive test of war, may qualify it as precept for all subsequent political activity.

In a centralized state, however "democratic" it may represent itself, it is enough to smash a head or the few heads of government, in order that the State collapse: witness France. But in a federalist democracy, as a Swiss statesman once told me, you would have as many heads to smash as there are citizens attached to their commune, their parish, or their local roots.[77]

The classic case of a collapse of a great centralized economy is ancient Peru. A nation larger and more populous than any in Europe had a high discipline and a great military force. Less than two hundred Spanish adventurers, coming in the guise of friends bringing greetings from their king, captured the person of the Inca, as he entertained them unarmed, and then, through his sacred person, dictated to the vast empire. An army of fifty thousand close at hand dared not act against the sacred head of the state, and so the empire collapsed.

[77] Denis de Rougemont, "Federalism vs. Totalitarianism," *Common Sense*, X, No. 6 (June, 1941), 182, 183. By permission of the publisher.

In Russia, under the centralized Czarist regime, a fanatic priest, Rasputin, could get the ear of the Czar and greatly affect national policies. Even in a democracy, under a "strong" administration there is incessant conjecture as to what forceful men have the ear of the executive. The comment of Bellamy in one of his earliest statements, "The fabric of society is as delicate and sensitive as it is vast," [78] applies especially to highly centralized governments. Such governments are unstable, vulnerable; they tend to be without roots in the soil.

The alternative is indicated by de Rougemont:

The tactic of federalism consists first, and from now on, in developing all existent local strongholds. The totalitarian tactic is long-range: it succeeds only on the day when the whole mass of a nation has been unified by force. But the federalist tactic has the advantage of succeeding immediately, wherever a stronghold is maintained and whenever it encourages a new one. Federalism begins, and indeed already exists, wherever a man affirms himself, in the consciousness of his rights and his responsibilities.

The average man can only be concretely *himself* within the framework of a local community (commune, parish, club, political group, syndicate) where he can make himself heard in a practical way and where he can act. Local communities, therefore, are the vital cells of every federation. . . . man can realize himself completely only within a federalist organization of society, because the latter alone provides both obligation and freedom.

Individualist democracy offers only freedom, without concrete obligation. It has crumbled to dust. Fascism and communism tolerate only obligation, without freedom. They mutilate the individual. Only where man wishes to be whole will the state never be totalitarian. But man can be whole only in a community his size. . . . Let us learn to think politically in terms of concrete communities, of local strongholds.[79]

The primitive independent community has fallen before the tribe, the feudal army, and the nation; and small nations fall before great ones. Can we recover and develop the autonomous local community, region, and state, and the larger units of human society, such as the nation? That is, and for long will continue to be, a dominant social issue.

[78] Unpublished papers (B-3B, First Lyceum Address, p. 4).
[79] Denis de Rougemont, "Federalism vs. Totalitarianism," pp. 183, 186. Reprinted by permission.

Society is in the throes of making itself into an organism. This movement is inexorable. Combinations of capital and labor and of agriculture are straws in the wind. The question is not whether this change comes, but *how* it comes, and in what form. The same evolutionary urge which produced men, produced rattlesnakes. There is no one form society must take in becoming an organism. The plans of men will partly determine which of many forms is taken. Much of the conflict of men is over competitive plans for personal and social life.

Centralization has become an absolute, but a limited, necessity. Its best use is to protect the freedom of smaller units of society and of individuals. Contagious disease leaps across local boundaries. Only the great state can keep its many communities free from danger of pestilence. Small communities, by setting up tariff or other barriers, may destroy freedom of commerce and of communication. Only a central government can protect its subdivisions against such restrictions. Small communities, by programs of armament and aggression, may put their neighbors under unwilling heavy servitude to military preparedness. The great central state can give freedom from such local military competition. Other necessary functions of the great centralized state might be cited. To abandon such values would be surrender of great social gains. The problem of society is how to become an organism while retaining the advantages of freedom and individuality.

The ideal central government will be modest in its demand for power. The wisely governed state will distinguish between necessarily centralized functions and those which can better be administered by smaller units. The ideal state will be a hierarchy—from the individual up through the family, the local community, the small region, larger regions or natural subdivisions, up to the one central authority. Each subdivision will receive from above, or will protect from loss to the central authority, all the power and functions not necessarily exercised by superior institutions, will retain only those which cannot well be exercised by any smaller unit, and will pass on to subordinate social units all that they or their members can exercise effectively. Always the greatest possible wholesome degree of autonomy, freedom, and responsibility will be the aim. Thus will be realized a union of efficiency and freedom.

Because conditions vary endlessly, such a social order will have endless variety. Its stability will rest, not on the simplicity of enforcing uniform rules, but from habits of integrity and good will so deeply rooted that they are the prevailing folkways. In fact, just such folkways now provide the living fiber of society, and the quality and strength of any society is determined by the quality of such folkways.

One of the difficulties of Bellamy's program is that complete nationalization of industry would tend to result in the absorption of all functions by the state. Would it not be possible to expand constitutional guarantees, so that fundamental rights would be protected by the central power, and then to leave the rest of life free to autonomous administration of local communities and regional divisions of government, with a large degree of personal freedom? Today every man is guaranteed equal protection of the laws. The national government exercises quarantine against disease and plant pests. It undertakes to prevent tariff barriers between states. To such existing constitutional guarantees might be added the assurance to every person of an income commensurate with the productive capacity of society—adequate for food, shelter, clothing, education, medical care, and a margin for incidentals of his own choice. Beyond that, life might be free, with local self-government and local responsibility unabridged. Then the aspiration to rise above the insured level of living probably would be as strong as is the desire today not to live in a disreputable house or wear rags.

BELLAMY AND AGRICULTURE

Edward Bellamy, having grown up in a small Massachusetts manufacturing town, had seen almost nothing of western farming, or of any farming beyond the small plots of New England. Yet his picture of the farming of the future more accurately represents present-day tendencies than does that of almost any agricultural writer of his time. Passages in *Equality* are typical:

I saw a large field from which the crops had been cut. Over its surface was moving a row of great machines, behind which the earth surged up in brown and rigid billows. On each machine stood or sat in easy attitude a young man or woman with quite the air of persons on a pleasure excursion.

"Nobody would certainly do farm work . . . if it had continued to be either more lonesome or more laborious than other sorts of work. As regards the social surroundings of the agriculturist, he is in no way differently situated from the artisan or any other class of workers. He, like the others, lives where he pleases, and is carried to and fro just as they are between the place of his residence and occupation by the lines of swift transit with which the country is threaded. Work on a farm no longer implies life on a farm, unless for those who like it."

"One of the conditions of the farmer's life, owing to the variations of the season," I said, "has always been the alternation of slack work and periods of special exigency, such as planting and harvesting, when the sudden need of a multiplied labor force has necessitated the severest strain of effort for a time. This alternation of too little with too much work, I should suppose, would still continue to distinguish agriculture from other occupations."

"No doubt," replied the doctor, "but this alternation, far from involving either a wasteful relaxation of effort or an excessive strain on the worker, furnishes occasions of recreation which add a special attraction to the agricultural occupation. The seasons of planting and harvesting are of course slightly or largely different in the several districts of a country so extensive as this. The fact makes it possible successively to concentrate in each district as large an extra contingent of workers drawn from other districts as is needed. It is not uncommon on a few day's notice to throw a hundred thousand extra workers into a region where there is a special temporary demand for labor. The inspiration of these great mass movements is remarkable, and must be something like that which attended in your day the mobilization and marching of armies to war." [80]

These very farming methods prophesied by Bellamy are now in use to a constantly increasing extent, but as yet without the social controls he proposed. As for farming conditions in the country as a whole where these modern methods have not penetrated, the picture Bellamy presented in 1897 still is substantially accurate, except as it is relieved by government payments, or by the continued process of "mining the soil," the farmer's income being balanced largely by the depletion of fertility. Bellamy wrote in *Equality:*

[80] *Equality,* pp. 298, 302.

"From the beginning of the world until the last century the tiller of the soil has been the most pathetic figure in history. In the ages of slavery his was the lowest class of slaves. After slavery disappeared his remained the most anxious, arduous, and despairing of occupations. He endured more than the poverty of the wage-earner without his freedom from care, and all the anxiety of the capitalist without his hope of compensating profits. On the one side he was dependent for his product, as was no other class, upon the caprices of Nature, while on the other in disposing of it he was more completely at the mercy of the middleman than any other producer. Well might he wonder whether man or Nature were the more heartless. If the crops failed, the farmer perished; if they prospered, the middleman took the profit. Standing as a buffer between the elemental forces and human society, he was smitten by the one only to be thrust back by the other. Bound to the soil, he fell into a commercial serfdom to the cities well-nigh as complete as the feudal bondage had been. By reason of his isolated and unsocial life he was uncouth, unlettered, out of touch with culture, without opportunities for self-improvement, even if his bitter toil had left him energy or time for it. For this reason the dwellers in the towns looked down upon him as one belonging to an inferior race.

"From time to time in the progress of history the condition of the farmer has for brief periods been tolerable. . . ." [81]

The decadence of relative agricultural income which has gone along with constant increase in efficiency of agricultural production is nearly everywhere evident. Through the fertile lands of Ohio and Indiana, for instance, it is doubtful whether ten per cent of the farmhouses have been replaced, except in case of fire, for fifty years.

If agriculture should be absorbed into the national economy in the manner Bellamy describes, and if reasonable production could be maintained, there would seem to be reason for agreeing to his comment as to the outcome:

"While in one sense economic equality brought an equal blessing to all, two classes had especial reason to hail it as bringing to them a greater elevation from a deeper degradation than to any others. One of these classes was the women, the other the farmers." [82]

In the main both Bellamy's appraisal of the condition of agriculture, and his prophecy of the direction of its development, are sound in the light of subsequent history.

[81] *Ibid.*, pp. 303, 304.   [82] *Ibid.*, p. 304.

OSTENTATIOUS PUBLIC EXPENDITURES

A serious fault in Bellamy's program is his anticipation of a vast increase in elaboration and ostentation of public expenditures. In *Looking Backward* he has Julian West describe how, in exploring the new social order into which he had been translated, he had dinner with his new-found friends in one of the public dining halls. Then the story continues:

> After dinner my entertainers conducted me about the building, of which the extent, the magnificent architecture and richness of embellishment, astonished me. . . .
>
> "You find illustrated here," said Dr. Leete, when I had expressed my admiration, "what I said to you in our first conversation, when you were looking out over the city, as to the splendor of our public and common life as compared with the simplicity of our private and home life, and the contrast which, in this respect, the twentieth bears to the nineteenth century. To save ourselves useless burdens, we have as little gear about us at home as is consistent with comfort, but the social side of our life is ornate and luxurious beyond anything the world ever knew before. All the industrial and professional guilds have club houses as extensive as this, as well as country, mountain, and seaside houses for sport and rest in vacations." [83]

This description confirmed his earlier impressions, for in first looking over the Boston of the year 2000 he observed, "Public buildings of a colossal size and an architectural grandeur unparalleled in my day raised their stately piles on every side," while Dr. Leete explained, "There is no destination of the surplus wealth so popular as the adornment of the city." [84]

Love of public ostentation seems to be a weakness of utopians. In Bacon's *New Atlantis*, in More's *Utopia*, in the memoirs of Gaudentio di Lucca, in Campanella's *City of the Sun*, and in other utopian writings, we find this same tendency. The program in ancient Peru actually worked out in that way. Private living was kept extremely simple, but there was lavishness of expenditure on public temples.

We have here the suggestion of a new tyranny, which might be the product of equality and of unity of social action. Unless both motives and taste should be refined, public officials in positions of

[83] *Looking Backward*, pp. 157, 158.   [84] *Ibid.*, pp. 38, 42.

authority naturally would compete in elaborateness and magnitude of expenditures as a way of expressing their sense of importance and their feeling of power. Public taste, never having passed through the long, slow process of education and refinement, and perhaps debased by ostentatious architectural proliferation, probably would approve such competition, with each community and guild anxious not to be outdone by its neighbors. Average public taste likes the grand and the obvious, rather than the disciplined and the refined. The man with intelligent and discriminating taste might find himself isolated and disregarded in a blatant world, robbed of his personal freedom by the necessity for working to produce and sustain that ostentation. The pyramids of Egypt were the result of a vast demand on the time and labor of the people. Had their construction been a popular movement to express the new system of equality, they still would represent a tyranny of public over private life.

How refreshing to turn to a contrasting utopian ideal, from the new land of California where ostentation was not yet intrenched, as expressed in *Utopia; or, The History of an Extinct Planet*, by Alfred Denton Cridge, published in 1884, four years before *Looking Backward*:

> You are used, my son, to useless and expensive display of massive and empty public buildings. Here [in Utopia] the people have learned that it is more than useless to put the wealth of the nation into piles of stone, only to be used a few days out of a period.
>
> Rear a mountain of granite over the body of a dead ruler, and you mix the mortar with the blood of slaves. Pile up national buildings costing millions of days of labor, and you build a sepulcher for liberty. Borrow of the future to commemorate the past, or to satisfy the arrogant assumptions of the present entrusted with the country's welfare, and you enslave unnumbered generations, plant the seeds of tyranny and corruption, bind liberty in chains, and destroy the prosperity of a nation. These people have learned that they can but show their strength and prosperity to others by prosperous communities, equal wealth and intelligent citizens.[85]

In a regime of equality, if the state should be abstemious, one could live his own life as elaborately or as simply as he pleased

[85] Alfred Denton Cridge, *Utopia: or, The History of an Extinct Planet*, p. 19.

within the limits of his income; but if public lavishness, ornateness, and ostentation should become settled public policy, then the work one would be compelled to do to keep up his share of such expenditures would be a compulsion against which a wise man would protest. The true purpose of human association is the increase of freedom and of the quality of individual life. Men working in organized co-operation can be so productive that the time required for economic sustenance at a high level could be less than the time required even by a Thoreau or a Gandhi to meet very simple needs by individual effort. On the other hand, if ostentation has full play it may expand to astronomical proportions, and be as consuming as universal war. The co-operative commonwealth should be a co-operative way to freedom, not co-operative bondage to ambition and ostentation, and to the vast expenditures they might entail. One of the cardinal principles of the new society should be great restraint in noneconomic public undertakings, so that restriction of freedom, and public demand upon the individual, would be at a minimum.

If economic products are fit and beautiful and appropriate, then ornamentation and elaboration will not be necessary to aesthetic expression. Plutarch, in his *Life of Lycurgus*, describes such an aim for Sparta, "Their lawgiver . . . by relieving the artisans of the trouble of making useless things, set them to show their skill in giving beauty to those of daily and indispensable use." [86] In modern life the opportunities for doing this are many. In the modern automobile the useful is made beautiful. In a modern utopia, for instance, original food packages would not need to compete in spectacular colors for advertising, but could be so beautiful as to be worthy of places on the finest tables, and their design might well establish national reputations of artists. Factories could be more beautiful than monuments or cathedral towers, for theirs would be a living, functioning beauty, not dead art for its own sake. A beauty inherent in the processes of living should displace much of the art of the past, which to a large degree unconsciously assumed that life as such is ugly and must be supplemented or overlaid by separate creation.

[86] *Plutarch's Lives* (Translated by John Dryden), p. 56.

This dread of the consumption of social resources in public ostentation is no idle fear. Next to war it has been one of the commonest ways for expressing power, and is to be expected of ambitious men who, having gained power and authority, seek the thrill of directing vast organizations of men and materials, and desire monuments to themselves. Also, the masses of people crave a sense of validity which may be gained by participating in what seems big and important. Mussolini fed the craving of his people for the grandiose with expansive plans for the rebuilding of Rome, Hitler took a similar course with Berlin and other cities, while Stalin undertook to build a skyscraper to be the highest in the world. American courthouses and state capitals throughout the country have been designed more for ostentation than for usefulness. The public architect is particularly susceptible to this temptation, since he would be the agent for giving it expression. Except for the soldier, no one is more inclined to consume public resources in creating and executing vast designs. One of them, in an article on "The Artistic Aspects of Bellamy's *Looking Backward*," gladly drew attention to the "important complement to this simplicity of private life . . . the simultaneous development of splendour in public life." [87]

Many utopians in the field of aesthetics were imitative. They desired to capture for every man what had been within reach only of the favored few. Without asking themselves whether this art of the aristocrats was really worth while in itself, they indiscriminatingly adopted current appraisals of value. That is one of the weaknesses of rebellion from servitude. The first craving of an inferior person is to possess what his superior already has. In the court of the French Empire rank was indicated by the height of heels. With the winning of freedom and equality, every woman now can demonstrate her equality by wearing shoes with heels as high as those formerly worn only by persons closest to the throne. The custom has survived, even when its origin has been forgotten.

Bellamy wrote in *Looking Backward* that if men refused to work they would be put on bread and water. Do we want bread and water

[87] Henry Holiday, "The Artistic Aspects of Edward Bellamy's *Looking Backward*," *Transactions of the Guild & School of Handicraft*, I, 62.

to be the alternative to making public life "ornate and luxurious beyond anything the world ever knew before"? When we get down to it, that is Bellamy's proposal.

Yet it would not be wise to set up a contrary doctrine, that public expenditures should be kept at a bare minimum, so that a maximum of time and resources would be available for individual freedom and for private use. Many of the finest of human achievements would continue to be in great public undertakings. Co-operative society should seek neither the maximum nor the minimum, but the optimum of public expenditure on things of beauty. The only reliances for keeping a wise course are the gradual development of respect for individuality, education in all areas of excellence, and a sense of relative values, which will keep public and private expenditures in good proportion to each other.

In the long run public taste is not a negligible guide to excellence. It is probable that for a few generations a people living in economic equality would have an orgy of building for themselves the kinds of monuments for which they had envied the ostentatious rich. Then, observing that good taste is marked by simplicity, and that ostentation and ornateness are essentially vulgar, they would cease to build such structures. For a time they would continue to use those already built, then they would dislike them, then barely tolerate them, and finally they would tear them down.

Whereas in choosing public officials Bellamy would eliminate popular elections and rely on the judgment of mature, experienced, and tested men, yet in the selection of public art and of artists to execute it he would rely on popular votes, and would tend to appraise art by its immediate popularity. In *Looking Backward* he says: "In art . . . as in literature, the people are the sole judges. They vote upon the acceptance of statues and paintings for the public buildings, and their favorable verdict carries with it the artist's remission from other tasks to devote himself to his vocation." [88] His comparison of literature with public art is mistaken, for whereas in literature each would purchase the book he wanted from his personal income, public art would be provided by general public taxation or its equivalent, and everyone must see it whether he liked it or not. Would not artists even more than now incline to

[88] *Looking Backward*, pp. 163–64.

produce "potboilers," that is, what would please the immediate public taste, rather than what they considered to be their best? Might not generations of economic equality pass by before democratically guided public taste would reach a very high level?

Plato in the *Republic* expressed his (or Socrates') opinion of that process. Treating of men who strive only to please the multitude, he has Socrates say:

> I might compare them to a man who should study the tempers and desires of a mighty strong beast. . . . Good he pronounces to be that in which the beast delights and evil to be that which he dislikes. . . .
> And in what way does he who thinks that wisdom is the discernment of the tempers and tastes of the motley multitude, whether in painting or music, or, finally, in politics, differ from him whom I have been describing? For when a man consorts with the many, and exhibits to them his poem or other work of art or the service which he has done the State, making them his judges when he is not obliged, the so-called necessity of Diomede will oblige him to produce whatever they praise.[89]

Oscar Wilde, in his *Soul of Man under Socialism*, also had a view of art strikingly different from that Bellamy expressed in *Looking Backward*. He wrote:

> *A work of art is the unique result of a unique temperament. Its beauty comes from the fact that the author is what he is. It has nothing to do with the fact that other people want what they want.* Indeed, the moment that an artist takes notice of what other people want, and tries to supply the demand, he ceases to be an artist, and becomes a dull or an amusing craftsman, an honest or a dishonest tradesman. He has no further claim to be considered as an artist.[90]

Wilde failed to realize that "It is only under limitation that the artist appears." The architect is more of an artist, rather than less, if the house he plans is suitable to live in. The highest beauty expresses fitness for a purpose, but fitness revealed to the genius of the artist, not as appraised by the relatively undiscriminating impressions of the populace.

The best course is not that of Plato or that of Wilde or that of Bellamy, but something more universal and discriminating than any of them. Would not the art of genius have its best opportunity

---

[89] *The Works of Plato* (Translated by Benjamin Jowett), pp. 237–38. Reprinted by permission.

[90] Oscar Wilde, *The Soul of Man under Socialism*, p. 34. Italics in original.

under a regime of equality if public expenditures were held to near a minimum, with much free time and considerable income with which the artist might work as he should choose?

In one of Bellamy's notebooks is an item reminiscent of Wilde:

I hold that the object of life is to live, and nothing else [counts], save as a means thereto. We are not here to work, but to live, to live the fullest, freest, most developed life we can. Life is its own end. To have accomplished this or that work, be it material or artistic, is well enough, only let it not be forgotten that we do not live to work, but work to live. Naturally the enjoyment of life necessitates culture of the faculties and their occupation, only let us not so exaggerate the importance of our work so as to make that which is a means an end in itself, so that at last the occupations which should be but the ministers and pastimes of life become a cruel and exacting deity to which life itself is sacrificed.[91]

The capacity of the public taste to improve with opportunity and experience may be underestimated. Already it is on a higher plane than when Bellamy wrote. In his later years Thomas Edison told the writer that in making phonograph records to sell to the public it was necessary to make them to the taste of the lowest and most ignorant immigrant from eastern Europe. Anything of a higher order, he said, would not sell. He tended to work on that basis, while a competing firm produced the world's great master-pieces; and Edison lost out in the field of recorded music. Doubtless in Bellamy's new society cultural associations would be organized for contributing from their annual incomes to the support of promising artists, just as Bellamy proposed for publishing jour-nals or for maintaining religious ministers.

Since Bellamy was a man of essential refinement, it is reasonable to believe that he himself would have seen the incongruity of the public ostentation he prophesied, if the issue had once been clearly presented to him. In *Equality* he gives us a suggestion which sup-ports such a judgment:

"In proportion to the increase of this abundance there has been through culture a development of simplicity in taste which rejects ex-cess and surfeit and ever makes less and less of the material side of life and more of the mental and moral. Thanks to this co-operation of

91 Unpublished papers (B1-1-31).

the material with the moral evolution, the more we have the less we need." [92]

In an editorial on "The Unfitness of Things" in the *Springfield Union* we read:

People are often strangely destitute of the power or habit of perceiving the proprieties of a situation . . . as the other day near Boston, where one thousand dollars worth of rare flowers were displayed at a burial . . . It is well enough to relieve the sombreness of funeral rites with a modest and tasteful use of these beautiful things. . . . But here was an extravagance, the very richness of which degenerated into vulgarity. It makes one think of the shoddy wealth which loads itself down with huge finger rings, and stuns the drawing room or the street with the flare of a walking jewelry shop. [93]

Such expressions as these concerning ostentatious luxury are among the clearest memories of his wife and children.

In the chapter in *Equality*, "Can a Maid Forget Her Ornaments?" Bellamy indicates that in his utopia of the year 2000 the process of refinement of public taste already had been active with reference to personal adornment:

"I imagine," said the doctor, "that good taste, which we understand even in your day rather frowned on the use of such ornaments, came to the aid of the economic influence in promoting their disuse when once the new order of things had been established. The loss by the gems and precious metals of the glamour that belonged to them as forms of concentrated wealth left the taste free to judge of the real aesthetic value of ornamental effects obtained by hanging bits of shining stones and plates and chains and rings of metal about the face and neck and fingers, and the view seems to have been soon generally acquiesced in that such combinations were barbaric and not really beautiful at all." [94]

In this Bellamy was expressing his own dislike for personal adornment by stones and metals.[95] If the issue had been brought clearly to his attention he might have taken the same attitude with reference to public ostentation.

[92] *Equality*, p. 266.
[93] "The Unfitness of Things," *Springfield Union*, May 11, 1875.
[94] *Equality*, p. 126.
[95] Bellamy's optimism prevented him from imagining a time like the present when precious jewels would be left in strongboxes, while inexpensive "costume jewelry" would enable both rich and poor to satisfy their tastes "by hanging bits of shining stones and plates and chains and rings of metal about the face and neck and fingers."

THE TIMING OF THE REVOLUTION

Edward Bellamy expected his utopia to be realized very soon. That sincere expectation, movingly expressed, probably was one of the reasons for the tremendous interest in his book. Had the fulfillment been set two thousand years ahead, it would have seemed to most men to be an interesting tale, but of no practical consequence.

About two months after the publication of *Looking Backward*, in reply to a criticism that the time allowed for so great a change was too short, he stated in a letter in the *Boston Transcript:*

Instead of placing the realization of the ideal social state a scant fifty years ahead, it is suggested that [the author] should have made his figure seventy-five centuries . . . No part of [*Looking Backward*] is believed by the author to be better supported by the indications of probability than the implied prediction that the dawn of the new era is already near at hand, and that the full day will swiftly follow. . . . Our children will surely see it, and we, too, who are already men and women, if we deserve it by our faith and by our works.[96]

In 1889, in a letter printed in the first issue of the *Nationalist*, he gave vigorous emphasis to his belief. He condemned those who talk of "needless centuries to make over society. No sort of talk, not even open opposition, is so foolish or so demoralizing as this. Fifty years will see our entire program accomplished." [97]

Bellamy had not always possessed such optimism. In 1875, reviewing a utopian plan by Ruskin, he wrote in the *Springfield Union:* "We are not going to join in the laugh at Mr. John Ruskin and his St. George's fund toward a social millennium . . . although we greatly fear it would take a journey of a full thousand years to come upon its reality." [98]

During that same year, in reviewing the memoirs of Charles Greville, who kept a remarkable diary in the reigns of George IV, William IV, and Victoria, he commented with obvious approval: "Mr. Greville is apparently profoundly penetrated with the truth of the remark by Chancellor Oxenstiern [the great Swedish states-

---

[96] *Looking Backward*, Postscript, pp. 333, 334, 337.
[97] "Editorial Notes," *Nationalist*, I, No. 1 (May, 1889), 21.
[98] "Editorial," *Springfield Union*, March 24, 1875.

man], 'You do not know yet, my son, with how little wisdom the world is governed.' " [99] Such a state of affairs would not seem to promise a quick approach to Utopia.

Of his first draft of *Looking Backward*, Bellamy wrote:

> I fixed the date of the story in the year A. D. 3000. . . . It was not till I began to work out the details of the scheme [of the industrial army] . . . that I perceived the full potency of the instrument I was using . . .
>
> Ten centuries had at first seemed to me none too much to allow for the evolution of anything like an ideal society, but with my new belief as to the part which the National organization of industry is to play in bringing in the good time coming, it appeared to me reasonable to suppose that by the year 2000 the order of things which we look forward to will already have become an exceedingly old story. This conviction as to the shortness of the time in which the hope of Nationalization is to be realized by the birth of the new, and the first true, nation, I wish to say, is one which every day's reflection and observation, since the publication of *Looking Backward,* has tended to confirm.[100]

The most favorable explanation of Bellamy's expectation for rapid social change is that it had been long in process, and was now coming to maturity. Bellamy held that the social organization which he proposed did not represent a new movement, but was the last phase of an evolutionary process which already was vigorously under way, and which shortly might be completed. In his mind, the development of great trusts and combinations was a movement which should not be checked by anti-trust laws, but rather welcomed as an approach to the one great trust including all the people.

Further pursuing that idea, he saw in the centralizations and the economic conflicts of his day a process of social evolution, not "a mere chaos of conflicting forces, but rather a stream of tendencies through ever larger experiments in concentration and combination toward the ultimate complete integration of the nation for economic as well as for political purposes." And then he added, "The sentiment of faith and good cheer born of this clear vision of the glorious end, and of the conviction that the seemingly contradictory and dangerous phenomena of the times are necessary means

---

[99] "Literary Notices," *Springfield Union,* January 30, 1875.
[100] Bellamy, "How I Came to Write *Looking Backward,*" pp. 1, 3, 4.

to that end, distinguishes the temper of the Nationalist as compared with that of other schools of reformers." [101]

It may be that Bellamy had inherited from the spirit of the preceding generation an unconscious inclination toward quick millennial changes. Referring to that period, he wrote:

. . . in a broad sense of the word the Nationalist movement did arise fifty years ago, for in spirit if not in form it may be said to date back to the forties. Those who are not familiar with the history of the extraordinary wave of socialistic enthusiasm which swept over the United States at that period and led to the Brook Farm Colony and a score of phalansteries for communistic experiments, have missed one of the most significant as well as most picturesque chapters of American history. [102]

Many people of that day expected a quick coming of a good social order.

His error in timing a profound social revolution in America had other and deeper causes. Among these were unforeseeable changes in social and economic conditions which postponed the crisis. He himself drew attention to the fact that the slavery issue, the Civil War, and the concentration of wealth resulting from it, set back the social movement of the 1840s. Unexpected inventions, such as the automobile, which created a new industrial frontier, the discovery of African gold and consequent reduction in the value of money, the growing ability of government to control great wealth, as through the Interstate Commerce Commission, and perhaps a limited checking of wealth concentration through anti-trust laws— all these postponed the climax of social change and tended to invalidate his predictions. Changes so postponed, however, might come with increased suddenness. Very few persons in 1928 would have foretold the rapidity of the social changes which were to take place by 1943. "The mills of the gods grind slowly," but sometimes they quickly turn out accumulated big grists. So far as external changes go, the year 2000 may yet make Bellamy seem like a conservative.

An even more serious criticism is that Bellamy misjudged the

[101] Bellamy, "Progress of Nationalism in the United States," *North American Review*, CLIV (June, 1892), 746.

[102] *Ibid.*, p. 743.

toughness and persistence of cultural patterns, and underestimated the cultural lag. A typical example of that inaccurate appraisal is his prophecy of the use of broadcasting. In technical imagination he was decades ahead of the scientists, but psychologically he was far behind. In *Equality* he wrote concerning the use made of broadcast programs: " 'Being able to pick from the choicest intellects, and most inspired moralists and seers of the generation, everybody of course agrees in regarding it a waste of time to listen to any who have less weighty messages to deliver.' " [103] What Bellamy expected, as compared with the actualities of modern radio programs, supplies an epitome of the fallacy of his judgment of the nature of social change. Nor is this low taste any evanescent condition due to the immaturity of the art. It might as well have been assumed in the year 1400 that when printing should be invented and the wisdom of great literature should be available to the world in inexpensive volumes, only masterpieces would be read, and all triviality in books would disappear.

Bellamy expected a prodigious extension of his views because he assumed unconsciously that the minds of men are largely uncommitted, open, and receptive. Instead they already are filled with the beliefs and opinions they have taken over from current society. They have taken their set, and are largely immune to new impressions which would require giving up the old. The toughness of this complex fabric of opinion, belief, skepticism, prejudice, and inclination can be learned only by experience.

Apparently he did not fully realize the competition with other minds which he had to meet. Writers have pointed out the relatively small impression left on the mind of the race by the life and mind of Jesus. Yet when we think of the thousands of millions of men who have lived, each one tending in some degree to transmit his life and mind to his associates, the fact that one individual should have so impressed his view of life on the race is very remarkable. This tendency to overlook the vast competition which individuals meet when they seek to gain acceptance for their views has led many men to undue expectations.

Bellamy had given such intense attention to his own plan for a

[103] *Equality*, p. 256.

unified society that he thought of it as unique, as the plan toward which all others must converge. On the contrary, it had to compete with several other concepts: single tax, Marxian socialism, regulated private industry, laissez-faire competition, the co-operative movement, and an eclectic, pragmatic policy of selecting any method or any combination of methods which should be found to work well in practice. The choice then in the public mind was not between Bellamy's program and chaos, but between his and several others, each of which had promise. Americans of his day were characterized by a tough common sense which was determined to hold onto what it had until it should be persuaded by tentative practical experience that some other course was better. Quite largely, also, they were too busy and too occupied with immediate concerns to give attention to new theories of any kind. Bellamy could not measure the readiness of America for fundamental social change. He made an obvious miscalculation, but, given his degree of understanding, his course of acting on great expectations was perhaps the wisest strategy.

Bellamy failed to realize at first the extent to which any promising movement can be hampered by human frailty and be debased and compromised by self-seekers. The editor of the *New Nation*, whom he personally selected, and the first editor of the *Nationalist*, were heavy drinkers, and for that reason were frequently incapacitated. He saw the People's party diluted, debased, and dissipated by demagogues, self-seekers, and "crackpots." His own frail health did not allow vigorous prosecution of his plans.

From all these and other causes he saw the road to Utopia grow more difficult. His widow is of the opinion that in his last days he was coming to realize that the social process with which he was dealing was long and complex. He was still young, and had he been of vigorous constitution, that realization might have been the beginning of a productive period, perhaps more significant than that which had gone before. As it was, however, it was only by extreme effort, and by paying for that effort with his life, that he was able to complete the book *Equality*, in which he hoped to give more adequate expression to his ideas. He had not the strength to reconstruct his program.

How much time should be allowed for so great a change of social outlook and structure as that pictured by Bellamy? Macnie in his utopia, *The Diothas*, gave seventy-six hundred years for less fundamental changes. A greater part of the mechanical changes he predicted for that long period not only have been achieved, but have been far surpassed in less than one per cent of that time. When our great-grandfathers were born, the control of the physical world was nearer that of the late Stone Age than of the present day. Two centuries have achieved more in that field than the preceding ten thousand years. Given favorable circumstance and a dominant current of world interest, with attention focused on reforming human thought and feeling along the best lines that can be determined by open-minded inquiry, change in social and economic temper and structure might be as rapid and as fundamental as the technological changes of the last century and a half. Should the mind of the people once enthusiastically adopt the attitude of open-minded inquiry, and of intolerance of propaganda and authoritarian teaching, the movement of social advance might be rapid, discriminating, and irresistible. If at such a time sociology should be supported by sound eugenics, it would seem that human society might reach a permanently higher level.

To paraphrase Bellamy's remark about Ruskin: we are not going to join in the laugh at Mr. Edward Bellamy because of his hopes for a good social order. Factors for social evolution are working today which never before existed. It might turn out that Edward Bellamy was not more than a century or two in error in his predictions.

XIII · Edward Bellamy and Karl Marx

In 1891, three years after *Looking Backward* was published, and when the resulting Nationalist movement was near its peak, Bellamy undertook to define the relation of "Nationalism" to socialism. In the *New Nation* he wrote:

Socialism has become a term too broad and inclusive to serve any longer as a specific definition. In its dictionary sense it stands for any theory which advocates a more orderly, just, and harmonious arrangement of society. In that sense it includes all schools of radical social reformers, and among them nationalists. With that understanding nationalists may be properly called socialists, but not when speaking specifically, for the reason that among the many schools of reform which claim the name of socialists, there are some which differ broadly from nationalists. To use the same term for groups so different in aims only produces confusion.[1]

In that statement he is in substantial harmony with the *Encyclopedia of the Social Sciences*, which states, "The terms socialism, communism and collectivism, which have often been used inter-

---

[1] Bellamy, "Talk on Nationalism," *New Nation,* I, No. 27 (August 1, 1891), 425. Because of the dominance of Marxian socialism in European and American literature, the word "socialism" commonly is associated with Marxian or so-called "scientific" socialism. However, the term in its modern sense originated in England in 1827, with Robert Owen and his associates, from whom Marx got a large part of his ideas. According to the *Britannica* article quoted by Bellamy, it was not commonly used until 1835 in connection with Owen's organization, the "Association of All Classes of All Nations." The word was taken to France by Rebaud, in his *Réformateurs Modernes* (1839), through which it gained general European distribution. A considerable element of English socialism has continued to follow the lead of Robert Owen and his school and is strikingly different from that of Marx and Engels and from Russian communism, which took its color from Marxian socialism. Until about 1875 the English type of socialism, represented in general by Robert Owen, by the Frenchman François Fourier, and by the American Albert Brisbane, dominated American social reform thinking. Then, with the migration of German Marxian socialists to American cities, the formal organization of American socialism tended strongly to be orthodox Marxian, though the socialist spirit which pervaded the American mind continued to be more nearly like the English type, to the often expressed regret and disapproval of Marxian socialists.

changeably, are ambiguous and ill defined . . ." [2] However, in adopting the name "Nationalism" for his own movement Bellamy left himself open to a similar charge of using a name that has various meanings.

On another occasion, in an introduction to the American edition of the *Fabian Essays*, Bellamy gave a more specific statement of his understanding of socialism. In that case he wrote:

Socialism may be said to be the application of the democratic method to the economic administration of a people. It aims by substituting public management of industry and commerce in the common interest, for private management in diverse personal interests, to more nearly equalize the distribution of wealth, while at the same time increasing the volume of wealth produced for distribution.[3]

On another occasion he said:

Socialism is a general or generic term for many social reform plans which agree in favoring the abolition of private capitalism and the substitution of some form of co-operative industry.[4]

These definitions all differ in some degree. The last, for instance, would include administration by non-governmental co-operatives, such as are not contemplated in the preceding definition or in *Looking Backward*.

When he was attacked by a Marxian socialist paper for calling socialism a generic term, Bellamy countered with a long article supporting his position by quotations from the article on socialism in the *Encyclopaedia Britannica*, by an author friendly to the movement. This author included in socialism the schools of Owen, Louis Blanc, and Marx, as well as anarchism, nihilism, and Christian socialism, and summed up his definition: "Having seen, then, how wide a social revolution is implied in the socialistic scheme of reconstruction, let us repeat that the essence of the theory consists in this: Associated production with a collective capital with a view to an equitable distribution." [5]

[2] *Encyclopedia of the Social Sciences,* XIV, 188.
[3] Bellamy, "Introduction to the American Edition," G. B. Shaw, ed., *The Fabian Essays in Socialism,* p. xi.
[4] *Boston Post,* Reprinted interview. May 22, 1898.
[5] Bellamy, "Is 'Socialism' a Definite or an Indefinite Term?" *New Nation,* II, No. 1 (January 2, 1892), 2.

There has been much difference of opinion as to how much Bellamy knew about socialism at the time he wrote *Looking Backward*. Heywood Broun in his introduction to a 1926 edition of that book, wrote: "Bellamy, of course, was familiar with the pioneer work of Marx. And that part of it which he liked he took over." [6] Broun seems to have written casually, without careful study of his subject. On the other hand, Morris Hillquit, in his *History of Socialism in the United States*, states that when Edward Bellamy wrote *Looking Backward*, he "was not familiar with the modern socialist philosophy." [7] What direct evidence have we on this point?

Mention is made elsewhere of the fact that as a boy of seventeen Bellamy was reading John Stuart Mill, and may have been influenced by his favorable discussion of economic equality. In 1916 Bellamy's brother Frederick wrote, ". . . his letters to me during that period, [when Edward Bellamy was in Germany in 1868] were full of German Socialism, of which he had read and studied much at home." While this is a direct statement, it is from memory of what had happened forty-eight years before. His brother Frederick also wrote at the same time, "About 1871, when he was visiting me in New York, I introduced him to Albert Brisbane, the Fourieristic Socialist, whose theories interested him deeply, and are reflected in a measure in *Looking Backward*."

Fourier was one of the last of the pre-evolutionary philosophical school of socialists. He and his followers established several cells or "phalansteries," where groups of followers lived in large apartment-like buildings. One of these, at Guise, France, was very prosperous for a time, and lasted for about half a century. It was the inspiration for the utopia of Marie Howland, *Papa's Own Girl*, which preceded, and perhaps influenced, *Looking Backward*. While some applications of Fourier's theories were fantastic, yet there was much that was sound and penetrating in his teaching. Horace Greeley became a convert through Brisbane, and gave much space in the *New York Tribune* to Fourier's ideas. Bellamy at that time was an admirer of Greeley and the *Tribune*.

---

[6] *Looking Backward* (Introduction by Heywood Broun), p. iii.

[7] Morris Hillquit, *History of Socialism in the United States*, p. 289. Reprinted by permission

Bellamy joined the staff of the *New York Evening Post* just as one of the half-dozen staff writers, Charles Nordhoff, left the *Post* for the *Times*. Bellamy reviewed Nordhoff's *The Communistic Societies of the United States* when it was published about four years later. Members of the New York branch of the First International were then very active, and the newspapers were giving them much attention. Morris Hillquit writes that these German socialists in New York were exceedingly well versed in Marx's writings. Nearly all the leaders as well as members were Germans, and since Nordhoff was a newspaperman, a German, and for years a writer on labor matters, he doubtless knew them.

One of these German socialists was William Weitling. About 1850 he came to New York, where a branch of "The League of the Just" already existed, which he turned into "The Emancipation League," just as in Europe it was turned into "The Communist League" in 1847. Max Beer, in his *Social Struggles and Modern Socialism*, says of him:

The real thinker of the League [of the Just] in the years 1837–1844 was Wilhelm Weitling, an able and constructive mind and a selfless character—the only really great German communist of pre-Marxian times. . . . Weitling had learnt much from Fourier, Owen, and Blanqui, but he had also thought a good deal for himself and worked on original lines; he gave the German workers a distinct vision of the future, a plan of communist organization, and taught them the employment of the tactics of revolutionary dictatorship during the transitional period from individual property to communism.[8]

Some of the principles of Weitling's New York "Emancipation League" are very similar to the program of *Looking Backward*. Among those which Beer summarizes are: "Universal compulsory labour will be decreed . . . By means of the introduction of labour-tokens as money, the anti-revolutionary rich will soon be compelled to place their property at the community's disposal, as they will be unable to procure any food or enjoyments with their gold and silver. The whole of the able-bodied population will be grouped in industrial organizations . . ."[9] Weitling died in New

[8] Max Beer, *Social Struggles and Modern Socialism*, pp. 30–32.
[9] *Ibid.*, p. 36.

York in January, 1871, a few months before Bellamy went there to join the staff of the *Post*, but his organization continued, and Bellamy may have become familiar with it. Uncertain as is this possibility of socialist influence, it seems more likely than any other that has been discovered, except for Bellamy's association with Cyrus Willard.

The most explicit evidence we have of Bellamy's early interest in socialism is the manuscript of an address before the Chicopee Falls Lyceum in 1871 or 1872, when he was twenty-one or twenty-two years old. This is quoted in Chapter V, "The Rebel." The quotation ends: "If you expect from me this evening a theory of socialism . . . you will be disappointed. It is an undiscovered country . . . But the faith of humanity points to its existence—and we must find it." [10] Fifteen years later Bellamy believed he *had* found it.

During his middle twenties, while he was writing book reviews and editorials for the *Springfield Union*, we find occasional references to socialism. At the age of twenty-four he seemed to be aware of the alien temper of some of the socialism which had appeared in America. In reviewing Charles Nordhoff's *The Communistic Societies of the United States*, which he called "one of the most valuable contributions to American literature," Bellamy wrote:

The words socialist and communist fall unpleasantly on American ears, being generally taken as implying atheistic or superstitious beliefs and practices and abnormal sex relations. This prejudice, largely a mistaken one, has prevented anything like a general understanding of the nature and results of the communistic experiments in the country. . . . These societies have no less than seventy-two communes . . . number 5000 persons, own over 750,000 acres of land, and hold over $2,000,000 of property. [11]

The editorials of the *Penny News* in 1880, while Edward Bellamy was editor and his brother Charles was business manager, indicated a wide acquaintance with social movements and its news columns gave remarkably clear, concise summaries of European and American news in that field. Since the Marxian "Socialist Labor party

[10] Unpublished papers (B3B-2nd Lyceum Address). Quoted on p. 100.
[11] "Literary Notices," *Springfield Union*, December 31, 1874.

of North America" was organized in 1877 and, though short-lived, was followed by a succession of other efforts, it is almost certain that Bellamy had at least a passing knowledge of these.

Looking Backward was written shortly after the anarchist agitations and the Haymarket violence in Chicago, which for years largely discredited radical movements in America. That fact may have had something to do with the inclusion in that book of a much criticized passage:

"What part did the followers of the red flag take in the establishment of the new order of things? They were making considerable noise the last I knew."

"They had nothing to do with it except to hinder it, of course," replied Dr. Leete. "They did that very effectually while they lasted, for their talk so disgusted people as to deprive the best considered projects for social reform of a hearing. The subsidizing of those fellows was one of the shrewdest moves of the opponents of reform." [12]

Cyrus Willard, first secretary of the First Nationalist Club of Boston, an experienced newspaperman as well as a one-time Marxian socialist, has given accounts of the subsidies and spying which came to his attention, especially in Chicago, where he edited a socialist paper after he left Boston.

Willard states emphatically that at the time *Looking Backward* was written, Bellamy had not read Marx or the interpretation of his ideas in Gronlund's *Co-operative Commonwealth* and "did not know scientific socialism"; and that he introduced Bellamy to Gronlund's book. Again he wrote, "I know Bellamy was repelled by the materialistic philosophy of Marx." He tells of having tried unsuccessfully to convert Bellamy to economic determinism.

Shortly after *Looking Backward* was published Bellamy wrote to William Dean Howells:

I have never been in any sense a student of socialistic literature, or have known more of the various socialist schemes than any newspaper reader might. Mr. Gronlund's work I read only on having my attention drawn to it by a letter from him after my book came out. [He may have heard of the book both from Gronlund and from Willard.]

After *Looking Backward* was published, Bellamy's attitude toward the various phases of socialism was fairly well defined. He

[12] *Looking Backward,* pp. 251–52.

had the "feel" of the American mind, as the Marxian socialists, mostly city-dwelling German immigrants, did not. Cyrus Willard could participate in Marxian socialist meetings in Boston only because he spoke German. He wrote that one seldom heard any other language at their meetings. Most of the few American academic socialists of the time probably tended more toward the English or Fabian school.

When the Nationalist movement began to take form after the publication of *Looking Backward*, Bellamy was anxious that it retain its indigenous American character, and that it should not be absorbed by the movement for Marxian socialism in America. Apparently he expressed himself to that effect in March, 1889, in letters to two or more Nationalist clubs. While we do not have those letters, we have replies to them. One from Cyrus Willard throws light on the situation:

Boston, March 22, 1889

DEAR FRIEND BELLAMY:

Do not be alarmed about the Socialists capturing the Nationalist Club. I am a Socialist . . . but I have no desire to see the Club captured by them or any one else. . . . A number of the original members of the Club were avowed Socialists and largely instrumental in its formation. They are not all ignorant men but they have great influence with the wage workers to whom this question must ultimately go for settlement by the ballot. . . . The Socialists can get along without you but you cannot get along without the Socialists. Henry George tried it in New York when his ideas were better known than yours and after he had received 68,000 votes. He expelled the Socialists and consequence was his movement as a political movement flattened out. The tried and disciplined workers had gone. . . . If you were here on the ground I think you would see what an unjustice you are doing by these suspicions to men who are just as sincere as you are and who have suffered for the ideas as you have not *as yet* done. . . .

On the following day a letter was written from the Washington, D.C., Nationalist Club, which refers to socialist interest in the Washington and New York clubs:

At the last meeting [the letter ran] Mr. Clancey, the Secretary, took occasion to read to us a letter from you in which you state . . . that you would deplore it deeply if the Socialists got the control of your club.

I believe that Socialists were the first who recognized the immense value of your work, and the *Workmen's Advocate,* a socialistic paper, was among the first to call the attention of its readers to it.

In Washington Socialists were the first who started the circulation of your work; it was a Socialist who called Mr. Clancey's attention to the same and who with Mr. Clancey and another Socialist was instrumental in the organization of the Nationalist Club.

Bellamy rejected the name "socialism" for his movement, not only because he considered it indefinite, but because it was associated with certain attitudes which he did not approve, and had an unsavory reputation which he believed would make it a handicap. A few months after *Looking Backward* was published he wrote to William Dean Howells, as elsewhere quoted:

In the radicalness of the opinions I have expressed I may seem to outsocialize the socialists, yet the word socialist is one I could never well stomach. In the first place it is a foreign word in itself, and equally foreign in all its suggestions. It smells to the average American of petroleum, suggests the red flag and all manner of sexual novelties, and an abusive tone about God and religion, which in this country we at least treat with decent respect. . . . Whatever German and French reformers may choose to call themselves, socialist is not a good name for a party to succeed with in America. No such party can or ought to succeed which is not wholly and enthusiastically American and patriotic in spirit and suggestions.[13]

[13] Laurence Gronlund, Danish born and educated, author of *The Co-operative Commonwealth,* and one of the early interpreters of socialism in America, in indicating the reason for American dislike for socialism as brought from Germany, wrote in 1889:

"We all know that those who hitherto have preached Socialism in this country have been nearly all foreigners, and principally Germans; men with the best intentions, and always ready for all sorts of sacrifices . . . but brimful of Continental prejudices, and, most of them, from their position,—in the nature of things,—possessing but a superficial smattering of other knowledge than economics.

"It is no wonder that Americans have hitherto supposed that Socialism is in its very nature atheistic, since it is notorious that most Socialists are avowed atheists. . . . I declare, on the contrary, that Atheism, instead of being an integral part of Socialism, is an accretion upon it, like tartar on the enamel of the teeth.

"In the eyes of Continental Socialists, patriotism is not a virtue at all, but rather a vice. This is most natural in them, though I think deplorable. It results from the geographical position of the continental countries, which prevents Socialism from being successfully inaugurated,—say, in Germany, as long as the present regimes obtain in France and Russia. . . .

It is of interest to note the particular respects in which Bellamy took issue with the Marxian socialists of his day. First of all, he believed that the Marxians, having focused their attention on what he himself recognized to be a profoundly important and often overlooked influence—that of economic conditions on social change—lost their sense of perspective and overemphasized that factor. A common attitude of "scientific socialism" as developed by Marx and Engels is expressed in Engels's *Socialism, Utopian and Scientific*, long used as a major text book by American Marxians:

The materialist conception of history starts from the proposition that the production of the means to support human life and, next to produc-

"The same applies to another doctrine, closely allied to the previous one: that of Socialism being a class-movement, which is true in one sense and not in another. This time it is the historical evolution which has brought it on a false scent. They speak and act as if Socialism must necessarily be a conflict between those who work with their hands and the rest of the nation, thus making it a doctrine of hatred and spoliation, and this in spite of the fact that nearly all their leaders have belonged to the educated classes. This our Nationalists rectify. They insist that there need not be conflict at all, that a Socialist *regime* will prove a blessing to all . . .

"Again, it is a fact, not by any means true of all Continental Socialists, but of a great many of them, that they are inclined toward Free-love; and, therefore, many Americans have got the notion that Socialism will destroy the family relation. This, I contend, is precisely the reverse of what its effect will be.

"It follows, further, from the position of the Continental Socialists, that Socialism has often been confounded with confiscation. Yet no error is greater than this. Confiscation is not at all a Socialist *principle* . . ." Laurence Gronlund, "Socialism True and False," *The New Ideal*, II, No. 11, 184–85.

Notwithstanding Gronlund's limitations, concerning the traits of European socialists he was in a position to know whereof he spoke. There is a vast amount of evidence to support this appraisal of Gronlund. Mrs. Shipley (Marie A. Brown) in her book *The True Author of "Looking Backward,"* charges Bellamy with failure to be a true socialist because he rejects extreme materialism, class warfare, and anti-religion. Calverton, in his strongly Marxian book, *The Liberation of American Literature*, treats Bellamy almost with contempt and disdain as one of the "petty bourgeoisie" who failed of Marxian Socialism in all these respects. He wrote: "Even religion was to have place in his Utopia . . ." (V. F. Calverton, *The Liberation of American Literature* [New York, Scribners, 1932], p. 349). James Boyle in his *What Is Socialism?*, published in 1912, commented on Bellamy's system, "called 'Nationalism,' which was, in a way, a rival to Marxian socialism, and was much opposed by the followers of the latter. . . . The system was a combination of Opportunism and Idealism; it was Socialist in the sense that it involved the nationalization of industry and the communal ownership of property; but the Marxian philosophy of the materialistic conception of history and of the class struggle had no place in it; consequently, Nationalism is not considered genuine Scientific Socialism, but simply a form of Utopianism." (James Boyle, *What Is Socialism?* [New York, Shakespeare Press, 1912], pp. 89–90.)

tion, the exchange of things produced, is the basis of all social structure . . . The final causes of all social changes and political revolutions are to be sought, not in men's brains, not in men's better insight into eternal truth and justice, but in changes in modes of production and exchange. They are to be sought, not in the *philosophy,* but in the *economics* of that particular epoch.[14]

Bellamy gave greater weight to economic determinism than did most of the English socialists of his day, yet to him this was only one factor in what he called "the great revolution." He was convinced that a good society required that all impulses and interests of men, intellectual, ethical, and aesthetic, as well as economic, be taken into account. He held that the problem is to achieve right emphasis and proportion among all social factors.[15] The diffusion of intelligence which followed the invention of printing he held to be a primary cause of the great social movement. Also, he laid great stress on "enthusiasm for the social, not the personal, salvation, and for the establishment in brotherly love of the Kingdom of God on earth which Christ bade men hope and work for." [16]

Because of the tendency of the past to reproduce itself, social theories and social movements tend strongly to inherit the character and the color of the traditional cultures which already exist, and not simply to follow the influence of economic forces. The inaccuracy of the common interpretation of the Marxian doctrine of economic determination as the sole important influence in social change, may be illustrated by an analogy from nature. In an Ap-

---

[14] Frederick Engels, *Socialism, Utopian and Scientific,* p. 94.

[15] In this respect Bellamy was closer to the English socialists. The English statistician and economist H. Stanley Jevons, who calls himself a communist, is an example of the persistence of English radicals in their refusal to accept the typical Marxian view. In his *Economic Equality in the Co-operative Commonwealth* (pp. 13–14), published in 1933, he wrote: "The innate qualities of men, and the moral tradition and civilization, including education, of the people, are determining factors of the economic organization, and . . . the latter adapts itself to those determining factors and the physical conditions of the country. Physical conditions become of decreasing importance, however, as civilization advances." Could anything be further from the economic determinism expressed in the quotation from Engels? Jevons continues, "A stable order of society, consisting entirely of educated men and women having political equality, cannot be founded on self-interest, but can be built up only by reliance on the highest motives in work as well as in public service." Quotations reprinted by permission.

[16] *Equality,* p. 340.

palachian forest twenty-five or more native species of trees will be found growing side by side. Although the environment is identical for all, yet it does not constitute an economic (ecological) compulsion which eliminates all but the one most suitable species. Within wide limits the environment is tolerant of variety, and of that tendency to increasing divergence of types which is characteristic of all living things. Within those limits of tolerance the species which can live and grow are determined not solely by "economic determination" (ecology) but also by the trees and other plants that are already there to drop their seeds and so to continue existing types; that is, within limits, the species which grow are determined by inheritance from the past, and not by present external (economic) conditions.

There is an even more important evolutionary principle than the survival of the fittest. It is the survival of what already exists. The evolutionary process seldom makes sudden new creations. It works over, adapts, and uses what it has at hand. The same is true of social change. A social movement, no matter how radical or revolutionary, will tend strongly to imitate or to continue the particular cultural traits of the people involved, even against the economic current.

To a degree that Marx and Engels did not realize, their "principles" were not the outcome of objective logic, but were an unconscious taking over of the mental attitudes which had long prevailed in the environment in which they grew up. For instance, some German socialists and the Russian communists aimed at "the dictatorship of the proletariat." This doctrine was largely a reflection of the governments of arbitrary power under which central and eastern Europe long had lived. It was unconscious atavism and nostalgia. It turned toward the past, not toward the future. In England and America, where democratic and constitutional methods had deeper roots, this type of socialist doctrine was very slow in taking hold. Such interest in "the dictatorship of the proletariat" as does exist in America either is a borrowing from Europe, or was acquired by imitating the industrial dictatorship of private business.

The conflict between Bellamy and Marxism was more fundamental than a disagreement between logical systems. It has been a conflict between the spirit of force and dictatorship which ruled European politics and society, and which Marx accepted and imitated as a working method, and the spirit and temper of democratic consensus and agreement which to some degree had taken root in America. Because an American ruling class brought from Europe its mental atmosphere of feudalism, while disadvantaged classes brought bitter resentment at servitude, the American democratic temper has had difficulty in holding its own.

If we observe the actual practices of the Russian revolution and the subsequent Soviet administration, we find that to a considerable degree both good and bad traits are to be accounted for not so much by economic determinism, as by the continuance of old government folkways and of cultural patterns among the people. This is true of the bent for communal or co-operative action, as well as of the secret police, of purges, of decisions from above affecting masses of people, and of the regimentation of speech and thought. The adoption of technology, the chief new element in the Russian scene, was bursting upon the nation before the communist revolution. No experimental control group has existed to indicate what would have happened to Russia without violent revolution. Therefore violent revolution is given credit for what did occur. Similar comparisons could be made for Italy and Germany. *To a considerable degree, solemnly presented social reforms are but rationalizations of old established cultural patterns.*

Marx and his followers rebelled against an autocratic and exploiting church, which in central and eastern Europe often was a monopoly of an oppressive government and had created vast hatred and bitterness. Experience with that condition gave peculiar significance to Marx's expression, "Religion . . . is the opium of the people." It was natural that Bellamy should repudiate the Marxian attitude of anti-religion, because a very different situation prevailed in America. Except for Roman Catholicism and a few other sects, American churches were democratically governed. The administration of democratically organized churches, lodges, and voluntary societies constituted a greater and more intimate school for democracy than government itself, whereas authoritarian church organization tended to undermine democracy by developing contrary mental habits.

Some supposedly democratic city churches were powerful, conspicuous, rich and exclusive, if not arrogant; yet rich churches were relatively few, even in the cities, while two thirds or more of the nation's population was rural, and the great mass of American churches were self-governing organizations of neighbors with but moderate resources and with no subservience to higher, undemocratic clerical authority. Their limitations were those of a narrow theology in the pioneer American democratic culture, rather than of autocracy. While most of them had the very serious fault of an other-world theology which tended to divert people's attention to a utopia beyond the grave, yet to a large degree the church was a useful social agency. It promoted ethical standards in advance of those that could be embodied in law; it bred neighborliness and cooperation; it furnished places and occasions for social gatherings under wholesome conditions; it provided social opportunity for young men and women to find mates. The American church was a genuinely folk institution, and the anti-religion of Marxian socialism was repellent to its members.

Edward Bellamy also took definite issue with the Marxian socialists because of their stimulation of class hatred, though he was fully aware of its existence. While he was unalterably committed to economic equality and social justice, he held that the common interests which unite Americans are greater than the issues which divide them. When Marxian socialism came to America from Germany it gave great emphasis to class conflict. While in theory Marxian socialists conceived of the class struggle as an impersonal circumstance, beyond the control of individuals in either class, in practice they often played upon and deliberately aroused class hatred. Over and over again, in the most emphatic terms, Bellamy repudiated and condemned class warfare as a method of social change.[17]

[17] H. Stanley Jevons, in the introduction to his *Economic Equality in the Co-operative Commonwealth* (pp. xviii–xix, xx), wrote: "It is to be hoped that the term 'communism' will gradually lose its extension to connote the class war and dictatorship of the proletariat, which the Russian revolution, following Karl Marx, with some degree of misunderstanding, has given it. . . . I person-

Bellamy's way of approaching social problems had a philosophical background no less than did that of Marx and Engels. He was at one with modern biology in holding that the primal urge of man, as of any other living creature, is for the extension of his being. In one of his notebooks we find a summing up of this view, "Extension of being the great motive of all action, the key of all high pleasure." [18] In this recognition of the primary impulse of man he was at least no less fundamental than Marx or Engels, and more so than Nietzsche with his doctrine of "the will to power." With Marx and most socialists, Bellamy insisted that since men are social beings they can find fulfillment for their aspirations only as society becomes a true organism in which men "are members one of another."

Marxian theory to some extent was a product of the era of rationalism and of the early days of the scientific method, when men believed they could arrive at the truth by starting with a basis of historic facts and by following a chain of logical reasoning to a formal conclusion. Supposedly logical deductions very generally are intellectual sleight-of-hand tricks. Bellamy trusted more to informal, common-sense intuition, disciplined by critical observation of facts, and consciously freed, so far as possible, from the warping of tradition and prejudice. In taking economic determinism as the sole important factor in social change, Engels was far more metaphysical and more idealistic, in the technical sense of the word, than was Bellamy. On the other hand, Marx and Engels did do some careful, analytical thinking from a broad knowledge of history, from which Bellamy could have profited.

It seems very unfortunate that Bellamy and the abler socialists did not come to understand each other. While Bellamy in his own way understood and expressed the principle of surplus value, acquaintance with Marx's teaching would have made him more aware

---

ally am entirely and absolutely opposed to propaganda advocating the class war and dictatorship of the proletariat as the only means of obtaining communism. A violent uprising is much more likely to damage all classes and destroy the progress of a generation. The purpose of this book is just the opposite, to point a constitutional way of realizing the legitimate aspirations of the people for social, and hence economic, equality in a system of democratic communism." Reprinted by permission.

[18] Unpublished papers (B2-EC-1).

of the importance of that principle. In other respects, too, he could have profited by socialist economic thinking. Moreover, his movement greatly needed the trained leaders and disciplined workers which socialism might have supplied. The German socialists in American cities, on the other hand, were isolated from the American life and spirit. They could only blindly apply doctrines developed in Europe to a new country they did not understand. Bellamy unerringly knew the genius of American life, and he had a tremendous popular following.

Lacking mutual support, Bellamy's organized Nationalist movement died, while it required nearly two generations, with disastrous organizational splits, for American socialism to free itself from domination by the spirit of German and Russian socialism and to emerge American in spirit but still weak in following and resources.

The American spirit still repudiates the class conflict. Most Americans still feel a national solidarity. In a recent article in the *New York Times* George Gallup summed up the situation:

Americans like to think of themselves as belonging to the "middle class." In one of the most interesting studies the Institute ever conducted, 88 people in every 100 said they thought of themselves in this way, while only 6 referred to themselves as belonging to the "upper" class, and 6 to the "lower." [19]

Edward Bellamy gave consciousness, form, and definition to deep-running currents of social temper in America. At a time when more than two thirds of the population of America was rural, and when much of the rest had a rural background, Bellamy pictured a social order which, while much urbanized in its character, harmonized with American folkways to a remarkable degree.

Bellamy's socialism was neither English nor Marxian—it was his own. In not encouraging class warfare, in holding to constitutional methods rather than to dictatorship with the violence and the suppression of civil liberties inherent in that process, in emphasizing ethical incentives and good will, and in the absence of anti-religion, it was at one with the American temper. He saw that those elements of Marxian socialism were not scientifically derived but were simply a continuation of the inherited cultural temper of

[19] New York *Times Magazine,* June 8, 1941. Reprinted by permission.

continental Europe. In refusing to adopt them or to treat economic determinism as the sole important factor in social change, Bellamy was more "scientific," though less involved and abstruse, than conventional Marxian socialism. On the other hand, Bellamy was far closer to Marxian socialism than were William Morris or the English Fabians. He gave greater weight to economic factors, and, except for Owen and a few others, he gave greater emphasis to the organic nature of society, and less to individual self-determination, than did the English.

Mason Green wrote:

Certain critics would have it that only a thin wall of paper separates Bellamy nationalism from Karl Marx socialism. And yet upon that thin wall are written the whole federal constitution and provision for orderly amendments.[20]

By supplying an alternative picture in *Looking Backward*, to no small degree Bellamy saved America from the cultural atavisms of the socialism of central Europe, which otherwise would have had a near monopoly of the field. In *Looking Backward*, in *Equality*, and in the Nationalist movement, he gave America a concept of the possibility of a good social order by means of those qualities and traits which tended to be characteristic of America, rather than through the destruction of those traits.

As charged by the Marxians, it was largely through the tremendously widespread reading of *Looking Backward*, and through the Nationalist movement, that the American tradition in the social movement became so thoroughly established that half a century has not done away with it. When one observes how slavishly many leaders in American higher education have tended to worship and to imitate the German university, and the extent to which American philosophy before James, and American political economy, similarly imitated Europe, the significance of the conscious, deliberate achievement of Bellamy in holding to the values of the American genius against the pressure of European prestige and tradition begins to be apparent. The tremendous hammering of indoctrination which the American social movement has received from European sources, with the ever-present help of academic doctrinaires

20 Green, pp. 3–4.

to whom nothing homely and indigenous can be important, until recently has had very little effect on the American program. Even today, while most European labor songs breathe a spirit of antagonism, of which the clenched fist is a typical symbol, native American labor and social-movement songs are less stereotyped. They include humor, satire, and religious motives, as well as revolt and challenge.

On some of his major issues Bellamy failed, in part, at least, to carry America with him. He clearly foresaw and urged the need for greater integration of economic life. The more favored classes resented his insistence that some of the freedom they clung to so tenaciously was freedom to exploit the less fortunate. On these points the country could learn only by the hard, compelling experience of later years.

Was Bellamy "seeing ghosts" in fearing that the socialists would capture his movement, and was that a possibility? Morris Hillquit in his *History of Socialism in the United States* wrote:

It is estimated that no more than ten per cent of the members of the Socialist Labor Party, during the period described [ten years or more beginning with 1877], were native Americans. All the rest, including the most active and influential leaders, were men of foreign birth, insufficiently acquainted with the institutions, customs, and habits of the country of their adoption, and frequently ignorant of its very language. . . . The endeavor to "Americanize" the socialist movement is the main keynote of the activity of the Socialist Labor Party throughout its entire career.[21]

To "Americanize" did not mean to discover the genius of America and to adapt socialism to that genius, but rather to make America accept European Marxian socialism, which was an exotic from another culture, including the elements of the "dictatorship of the proletariat," class antagonism, and anti-religion.

Many of the Marxians of Bellamy's day despised him. Theirs was "enlightened selfishness." They did not see that selfishness never can be enlightened enough to guide human affairs. He saw,

---

[21] Hillquit, *History of Socialism in the United States,* pp. 193, 194. Reprinted by permission.

as they did not, that "they that take the sword, shall perish by the sword"; that violence is inherently atavistic. Bellamy persistently held to the belief that mutual confidence and regard and good will must be the foundation of any stable social order. Without them, bureaucracy with its vested interests, jealousies, ambitions, and intrigues, from which there may be no escape, may well be worse than the evils from which society might have fled.

A great contribution of Bellamy to the social question was his insistence that the founding of a good social order is not just a concern of the head, but also of the heart, and not at best a concern of attitudes such as hate, which would be out of place in a good social order, but of good will. He saw, as the Marxians did not, that *the attitudes we take in bringing about a social order will be the attitudes that will be native and natural to us, and that we will continue to hold in that social order after it is created.* He looked upon his work as being in the spirit of Isaiah and of Jesus, rather than of the clenched fist.

It was Bellamy's own individual judgment and determination which led him to keep his movement distinct from that of the Marxian socialism of his day. But by the time that issue became acute he was used to the lonely road. A lonesome man, his projects failed, his last years were an anticlimax. Which would be more productive, to pass on his ideas, uncompromised but unrealized in action, or by compromise and strategy to acquire power and so bring some of them to partial realization, perhaps passing on his mantle of prestige to the unworthy shoulders of someone who might use it as the cloak of a demagogue? That is a problem many a man has had to face. Perhaps only very long-time results will disclose the true balance of values. In the meantime a man must live by his intuitional convictions; that is, by faith. In the long run the world gives its highest allegiance to men whose faith was "the substance of things hoped for, the evidence of things not seen."

XIV · The Object of Criticism

MANY public men took occasion to criticize Bellamy's views. Some of their objections are no less pertinent today, while others reflect the obsolete theories of a past generation. Generally the appraisals have some of both characteristics, as did the mouse theology described by Eugene Field, which had for its two cardinal doctrines that the moon is made of green cheese and that mice should beware of cats. A glance at some of these criticisms will throw light both on Bellamy's views and on his times.

William T. Harris was the intelligent, well-educated, and public-spirited United States Commissioner of Education. His appraisal of *Looking Backward*, in a review in the *Forum* for October, 1889, is a typical expression of the explicit, simple economic thinking of the period. It is better written, with less ranting and abuse than most contemporaneous reviews. He wrote:

> The results of thrift and economy are such as to benefit the unthrifty and the prodigal as well as the rich. Wealth begins with self-denial which saves a surplus, and it is preserved and increased by sagacity in investment. The unthrifty invests in what is consumed as means of gratification and enjoyment; the thrifty denies himself and invests his money in the means of production, and thereby increases the total productive power of the community. . . . Of course, with the accumulation of capital invested in permanent improvements and instruments of production the means of comfortable living are cheapened and made constantly accessible, and labor becomes able to secure constant employment at remunerative wages.

> If competition and the system of private property are working the amelioration of all classes, poor and rich, there is no occasion for us to make rash experiments with an entirely different system.

> The true law of capital has been announced by Cary and Bastiat: "As capital increases it draws a smaller proportional amount from the product as its share, while labor gets a larger proportional amount."

> The age in which we now live is proclaimed to be an age of individualism and personal freedom. We have just completed a hundred years of

protest against all manner of restraints and impediments to individual liberty. . . . The highest individualism is the ideal of our civilization; we look forward to greater and greater possibilities for each person in the way of conquest over nature. At a less expenditure of power he shall provide himself with food, clothing, and shelter in greater abundance. In fact, at the present rate of increase of productive power we shall average over $2.50 per day for each man, woman, and child, by Mr. Bellamy's year 2000 A. D. . . .

Private property and free competition constitute the simple device by which civilization has been able to isolate individuals from one another and develop a sense of the sacredness of personality. Without this province for the free exercise of his will, and without a surrounding wall of privacy, the individual becomes attached to the social whole so closely that he can have no freedom of thought or action. An imperious public opinion watches all that he does or refrains from doing, and suspects any individual departure from the communal standard as treasonable in its intent. Wantonly to throw away these instrumentalities of our freedom, is to throw away all that the race has gained for eighteen hundred years.

Nationalistic socialism insists on giving up the freedom of private property that we have but recently secured, even for the slave, as a priceless boon. Such a system as Mr. Bellamy describes would prove more repressive to individual development than any despotism of which we have any knowledge in recent times.[1]

Looking back after fifty years we see how inadequate were such appraisals of the economic system. Men are interdependent in society to a degree which Harris and the "solid" men of his times were unable or unwilling to recognize. In some respects Bellamy's insight was much more penetrating. Daily it is becoming more evident that the alternatives are not Bellamy or the status quo, but the choice is between his program and some other great change. Yet, the ideal of freedom which Harris reasserts is too precious to be lightly given up. Bellamy made a real effort to get the benefits both of co-ordination and of freedom.

Again it was charged that economic equality would result in a downward leveling. Oliver Wendell Holmes held that equality would result in boredom. Arthur Dudley Vinton, in *Looking Further Backward*, held that the security and general prosperity resulting

---

[1] W. T. Harris, "Edward Bellamy's Vision," *Forum,* VIII (October, 1889), 202, 204, 205, 206, 207, 208.

from Bellamy's program would make Americans soft, and pictured America as being overrun by a hardy Chinese army. William Dean Howells would have preferred his utopia much simpler, with less government and less machinery.

Edward Everett Hale, who was a strong supporter of Bellamy, criticized him for assuming mechanical inventions. In a review of *Equality* he wrote, "Mr. Bellamy has no right, as it seems to me, when he wants to get out of a scrape, to invent an invention for that purpose." [2] In this Bellamy was wiser than Hale. If able people could not escape the "dirty work" by hiring servants, they would invent ways to eliminate the dirty work. A modern, simple, electrified home is less of a burden to a woman doing her own housework than was an old-fashioned southern plantation—with half a dozen servants, but with no thought of economy of labor—to the mistress who administered it. Most of Bellamy's rash assumptions as to inventions already have been realized, and many of them surpassed. Probably all would soon be surpassed if no man could employ others to do his drudgery.

Nicholas Paine Gilman in a review of *Looking Backward* in the *Quarterly Journal of Economics*, declared that the social problem largely owed its existence, under its present form, to a remarkable succession of men of letters—from Rousseau to Carlyle and from Shelley to Victor Hugo—who have exercised the function of prophets of a moral civilization with strange power and effect. He disposed very summarily of Bellamy's forecast of the disappearance of individual states and the supremacy of the national government:

That the author, however imaginative, should seriously suppose that within a hundred years the federal principle will be utterly neglected in the United States, and every state line abolished, is sufficiently curious. He evidently has as little hold upon reality in the sphere of politics as in that of economics. The abolition of state governments in America fully matches the abolition of private property. . . . The cornerstone of American freedom—the American State—will shipwreck every Utopia that strikes it.[3]

2 Hale, "Fraternal Government," *Book Buyer,* XV, No. 1 (August, 1897), 39.
3 Gilman, "Edward Bellamy and Nationalism in the United States," *Quarterly Journal of Economics,* IV (October, 1889), 70.

(We may wonder what this author would think of the present fading status of the individual states, with the "states' rights" commonwealths of the South as the backbone of support of that tendency.)

It is interesting to observe the absolute pontifical authority with which some of the professional economists scathingly disposed of Bellamy's economic ideas. Some of the economic axioms with which they demolished him are far from axiomatic today. Moreover, in a surprising number of cases those who wrote about him showed a marked lack of acquaintance with the facts of his life and work.

Though there were elements of genuinely critical appraisal, a considerable number of the contemporaneous adverse criticisms of his books, even when written by men of national reputation, were largely tirades, often uncritical, and frequently misstating both the content and the spirit of Bellamy's message. Bellamy called for such a great departure from prevailing habits of thinking that the subconscious emotional revolt from those strange ways often ruled the conscious thinking of conservative men.

In addition to the general criticisms of Bellamy's proposals, some of which were the result of uncritical opposition to change or opposition to the obvious disadvantages of regimentation, Bellamy met the more or less critical opposition of men who, often with equal sincerity, were trying to improve the social order and expected to bring about profound changes in doing so.

Among the most interesting criticisms of Bellamy's views are those of Laurence Gronlund, pioneer in American socialism. His *Co-operative Commonwealth*, published in 1884, two years before the first edition in English of *Das Kapital*, was among the earliest efforts to present Marxian socialism to American readers in simple, orderly form. It was eagerly read in American universities and by the socialistically minded and went through two or three editions in a few years.

When Gronlund came in contact with the American spirit and outlook, and especially after reading *Looking Backward*, he was deeply influenced and tended to repudiate the class conflict of Marxian socialism. From then on his writings displayed a never-

ending conflict in himself between Marxism and the American spirit
as represented by Bellamy. In that respect he epitomizes the entire
social movement in America, which was powerfully influenced by
the aggressive propaganda of unreconcilable class conflict of European Marxian socialism, a propaganda greatly accelerated and
intensified by the exploitation of labor by American capital. On
the other hand, the American social movement was much influenced
by the American spirit of social change by free discussion, and by
the orderly progress of self-government within the framework of
a liberal constitution. It was inclined to hold to the American doctrine that the interests which unite Americans are greater than
the differences which divide them into warring classes. The American social movement for half a century has vacillated between
these two positions, and still does so. The attitudes of the pioneer
socialist Gronlund are interesting as illustrating that process,
though he differed from Bellamy also on matters which had no
relation to that issue.

Gronlund's friendliness to Bellamy after he read *Looking Backward* is evident in various articles of his in the *Arena* and the
Nationalist. Though at first he ordered the sale of his *Co-operative
Commonwealth* to be stopped in favor of pushing the sale of *Looking
Backward,* yet later he decided to continue the circulation of his
own book, and a second edition appeared in 1890, about two years
after *Looking Backward*. In the preface to the second edition we
read:

There are three ideas in that novel [*Looking Backward*] for which socialism should not be held responsible . . . These are a love for militarism, equal wages, and appointments by the retired functionaries.
They are decidedly unsocialistic notions, belong exclusively to Mr. Bellamy . . .[4]

Also in the second edition, chiefly in footnotes, he wrote:

Many worthy persons . . . entertain the fear which shines forth in
Mill's famous essay on "Liberty"—the fear lest freedom should be
drilled and disciplined out of human life, in order that the great mill of
the commonwealth should grind smoothly . . . It is a great pity that

[4] Gronlund, *The Co-operative Commonwealth; an Exposition of Socialism,*
p. viii. This and following quotations used by permission.

Bellamy seems to justify this fear by the love of militarism he displays in *Looking Backward*. But this is not socialism; it is the very reverse of it.[5]

The second of Gronlund's criticisms is:

The . . . *decidedly unsocialistic* idea which Bellamy introduces in *Looking Backward,—equal wages*. . . . Socialism must not be saddled with this proportion, which is both impracticable and unjust.[6]

As Gronlund undertakes to state his own position on this question, he falls into utter confusion. First, he sees society as a great organism. In *The Co-operative Commonwealth* he says:

The State is a living organism, differing from other organisms in no essential respect.

. . . .

A man's sphere, as far as himself is concerned, consists in caring for his own well-being. If that be properly done, then his brain, his lungs, and his stomach will have nothing of which to complain. So with the State. Its whole sphere is the making all special activities work together for one general end,—its own welfare, or the public good.[7]

Yet Gronlund holds that in this social organism, "the workers will be rewarded according to results." [8]

How are the "results" to be measured individually for each person after society has dispensed with fixing wages by supply and demand? Gronlund evades this most vital and critical question of socialist economics in several ways. He suggests:

The leaders . . . cannot better show their practical common sense than by . . . retaining for an unlimited period the ratio of wages which, at the time of the change, will obtain in the various branches of manual work and for the different qualities of workmen. This ratio will furnish them a sufficiently accurate "gradation of labor." [9]

That is, he would begin with wage relations fixed competitively and would freeze that status quo, regardless of inequities or of changed conditions. As to reaching an enduring principle of compensation, he says: "When the co-operative commonwealth has

---

5 *Ibid.*, p. 99.
7 *Ibid.*, pp. 79, 83.
9 *Ibid.*, p. 158.

6 *Ibid.*, p. 158 (footnote).
8 *Ibid.*, p. 157.

worked for a couple of generations . . . then another rule may obtain . . . to speculate upon that in our generation can properly be termed 'utopian.' " [10]

To freeze the prevailing rates of wages "for a couple of generations" in an actively evolving industrial society would seem to be impractical, yet it is to such expedients that men are driven who try to devise a substitute for economic equality in a noncompetitive society.

How to measure the "actual" production of wealth by individual workers of all kinds in an organized society by any other than the competitive method of supply and demand, is a nut which never has been cracked. Bellamy frankly admitted the fact, and fell back on the policy of equality of income. He would have the relative attractiveness of the work measured by supply and demand, with the less attractive service calling for shorter working periods. Gronlund actually gets close to equality of income by some process he does not disclose or admit. He says:

Do not here object that if the rewards of captains of industries and of the professions are thus reduced to a level with manual labor, men of genius and of natural gifts will then part with the management of affairs and with the professions. . . . They will find their ulterior reward in the zest of intellectual activity, the joys of creative genius, the honor of directing affairs, and the social distinction they will enjoy.[11]

There will be no more $50,000 or $25,000 or even $10,000 salaries paid. . . . In the co-operative commonwealth the Postmaster-General will not receive $10,000 while letter-carriers must be satisfied with $800.[12]

It would be as difficult to measure "actual" production in an organized society without competition as it would be to determine for the human body how much of personal achievement is to be credited to heart, to brain, to bones, to skin, or to adrenal glands. This discussion is included, not primarily because of the importance of Gronlund's work, but because his inconsistency is characteristic.

Gronlund's other difference from Bellamy he states as follows: "The third idea in *Looking Backward*, for which Bellamy alone must be personally responsible, is that of electing the officers of

[10] *Ibid.*, p. 161.   [11] *Ibid.*, p. 160.   [12] *Ibid.*, pp. 159–60.

government by the retired functionaries. . . . Socialism distinctly demands appointments from below . . ." [13] He then outlines a plan in which appointments would be made from below and the workers in a factory would elect their foreman, teachers their superintendent, and so forth and adds his personal suggestion: "While the subordinates elect, the superiors dismiss." [14] In *Looking Backward* we find a fundamentally different concept of succession to authority. Let Bellamy speak for himself:

"It is simply by the excellence of his record as a worker that one rises. . . . by appointment from above, strictly limited to the candidates of the best records. The general of the guild appoints to the ranks under him, but he himself is not appointed, but chosen by suffrage."

"By suffrage!" I exclaimed. "Is not that ruinous to the discipline of the guild, by tempting the candidates to intrigue for the support of the workers under them?"

"So it would be, no doubt," replied Dr. Leete, "if the workers had any suffrage to exercise, or anything to say about the choice. But they have nothing. . . . The general of the guild is chosen from among the superintendents by vote of the honorary members of the guild, that is, of those who have served their time in the guild and received their discharge. As you know, at the age of forty-five we are mustered out of the army of industry . . . the nation entrusts to the honorary members of each guild the election of its general . . . no previous form of society could have developed a body of electors so ideally adapted to their office, as regards absolute impartiality, knowledge of the special qualifications and records of candidates, solicitude for the best result, and complete absence of self-interest." [15]

Similarly, in Bellamy's plan the retired heads of departments elect the President. The working body of the people is not allowed to vote, for "That would be perilous to its discipline, which it is the business of the President to maintain." [16]

Here we see two strikingly different concepts of democracy. Both Gronlund and Bellamy make them clear. Shall those who are to be disciplined select the persons who are to discipline them? Gronlund says "Yes." Bellamy says "No."

Henry George and Edward Bellamy were seated together at a public dinner when Bellamy turned to George and asked, "Mr.

[13] *Ibid.*, p. 193 (footnote).   [14] *Ibid.*, p. 197.
[15] *Looking Backward*, pp. 188–90.   [16] *Ibid.*, p. 191.

George, why are you not a Nationalist?" The answer was, "Because I am an individualist," to which Bellamy replied, "I am a Nationalist because I am an individualist." This exchange was typical, for the two men never came to agreement on the solution of social issues. George said, "*Looking Backward* is a castle in the air with clouds for its foundation." [17]

The general criticism which Henry George and his single tax followers made of Bellamy and Nationalism was that the latter represented collectivism, an unnecessary and menacing extension of the state, and an infringement on personal freedom and individuality. What was needed, George held, was not a revolution of government and society, but elimination of all monopoly and privilege in the use of the earth and its raw materials, and the taking over of natural monopolies by the state. This discussion, generally in a good spirit on both sides, ran through the literature of both movements.

Henry George was nearly eleven years older. He arrived in New York about three years before Bellamy did, like him to try his hand there at journalism. Each, after returning to his home town, started a penny newspaper of his own. Each had difficulty in getting an economic basis for his life. Each came suddenly into world view by writing a best seller. *Progress and Poverty* was published eight years before *Looking Backward*. The two authors were first stirred to social conscience in 1869 by seeing striking contrasts between wealth and poverty, Bellamy in Europe and George in New York City, and they described these first impressions in almost identical terms. However, the remedies they offered were not the same.

For years Henry George had a strong urge to social reform, but did not see his way. He was a prophet without a clear message. Then, as he was horseback riding one day near San Francisco in a locality where land speculation was rife, his great idea came to him in a flash of inspiration. To quote his own words:

Absorbed in my own thoughts, I had driven the horse into the hills until he panted. Stopping for breath, I asked a passing teamster, for want of

[17] J. Foster Biscoe, "Attitude of the Press," *Nationalist*, I, No. 6 (October, 1889), p. 220.

something better to say, what land was worth there. He pointed to some cows grazing off so far that they looked like mice, and said: "I don't know exactly, but there is a man over there who will sell some land for a thousand dollars an acre." Like a flash it came upon me that there was the reason of advancing poverty with advancing wealth. With the growth of population, land grows in value, and the men who work it must pay more for the privilege. I turned back, amidst quiet thought, to the perception that then came to me and has been with me ever since.[18]

Thereafter the idea of the single tax was the central theme of his social theories. The rest of his life work in effect was a process of developing, refining, and rationalizing that flash of insight, explaining it, supporting it, promoting it. Except, perhaps, for the item of public ownership of natural monopolies, no important new element was added.

In many respects Henry George and Edward Bellamy saw alike, though Bellamy had a way of driving his ideas to an ultimate conclusion which Henry George lacked. On the subject of monopolies and the growing dimensions of business, Henry George wrote:

That concentration is the order of development there can be no mistaking—the concentration of people in large cities, the concentration of handicrafts in large factories, the concentration of transportation by railroad and steamship lines, and of agricultural operations in large fields. . . . All the currents of the time run to concentration. To resist it successfully we must throttle steam and discharge electricity from human service.[19]

Henry George held that, ". . . businesses which are in their nature monopolies are properly part of the functions of the State, and should be assumed by the State." [20] Beyond that he seemed to rely on the policy commonly known as the single tax—that the income from land in rent or royalties, or profits from the ownership of natural resources such as minerals, should all accrue to the state, to be collected as a tax which would be approximately the sole income of government.

Compare this with Bellamy's attitude, as expressed in *Equality*:

[18] George Raymond Geiger, *The Philosophy of Henry George*, pp. 42–43.
[19] Henry George, *Progress and Poverty*, p. 327. Reprinted by permission.
[20] *Ibid.*, p. 412.

"March with the course of economic evolution, not against it. The competitive system can never be restored, neither is it worthy of restoration, having been at best an immoral, wasteful, brutal scramble for existence. New issues demand new answers. It is in vain to pit the moribund system of competition against the young giant of private monopoly; it must rather be opposed by the greater giant of public monopoly. The consolidation of business in private interests must be met with greater consolidation in the public interest, the trust and the syndicate with the city, State, and nation, capitalism with nationalism. The capitalists have destroyed the competitive system. Do not try to restore it, but rather thank them for the work . . ." [21]

Both George and Bellamy were inclined to rest their cases on supposedly absolute principles. In *Progress and Poverty* we read:

The equal right of all men to the use of land is as clear as their equal right to breathe the air—it is a right proclaimed by the fact of their existence. For we cannot suppose that some men have a right to be in this world and others no right.

If we are all here by the equal permission of the Creator, we are all here with an equal title to the enjoyment of his bounty . . . [22]

Compare this with Bellamy's statement in *Looking Backward* which, for the sake of this comparison, is quoted again:

"The right of a man to maintenance at the nation's table depends on the fact that he is a man, and not on the amount of health or strength he may have, so long as he does his best."

"I am to understand, then, that the lame, the blind, the sick, and the impotent, are as well off as the most efficient, and have the same income?"

"Certainly," was the reply. [23]

Right here we have the essential difference between George and Bellamy. George saw men as having right to equality in one particular respect—to the use of the land. Bellamy saw the "right" to equality as relating to the whole of human inheritance, both physical and cultural. Henry George went part way toward the same position, but, as in the case of his attitude toward monopolies, he stopped short of the logical conclusion.

Here we have Henry George on the nature of man's cultural inheritance:

[21] *Equality*, p. 333.
[22] *Progress and Poverty*, p. 338. Reprinted by permission.
[23] *Looking Backward*, p. 133.

That each society, small or great, necessarily weaves for itself a web of knowledge, beliefs, customs, language, tastes, institutions, and laws. Into this web, woven by each society, or rather, into these webs, for each community above the simplest is made up of minor societies, which overlap and interlace each other, the individual is received at birth and continues until his death. This is the matrix in which mind unfolds and from which it takes its stamp. This is the way in which customs, and religions, and prejudices, and tastes, and languages, grow up and are perpetuated. This is the way that skill is transmitted and knowledge is stored up, and the discoveries of one time made the common stock and stepping stone of the next.

Human progress goes on as the advances made by one generation are in this way secured as the common property of the next, and made the starting point for new advances.[24]

While Henry George got a glimpse of the significance of the cultural inheritance, he did not see that man inherits his world as a unity—its culture as well as its physical property. He explicitly rejected the idea of such unity when he wrote, "There is a fundamental and irreconcilable difference between property in things which are the product of labor and property in land . . ." [25]

Bellamy saw further than George. He saw that the cultural inheritance—education, breeding, craftsmanship, thrift—all that adds character to the genetic inheritance of people—is a social inheritance, and not the creation of each generation for itself. He saw that any rights of the individual, which George in practice limited to land, apply also to the common inheritance of culture. This point of view Bellamy made clear in *Looking Backward,* in a passage already quoted at greater length in the chapter on "The Political Economist":

"There is no such thing in a civilized society as self-support. . . . From the moment that men begin to live together, and constitute even the rudest sort of society, self-support becomes impossible. As men grow more civilized, and the subdivision of occupations and services is carried out, a complex mutual dependence becomes the universal rule. . . . The necessity of mutual dependence should imply the duty and guarantee of mutual support . . ." [26]

[24] *Progress and Poverty,* pp. 504, 505. Reprinted by permission.
[25] *Ibid.,* p. xv.
[26] *Looking Backward,* p. 132.

The same concept is expressed much more fully in *Equality*.[27]

Bellamy did not mention Henry George by name in his books, but there is a clear reference to him in a passage in *Equality:*

"The idea of an unearned increment given to private properties by the social organism was talked of in my day," I said, "but only, as I remember, with reference to land values. There were reformers who held that society had the right to take in taxes all increase in value of land that resulted from social factors, such as increased population or public improvements, but they seemed to think the doctrine applicable to land only."

"Yes," said the doctor, "and it is rather odd that, having hold of the clew, they did not follow it up." [28]

When Henry George's magazine, the *Standard*, suspended publication in 1892, the comment in Bellamy's *New Nation* was a fair statement of the attitude of the Nationalists:

Nationalists believe of course in the ultimate nationalization of all land, as of all other forms of capital, each individual holding what land he wishes as tenant, for as long as he pleases to pay its rental to the nation.

The nationalization of land however, from our point of view, is only a part of the general scheme for the nationalization of all capital and labor.[29]

Henry George had an intuitive dread of big government, and he tried to avoid any element of collectivism. "What I have done . . . ," he wrote in a preface to the fourth edition of *Progress and Poverty*, "is . . . to show that *laissez faire* (in its full true meaning) opens the way to a realization of the noble dreams of socialism . . ." [30] Again he wrote:

As to the truths that are involved in socialistic ideas I shall have something to say hereafter; but it is evident that whatever savors of regulation and restriction is in itself bad, and should not be resorted to if any other mode of accomplishing the same end presents itself.[31]

We have passed out of the socialism of the tribal state, and cannot re-enter it again except by a retrogression that would involve anarchy

[27] *Equality*, pp. 88, 89, 91.   [28] *Equality*, p. 91.
[29] *New Nation*, II, No. 37 (September 10, 1892), 567.
[30] George, *Progress and Poverty*, pp. xvi, xvii.   [31] *Ibid.*, p. 320.

and perhaps barbarism. Our governments, as is already plainly evident, would break down in the attempt.[32]

An ardent disciple and contemporary of Henry George dealt specifically with Bellamy's program. William Lloyd Garrison, son of the abolitionist of the same name, was a typical reformer. Sincere, intelligent, and active, he worked for the single tax, free trade, and woman's suffrage, and against imperialism. An intense advocate of personal freedom, he looked with fear and repugnance on any extension of government and any restriction of free initiative. One of the fairest and yet most caustic criticisms of Bellamy and the Nationalist movement was an article by him in the *Arena*, entitled "The Mask of Tyranny."

To the question, "And what records do human governments present to sustain their right to the assumption of further responsibilities?" Garrison's answer is unequivocal:

In all history, wherever they have undertaken to meddle with industrial functions, disaster has followed. The clumsy feet of legislation mark a pathway of woe. In despotic governments the people have been impoverished and fertile fields forced into sterility. In partial republics,—for no real republic has ever yet existed,—the governing power has acted on crude and havoc-making theories of commerce and finance. . . .

It is complacently assumed by Nationalism that all will be well when government is the one grand monopolist. It is of course to be an ideal government possessing wisdom, benevolence, and the highest economic sense. But is it not patent that in a democracy the representatives of the people must reflect the intelligence of the average voter? The fountain cannot rise higher than its source. If men left unhampered to their own devices of trades are failures, how can similar men chosen to govern for all be successes?

It does not follow that because great trusts have flourished, equal management can be secured for a government trust. Ability is costly. "Wealth beyond the dream of avarice" tempts the Rockefellers to assume the cares of the Standard Oil Co., and if the managers were chosen by popular vote, how long would the trust live? The great captains of industry are not to be had for the asking. They are as rare as great authors, generals, or men of science. The genius to grasp oppor-

[32] *Ibid.*

tunities and to co-ordinate masses of material and armies of men in harmonious production cannot be commanded by popular vote.[33]

The example of ancient Peru, which, by the methods Bellamy proposed, under extremely adverse physical conditions achieved miracles in production, and a higher degree of economic security than the world had known before, is a telling answer to the claim that government cannot be efficient, though it is no guarantee of freedom.

Garrison's condemnation of Bellamy's Nationalism is unequivocal:

The effort of Nationalism aims at an equality of human condition through law. Were such equality attainable, who can compute its cost? What must be bartered for it? How much individual character, what incentives to exertion, what suppression of personal force? "If men should take these moralists at their word," says Emerson, "and leave off aiming to be rich, the moralists would rush to rekindle at all hazards this love of power in the people, lest civilization should be undone." [34]

Emerson said more in this short sentence than is included in whole volumes on political economy. In California and Florida, and in many a rural nook, today there are successful executives who, weary and disgusted with labor conflicts, government interference, and general denunciation of their methods, have chosen simple quietude, rather than continue to be the objects of defamation and abuse. A much larger number of such men would take the same course but for their sense of responsibility to employees and investors. Why, they ask, should they be the drudges and choremen of economic production if scorn and hatred is to be their lot. This feeling on the part of business men of deep hurt and unjust accusation is a larger element in the national pattern than generally is realized. Just as children growing up criticize their parents, not dreaming that the time ever can come when the parents may feel hurt and inferior, so the public cannot realize that the vogue of

[33] William Lloyd Garrison, "The Mask of Tyranny," *Arena*, I (April, 1890), 555–56.
[34] *Ibid.*, pp. 556, 557.

condemning business management may go so far as to destroy all joy and zest in work on the part of management.

In the passages quoted, Emerson and Garrison did not distinguish between love of riches and love of power. The fact that love of power has many other forms than love of riches is both the hope and the despair of such programs as that of Bellamy. What men crave is not primarily great wealth, but honor and respect; and whatever promises those rewards will induce their greatest efforts. Under economic equality men still would do their utmost to excel. But just as today men use intrigue and make-believe to gain riches, will they not use like methods when their ends are high position and places of leadership, rather than money? However, admitting that economic equality would not bring the millennium, whenever a crude kind of compulsion is removed, such as personal slavery or economic slavery, competition for the respect of men may take higher and more wholesome forms of expression.

The craving for individual freedom, which runs all through Garrison's protest against Bellamy's Nationalism, arouses a vigorous response in every person of independent temper. "Individual freedom alone," he concludes, "will bring the ideal government." [35] As we examine closely the proposals of Henry George and William Lloyd Garrison in the light of the steady drift toward concentration and consolidation of industry—much of which is almost entirely independent of ownership of land and raw materials—we find no remedy offered except single tax and a grudging acceptance of public ownership of natural monopolies. We are forced to the conclusion that it is not Bellamy but the single taxers and other individualists to whom the term "utopian" in its invidious sense must be applied. A writer in the *Arena,* answering Garrison's criticism of Bellamy and Nationalism, wrote very truly, "In the marvelously complex interdependence of our industrial relationships, to talk of a 'private business' is to be guilty of a contradiction in terms." [36]

If the exigencies of society will but give us time, a gradual organic development such as Henry George proposed would have great advantages over a vast governmental organization controlled

---

[35] *Ibid.,* p. 559.
[36] Edward P. Foster, "Behind the Mask," *Arena,* II (October, 1890).

from a central office. But such a course would require many other controls than the proper control of land. Human ingenuity is so versatile that it can take any given system and turn it to its purpose, whether that purpose be selfish or humane. No simple, arbitrary system will protect society against such ingenuity. The only dependable protection is a way of life generally followed by the people, supported by social controls. In a modern society individualism cannot remain as undisciplined as Henry George supposed.

Among all critics of *Looking Backward* and *Equality*, none have been more persistent than those who charge that Bellamy's writings reflected an essentially dull and commonplace mind, insensitive to nature and to beauty; one that was enamored of machines and was under the spell of soulless material civilization. Typical of such critics is the great William Morris, lover and creator of beauty. In his review of *Looking Backward* in his magazine, the *Commonweal*, Morris wrote:

The only safe way of reading a utopia is to consider it as the expression of the temperament of its author. . . . [Bellamy's] temperament . . . may be called the unmixed modern one, unhistoric and unartistic; it makes its owner . . . perfectly satisfied with modern civilisation, if only the injustice, misery, and waste of class society could be got rid of; which half-change seems possible to him. The only ideal of life which such a man can see is that of the industrious *professional* middle-class men of to-day purified from their crime of complicity with the monopolist class, and become independent instead of being, as they now are, parasitical. . . .

He shows unconsciously that he has his mind fixed firmly on the mere *machinery* of life . . .

His scheme may be described as State Communism, worked by the very extreme of national centralisation. The underlying vice in it is that the author cannot conceive, as aforesaid, of anything else than the *machinery* of society . . . Though he *tells* us that every man is free to choose his occupation and that work is no burden to anyone, the *impression* which he produces is that of a huge standing army, tightly drilled, compelled by some mysterious fate to unceasing anxiety for the production of wares to satisfy every caprice, however wasteful and absurd, that may cast up amongst them. . . .

Mr. Bellamy's ideas of life are curiously limited; he has no idea beyond existence in a great city; his dwelling of man in the future is

Boston (U.S.A.) beautified. In one passage, indeed, he mentions villages, but with unconscious simplicity shows that they do not come into his scheme of economical equality, but are mere servants of the great centres of civilisation. This seems strange to some of us, who cannot help thinking that our experience ought to have taught us that such aggregations of population afford the worst possible form of dwelling-place.[37]

In short, a machine-life is the best which Mr. Bellamy can imagine for us on all sides; it is not to be wondered at then that his only idea of making labour tolerable is to decrease the amount of it by means of fresh and ever fresh developments of machinery. . . . Mr. Bellamy worries himself unnecessarily in seeking (with obvious failure) some incentive to labour to replace the fear of starvation, which is at present our only one, whereas it cannot be too often repeated that the true incentive to useful and happy labour is and must be pleasure in the work itself.[38]

William Morris' appraisal was most inaccurate. From the time of Bellamy's earliest extant journals, at the age of twenty—some of which are quoted in the chapter on "The Rebel"—until nearly the time of his death, we find constantly recurring expressions of his craving for freedom. His own life bore out this theme. A careful reading of *Looking Backward* and *Equality* will disclose a spirit not out of harmony with these expressions.

Why then did Bellamy picture a society in which work is compulsory and regimented? The answer is clear. He was determined to

[37] In *Equality*, which was written after Morris' criticism, Bellamy makes very clear his attitude toward great cities:

"It was only necessary that the era of private capitalism in America should last long enough for the rural districts to have been reduced to what they were in the days of the Roman Empire, and of every empire which achieved full development—namely, regions whence all who could escape had gone to seek their fortunes in the cities, leaving only a population of serfs and overseers."

"But you have cities yet!" I exclaimed.

"Certainly—that is, we have localities where population still remains denser than in other places. None of the great cities of your day have become extinct but their populations are but small fractions of what they were.

"There are in Boston to-day perhaps a quarter as many people as lived in the same limits in the Boston of your day . . . Manhattan Island . . . is rather thickly built up according to modern notions, some two hundred and fifty thousand people living there among the groves and fountains." *Equality*, pp. 292–93, 294.

[38] Morris, "*Looking Backward*," *Commonweal*, V, No. 180 (June 22, 1889), 194.

claim for himself only what would be possible for all men. It was for that he denied his intense, life-long craving for quiet and solitude, and gave some of the most active years of his life to the Nationalist movement, playing a part most distasteful to himself. Bellamy proposed a degree of regimentation for everyone, not because he liked regimentation or because he was dull to a feeling for freedom, but for the very opposite reason. The freedom he craved as of the very essence of life he was ready to surrender in part in order that others might have their fair share of freedom.

William Morris called *Looking Backward* "a horrible cockney dream" and was so agitated by it that he proceeded to supply an antidote in *News from Nowhere*, a utopia of his own. This was a true expression of his own personality. He was one of the most refining influences of the England of his day, an influence felt in a surprising range of activity. But he did his work as one of a favored class. In his social attitude he was a romanticist, and could not face the facts.

Morris was a product of privilege and exploitation. From his childhood until his death the quiet, luxurious beauty of his environment, and his own freedom from regimentation, were sustained by the regimentation and friendly servitude and drudgery of servants, and by that large part of the population which worked in bitter poverty. William Morris felt revulsion against that vast injustice. He called himself a socialist and wanted to feel the humanitarian thrill of sharing his lot with others, yet neither in action nor in theory did he bring himself to pay the necessary price.

Bellamy faced this issue. Morris, not seeing how to surrender either his concern for social improvement or his privileged status, escaped in imagination from the real society of wealth and poverty, of privilege and servitude, in which he actually lived, with all its real good and its real evil, to a romantic and fanciful world. There he imagined that he shared the common lot of men, but he did not give up his accustomed luxury or the privilege of self-expression made possible by the servile toil of others, many of whom were in dire poverty.

William Morris' utopia records this flight of his mind. A modern industrial time-study of the labor actually necessary to maintain the quiet, luxurious, country-club life described in that book would show conclusively that such bountiful simplicity could not result from the amount of work he describes and with the primitive fourteenth-century methods he would use. Instead of six hours' work a day, probably not less than sixteen would be required.

Graham Wallas, in his book, *The Great Society*, has given a fair appraisal of William Morris:

It was true that Morris, for all his greatness, never faced the fact that we cannot both eat our cake and have it, cannot use slow methods of production and also turn out without overwork large quantities of consumable wealth. Once, while I listened to him lecturing, I made a rough calculation that the citizens of his commonwealth, in order to produce by the methods he advocated the quantity of beautiful and delicious things which they were to enjoy, would have to work about two hundred hours a week. It was only the same fact looked at from another point of view which made it impossible for any of Morris's workmen, or indeed for anyone at all whose income was near the present English average, to buy the products either of Morris's workshop at Merton or of his Kelmscott Press.[39]

Morris hints at factories for the mass production of necessities that have no aesthetic quality, probably such as sewer pipe, cement, and nails, but these are left as vague shadows in a misty background. With the medieval handicraft methods he prescribes for nearly all productive work, to maintain for all men the environment he pictures—the well-kept roads and streets; expansive, well-groomed lawns, vast flower gardens; spacious homes; good and varied food, daintily served; boats, horses, music, and art—would mean drudgery for all. So completely had his mind departed from reality that his chief concern in *News from Nowhere* is that when all necessary work is done, men will have no way left for making themselves feel needed or useful. In reality, even assuming that today ninety per cent of human effort is wasted, and that Morris' utopia could eliminate three quarters of all waste from all causes, his picture of utopian life still would be romantic and unreal. Several persons living in economic servitude would be required to maintain one of his utopians in his leisurely and luxurious English country-life existence.

[39] Graham Wallas, *The Great Society*, p. 326. Reprinted by permission.

In his own actual productive life William Morris followed this same romantic pattern. In an environment of simple, friendly craftsmanship he made beautiful things for rich men who were supported by a vast number of the poor. His workshop spent nearly a year making one luxurious carpet, and he produced beautiful books to sell for from five dollars to one hundred dollars a copy.

That Bellamy was by no means insensitive to that charm of old ways around which William Morris built his romantic utopia, is evident from his review of the Paston Letters in the *Springfield Union* of August 19, 1876. It is clear, too, that his facing of the issue is far more realistic.

Not a little of the picturesqueness of life has been lost in the progress of modern improvement; and with this there has been a loss of enjoyment, in exchange, doubtless, for a large amount of inconvenience. The very rudeness of old-time ways of keeping time, and traveling, and getting on generally, has in it a racy relish, like the taste of wild berries and of forest game. It is easy to see beyond the time where the inconveniences override the pleasures, as, for instance, in the most graphic and minute picture of English society and public affairs which has come down to us from the reigns of Henry VI and Edward IV, full four hundred years, in the Paston Letters. The roughness and the polish, the squalor and the extravagance, the glitter and the brutality of those days of the "wars of the roses" leave the balance on the wrong side too heavily for a second thought as to their fascination.

Between then and now there have perished or mostly vanished, some things which were pleasant to the eyes, and enjoyable both by the body and the mind. It is the charm of the simplicity of a state of things in which people have to depend on their own resources very much for what they need, or else go without it. It comes out strongly in Homer's old epics; and constitutes largely their universal and endless attraction. . . . But not to belittle our theme, the modern railroad has ruined much of this picturesque quality of earlier days . . . You have to get away within these Alpine districts to find the ancient glory of New England turnpikes in its unabridged integrity. These coaches (stage-coaches) wind among the deep valleys with practiced drivers, who grasp the handfulls of intricate ribbons, like the threads of destiny. . . . Certainly our country is too large to be used for travel by this vanishing kind of conveyance. We are the children of steam and the iron track. But there is no harm in being glad that there will always be sections of the world where the engineer's whistle will never expel the more primitive ways of getting around.[40]

When we see the travail of soul with which Edward Bellamy accepted limitations of personal freedom, how cheap seem the sneers of the academic and aesthetic dilettantes who neither had his great craving for freedom, nor ever paid the hard price that Bellamy did of achieving it in their personal lives.

But there is another element of Morris' criticism of Bellamy which is far more substantial. In his review of *Looking Backward* he continued:

It is necessary to point out that there are some Socialists who do not think that the problem of the organisation of life and necessary labour can be dealt with by a huge national centralisation, working by a kind of magic for which no one feels himself responsible; that on the contrary it will be necessary for the unit of administration to be small enough for every citizen to feel himself responsible for its details, and be interested in them; that individual men cannot shuffle off the business of life on the shoulders of an abstraction called the State, but must deal with it in conscious association with each other. That variety of life is as much an aim of true Communism as equality of condition, and that nothing but an union of these two will bring about real freedom. That modern nationalities are mere artificial devices for the commercial war that we seek to put an end to, and will disappear with it.[41]

In the present current of society it would appear that an interval —perhaps a long one—of highly regimented living under a powerful centralized state may be in store. Yet there is a pattern of freedom in the spirit of man which refuses to fade, and he will continue to look and to work for the time when the Frankenstein state will rust away and leave the human spirit free.

More than twenty-five hundred years ago the prophet Hosea went up and down the land crying: "The Lord hath a controversy with the inhabitants of the land, because there is no truth nor mercy, nor knowledge of God in the land. . . . And there shall be, like people, like priest: and I will punish them for their ways. . . . For

40 "Old, but Worth Saving" (editorial), *Springfield Union,* August 19, 1876.
41 Morris, *"Looking Backward,"* pp. 194–95.

I desired mercy, and not sacrifice; and the knowledge of God more than burnt offerings." [42]

That conflict between priest and prophet seems never to cease, and it gives a key to the treatment of Bellamy's writings in the pulpits and the religious press. While there was much intelligent objective criticism of his views, two characteristic attitudes appeared. Many ministers shared his passion for social betterment and gave eager support to his message, their only question being the wisdom of the means he proposed. Others, who were in the priestly tradition, denounced his desire to improve the social order as having nothing to do with religion or even as being opposed to its interests. Such persons gave meaning to Karl Marx's expression, "Religion . . . is the opium of the people."

The most striking criticism of Bellamy's program by the orthodox churchmen might be expressed in a comment, intended to be complimentary, in the *Overland Monthly Magazine* of June, 1890: "Plato demanded that men be as gods; More that they be good; Bellamy that temptation be removed."

A not uncommon attitude of conventional orthodox religious journals was expressed in a long and hostile review of *Looking Backward* by Anna L. Dawes in the *Andover Review*, a ranking theological journal published by the Andover Theological Seminary: "Jesus was a peasant with nowhere to lay his head, teaching an absolute unregard for environment. It is certainly a new idea in the world that virtue is the child of comfort." [43] One might hazard a guess that the writer of this article was in comfortable economic circumstances when she wrote it. Bellamy, according to Mason Green, said of this review that "Such criticism makes my blood boil."

A somewhat more scholarly criticism of Bellamy of the same import appeared in the *New Englander and Yale Review:*

And first of all Christianity sets before men, as its one aim, the creation of an ideal condition of character, not an ideal condition of environment. To the evolution of this character all other things are sub-

---

[42] Hosea, 4: 1; 4: 9; 6: 6.

[43] "Mr. Bellamy and Christianity," *Andover Review*, XV (April, 1891), 418.

servient; beside it the materialistics of life—conditions of pain and pleasure—are insignificant. Not only so: pain in the evolution of this character is looked upon as often a high contributory element—the exaggeration of which feeling led, in earlier ages, almost to its deification. Granted that the environment of man is strenuous, granted that man is well nigh perishing of want, it by no means follows—sad as this latter case would seem to be, and abhorrent to every proper feeling of the tender soul;—that that which differentiates man peculiarly from the animals is thereby imperilled. Testimony is not wanting from the most practical of lay workers among the London poor to the beneficial effect upon the springs of character of the most strenuous circumstances and even the most constant and immedicable pain. . . . Christianity recognizes that the removal of moral evil is a condition precedent to the extinction of industrial and social evil, and acts upon this theory.

. . . .

The Christian conception of the Universe recognizes that man's position here is not a final one; that hence for the obliteration of every evil external to the human heart itself the Christian thinker is content to wait.

. . . .

In its treatment of all problems relating to the improvement of the race, Christianity is individualistic and not communistic. With true scientific and psychologic insight it works from within outward, commencing with the evil in the individual heart; and hence toward everything purely structural in human society its attitude is unaggressive.[44]

This writer was conservative in other fields as well as in religion. Referring to Bellamy's prophecy of the broadcasting of music and of the human voice, he wrote:

As well have our portfolios filled with the production of the oleotype press, instead of with the watercolors of our sisters, our wives, our children—because of their superiority in perspective—as have our music laid on by telephone as we lay on our gas; or hear what in Mr. Bellamy's Utopia passes muster for preaching—without any of the inspiration of common worship, or the speaker behind the voice.[45]

Bellamy was attacked about equally by those Marxians who saw moral evil as almost solely the result of economic and social evil, and by those who saw social and economic misfortune as almost

---

[44] William Higgs, "Some Objections to Mr. Bellamy's Utopia," *New Englander and Yale Review*, CCXL (March, 1890).
[45] *Ibid.*

entirely the outcome of shortcomings of individual character. He held that personal quality and social and economic conditions are interrelated and inseparable, and must equally be the concern of men. He did not give comfort to that large class of social reformers who excuse their own slovenly and undisciplined characters on the ground that personal character is a by-product of social conditions. His opinion in this regard is expressed in a letter to Thomas Wentworth Higginson:

Not only is it the Nationalist idea that the Nation should become an economical organism, but a *moral* organism as well. Before this last point I would lay extraordinary stress. This is, of course, necessarily an economic reform, but its most important aspect is that of a moral movement for uplifting, enlarging and ennobling the individual life by making every individual contribute his efforts first and directly to the common or national wealth, and himself dependent for his livelihood upon his equal chance in it, so that he is rich as the nation is rich and poor as his fellow citizens are poor and never otherwise. Then all the issues of life will be first from the individual to the nation, then from the nation back to him. As the hand profits not directly by what it seizes nor the mouth by what it devours, but only by sending its booty to the common treasury to be nourished in return by red blood from the heart, so the members of the coming nation will serve and live in constant remembrance and realization of their common life and mutual dependence. The great heart will beat in the pulse of the smallest member.

Neither did Bellamy support those who evade social responsibility by holding that the socially oppressed are but suffering for their faults of character. Therefore he could not found an escapist cult, and most cults would shrivel up if the element of escape were removed. Wholeness was a passion of his life.

XV · In Conclusion

To be a recognized member of any cult one must know the passwords. In the cult of philosophy, for instance, John Dewey made havoc of classical and conventional doctrines. His mastery of the language and of the processes of conventional philosophy gave him entrance to the cult, and recognized standing in it. Had he expressed the same ideas without first giving the esoteric passwords, it is doubtful whether innate quality of ideas would alone have been recognized quickly enough to win acceptance among philosophers.

Edward Bellamy was an original, creative-minded genius in more than one field, but he never adopted the passwords of the cults, and so never gained professional recognition. He tried to preserve that precious heritage of untaughtness which sometimes keeps the common man from the worship of mummeries in philosophy and economics. He was free from that supine acquiescence before a teacher which sometimes goes by the name of education. For this we may well be thankful.

Few things in life are rarer than the intelligent, inquisitive, curious, unspoiled mind of a boy. Most boys are never curious in an intellectual sense, and that counts them out. Of the few remaining, most are docile and impressionable, so that as they learn the native tongue they also adopt without question the prevailing concepts and interpretations of the world. Their intellectual life consists in elaborating, refining, organizing, and using prevailing ideas and habits, not in looking at them with fresh, curious questioning. This seems to be true also of erudite scholars.

Even the spirit of rebellion against prevailing viewpoints and mores is seldom evidence of intellectual curiosity. What is more stereotyped and more barren of such quality than the usual "revolt of youth" or the orthodoxy of standardized radicalism! A long-established prevailing interpretation of life often has at least the virtues of intellectual discipline and of a certain elimination of the crude and trivial. Too often a popular "revolt of youth," which is general enough to become a vogue, is but daydreaming, or a relapse to animal impulse, and a revolt from the inconvenience of self-discipline.

The unspoiled, intelligent curiosity of a boy seldom is a mass phenomenon. Generally it is a rare, single, and individual emergence, and of itself it constitutes genius. That quality of mind characterized Edward Bellamy throughout his life.

Perhaps the controlling limitation of Edward Bellamy was that of personal vigor. His tendency to see things as would an intelligent, curious, unindoctrinated boy; to see the simple realities of pompous and revered dogmas in religion, philosophy, society, and government—this way of seeing the world developed suggestions and implications of great importance. Had Bellamy possessed the vigor of mind and body of Victor Hugo or Karl Marx or Immanuel Kant, and had he been able to follow these fresh concepts to their full implications with rigorousness, vigor, and sureness, he might have presented a more vital, more natural, and more significant philosophy than either Kant or Marx. During most of his short life of forty-eight years he was so restricted in energy output that he could not throw himself with forgetfulness into his work. The drive of a Macaulay or of a Gladstone could make commonplace thinking almost illustrious. The limited vigor of Bellamy prevented him from revealing, even to himself, the full possibilities of his fresh and direct creative thinking.

Edward Bellamy was a social engineer. An important element in the success of *Looking Backward* was the sheer creative ingenuity of its author. No sooner does a difficulty arise in his program than he sees a normal and reasonable way out. It is largely that genius of his which gives the atmosphere of common-sense reality to his picture. In that respect he was supreme among all creators of utopias.

The drafting of legislation for large social undertakings is like the invention and design of complex mechanical equipment. Just as a schoolgirl steps into a powerful automobile and drives away, or picks up the telephone receiver to call a friend, totally uncon-

scious of the enormous technical achievement on which she relies;
so, in case of well-drafted legislation, men live and work under it
without friction or waste motion, quite unaware of the skill of legislative design on which this convenience rests.

A chief fault of democratic, as well as of most other government,
is the common lack of fine legislative design. One of the principal
reasons why our laws work so badly is that they are stupidly and
unskillfully conceived and formulated. While mechanically we live
in the automobile and airplane age, much of our legislative drafts-
manship is of the age of the ox cart.

In skill of adapting means to ends in the design of a social system, Edward Bellamy was more than unusual—he was a genius.
Only persons who have worked at the preparation of legislative
codes can appreciate the extent to which this is true.

An instance of Bellamy's skill is his device of making working
hours shorter or longer depending on the degree of attractiveness
or unattractiveness of the work, so that without regimentation or
other compulsion the supply of labor in any field will balance the
demand, with extra-hazardous jobs made attractive by being especially honorable. One could raise many questions about the
working in detail of such a plan, but creative imagination such as
Bellamy's would find common-sense solutions.

Had Bellamy set up an office in Washington to be of service
to members of Congress in drafting legislation, he might have become a national institution as clearly unique as Thomas Edison or
Gilbert and Sullivan. Where the art of designing legislation is
studied, as it should be (and usually is not) in law schools, *Looking
Backward* and *Equality* might well be used as texts to illustrate
the exercise of skill in relating means to ends. Very often Bellamy
is so skillful that his methods are not quickly obvious. Only a careful study of *Looking Backward* and *Equality* disclose the rare quality of creative imagination which they express.

Bellamy's ability in this respect was also his weakness. The
writer has known an exceptionally competent engineer whose un-
failing ingenuity in meeting difficulties resulted in his doing his work
with great economy. However, when he estimated the cost of work
to be done under the supervision of others, he would expect the same

ingenuity and economy to be exercised, and as a result his estimates were habitually too low until he deliberately corrected that weakness. So Bellamy, in thinking of the administration of his new social state, assumed that the rare creative ingenuity which he possessed would characterize legislation and administration. He did not imagine how stupid and uncreative men can be, and with how little imagination the world is governed.

Even such creativeness as his, however, is but an instrument for realizing the controlling desires of men. If such desires be antisocial, that creativeness may achieve them at great cost to society. His various skills and powers added current effectiveness to his writing, but what gave permanent value was an underlying philosophy, and what might be called his religion—that is, the commitment of his mind and spirit to the concept of the brotherhood of man as an expression of that unity of all things which he called "The Soul of Solidarity." Practical politicians may scorn a philosophy which extends beyond immediate issues, but the enduring loyalties of men are given to ways of life which are the result of facing the eternal problems and of finding answers which satisfy the whole nature of man. Karl Marx saw clearly that politics and economics could not be isolated phenomena, but to be enduring must be expressions of a philosophy which is concerned with the whole of reality. Edward Bellamy aimed at nothing less.

By many historians of economics and sociology, Bellamy is dismissed as "only one of the utopians," and the breed in general is given short shrift. Without doubt today "utopian" is a word of reproach. It implies visionariness and the expectation of impractical perfection. Beyond that, the distinctions between realism and utopia are as vague as between orthodoxy and heterodoxy.

Bellamy was a utopian. He looked upon the tragedies of human affairs as mostly due to causes under human control, and not irremovably innate in nature. As to the physical world, he risked making a fool of himself by carelessly assuming many inventions which were necessary to his purpose. He almost implied that in the physical world the limits of man's desire set the only limits to what he might create. At a time when "sensible" men protected themselves against the charge of being utopian by refraining from such wild suggestions, Bellamy assumed the existence of television, broadcasting, air travel, air conditioning, automobiles, mechanical calculators, concrete highways, farm tractors, and the controlled acceleration of plant growth.

Being by no means a physicist or an engineer, except for his wide scientific reading, he was in a strange and unknown land when he discussed physical inventions, and the chance for him to make himself ridiculous would seem to be very great. In dealing with human motives and actions, however, he was in the field of his lifetime interest, and there would seem to be less danger that he would expose himself to valid criticism. Few men of his day had more penetratingly observed or more acutely thought upon the springs of human action. His assumption that "human nature" is but the raw material out of which culture and purpose may form motives, bents, habits, and desires—this was the deliberate conclusion of one who had thought long and incisively on the matter.

During the more than half a century since *Looking Backward* was written, the steady drift of scientific opinion has been in Bellamy's direction. The psychologist no longer asks whether "human nature"—in the everyday meaning of the term—can be changed. He knows that, even in a year-old baby, we never see human nature that has not been profoundly modified. He knows that the ethics, the prejudices, the likes and dislikes, the loyalties, the motives, and many of the springs of action which have been included in the term "human nature" by the public, are not inborn, but are the results of cultural training and inheritance. As a clear pattern of life emerges in human thinking it will be feasible to transmit that pattern to the oncoming generation by methods that are not abstruse or farfetched.

Just as man's control of physical forces grew with almost imperceptible slowness during hundreds of thousands of years, and then in the course of two centuries leaped forward to the present still accelerating rate of progress, so it seems entirely reasonable to expect that rapidly increasing control of the cultural inheritance, including what in common parlance has been called "human nature," may soon result from the increase of the scientific temper which is steadily permeating human outlook.

Bellamy was so rash as to predict that by the year 2000 a universal language would exist, so that a man need learn only two languages, his own and the universal, in order to speak to the whole world. During the past decade I have heard scholarly men speak with derision of such a possibility. Yet in about 1931 I attended a meeting of the International Auxiliary Language Association, at which a prominent European Esperantist pleaded with the association not to hinder the triumphant march of Esperanto as the universal language, because after half a century of faithful effort more than two hundred thousand persons had some knowledge of Esperanto, and that it would be a tragic loss to humanity for that great gain to be wasted. The late General Carthy of the Radio Corporation of America answered him in the spirit of the present age. He said that the chief handicap to the spread of Esperanto is lack of conviction that it is the most suitable instrument for the purpose. General Carthy added that given assurance that some synthetic language was the considered choice of the western world as an international auxiliary language, he could provide a course by radio which would result in two or three million persons learning the language within a year.

This incident is significant. The scientific temper, as it emerges more and more into dominance in ever increasing areas of human affairs, tends constantly to bring about unity of opinion on issues where the theological and the traditional tempers tended to maintain isolation or conflict. A growing unity of opinion concerning essentials of social and economic policy seems not impossible. As fast as that unity is achieved, it will find at hand the instruments of universal dissemination, and a growing knowledge of effective methods for the creation of a new cultural inheritance. Within a century the "utopian" viewpoint with reference to our cultural inheritance may seem no less reasonable and feasible than Bellamy's forecast of material mastery does today. Even the existence of totalitarian governments and their effort to regiment thought may prove to be frail barriers against the pervasiveness of intelligence.

It is to the credit of Bellamy that in his opinion the unification of opinion which is to so change "human nature" is not to come by political compulsion or by dictatorship, but by an intense though informal revival of interest in human values, and by the processes of peaceful and voluntary action on the part of large numbers. It is to his credit, also, that he indicates great restraint in the dissemination of official ideas. In his utopia agreement arises out of experience and education, rather than from imposed dicta. The processes of Hitler, Mussolini, and Stalin may seem more rapid, but the process of Bellamy, which to a considerable degree expresses the genius of American idealism, is sounder and more persistent. It provides a freer play of outlooks and less arbitrary suppression of elements which may have great value, but which are slow in maturing.

His being a utopian will less and less be held against Bellamy as evidence that he was unsound. Yet a blemish remains. Bellamy was a zealot. His program seemed nearly perfect in his eyes. Almost every criticism is completely answered. His solutions are to him ideal. He does not see them as simply the most practicable and least faulty of several ways, every one of which in some degree is faulty.

A great fact of human life which Bellamy did not fully appreciate is the existence of dilemmas. Repeatedly men find themselves in situations from which there is no good way out. A sick man needs strength for recovery, yet his stomach may need rest from digesting food. Either feeding him or starving him is perilous. Society needs freedom from the tyranny of traditional beliefs and restrictions in order to develop discrimination and self-control, yet if freedom comes before discrimination and self-control are developed, we may have license and disorder. In reading *Looking Backward* and *Equality* one seldom gets a hint that life is sometimes the choice of two or more evils. The open-minded scholarship which characterizes his early *Duke of Stockbridge* began to fade as he came to see himself as the prophet of a new day. Were his writings to have exclusive right of way to the degree which Marxism did in Russia, this defect would be serious. In a world of freely competitive ideas his fallacies will be exposed, while the vision and belief in a possible better world will remain a powerfully motivating force, and the intelligent creativeness of his solutions will be a very helpful guide to less imaginative persons.

At the time of Edward Bellamy's death, Katherine Pearson Woods in the *Bookman* expressed a notable characteristic of his writing:

Mr. Bellamy's great and distinctive merit is that by clothing the Ideal in the apparel of the Real, he inspired us with a hope of its speedy attainment. It was this note of hope, the hope which his gospel had brought to his own soul, that took the world by storm; for who would not find his own burden light, in the belief that his children should be delivered from it? [1]

To make a great and real picture of what might be, so that men may have a basis for comparison, and therefore a basis for a wholesome aspiration, is a significant achievement. That contribution Bellamy made.

Shortly after his death a reform magazine in a small Nebraska town changed its name to the *Bellamy Review*, and on doing so made the following statement:

In rechristening our Review we have chosen a name that cannot be bettered. We count ourselves very fortunate in being the first to use it.

No man has done as much as Edward Bellamy to open the eyes of the people to that vision of social justice and goodwill which every prophet has beheld.

Without uttering an angry syllable he has shown the horrors of the struggle for wealth.

Without ceasing for a moment to be guided by common sense, he has given us a picture of society as it might be, if it were based on equality and labor.

Without the use of a word which the ordinary reader could not understand, he has made plain certain economic laws which professors and philosophers have vainly tried to make clear, either to other people or to themselves.

He had clearer and keener sight than the over-praised Marx. His idealism never became whimsical, as was the case with William Morris.

[1] Katherine Pearson Woods, "Edward Bellamy, Author and Economist," *Bookman*, VII (July, 1898), 401.

His abhorrence of present evils never warped him to reactionary convictions, as happened to John Ruskin.

Unlike Lassalle, he never allowed his passion for the poor to become a flame of destructive revolution; and unlike Henry George, on the other hand, he never became so heavily practical that he neglected his ideal in the attempt to secure a small immediate reform.

Though an explorer in unmapped fields of thought, he never preferred ideas to men, as did Emerson and Carlyle. And though in many senses the most extreme of social reformers, his indignation never became bitter and frenzied, as did that of William Lloyd Garrison.

Edward Bellamy was one of the sanest men of the century. No prophet ever spoke his message as wisely or as well as did the modest seer of Chicopee Falls.

As the years roll on, men will speak less of his imagination and more of his practical sense.[2]

Bellamy had the fresh mind of a boy, but not the mind of a dullard. He did not imagine that in these two books he had covered the issues of a good life. During all his days this problem, of what lay beyond utopia, was ever present. In one of his notebooks of the year 1878, when he was twenty-eight years old, we find the note, "The uselessness of any further labor-saving inventions until men learn how to enjoy their leisure." [3] In one of his still earlier journals he wrote:

We are envious of happiness only as we think we see the means whereby it was attained, and that, having them, we might be happy. An error: the means we ascribe happiness to could not produce it. It is a miracle, a subtle compounding of unknown essences, the secret of which no philosopher can fathom.[4]

In the prime of his life these impressions of his youth were deepened into convictions. He saw a good society as only a secure ground on which men might stand in order to face the greater issues of life. In *Looking Backward* he did not allow his readers to lay down the book with the feeling that he had taken them to the end of the road. Near the close of his great utopia we find this passage:

"The solution of the problem of physical maintenance so as to banish care and crime, so far from seeming to us an ultimate attainment, ap-

---

[2] "Bellamy's Prophecy," *Bellamy Review; a Monthly Journal of Progress*, I, No. 7 (October, 1900), 210–11.

[3] Unpublished papers (B2-HI-p. 13). [4] *Ibid.* (B1-2-16).

pears but as a preliminary to anything like real human progress. We have but relieved ourselves of an impertinent and needless harassment which hindered our ancestors from undertaking the real ends of existence. We are merely stripped for the race; no more. We are like a child which has just learned to stand upright and to walk. It is a great event, from the child's point of view, when he first walks. Perhaps he fancies that there can be little beyond that achievement, but a year later he has forgotten that he could not always walk. His horizon did but widen when he rose, and enlarge as he moved. A great event indeed, in one sense, was his first step, but only as a beginning, not as the end. His true career was but then first entered on.

"Do you ask what we look for when unnumbered generations shall have passed away? I answer, the way stretches far before us, but the end is lost in light. For twofold is the return of man to God 'who is our home,' the return of the individual by the way of death, and the return of the race by the fulfilment of the evolution, when the divine secret hidden in the germ shall be perfectly unfolded." [5]

Had Edward Bellamy been given twenty additional years, and vigorous life, it is reasonable to believe that he would have reached out beyond his utopia and would have turned his mind and spirit again to those agelong problems of human life which so intensely concerned his earlier years. His work and thought as a whole incline us to this belief. His vision did not fade, nor did his sense of proportion fail him. R. E. Bisbee, his friend and neighbor, has given us a glimpse of his later mind:

Those who think that Bellamy looked upon socialism as the ultimate goal and destiny of humanity utterly failed to comprehend him. With him socialism was but the next and necessary step in human progress. I am not sure but that he regretted the necessity of the step. If all men would do right there would be no need of socialism, no need of economic equality. To prevent a few from doing wrong, we make laws for the many. Because some will oppress their fellows if they can, we must make it impossible for any to do so. The highest ideal of society is one in which all live together as brothers, in which love is the one motive for action. The path to this ideal state leads through socialism, but this ideal state is not socialism. In this ideal state there will be no division of property, and no statute law; but all shall have enough, and the law will be written on men's hearts. The family is the prototype of this far-off but coming civilization.

Mr. Bellamy understood and accepted this view. When I brought

5 *Looking Backward*, pp. 291, 292.

out this point in some published comments on *Equality,* he wrote to thank me for my criticism. In my last conversation with him I put the question to him plainly, "Mr. Bellamy, you do not consider the social state pictured in *Equality* the end of human progress, do you?" "Oh, no," he replied, with what I felt to be almost a touch of impatience; "it is only the beginning. When we get there we shall find a whole infinity beyond." These were his last words to me. He had opened the door to let me out when I asked the question. His hand was still on the knob when he answered. There he stood, that little pale man, within eight months of his death, with a far-away look in his eyes which I shall never forget, as he repeated—"A whole infinity beyond." [6]

Those who enter into the mind and spirit of Edward Bellamy will be his friends but not his worshipers. They will see him as having thrown strong light upon the way ahead, but not as having revealed a perfect plan. They will not draw a line below the last word he wrote and inscribe thereunder

FINIS

[6] R. E. Bisbee, "Some Characteristics of Edward Bellamy," *Coming Age,* I, No. 2 (February, 1899), 185.

Appendix

SOME of the source material used or consulted in preparing this biography is deposited in the Harvard College Library, and duplicates of parts are deposited in the Library of Congress, in the Huntington Library, and in the library of Antioch College.

The typed copies of notebooks and other manuscripts were bound temporarily for current use, with no logical system. Later it was found more convenient to continue this order than to reclassify the material.

Both the original manuscripts and typed copies are in the Harvard College Library. Only typed copies are in the Library of Congress, the Huntington Library, and the Antioch College Library. Footnote references are to the bound typewritten copies. A footnote reading "Unpublished papers (B1-2-20, 21)" refers to Binder No. 1, Notebook No. 2, pages 20 and 21. A footnote reading "B1-B-3" refers to Binder No. 1, Notebook B, page 3. A footnote note reading "B3B, Liberty of the Press, 11," refers to Binder No. 3B, page 11 of the article on "Liberty of the Press."

Of these, copies are in the Harvard College Library, Library of Congress, Huntington Library, and Antioch College Library.

UNPUBLISHED WRITINGS OF EDWARD BELLAMY

Binder No. 1 (B1), Notebooks A, B, and C, and 1, 2, and 3.
Binder No. 2 (B2), Notebooks 4, 5, 6, and 7. Also:
  Story of Eliot Carson (E.C.)
  Hawaiian Island notebook (H.I.)
  Thoughts on Political Economy (Pol. Ec.)
  Plots for Stories—No. 1 (Plots 1)
  Plots for Stories—No. 2 (Plots 2)
  Paul Bellamy's notebook (readings suggested by Edward Bellamy
    for his son, Paul)
Binder No. 3A (B3A), copies of published articles by Edward Bellamy.
Binder No. 3B (B3B), unpublished manuscripts by Edward Bellamy:
  Almost a Suicide
  Autobiographical Sketch Written at about the Age of Twenty-five
  A Dream That Was not All a Dream
  The Dual Life
  Faneuil Hall Address

How Many Men Make a Man?
Liberty of the Press
First Lyceum Talk
Second Lyceum Talk
Original Introduction to *Equality*
Religion: Original Draft of Chapters 23, 24 and 25 of *Equality*
Religion of Solidarity
Selectman Danforth and Aurora Day
The Spring Feeling
Miscellaneous Fragments
Boyhood Essays (1860–70)

COLLEGE AND GRADUATE THESES CONCERNING EDWARD BELLAMY

(Copies in the Harvard College Library.)

Blaufarb, Douglas. "The Mind of Edward Bellamy." Harvard College, 1939, 158 pp. including bibliography.

Franklin, John Hope. "Edward Bellamy and the Nationalist Movement." Harvard University, 1937, 53 pp. and bibliography.

George, James T. "Edward Bellamy and the Nationalist Movement." Divisional Honors, Amherst College, 1938, 149 pp. and bibliography.

Smith, Walter A. "The Religion of Edward Bellamy." Columbia University, 1937, 107 pp.

ADDITIONAL BIOGRAPHICAL DATA

(The first two are in all the libraries mentioned, the third in the Harvard College Library only.)

Green, Mason A. *Edward Bellamy: a Biography of the Author of "Looking Backward,"* 207 pp., unpublished, evidently written or finished in the 1920's or early 1930's.

Willard, Cyrus Field. Chapters from an *Autobiography,* written in the 1930's, and typed from the manuscript for the author of this biography. (Chapters 10, 11, 12, and 13 deal with Bellamy and his movement.)

Luntz, Lester. *Daniel De Leon and the Movement for Social Reform.* 1939, 47 pp., unpublished. (Chapter III, "The Nationalist Movement," discusses De Leon's association with Nationalism.)

Additional material placed in the Harvard College Library includes:
Unbound fragments of manuscripts by Edward Bellamy that have not been deciphered. (These may contain interesting new material.)
A larger manuscript of this biography, exceeding it in length by about 50 percent, and including further selections from Bellamy's unpublished writings

Letters to and from Edward Bellamy

Letters to and from members of the Bellamy family

Correspondence with Cyrus Field Willard concerning Bellamy, Nationalism, and the Theosophical Society

Miscellaneous letters about Edward Bellamy, *Looking Backward* and Nationalism

Correspondence with associates of John Macnie, author of *The Diothas,* concerning the charge of plagiarism of *Looking Backward*

Originals or copies of legal papers relating to Edward Bellamy or to members of his family, concerning admission to the bar, adoption, births, marriages, deaths, etc.

Memoranda concerning the life and personality of Edward Bellamy by Mrs. Edward Bellamy and by their son Paul Bellamy and their daughter Mrs. Marion Bellamy Earnshaw

Correspondence with Theosophists concerning the Nationalist movement in California.

Excerpts from book reviews and editorials in the *Springfield Union* attributed to Edward Bellamy

Excerpts from the Springfield *Penny News* and *Daily News,* mostly of the period when Edward Bellamy was editor

Correspondence with and about persons particularly influenced by Edward Bellamy

Miscellaneous correspondence throwing light on Bellamy and his movement and influence

Book reviews and comments on *Looking Backward* and *Equality* and obituary comments on Edward Bellamy

Copies of little known magazines containing articles concerning Bellamy and his movement

Miscellaneous source material used in writing this biography

The following material has been placed in the Antioch College Library:

Files of the *Nationalist*

Files of the *New Nation*

A collection of utopias

Some notebooks used by the author in preparing this biography

Bibliography

I. BOOKS AND ARTICLES QUOTED OR REFERRED TO IN THIS
BIOGRAPHY

Aeschylus. Agamemnon. Gilbert Murray, trans. New York: Oxford University Press, 1920.

Alger, William R. The Genius of Solitude. Boston: Roberts Brothers, 1867.

Andreae, Johann Valentin. Christianopolis. Translated from the Latin by Felix Emil Held. New York: Oxford University Press, 1916.

Aristophanes. The Ecclesiazusae. Benjamin B. Rogers, trans. London: Heinemann; New York: Putnam, 1924.

Bacon, Francis. New Atlantis. Vol. 3, pp. 151–91. New York: P. F. Collier, 1910. The Harvard Classics.

Baxter, Sylvester. "The Author of *Looking Backward*," *New England Magazine,* n.s. Vol. 1 (September, 1889).

—— "Edward Bellamy's New Book of the New Democracy," *American Monthly Review of Reviews,* Vol. 16 (July, 1897).

—— "What Is Nationalism?" *The Nationalist,* Vol. 1, No. 1 (May, 1889).

Bebel, August. Woman in the Past, Present, and Future. London: William Reeves, n.d.

Beer, Max. Social Struggles and Modern Socialism. Boston: Small, Maynard, 1926.

Bell, Fred W. "Edward Bellamy and 'The Bellamy Plan,'" *The Theosophist,* Vol. 55 (August, 1934).

Bellamy, Charles J. The Breton Mills. New York: Putnam, 1880.

—— The Way Out. New York: Putnam, 1884.

Bellamy, Joseph. The Works of the Rev. Joseph Bellamy, D.D. 3 vols. New York: Stephen Dodge, 1811.

"Bellamy's Prophecy," *The Bellamy Review; a Monthly Journal of Progress,* Vol. 1, No. 7 (October, 1900).

Berington, Simon (pseud. George Berkeley). The Adventures of Signor Gaudentio Di Lucca. Dublin: John Cumming, 1821.

Bhagavad-Gita or The Lord's Lay, The. Translated from the Sanskrit by Mohini M. Chatterji. Boston: Houghton, Mifflin, c.1887.

Bisbee, R. E. "Some Characteristics of Edward Bellamy," *The Com-*

ing Age, Vol. 1, No. 2 (February, 1899). (With Bellamy source material in Harvard College Library.

Biscoe, J. Foster. "Attitude of the Press," *The Nationalist,* Vol. 2, No. 4 (March, 1890).

Blanc, Louis. L'Organisation du travail. 9th ed. Paris: 1850. (Included in J. A. R. Marriott, The French Revolution of 1848 in Its Economic Aspect, Vol. 1, Oxford, Clarendon Press, 1913.)

Blavatsky, H. P. The Key to Theosophy. Point Loma, California: Theosophical University Press, 1939.

—— "The Nationalist," *Lucifer,* Vol. 4 (July 15, 1889).

Bouvé, Edward T. Centuries Apart. Boston: Little, Brown, 1894.

Burnham, Collins G. "The City of Chicopee," *New England Magazine,* n.s. Vol. 18 (May, 1898).

Calverton, V. F. The Liberation of American Literature. New York: Scribner, 1932.

Campanella, Thomas. The City of the Sun. In *Ideal Empires and Republics,* pp. 273–317. New York: Aladdin Book Company, 1901.

Carey, Thomas. The History of the Pirates. Hartford: Henry Benton, 1834.

Carnegie, Andrew. Triumphant Democracy. New York: Scribner, 1886.

Carpenter, Frederic Ives. Emerson and Asia. Cambridge: Harvard University Press, 1930.

Chambers, R. W. Thomas More. New York: Harcourt, Brace, 1935.

Chapman, Clowry. "Learning While Earning," *The Munsingwear News,* August, 1919. (With Bellamy source material in Harvard College Library.)

Christy, Arthur. The Orient in American Transcendentalism. New York: Columbia University Press, 1932.

Clemens, Samuel L. (Mark Twain). The Curious Republic of Gondour. New York: Boni and Liveright, 1919.

Cridge, Alfred Denton. Utopia; or, The History of an Extinct Planet. Oakland, California: Winchester and Pew, 1884.

Dawes, Anna L. "Mr. Bellamy and Christianity," *The Andover Review: a Religious and Theological Monthly,* Vol. 15 (April, 1891).

Deutsche Arbeiterpartei, Die; ihre Prinzipien und ihr Programm (a pamphlet). Berlin: 1868. (In New York Public Library.)

Dewey, John. Freedom and Culture. New York: Putnam, 1939.

—— "A Great American Prophet," *Common Sense,* Vol. 3, No. 4 (April, 1934).

Dexter, Franklin Bowditch, ed. The Literary Diary of Ezra Stiles. 3 vols. New York: Scribner, 1901.

Dombrowski, James. The Early Days of Christian Socialism in America. New York: Columbia University Press, 1936.

Dorfman, Joseph. Thorstein Veblen and His America. New York: Viking Press, 1934.

"Edward Bellamy," *Good Housekeeping,* Vol. 10, No. 4 (December 21, 1889).

"Edward Bellamy," *The Literary Weekly,* Vol. 5 (January 4, 1894).

Ellis, G. New Britain; a Narrative of a Journey. London: W. Simpkin and R. Marshall, 1820.

Engels, Frederick. Socialism: Utopian and Scientific. Chicago: Charles H. Kerr & Co., 1908.

Etzler, J. A. The Paradise within the Reach of All Men. Pittsburgh: Etzler and E. Reinhold, 1833 or 1883.

Fiske, A. K. "Old Time Factory Life in New England," *New England Magazine,* n.s. Vol. 18 (April, 1898).

Fiske, John. A History of the United States. Boston: Houghton, Mifflin, 1894.

Foss, Sam Walter. "The Songless Poet," in Whiffs from Wild Meadows. Boston: Lothrop, Lee, & Shepard, 1895.

Foster, Edward P. "Behind the Mask," *The Arena,* Vol. 2 (October, 1890).

Gallup, George H. "We, the People, Are Like This," *New York Times Magazine,* June 8, 1941.

Garrison, William Lloyd. "The Mask of Tyranny," *The Arena,* Vol. 1 (April, 1890).

Geiger, George Raymond. The Philosophy of Henry George. New York: Macmillan, 1933.

"General Gossip," *Current Literature,* Vol. 4, No. 3 (March, 1890).

George, Henry. Progress and Poverty. New York: Robert Schalkenbach Foundation, 1935.

Georgii, Max. "Nationalism Versus Prohibition," *The Nationalist,* Vol. 2, No. 6 (May, 1890).

Gilman, N. P. "Edward Bellamy and Nationalism in the United States," *Quarterly Journal of Economics,* Vol. 4 (October, 1889).

Gosse, Philip. The Pirates' Who's Who. London: Dulau and Co. Ltd., 1924.

Green, Mason A. Edward Bellamy; a Biography (unpublished). (With Bellamy source material in Harvard College Library, Library of Congress, Huntington and Antioch.)

Griffith, Mrs. Mary. Three Hundred Years Hence (part of a volume entitled Camperdown; or News from Our Neighborhood). Philadelphia: 1836. Republished in *The Colophon,* summer, 1935.

Gronlund, Laurence. The Co-operative Commonwealth; an Exposition of Socialism. Boston: Lothrop, Lee, and Shepard, c.1890.

—— The New Economy. Chicago & New York: Herbert S. Stone & Co., 1898.

Gronlund, Laurence. Our Destiny. Boston: Lothrop, Lee, and Shepard, 1891. Appeared serially in the *Nationalist,* Vol. 2 (March–September, 1890).

Hale, Edward Everett. "The Best Government," *The Nationalist,* Vol. 1, No. 2 (June, 1889).

—— "Fraternal Government," *The Book Buyer,* Vol. 15, No. 1 (August, 1897).

Harrington, James. Oceana. In *Ideal Commonwealths,* pp. 181–416. New York: the Colonial Press, 1901.

Harris, W. T. "Edward Bellamy's Vision," *The Forum,* Vol. 8 (October, 1889).

Hart, Albert Bushnell, ed. American History Told by Contemporaries. 4 vols. New York: Macmillan, 1923.

Henderson, Archibald. Bernard Shaw, Playboy and Prophet. New York: Appleton, c.1932.

Hertzka, Theodor. Freeland. New York: Appleton, 1891.

Higgs, William. "Some Objections to Mr. Bellamy's Utopia," *New Englander and Yale Review,* Vol. 240 (March, 1890).

Hillquit, Morris. History of Socialism in the United States. New York: Funk and Wagnalls, 1910.

Holiday, Henry. "The Artistic Aspects of Edward Bellamy's *Looking Backward." Transactions* of the Guild & School of Handicraft (London, Guild & School of Handicraft, Essex House, Mile End, 1890), Vol. 1, p. 62.

Holmes, Oliver Wendell. Pages from an Old Volume of Life. Boston: Houghton, Mifflin, c.1891.

Houghton, Mifflin & Co. Literary Bulletin, March, 1890. (With Bellamy source material in Harvard College Library.)

Howells, William Dean. "Edward Bellamy," *Atlantic Monthly,* Vol. 82 (August, 1898).

Howland, Marie. Papa's Own Girl. New York: John W. Lovell Co., c.1874.

James, William. "The Moral Equivalent of War," Memories and Studies. London: Longmans, Green. Reprinted in Representative Essays in Modern Thought, H. R. Steeves and F. H. Ristine, eds., New York, American Book Co., 1913.

Jameson, John Franklin. Privateering and Piracy in the Colonial Period. New York: Macmillan, 1923.

Jevons, H. Stanley. Economic Equality in the Co-operative Commonwealth. London: Methuen, 1933.

Lanier, Sidney. Poems. New York: Scribner, 1900.

Lao-Tze. Tao Teh King (Canon of Reason and Virtue). Paul Carus, ed. and trans. Chicago: Open Court Publishing Co., 1927.

"Late Mr. Bellamy, The," *The Critic,* Vol. 32, No. 849 (May 28, 1898).

London, Jack. The Iron Heel. New York: McKinlay, Stone & Mackenzie, c.1907 and 1924.

—— The People of the Abyss. New York: Grosset & Dunlap, c.1903.

"Looking Backward" (review), *New Orleans Times-Democrat,* February 5, 1888.

"Looking Backward" (review), *The Saturday Review,* March 24, 1888.

"Looking Backward" (review), *Science,* July 20, 1888.

Macnie, John (pseud. Ismar Thiusen). The Diothas; or, A Far Look Ahead. New York: Putnam, 1883.

Marquis, Don. The Almost Perfect State. Garden City, N.Y.: Doubleday, Doran, 1927.

Marshall, John. The Life of George Washington. 5 vols. Fredericksburg, Va.: the Citizens Guild of Washington's Boyhood Home, 1926.

Menninger, Karl. "Death of a Prophet," *The New Republic,* Vol. 100 (August 9, 1939).

Michaelis, Richard C. Looking Further Forward; an Answer to *Looking Backward.* Chicago: Rand, McNally & Company, 1890. London: William Reeves, c.1893 (The Bellamy Library, No. 10).

Mitchell, Edward Page. Memoirs of an Editor; Fifty Years of American Journalism. New York: Scribner, 1924.

More, Thomas. Utopia. New York: Dutton. (Everyman's Library, Vol. 461.)

Morris, William. *"Looking Backward," The Commonweal,* Vol. 5, No. 180 (June 22, 1889).

—— News from Nowhere. New York: Vanguard Press, 1926.

Mumford, Lewis. The Story of Utopias. New York: Boni and Liveright, 1922.

"New Utopia, A," *New York Tribune,* February 5, 1888.

Nordhoff, Charles. The Communistic Societies of the United States. New York: Harper, 1875.

Owen, Robert. The Book of the New Moral World. New York: G. Vale, 1845.

Page, Elizabeth. The Tree of Liberty. New York: Farrar & Rinehart, 1939.

Peebles, H. P. "The Utopias of the Past Compared with Theories of Bellamy," *Overland Monthly,* 2d ser., Vol. 15, No. 90 (June, 1890).

Plato, Works. Benjamin Jowett, trans. New York: Tudor Publishing Company, n.d.

Prescott, William Hickling. The Complete Works, edited with the author's latest corrections, by John Foster Kirk. 12 vols. London: Gibbings & Company, 1896. Vol. 5, "The History of the Conquest of Peru."

Rougemont, Denis de. "Federalism vs. Totalitarianism," *Common Sense*, Vol. 10, No. 6 (June, 1941).

Sears, Lorenzo. John Hancock: The Picturesque Patriot. Boston: Little, Brown, 1912.

Shaw, George Bernard, ed. The Fabian Essays in Socialism. Boston: Charles E. Brown & Co., c.1894.

Shipley, Marie A. (Mrs. John B.) The True Author of *Looking Backward*. New York: John B. Alden, c.1890.

—— "Bebel's Bricks or Bellamy's?" *Liberty*, Vol. 7, No. 4 (June 21, 1890).

Shurter, Robert L. The Utopian Novel in America, 1865–1900. Doctor's Dissertation, Western Reserve University, May, 1936.

Smith, Ralph D. "Matthew Bellamy of New Haven, Conn., and His Descendants," *The New England Historical and Genealogical Register*, Vol. 61, No. 244 (October, 1907).

Smith, Walter A. The Religion of Edward Bellamy. Unpublished M.A. thesis, Columbia University, June, 1937.

Sophocles. Oedipus, King of Thebes. Gilbert Murray, trans. New York: Oxford University Press, 1911.

Stiles, Ezra. The Literary Diary of Ezra Stiles. 3 vols., Franklin Bowditch Dexter, ed. New York: Scribner, 1901.

Tawney, R. H. The Acquisitive Society. New York: Harcourt, Brace, 1920.

"Theosophical Aspects of Contemporary Thought and Literature," *The Path* (March, 1889).

Thomson, J. Arthur. The Outline of Science. New York: Putnam, 1922.

Utter, Ruth, and Matilde Kelly. "Books That Have Changed the Modern World," *Wilson Bulletin for Librarians*, Vol. 10 (October, 1935).

Vassault, F. I. "Nationalism in California," *Overland Monthly*, 2d ser., Vol. 15, No. 90 (June, 1890).

Veblen, Thorstein. The Place of Science in Modern Civilization. New York: B. W. Huebsch, 1919. (Includes "Some Neglected Points in the Theory of Socialism.")

Wallas, Graham. The Great Society. New York: Macmillan, 1923.

Weeks, Edward. This Trade of Writing. Boston: Little, Brown, 1935.

Who's Who in America, 1903–5.

Wilde, Oscar. The Soul of Man under Socialism. Boston: John W. Luce and Company, n.d.

Willard, Cyrus Field. Autobiography. (Unpublished; with Bellamy source material in Harvard College Library, Library of Congress, Huntington Library, and Antioch College Library.)

Willard, Cyrus Field. "The Nationalist Club of Boston (a Chapter of History)," *The Nationalist,* Vol. 1, No. 1 (May, 1889).
—— "News of the Movement," *The Nationalist,* Vol. 2, No. 7 (June, 1890).
—— "A Retrospect," *The Nationalist,* Vol. 2, No. 1 (December, 1889).
Willard, Frances E. "An Interview with Edward Bellamy," *Our Day,* Vol. 4, No. 22 (October 10, 1889).
Woods, Katherine Pearson. "Edward Bellamy: Author and Economist," *The Bookman,* Vol. 7 (July, 1898).
World Almanac and Encyclopedia, The. New York: 1903.
Zarovitch, Vera (Mary E. Bradley Lane). Mizora; a Prophecy. New York: G. W. Dillingham, 1889.

II. WORKS OF EDWARD BELLAMY

Address to Mass Meeting Held at Cooper Union, February 12, 1890, to parents protesting cutting down of schools.
"At Pinney's Ranch," *Atlantic Monthly,* Vol. 60 (December, 1887). Republished in *The Blindman's World.*
"Blindman's World, The," *Atlantic Monthly,* Vol. 58 (November, 1886). Republished in *The Blindman's World.*
Blindman's World, The, and Other Stories, with a Prefatory Sketch by W. D. Howells. Boston: Houghton, Mifflin, 1898.
"Brief Summary of the Industrial Plan of Nationalism Set Forth in *Looking Backward,* for Class Study," *The Dawn,* Vol. 1, No. 5 (September 15, 1889). In Boston Public Library.
"Christmas in the Year 2000," *The Ladies' Home Journal,* Vol. 12, No. 2 (January, 1895).
"Cold Snap, The," *Scribners Monthly,* Vol. 10 (September, 1875). Republished in *The Blindman's World.*
"Deserted," *Lippincott's Magazine,* Vol. 22 (November, 1878). Republished in *The Blindman's World.*
Dr. Heidenhoff's Process. New York: Appleton, 1880.
The Duke of Stockbridge. New York: Silver, Burdett, 1900.
"Echo of Antietam, An," *Century Magazine,* Vol. 38 (July, 1889). Republished in *The Blindman's World.*
Edward Bellamy Speaks Again. Kansas City, Missouri: the Peerage Press, 1937.
Equality. New York: Appleton, 1934.
"Extra Hazardous," *Appleton's Journal,* n.s. Vol 3 (November, 1877).
"First Steps toward Nationalism," *The Forum,* Vol. 10 (October, 1890). Republished in *Edward Bellamy Speaks Again.*

"Fourth of July, 1992," *Boston Globe,* July 4, 1892. Republished in *Edward Bellamy Speaks Again.*

"Hooking Watermelons," *Scribner's Monthly,* Vol. 14 (September, 1877). Republished in *The Blindman's World.*

"How I Came to Write *Looking Backward,*" *The Nationalist,* Vol. 1, No. 1 (May, 1889). Republished in *Edward Bellamy Speaks Again.*

"How I Wrote *Looking Backward,*" *The Ladies' Home Journal,* Vol. 11, No. 5 (April, 1894).

How to Employ the Unemployed in Mutual Maintenance (a pamphlet). Republished in *The Golden Book,* June, 1933, and also in *Edward Bellamy Speaks Again,* in the version which first appeared in the *Boston Traveler,* November 4, 1893.

"How We Shall Get There," *Twentieth Century,* Vol. 2, No. 18 (May 11, 1889).

Interview, *Boston Post,* May 22, 1898.

"Introduction to the American Edition," *The Fabian Essays in Socialism,* George Bernard Shaw, ed. Boston: Charles E. Brown and Co., c.1894. Republished in *Edward Bellamy Speaks Again.*

"Is 'Socialism' a Definite or an Indefinite Term?" *The New Nation,* Vol. 2, No. 1 (January 2, 1892).

"Letter from Edward Bellamy," *The Dawn,* Vol. 1, No. 1 (May 15, 1889). In Boston Public Library.

Letter to William Dean Howells, in the Harvard Library collection of Howells' correspondence.

Looking Backward 2000–1887. Boston: Houghton, Mifflin, 1926.

"*Looking Backward* Again," *North American Review,* Vol. 150, No. 400 (March, 1890). Republished in *Edward Bellamy Speaks Again.*

"Looking Forward," *The Nationalist,* Vol. 2, No. 1 (December, 1889). Republished in *Edward Bellamy Speaks Again.*

"Lost," *Scribner's Monthly,* Vol. 15 (December, 1877). Republished in *The Blindman's World.*

"Love Story Reversed, A." Republished in *The Blindman's World.*

Miss Ludington's Sister. Boston: James R. Osgood and Company, 1884.

"Nationalism—Principles, Purposes," *The Nationalist,* Vol. 2 (April, 1890); address at Tremont Temple, Boston, on the Nationalist Club Anniversary, December 19, 1889. Published in pamphlet form by B. F. Hunter, Philadelphia, 1889 (copy in New York Public Library). Republished in *Edward Bellamy Speaks Again.*

"Old Folks' Party," *Scribner's Monthly,* Vol. 11 (March, 1876). Republished in *The Blindman's World.*

"Our Prospective Sovereigns," *The Nationalist,* Vol. 1 (July, 1889). Republished in *Edward Bellamy Speaks Again.*

"Outcome of the Battle of Standards, The," *Boston Globe,* July 16, 1893. Republished in *Edward Bellamy Speaks Again.*

"Plea of Insanity, The," *Christian Union*, May 8, 1872. Unsigned, but reported to be by Edward Bellamy.

Plutocracy or Nationalism, Which? Address at Tremont Temple, May 31, 1889, published in pamphlet form by the Nationalist Club of Boston. Also published as No. 18 of Pocket Library of Socialism, Kerr & Co., Chicago. Republished in *Edward Bellamy Speaks Again*.

"Positive Romance, A," *Century Magazine*, Vol. 38 (August, 1889). Republished in *The Blindman's World*.

"Potts's Painless Cure," *Scribner's Monthly*, Vol. 17 (February, 1879). Republished in *The Blindman's World*.

"Programme of the Nationalists, The," *The Forum*, Vol. 17 (March, 1894). Republished in *Edward Bellamy Speaks Again*.

"Progress of Nationalism in the United States," *North American Review*, Vol. 154 (June, 1892). Republished in *Edward Bellamy Speaks Again*.

"Rate of the World's Progress, The," letter to the editor of the *Boston Transcript* in reply to a review of *Looking Backward*. March, 1888. Republished as "Postscript" in later editions of *Looking Backward*.

"Should Every Boy Learn a Trade?" *Boston Herald*, August 9, 1892. Republished in *Edward Bellamy Speaks Again*.

Six to One; a Nantucket Idyl. New York: Putnam, 1878. Published anonymously.

"Some Misconceptions of Nationalism," *Christian Union*, November 13, 1890. Republished in *Edward Bellamy Speaks Again*.

State Management of the Liquor Traffic (leaflet), Black Temperance Collection, No. 21. In New York Public Library.

"Summer Evening's Dream, A," *Lippincott's Magazine*, Vol. 20 (September, 1877). Republished in *The Blindman's World*.

"Superfluity of Naughtiness, A," *Lippincott's Magazine*, Vol. 19 (May, 1877).

"Talk on Nationalism," *The New Nation*, Vol. 1, No. 27 (August 1, 1891). One of a series republished in *Talks on Nationalism* (Chicago: the Peerage Press, 1938).

"To Whom This May Come," *Harpers Monthly*, Vol. 78 (February, 1889). Republished in *The Blindman's World*.

"Two Days' Solitary Imprisonment." Republished in *The Blindman's World*.

"Vital Domestic Problem, A—Household Service Reform," *Good Housekeeping*, Vol. 10, No. 4 (December 21, 1889).

"What Nationalism Means," *The Contemporary Review*, Vol. 58 (July, 1890). Republished in *Edward Bellamy Speaks Again*.

Why Every Workingman Should Be a Nationalist, Building Trades' Council Souvenir, April, 1893. Republished in *Edward Bellamy Speaks Again*.

"With the Eyes Shut," *Harpers Monthly,* Vol. 79 (October, 1889). Republished in *The Blindman's World.*

"Woman in the Year 2000," *The Ladies' Home Journal,* Vol. 8, No. 3 (February, 1891).

Periodicals

Nationalist, The, published monthly by the Nationalist Educational Association, Boston, from May, 1889, to April, 1891. Edward Bellamy contributed frequent articles.

New Nation, The, edited and published by Edward Bellamy, January 31, 1891 to February 3, 1894. In Springfield Library, Springfield, Massachusetts.

New York Evening Post. An examination of the files of the *Post* during the period when Bellamy worked there (1871–72) failed to disclose any writing which can be identified as his.

Penny News, The, edited and published by Edward and Charles Bellamy, beginning February 24, 1880. No copies available between issues of March 20 and September 24, 1880. Became *Springfield Daily News* during this period. Edward Bellamy's connection with the paper extended from the first issue to about the end of 1880.

Springfield Daily Union. Bellamy's editorials and book reviews appear from August, 1872, to December, 1877.

III. BOOKS AND ARTICLES RELATING TO EDWARD BELLAMY
OR TO THE NATIONALIST MOVEMENT

Arden, Edward. "Propositions of Nationalism," *The Chautauquan,* Vol. 14 (January, 1892).

Austin, Henry. "Edward Bellamy," *National Magazine,* Vol. 9 (October, 1898).

"Author of *Looking Backward,* The," *The Book Buyer,* Vol. 5, p. 275.

Bakeless, John. "Edward Bellamy," *Dictionary of American Biography,* Vol. 2, pp. 163–64. New York: Scribner, 1929.

Baxter, Sylvester. "Edward Bellamy: His Writings," *Book News,* Vol. 8 (August, 1890). Reprinted from *New England Magazine,* September, 1889.

Beard, Charles A., and Mary R. Beard. The Rise of American Civilization, pp. 253, 442, 547. New York: Macmillan, 1927.

Bell, Fred W. "Edward Bellamy and His Works," *The Indicator* (February, 1935). Johannesburg, South Africa. Copy included with Bellamy material in Harvard College Library.

Bellamy Nieuws, bimonthly publication of the Internacia Asocio Bellamy. Driehuis, Netherlands. Copy included with Bellamy material in Harvard College Library.

"Bellamy's Utopia" (a review of Equality), *The Nation,* Vol. 65, No. 1678 (August 26, 1897).

Blaufarb, Douglas. The Mind of Edward Bellamy, Honors Essay, Harvard College, March, 1939.

Bloomfield, Paul. Imaginary Worlds. London: Hamish Hamilton, 1932.

Bogardus, Emory S. A History of Social Thought. Los Angeles: University of California Press, n.d.

Bok, Edward. The Americanization of Edward Bok, pp. 117–18. New York: Scribner, 1924.

Boyle, James. What Is Socialism? pp. 89–90. New York: the Shakespeare Press, 1912.

Brooks, John Graham. The Social Unrest; Studies in Labor and Socialist Movements, pp. 230–32, 240–41. New York: Macmillan, 1903.

Case, C. M. Outlines of Introductory Sociology, pp. 594, 598–603. New York: Harcourt, Brace, 1924.

Chamberlain, John. Farewell to Reform. 2d ed., pp. 55–56. New York: the John Day Co., 1933.

Chandler, Alfred Dupont. Municipal Control of Commercial Lighting: Nationalism Analyzed. Boston: Massachusetts Legislature, Session of 1889, April, 1889.

Cobb, John Storer. "General Walker and 'The Atlantic,'" *The Nationalist,* Vol. 2 (March, 1890).

Coleman, McAlister. Eugene V. Debs. New York: Greenberg, Publisher, c.1930.

Damon, Bertha. Grandma Called It Carnal. New York: Simon and Schuster, c.1938.

Davis, Jerome. Contemporary Social Movements, pp. 37–50. New York: Century, 1930.

"Death of Edward Bellamy" (editorial), *Twentieth Century,* Vol. 20, No. 23 (June 4, 1898).

De Laveleye, Emile. "Two New Utopias," *Contemporary Review,* Vol. 57 (January, 1890). Also in *Littells Living Age,* Vol. 184 (February, 1890). Republished in *Edward Bellamy Speaks Again.*

Dougan, P. "Where Nationalism Fails," *Westminster Review,* Vol. 171 (January, 1909).

Earnshaw, Marion Bellamy. Edward Bellamy Today. Kansas City, Missouri: the Peerage Press, 1936.

"Edward Bellamy." *American Fabian* (June, 1898). Republished in *Edward Bellamy Speaks Again.*

"Edward Bellamy: Author of *Looking Backward* and Editor of *The New Nation,*" *The Literary Weekly,* Vol. 5 (January 4, 1894).

Ely, Richard T.   Socialism and Social Reform. New York: Thomas Y. Crowell, 1894.

"*Equality,* by Edward Bellamy" (a review), *The Saturday Review,* Vol. 84 (July 10, 1897).

Filler, Louis.   Crusaders for American Liberalism, p. 25. New York: Harcourt, Brace, 1939.

Flood, N. A.   "Nationalism as an Economic Factor," *American Journal of Politics,* Vol. 1, No. 2 (August, 1892).

Flower, B. O.   "The Latest Social Vision; a Review of *Equality,*" *The Arena,* Vol. 18 (1894). Reprinted in pamphlet form by the Arena Publishing Co., Boston, 1897.

—— Progressive Men, Women, and Movements of the Past Twenty-Five Years. Boston: the New Arena Publishing Co., 1914.

Franklin, Fabian.   People and Problems, pp. 149–54, New York: Henry Holt, 1908.

Franklin, John Hope.   "Edward Bellamy and Nationalism," *New England Quarterly,* Vol. 11 (December, 1938).

—— Edward Bellamy and the Nationalist Movement. Cambridge: Harvard University, December, 1937.

Geissler, Ludwig A.   Looking Beyond. New Orleans: L. Graham & Son, 1891.

George, James T.   Edward Bellamy and the Nationalist Movement, Divisional Honors Thesis, Amherst College, May, 1938.

Gillette, King C.   The People's Corporation. New York: Boni and Liveright, 1924.

Gilman, N. P.   "Bellamy's Social Equality," *Quarterly Journal of Economics,* Vol. 12 (October, 1897).

—— Socialism and the American Spirit, pp. 191–221. Boston: Houghton, Mifflin, 1893.

Gittleman, David.   "A Yankee's Way to Utopia," *Unity,* Vol. 116, No. 11 (February 3, 1936).

Griffin, C. S.   Nationalism. Boston: published by the author, 1889.

Gronlund, Laurence.   "Nationalism," *The Arena,* Vol. 1 (January, 1890).

Harvey, William P.   "Current Economic Issues Raised by Edward Bellamy Back in 1887," *Railroad Trainman,* January, 1938 (reprinted from the *Kansas City Journal-Post*).

Hertzler, Joyce Oramel.   History of Utopian Thought, pp. 225–36. New York: Macmillan, 1926.

Hicks, Granville.   The Great Tradition. Revised ed., pp. 139–42. New York: Macmillan, 1935.

Hicks, Granville, and Richard M. Bennett.   The First to Awaken. New York: Modern Age Books, 1940.

Higginson, T. W. "Edward Bellamy's Nationalism," *Our Day*, Vol. 5 (April, 1890).

Hills, William, Ed. "Literary News and Notes," *The Author*, Vol. 1, No. 10 (October 15, 1889) (includes item on Bellamy).

Hovey, Carl. "Edward Bellamy's *The Duke of Stockbridge*," *The Bookman*, Vol. 12 (January, 1901).

Howells, William Dean. "Review of *Looking Backward*," *Harpers Magazine*, Vol. 77 (June, 1888).

—— "Review of *Miss Ludington's Sister*," *Century Magazine*, Vol. 28 (August, 1884).

Johnson, Oliver Warren. An Answer to Chaos; the Coming Economic Life (Edward Bellamy's Theory Reduced to Working Form). Geneva, Ohio: published by the author, 1888, 1933.

Lloyd, Henry Demarest. Wealth against Commonwealth. Washington, D.C.: National Home Library Foundation, 1936.

"Look Ahead, A" (a review), *The Literary World*, Vol. 19 (March 17, 1888).

"Looking Backward" (review), *Atlantic Monthly*, Vol. 61 (June, 1888).

"Looking Backward" (review), *The Nation*, Vol. 46, No. 1187 (March 29, 1888).

"Looking Backward; a Socialistic Dream," *The Christian Union*, Vol. 37, No. 20 (May 17, 1888).

Luntz, Lester. Daniel De Leon and the Movement for Social Reform. New York: Columbia University, 1939.

Mackail, J. W. Life of William Morris. London: Longmans, Green, 1922. Vol. 2, pp. 248, 256–57.

Martin, Prestonia Mann. Prohibiting Poverty. New York: Farrar & Rinehart, c.1932.

McKenzie, Esther Elizabeth. History of the Nationalist Movement. Urbana: M. A. Thesis, University of Illinois, 1936.

"Miss Ludington's Sister" (review), *The Literary World*, Vol. 15, No. 16 (August 9, 1884).

Moore, Margaret Elsie. The Socialistic Utopias of Bellamy and Howells, Master of Arts Thesis, Columbia University, 1925.

Morgan, Arthur E. Plagiarism in Utopia; a Study of the Continuity of the Utopian Tradition, with Special Reference to Edward Bellamy's *Looking Backward*. Yellow Springs, Ohio: published by the author, 1944.

—— The Philosophy of Edward Bellamy. New York: King's Crown Press, 1944.

—— Nowhere Was Somewhere; an Exploration of the Utopian Tradition, with a Discussion of Thomas More and the Inca Civilization. Not yet published.

"Mr. Bellamy's Critics," *Lend a Hand,* Vol. 6, No. 1 (January, 1891) (unsigned article, presumably by Edward Everett Hale, editor of the periodical).

"Nationalism," *Our Day,* Vol. 5 (January, 1890) (addresses by Edward Everett Hale and Edward Bellamy).

"Nationalism at Des Moines, Iowa," *American Architect and Building News,* Vol. 29 (August 16, 1890).

"Nationalist Movement, The" (editorial), *The Dawn,* Vol. 1, No. 1 (May 15, 1889). In Boston Public Library.

"New Dealers of the 'Seventies: Henry George and Edward Bellamy," *The Forum,* Vol. 92, No. 3 (September, 1934).

Parrington, V. L. Main Currents in American Thought, Vol. III, pp. 302–15, New York: Harcourt, Brace, 1930.

Reeve, Sidney Armor. Modern Economic Tendencies; an Economic History of America, p. 711. New York: Dutton, c.1921.

Ridpath, John Clark. "Is the Prophet Dead?" *The Arena,* Vol. 20 (August, 1898). Republished in *Edward Bellamy Speaks Again.*

Roberts, J. W. Looking Within; the Misleading Tendencies of *Looking Backward* Made Manifest. New York: A. S. Barnes & Co., 1893.

Ross, J. Elliot. "On Rereading Bellamy," *Commonweal,* Vol. 23 (February 14, 1936).

Russell, Frances Theresa. Touring Utopia; the Realm of Constructive Humanism. New York: Dial Press, 1932.

Samson, Leon. Toward a United Front. New York: Farrar & Rinehart, c.1933.

Sanders, George A. Reality; or, Law and Order vs. Anarchy and Socialism. Cleveland: The Burrows Brothers Co., 1898.

Schindler, Solomon. "What Is Nationalism?" *New England Magazine,* n.s. Vol. 7 (September, 1892).

—— Young West. Boston: Arena Publishing Co., 1894.

Scudder, Vida D. Social Ideals in English Letters. Boston: Houghton, Mifflin, 1898.

Shurter, Robert L. "Literary Work of Edward Bellamy," *American Literature,* Vol. 5 (November, 1933).

Spargo, John, and George L. Arner. Elements of Socialism, p. 198. New York: Macmillan, 1912.

Stockbridge, Frank Parker. "Edward Bellamy, Prophet of Technocracy," *American Press,* Vol. 51, No. 4 (January, 1933).

Symes, Lillian, and Travers Clement. Rebel America, pp. 186, 188. New York: Harpers, 1934.

Taylor, W. F. "On the Origin of Howells' Interest in Economic Reform," *American Literature,* Vol. 2 (March, 1930).

Thomas, Norman. America's Way Out, p. 146. New York: Macmillan, 1931.

Ticknor, Caroline. Glimpses of Authors. Boston: Houghton, Mifflin, 1922.

Twentieth Century, Vol. 4, No. 18 (May 1, 1890) (editorial on the writing of *Looking Backward,* and Edward Bellamy's letter in reply).

Twentieth Century, Vol. 20, No. 22 (May 28, 1898) (comments on Edward Bellamy in column, "Our Weekly News-Letter").

Van Dalsem, Newton. "Edward Bellamy and His Works," *Roman Forum,* Vol. 8, No. 5 (August, 1939).

Vinton, Arthur Dudley. Looking Further Backward. Albany: Albany Book Co., 1890.

Wakeman, T. B. "Is Nationalism a Sin against Hell?" *The Open Court,* Vol. 4 (May 29, 1890).

—— "Is Nationalism a Sin against Liberty?" *The Open Court,* Vol. 4 (July 10, 1890).

Walker, Francis A. "Edward Bellamy and the New Nationalist Party," *Atlantic Monthly,* Vol. 65 (February, 1890).

Walsh, Correa Moylan. Socialism, p. 58. New York: Sturgis and Walton Co., 1917.

Ward, L. F. Pure Sociology, pp. 83–84. New York: Macmillan, 1909.

Wells, H. G. A Modern Utopia, pp. 87, 100. New York: Scribner, 1905.

Wilbrandt, Conrad. Mr. East's Experiences in Mr. Bellamy's World. Translated from the German by Mary J. Safford. New York: Harpers, 1891.

Young, Alexander. "The Author of *Looking Backward,*" *Book News,* Vol. 8, No. 87 (November, 1889). Reprinted from *The Critic.*

Acknowledgments

A REPRESENTATIVE biography of a recent historical character can be successful only through the coöperation of many persons. To refer to all those who have contributed to this volume would unduly encumber the acknowledgments. A few to whom the writer is peculiarly indebted will be mentioned.

Mrs. Edward Bellamy made available the notebooks and other manuscripts of her husband which are the source of much of the substance of this biography. Also, from her memories she supplied information about his personality and habits. Throughout the preparation of the book she has been helpful.

Marion Bellamy Earnshaw, their daughter, in addition to giving an account of her memories of her father and gathering biographical material from friends and others who knew him, spent some months in examining the files of the *Springfield Union* of the period during which her father was editorial writer. Paul Bellamy, in addition to a statement of his memories of his father, has been helpful in many ways. Mrs. Edward Bellamy and her son and daughter read and criticized the manuscript when it was nearly finished. N. P. Ames Carter, a lifetime resident of Chicopee and long a neighbor of Edward Bellamy, supplied interesting information concerning his early life.

Cyrus Field Willard, first secretary of the First Nationalist Club of Boston, was most helpful in completing the record of Edward Bellamy's relation to the Nationalist Club and the Nationalist movement. He wrote voluminously of his memories, and friends of the writer who visited him in California testified to his clear and consistent memory. Before his death he read and criticized a nearly finished draft of the part of the book concerning which he had information. Abbott B. Clark, last surviving Theosophist who helped to promote the Nationalist movement in California, provided information concerning the relation of the Nationalist and Theosophical movements which would have been available nowhere else.

Vilhjalmur Stefansson, from his early memories at the University of North Dakota, and by introducing me to classmates there, helped to throw light on the possible association of Edward Bellamy and John Macnie, author of *The Diothas,* a utopia with similarities to *Looking Backward* which preceded Bellamy's book by four years. D. Joffo went to considerable effort to acquaint me with the influence of Edward Bellamy on prerevolutionary and early revolutionary Russia. Philip Ainsworth Means, authority on ancient Peru, read parts of the manuscript and supplied historical records concerning the first discovery of the Inca civilization from the Atlantic coast and concerning the nature of Inca society, from which, it appears, Bellamy may have taken some of his principal ideas.

In the process of writing the biography help was received from many sources. I wish to record my deep appreciation for the exceptionally competent and interested assistance of Grace Ostling Robinow. Her thoroughness in verifying citations and quotations and her discrimination in literary usage were of great value. Her death during the progress of the work was a deeply felt loss.

Mrs. Barton M. Jones deciphered and copied numerous Bellamy manuscripts which were so difficult to read that they had been omitted from the general process of transcribing his written papers. Mildred Kahoe compared most of the copied Bellamy manuscripts with the originals and corrected many errors of transcription. Walter Kahoe aided by acquainting me with much source material. Marguerite McGuire, because of her interest in Edward Bellamy's ideas, spent much time in the Congressional Library searching and copying reference material. Individual chapters of the manuscript were read and criticized by other persons familiar with the several fields.

Eleanor Switzer, my assistant, has ably directed the manuscript through its later stages. Also she has prepared the source material for deposit in the Harvard College Library. Without her interested and versatile help the book could scarcely have been finished.

From start to finish my wife, Lucy Griscom Morgan, and my son, Griscom Morgan, have given sympathetic encouragement to the undertaking. From their wide reading they have made me acquainted with relevant material and have criticized very helpfully both the form and the content of the book. My son has been especially helpful on the literature of social theory.

Finally, I wish to express my keen appreciation for the exceptionally competent and discriminating services of the Columbia University Press in editing the manuscript, and in general supervision of the book. It is a pleasure to be able to commit one's work to such hands.

Permission to use quotations has been kindly granted by the following persons and publishers. The works from which quotations were taken are given in parentheses.

D. Appleton-Century Company (Archibald Henderson, *Bernard Shaw;* Edward Bellamy, *Equality*); The Citizens' Guild of Washington's Boyhood Home (John Marshall, *Life of George Washington*); Dulau & Co., Ltd. (Philip Gosse, *The Pirates' Who's Who*); Harlem

Book Co. (*The Works of Plato: The Republic,* Benjamin Jowett, trans.); Funk & Wagnalls Company (Morris Hillquit, *History of Socialism in the United States*); Houghton Mifflin Company (Edward Bellamy, *Looking Backward* and *The Blindman's World;* John Fiske, *A History of the United States*); The President and Fellows of Harvard College (Aristophanes, *The Ecclesiazusae,* from the Loeb Classical Library); Lothrop, Lee & Shepard Co. (Laurence Gronlund, *The Co-operative Commonwealth*); Harcourt, Brace and Company (R. W. Chambers, *Thomas More*); The Macmillan Company (Albert Hart, *American History Told by Contemporaries;* Graham Wallas, *The Great Society*); Methuen & Co., Ltd. (H. Stanley Jevons, *Economic Equality in the Co-operative Commonwealth*); Mrs. Charmian K. London (Jack London, *The People of the Abyss*); G. P. Putnam's Sons (J. Arthur Thomson, *The Outline of Science;* Charles J. Bellamy, *The Breton Mills* and *The Way Out;* John Macnie, *The Diothas*); The Robert Schalken-bach Foundation (Henry George, *Progress and Poverty*); Charles Scribner's Sons (Franklin B. Dexter, *The Literary Diary of Ezra Stiles;* V. F. Calverton, *The Liberation of American Literature;* Andrew Carnegie, *Triumphant Democracy;* Edward Page Mitchell, *Memoirs of an Editor*); *The Atlantic Monthly* (William Dean Howells, "Edward Bellamy"); The Theosophical University Press (H. P. Blavatsky, *The Key to Theosophy*); *Common Sense* magazine (John Dewey, "A Great American Prophet"; Denis de Rougemont, "Federalism vs. Totalitarianism"); *Good Housekeeping* magazine ("Edward Bellamy," editorial); *Harper's Magazine* (William Dean Howells, "Review of *Looking Backward*"); *New York Times Magazine* (George Gallup, "We, the People, Are Like This").

Index